a guide to
Architecture in San Francisco
& Northern California

a guide to
Architecture in San Francisco
& Northern California

David Gebhard
Roger Montgomery
Robert Winter
John Woodbridge
Sally Woodbridge

Designed by Marc Treib

Peregrine Smith, Inc.
SANTA BARBARA AND SALT LAKE CITY

1973

Acknowledgments

The authors wish to thank the following institutions and individuals for their contributions to this Guide:

For Financial Assistance:
>   The Bank of America Foundation
>   The California Redwood Association
>   Kaiser Industries
>   The American Institute of Architects
>>   Northern California Chapter
>>   East Bay Chapter
>>   Santa Clara Valley Chapter

For Contributions in Research, Editing and Writing:
>   John Beach (noted authority)
>   Joseph Baird
>   Henrik Bull
>   Kenneth H. Cardwell
>   Richard Longstreth
>   Robert Marquis
>   Charles W. Moore
>   Thomas Owen
>   Richard C. Peters
>   Walter T. Steilberg
>   Claude Stoller
>   Harold A. Stump
>   William Turnbull, Jr.
>   Peggy Woodring

For Production:
>   Mary Ann Beach
>   Reiko Habe
>   Marjanne Pearson
>   Kajsa Uddenberg
>   Haydon Valdes
>   Charlene Welch

For General Editorial Assistance:
>   Dr. Clove Baker
>   James R. Burch
>   William Garnett
>   George Homsey
>   Harold Kirker
>   Jerry Kotas
>   Randell Makinson
>   Esther McCoy
>   Arthur B. Waugh
>   Margaret Wheaton
>   California Historical Society, San Francisco
>   California Society of Pioneers, San Francisco
>   California State Library, Sacramento
>   Monterey Savings and Loan Association, Monterey
>   Oakland Public Library, Oakland
>   University of California, Berkeley
>>   Bancroft Library
>>   Library, School of Environmental Design
>   Wells Fargo Bank, San Francisco
>   Women's Architectural League, San Francisco
>   Planning Departments of Fremont, Oakland, Richmond, San Francisco, Santa Clara County & Sunnyvale

Acknowledgments

Photographic Credits:

Morley Baer and Chronicle Books for permission to publish several photographs which first appeared in the book *Here Today, San Francisco's Architectural Heritage*, published by Chronicle Books, San Francisco, and sponsored by the Junior League of San Francisco, Inc., 1968.

Morley Baer
Jeremiah O. Bragstad
Ernest Braun
Calif. State Division of Highways
Roy Flamm
Les Flowers, Jr.
Joshua Freiwald
Alexandre Georges
Harrington-Olsen
Robert Hollingsworth
Kathleen Kershaw
Jack Laxer
Rondall Partridge
Karl Reik
Security First National Bank, Los Angeles
Ezra Stoller
Roger Sturtevant
Title Insurance and Trust Co., San Diego

Cover photo: Sam Davis

Contents

Inside Front Cover: Map Codes
Inside Back Cover: Authors

A Guide to this Guide

This is a Guide to the man-made structures, gardens, parks, and spaces that compose the physical structure of the towns, cities, and countryside of Northern California. Its time span begins with the missions of Spanish Colonial California and ends with projects which will be substantially complete in 1973.

GEOGRAPHIC ORGANIZATION

The authors assume that most users of the Guide will begin their travels in San Francisco. Therefore, the Guide has been organized in a geographic spiral around the Bay, beginning with San Francisco and moving south through the Peninsula, around the bottom of the Bay through Santa Clara County, and down the east side of the Bay from Marin County south through the East Bay. This first major section, the Bay Area, is followed by the rest of Northern California divided into 13 sections from north to south.

MAPS

Each of the two major sections, the Bay Area and Northern California, is divided into areas such as San Francisco, Peninsula, East Bay (Bay Area) and Area 1, etc. (Northern California). Each area is divided into numbered sub-areas: for example, SF-1, San Francisco-Presidio. Each sub-area is provided with a map locating the buildings by number. The map numbers correspond to the text entries.

We recommend the supplementary use of standard road maps, as the Guide maps are schematic to a certain extent and in large-scale areas show only major arteries. Cuts in streets indicate that map sections have been deleted. Road widths are not to scale. Arrows with numbers indicate entries which lie off the map. Areas with few entries have no maps.

KEY MAPS

Key maps showing the areas covered by regional guide maps appear on the following pages: San Francisco, 32-33; Peninsula and Santa Clara Valley, 103; East Bay, 223; Northern California, 315.

ENTRIES

Each entry lists the name of the building, the date, the name of the architect or designer if available, and the address. In some cases, buildings are listed which are not visible from a public thoroughfare. This is only done in cases where the importance of the building demands its inclusion, and should not be taken as permission to trespass. In fact, in no way does the listing of any private buildings in this Guide give the user permission to enter the grounds or building. In general, users who wish to see the interiors of private buildings should apply to the office of the architect, not the owner.

Federal, state, county and city public buildings are generally open between the hours of 10:00 A.M. and 5:00 P.M. on week days. A number of historic buildings open to the public are included in the Guide. In-

A Guide to this Guide

formation about these buildings is included in the introduction to the section or in the individual entry.

PHOTOGRAPHS

Photographs generally follow their entries and, in such cases, have not been captioned. Photographs which precede or are separated from entries have been captioned in all but obvious situations.

ARCHITECTURAL STYLES

A glossary of architectural styles is provided following a chronological photographic section showing buildings representative of each style.

INDEX

Significant places not listed in the table of contents; i.e., neighborhoods, public squares, parks, etc., as well as architects are indexed at the back of the guide.

SYMBOLS

● beside entries indicates that they have photographs in the Photo History section of the Guide.

B BART

 North

A Guide to this Guide

NOTE ON THE SELECTION OF BUILDINGS AND URBAN PLANS

Among the five authors who have collaborated on this Guide, there were quite naturally many different opinions as to what should or should not be included. Each of us has his own strong beliefs and points of view and tends to ride them. However since this was a group project, we have constantly criticized each other and have tried to force the more hard core zealots to be reasonable. If there seems to be an over-abundance of, say, the Moderne, it is not because we have allowed one of our group to run loose but because we think that this style has been misunderstood and historically under-rated and needs to be brought to the public's attention. We are well aware that in a few years this book will probably be looked at as a fascinating period piece. That would not be unusual. But we have tried assiduously to avoid pure crankiness. All of us are in complete agreement that every style and the work of every architect or planner has had its dull moments. In the selection process, we have sought to concentrate on the brighter moments.

We do, though, admit to certain bias, on the one hand toward the unusual and flamboyant, on the other to the simple, pure and chaste. The middle of the road just does not seem to affect us very much. And, within this bias, we have a predilection for those buildings and urban plans which exhibit a concern for details, whether large or small. A building or even an urban scheme can be monumental, or it can be playful, but it has no business being mindless; and a great deal in Northern California (and throughout the U.S.A.) during the past two hundred years has been mindless.

Another aspect of the Guide of which we are well aware is that we have been much more discriminating in our selection of buildings in the Bay area and in Sacramento than we have in smaller communities such as Red Bluff. We have not mentioned many houses in the Victorian sections of San Francisco which would, if transported to Red Bluff, equal and even in some cases surpass much of the domestic work there—though we should add that San Francisco would be far better off if it possessed a church of the quality of Ernest Coxhead's Red Bluff church. It seems to us that it is important to draw attention to the high quality of much of the work in the smaller towns, many of which are rich in things that please the eye. Indeed, there may be a better chance of saving the best in our smaller communities than there is in our larger cities. If only, in the 1950s, someone had told Marysville of the significance of her architecture, might not urban renewal have spared her wonderful Court House, her City Hall and other marvels?

We hope, in publishing this Guide, that we have not left out anything really important. But we know, since we have not covered every road in the state, that we may well have omitted some very good things. We invite your comments and criticisms. Everyone will profit from them in the next edition.

Introduction

Northern California evokes two images—one of a country of majestic mountains running to golden, oak-studded hills undulating toward the Pacific surf; the other of the get-rich-quick locale of the hell-bent exploiter, ravaging the land, jerry-building towns and cities, and generally setting aside all values except the profit motive. In 1840 Richard Henry Dana, with a Yankee eye toward progress, found California Indians lazy and the Mexicans generally lacking in ambition. By no means insensitive to scenery, he enjoyed riding into the hills, but he could not avoid remarking, "In the hands of an enterprising people what a country this might be." Almost a half-century later, Helen Hunt Jackson thought better of the Hispanic-Mexican era and ascribed to California's past the virtues of simplicity and quietude. To her the old California was a land untrammeled by acquisitive instincts. It was a good land, the perfect backdrop for the love of Ramona and Alessandro. The same beautiful country appears in Frank Norris' *Octopus* though it is a country corrupted by the aggressive passions of farmers and railroad magnates.

The truth is that both images—innocence and aggression—are hopelessly entangled in northern California's reality and myth. Californians have dealt harshly with their environment. Yet nature has not so far lost her visual hold, whether along rugged coastline, in the great Bay of San Francisco, or through the resort-strewn mountains. Though here and there, as around Sacramento, the area north of Monterey to Santa Cruz, and on the Peninsula, urban and suburban sprawl has desecrated the countryside, the traveler in northern California must be surprised that most of his journey leads, if not through virgin land, through rural, small-town America.

The only real intruder on this idyll is the road, be it freeway or an older winding highway. Everyday life, as well as vacation life, is oriented on the highway, while older, man-made objects—barns, fences, houses and towns—appear as far distant historic fragments. The road leads to the outskirts of town—the shopping centers, strip developments and acres of single family

San Francisco 1870s photo: Wells Fargo Bank

Introduction

houses. Consequently the older sections of town, especially those which have experienced urban renewal, seem forlorn, abandoned. Ironically, the older traditional court house center of the city has been replaced by fringe areas struck by nostalgia (often with Victorian fringes on top). Where fragments of the Victorian era still remain, as at Mendocino, Ferndale and Woodland they have been "discovered" and "enhanced" with Disneyland versions of the general store and establishments selling artsy-craftsy products.

What impression does the typical, automobile-oriented northern California town convey today? Like their midwestern counterparts, these towns were, with few exceptions, established on the basis of economic fact. Sites favorable to transportation, lumbering, mining and commerce were rarely selected for their beauty. Where a river, lake, or oceanfront was found to be a profitable commodity, it was seized by the entrepreneur and put to economic use, causing later residents to engage in expensive transactions to have even modest parks. Though mid and late 19th century Anglo northern California towns might indeed be located on a river or bay, they usually ended up turning their backs on their major visual asset.

Just as the sites selected for towns were seldom the most beautiful to be found in the locale, nor, in many cases, were they really healthy places to live. Here the difference between the sites selected by the Spanish for their California towns (usually made up of a Mission and a Presidio) and those selected by Yankee Anglos is strikingly different, for as a rule the earlier Hispanic settlers sought out agreeable locations, and when a site proved otherwise they pulled up stakes and moved on to another.

The checkerboard gridiron scheme was the prevalent pattern for these California towns whether of the Hispanic period or later—except it is difficult to escape the feeling that there is a harsh, cold relentlessness about the Anglo gridiron schemes that is never found in the Plaza-oriented Spanish towns.

Northern California participated to a limited extent in planning in the 19th century. Frederick Law Olmsted and others helped to establish one of the earliest of the state parks systems, and Yosemite Valley was set aside as a park as early as 1864. Olmsted was also involved with the early planning of Golden Gate Park (1865) which John McLaren successfully completed; with an unrealized scheme for the University of California and the city of Berkeley (1865); and with laying out the grounds of Stanford University in 1888. But it was only at the end of the century as an outcome of the City Beautiful movement that most northern California communities began to acquire land to build parks and boulevards on their hills, along side streams and rivers, or on parcels of land overlooking the ocean. Generally speaking these northern California towns (San Francisco in a way being an exception) do not make a strong urban impression. A few, like Eureka and Woodland, have fortunately preserved enough

Introduction

buildings of the 80s and 90s that their Victorian character has remained. But most of the cities and towns, particularly in their central business districts, are dull and uninteresting. Often what really makes them pleasant and at times beautiful are their residential streets with magnificent trees, shrubs, green lawns and flowers.

In their downtown areas, the two dominant architectural monuments seem invariably to be a Streamlined movie theater of the late 1930s or early 40s, and the Federal Post Office building, either Renaissance or Classical-Moderne in style. In scale and location, the post office buildings are slow in pace and pedestrian oriented, while the Streamlined theaters with high, brilliantly lighted tower-signs and neon-encrusted marquees are a product of commercial strip development and its orientation to the automobile.

Though many federal, county, and city governmental buildings have been constructed in northern California since 1945, it is discouraging to see how few of these make strong architectural statements or contribute anything except blandness to the visual quality of their respective urban scenes. The Streamlined Moderne movie house and the Classical post office buildings have not yet been replaced by other new or dominant building types.

This Guide is concerned with identifying that architecture past and present which by the fact of its existence lends interest and flavor to the northern California environment.

Recalling the simplicity and quietude of California's Hispanic past are the earliest remnants of architectural effort in California—the Spanish missions and adobes. Of the twenty-one Missions established in California, ten are located in northern California, and of these, three convey some architectural pretensions: the Carmel Mission (1793-1797), the Mission Dolores (1776-1784), and the Presidio Chapel at Monterey (1794). These three buildings mirror, in a provincial abbreviated fashion, late 18th century neo-classical taste derived from central and northern Mexico. In contrast to these Mission churches, the Mission San Juan Bautista (1803-1812) or the Mission San Antonio de Padua (1810-1813) represent something quite different, for these Mission compounds are composed of simple, domestic buildings merely enlarged in scale. These primitive Mission structures have, since the late 19th century, always been the most popular.

Early Yankees had little immediate appreciation of the indigenous adobe architecture, though they continued to use it until better materials could be found. An important "improvement" on the Mexican building was the "Monterey Style," so-called because of the many buildings in Monterey built in that mode. Essentially it consisted of the use of adobe brick in load-bearing walls with a roof extended and overhanging a balcony, thus protecting the friable adobe. Its style is simplified and attenuated Neo-Classical, and can be found in many areas of the eastern United States.

Introduction

When milled lumber and skilled carpenters were brought in, the new Californians showed their nostalgia for the tried and true in better imitations of eastern styles. At first they continued the Classical Revival, even trying awkward columns as in Colton Hall (1847) in Monterey. Usually, as in the Jenny Lind Theater (1851) and Montgomery Block (1853) in San Francisco (both destroyed), they followed the provincial eastern practice of stripping away classicism to post and lintel elements with little regard for classical detail or proportions. Though the Gothic Revival was by all odds the most popular style for churches throughout the nineteenth and into the twentieth century, it is relatively rare in secular architecture. When it appeared, it was usually, as in the Moss Cottage (1865) in Oakland, in the early phase of the eastern style that A. J. Davis had popularized twenty to thirty years earlier, or in the Ruskinian phase as in the Masonic Hall (1882) at Woodbridge.

In the late 60s and on through the 70s, the most fashionable packaging for governmental, commercial and domestic buildings was the Italianate style, with its strong commitment to vertical exterior elements and elongated, often asymmetrical floor plans. Some of the Italianate villas, such as the Bidwell house (1865) in Chico, were directly derived from the early eastern phase of the style, but most Italianate buildings in northern California are stylistically akin to what was being built in the 60s and 70s in eastern and midwestern cities. San Francisco was once resplendent with blocks of three to five story brick and cast iron Italianate commercial buildings, but these have all but disappeared. Now one can only gain a general feeling for what commercial San Francisco must have been like by walking around Jackson Square, or by visiting her provinces—Santa Cruz, Eureka, especially Petaluma.

The Italianate courthouses which once were the pride of almost every county have all but vanished. A few still survive at Bridgeport, at Napa (sans cupola), at Merced, and at Yuba City. The Italianate style was most persistent as a wood framed and sheathed row house, especially in San Francisco and Oakland. Rows of these were being built as late as the early 1900s, but by that time they hardly represented high fashion among the sophisticated.

Harold Kirker has noted in his *California's Architectural Frontier* that, while most of California lagged behind the East in architectural sophistication, San Francisco boasted a surprising number of commercial and governmental buildings that would have been perfectly in place in New York or Boston. A partial explanation of this phenomenon is the fact that many foreign as well as American architects joined the Gold Rush and when that was over they settled down to their profession. Victor Hoffman's four-story Globe Hotel (1857) and Peter Portois' Hibernia Society and Bank Building (1857), (both are gone), were very fine Renaissance Revival designs by gifted architects. This sophistication was sustained throughout the late 19th century.

Introduction

Palace Hotel, San Francisco 1873-74

By the 1870s California architects were numerous enough to establish their own professional journal of architecture, *The California Architect and Building News*, a gold-mine of information for the student of California's architectural history. By 1881 they had a professional society of architects. Actually there were two contingents, one, the aforementioned well trained San Francisco elite, the other, a much larger group of self-trained designers who often turned out to be at one time architects, builders and speculators. It was the latter group, together with carpenter-builders who relied on popular handbooks, which produced most of the domestic architecture of northern California, a situation by no means restricted to this area but characteristic of the entire United States.

Through the last three decades of the nineteenth century, northern California architects took up, combined and discarded the profusion of decorative styles that we today label Victorian. The Stick style was succeeded by Eastlake and Eastlake by Queen Anne. Then came Richardsonian Romanesque, the Shingle style, and in rapid succession the Colonial Revival, the Chateauesque, the Renaissance Revival, and finally the Craftsman, taking us into the twentieth century. The handling and mixing of these styles was not very much different from what was occurring in other parts of the United States, except for California's greater flamboyance in the mixture of Queen Anne and Eastlake forms, partially accounted for by the abundance of wood, particularly redwood, which allowed carpenters enormous freedom in developing lush designs. It goes without saying that no house was ever built in the East or Midwest which could compare in richness of form and detail with the often illustrated Carson house (1884) at Eureka, designed by Samuel and Joseph C. Newsom. Indeed, this design demonstrates a self-assurance

Introduction

S.C. BUGBEE AND SON ARCH'TS. HOUSE OF J. M. WALKER : OAKLAND CAL.

which has rarely been equaled in the history of American architecture.

In plan, materials used, and methods of construction, there was little to distinguish these Victorian houses from those in the rest of the country. Similarly, when the East took up the resort hotel craze, so did northern California, the famed Hotel del Monte (1879) near Monterey being one of the first of these. The great difference between California and the East was a more beneficient nature which endowed the hotels with dramatic scenery and allowed the buildings to be surrounded with palms, eucalyptus and acacia.

Northern California's contribution to architectural innovation was the use of concrete, especially Ernest Ransome's development of reinforced concrete. Ransome's Arctic Oil Works (1884) in San Francisco was the first reinforced concrete building in the United States. Although it no longer exists, Ransome's reinforced concrete Alvord Bridge (1889) in Golden Gate Park does, and it is likewise a first. From the 80s onward, reinforced concrete was increasingly used, first primarily in utilitarian structures and then after the 1906 earthquake in schools, churches and commercial buildings.

We have already noted the unusual sophistication of San Francisco architecture in the late nineteenth century. The Bay Area was a center of ideas and still is. If an outlying town had an important project, its leaders would usually go to San Francisco for their architect. The result was a certain unity of architectural values, though the smaller towns naturally engaged in culture with greater modesty than did the big city. The railroads, particularly the Southern Pacific Railroad, were, of course, a major vehicle which helped to bring about this cultural unity throughout the state. They created new towns and linked them together with old ones into an empire that is still visible. But by

Introduction

1900 economic expansion had, except for a few short-lived spurts, died down in most of northern California, leaving the physical and architectural character of a majority of towns pretty well set. At Red Bluff, for instance, were it not for a few motels, neon signs, and "modernization" of store fronts, you would feel correctly that you were in nineteenth century America. Some towns continued to grow—Sacramento, Stockton, Eureka, and the cities around San Francisco Bay. The result is a still visible gap between what happened architecturally after 1900 in and around San Francisco and other "growing" cities and the virtual stagnation of the building art in the smaller northern California communities—until the boom of the 20s and later of the 50s and 60s revived it again, particularly in the field of domestic architecture.

By the 1890s a second wave of well-educated architects—A. Page Brown, Ernest Coxhead, A. C. Schweinfurt, Willis Polk, John Galen Howard, Louis C. Mullgardt and Bernard Maybeck—arrived in the Bay Area. Their work at the turn of the century, particularly in domestic architecture, was characterized by the use of shingles and stained wood and by picturesque changes in spatial and axial arrangement. It has been loosely called the "First Bay Tradition," but this was hardly a strong unified style comprising, as it did, elements of the Shingle, Mission Revival, and Swiss Chalet styles. In fact, as the first decade of the new century came to a close, these younger Bay Area architects showed themselves to be as catholic in their taste as were their Victorian ancestors. They went from Shingle style and Craftsman work to the Renaissance Revival with no trouble at all, and they occasionally made forays into the Gothic and Tudor. In the late teens and 20s they even ventured into the Spanish Colonial Revival. Personally their work varied, ranging from the dry correctness of Howard, to the almost inexhaustible creative imagination of Maybeck. Notwithstanding the variety of styles which these men represented, a thread brought their work together. They tended to be highly unorthodox in their development of space and scale and equally unorthodox in their use of historic forms. Space was not for them, as it was for their great contemporary Frank Lloyd Wright, a matter of flowing from one visual experience to another, but was instead a series of horizontal and vertical explosions, often bewildering if not deafening. There is in much of their work an "Alice in Wonderland" quality that had occurred a little earlier but less radically in the architecture of the Englishman, Charles F. A. Voysey.

The Englishman's fairy-tale appears coherent and real in comparison to some of the Bay Area architects' designs in which classical columns, entablatures, Gothic windows and gargoyles, pieces of Islamic summer houses, Byzantine capitals, Roman sarcophagi, and other historical tid-bits were loosely, even carelessly applied to wood frame boxes. This "tradition" of heightened contrast, of sharp clashes of space, scale and historic ornament, is the element of continuity which

Introduction

crops up later in the 30s and 40s in the "Second Bay Tradition" of William Wurster and others and more recently in the vertical cut-out box architecture of Charles Moore.

This is not to say that the Bay Region architects were conscious of their intellectual relationships. Few of them wrote very much, so much must be left to dangerous surmise. But it is significant that the center of the woodsy Craftsman style was the elitist educational community at Berkeley, that its chief exponent, Bernard Maybeck, was at one time an instructor of architecture at the University of California, and that Maybeck's clients were very often professors and other cultural leaders. The rusticity of Berkeley was a cultivated one. In fact, there is much evidence that Berkeley's folksy humanists were fully aware and strongly influenced by what was going on in the way of avant-garde work not only in Chicago but also in England, Scotland, and Vienna. Maybeck's Lawson house (1907) in Berkeley, for example, has strong affinities with Secessionism. Even more direct connections can be made between the work of the Vienna group and the houses of the Berkeley architect John Hudson Thomas.

The popularization of the ideals of the Arts and Crafts movement is manifest in the California bungalow and in the stucco box stripped version of Frank Lloyd Wright's 1906 *Ladies Home Journal* Prairie house. The bungalow was essentially a southern California phenomenon, but its popularity in the north is fully documented by the hundreds that still exist in the Bay Area and that pop up occasionally in other places. In plan, these bungalows, often copied or adapted from the scores of bungalow books produced in Los Angeles, are identical with those in the south, though their elevations tend to be more blocky and stout.

This abstract volumetric quality is also to be found in the Prairie houses which frequently appear on the streets of Oakland and San Francisco. With the exception of Chicago, there is no urban community which contains as many examples of the Prairie style. Like the bungalow, it appears unexpectedly in other places —Chico, Petaluma, Hollister. Almost all of these were builder-designed, speculative houses. Very few were designed by architects.

Precisely contemporaneous with the First Bay Tradition and the Craftsman movement was the Mission Revival. Slowly, in the 80s and 90s, Californians began to take an interest in restoring the Missions which they had allowed to molder, sometimes literally into dust, since the American occupation. The inspiration for this activity has been ascribed to the popularity of Helen Hunt Jackson's romantic portrayal of life before the Yankee in *Ramona* (1884) and to the propagandizing efforts of Charles Fletcher Lummis who edited the widely read *Land of Sunshine Magazine* and who founded the California Landmarks Club (1894), one of the oldest preservation organizations in the United States.

Introduction

For Californians, the Mission Revival was the logical result of their desire for a simpler, indigenous architecture. Although a number of examples of the imitation of certain elements of Mission churches occur in the 80s and early 90s, the first great monument of the Mission Revival was A. Page Brown's California Building at the World's Columbian Exposition at Chicago in 1893. The Mission theme overwhelmed almost everything at the California Midwinter Exhibition at Golden Gate Park in 1894. By the late 90s, Mission gables and arches with neo-Moorish towers were being used for railroad stations, schools, libraries, commercial buildings, and houses. Although the style did not transform northern California as it did the southern part of the state, hardly a single town came out of the period without at least one building clothed in Mission Revival garb. As in southern California, the Mission Revival paved the way for the more urbane and elaborate Spanish Colonial Revival of the late teens and 20s.

Side by side with the Craftsman and Mission modes, and their gestures to a simpler America, was the Renaissance Revival stimulated by the Chicago fair of 1893—from the cultural point of view one of the most important events in American history. To anyone trying to make sense out of this period, the staggering effect of "The Great White City" on a people aspiring to simpler virtues must offer problems. The American mind has, of course, never been consistent. But there is a certain consistency beneath all of this. What Americans saw at the Fair was noble order, something that they had not seen in their cities since the 18th century. Like the return to fine workmanship, the City Beautiful promised a respite from the ugliness of modern life.

Daniel Burnham, the leading exponent of the City Beautiful movement, was engaged to develop a plan for San Francisco in 1904 and he presented it the next year. Even though the 1906 earthquake and fire seemed a God-given chance to carry out Burnham's ideas, the plan was never acted upon. Had it been, San Francisco would have been today a small scale version of Baron Hausmann's Paris. The only relic of Burnham's scheme is a symmetrically laid out Civic Center. Starting in 1912 with the domed City Hall by Bakewell and Brown and finishing in 1936 with the Federal Building, San Francisco was one of the few American cities to end up with monuments to the City Beautiful movement outside Washington, D. C., another Burnham project. Other northern California cities attempted to give classical order to their central city plan and its architectture, but few besides Stockton got very far. Naturally, the University of California picked up the idea in planning its campus, though, except for the prominence of Sather Tower at the end of University Avenue, it is difficult today to detect even a trace of the original Grand Design.

The Panama Pacific Exposition in 1915 gave San Francisco another chance at the City Beautiful, but axial symmetry was lost in richness. It was a sight to behold, and yet it had no lasting effect on architecture

Introduction

compared to the Fair the same year in San Diego.
Even the visual delight of Maybeck's Palace of Fine
Arts proved no popular match for Bertram Goodhue's
California building and the buildings of Goodhue's
allies at Balboa Park. Maybeck's work was too moody

Panama Pacific Exposition, San Francisco 1915

to become a prototype. Goodhue's way with the Churrigueresque suited perfectly the ebullient mood of an
affluent society and his buildings mark the emergence
of the Spanish Colonial Revival. Compared to the Southland, northern California was more reserved and circumspect in its use of Mediterranean forms. Yet, by
1930 it could boast an impressive array of monuments
in the style, buildings designed by Addison Mizner,
George Washington Smith, and Clarence Tantau. Impressive Hispanic-Moorish gardens were laid out on estates down the Peninsula, and Pebble Beach realized
its long held ideal of becoming a New World version
of the Riviera.

In the north the English Tudor, French Provincial and
even the Eastern clapboard Colonial Revival competed
on almost equal terms with the Hispanic. A high point
of sorts in northern California domestic architecture
during the twenties was the Hansel and Gretel Fairy-
land houses, stores, and cottages built in and around
Berkeley by W. R. Yelland and by Hugh Comstock in
Carmel. That these charming excursions into a conscious stage-set did indeed make a real contribution
to architecture via their space, scale, mystery and surprise is only beginning to be realized.

Being more conservative in its view of architecture, San
Francisco did not attract the "way-out" designers of the
twenties—R. M. Schindler, Richard J. Neutra, Lloyd
Wright and others—all of whom ended up in Los Angeles. But San Francisco did participate fully in the
Moderne (Art Deco) of the 20s, of which Miller and
Pflueger's 450 Sutter Street skyscraper of 1929 is, in its
quality of design and ornament, one of the major monuments in the United States.

William W. Wurster helped to return northern California to its earlier architectural eminence by initiating
the "Second Bay Tradition" of the 30s and 40s. Wur-

ster's design vocabulary eschewed the Shingle style, English Cottage, and Swiss Chalet forms of the earlier group and instead was derived from a number of seemingly incompatible sources—Monterey, American Colonial and Regency revivals, later mixed with board and batten, Moderne and International style details. By World War II an impressive group of architects formed around Wurster—Gardner Dailey, John Funk, John Dinwiddie, Joseph McCarthy, Michael Goodman—whose common ground was their use of a diversity of borrowed forms and their conscious creation of awkward spaces and strange proportions. The desire to produce liveable enclosed space was matched by the desire to create small scaled usable space out-of-doors. The garden as an informal out-of-doors living room developed hand in hand with the woodsy Bay Region house. Thomas Church, and later Garrett Eckbo and Lawrence Halprin, succeeded in bringing about as strong a revolution in the art of the garden as Wurster and his colleagues had for the house.

The experience of the 1930s brought together a group of Bay Area designers and planners to found the environmental design movement. Architects Burt Cairns, Vernon DeMars, Joseph McCarthy, landscape architect Garrett Eckbo, and town planners T. J. Kent, Jr. and Francis Violich formed the group called Telesis in 1939. Their landmark exhibition in the fall of 1940 at the San Francisco Museum of Art opened the campaign to define a broad new field based on interdisciplinary teamwork and to bring environmental issues before the public. After the War, a traveling exhibit organized by Kent helped build the case for regional planning in the Bay Area. It certainly contributed to achieving rapid transit (BART), strong regional planning (ABAG), Bay conservation (BCDC), and the current campaign for open space. But perhaps the most important contribution from Telesis to the world at large was the idea for the College of Environmental Design at University of California, Berkeley, an idea heard and copied 'round the world.'

Compared to Los Angeles, northern California's recovery from the Great Depression of the 30s was very slow. Perhaps that is the reason why the region corralled so many WPA and PWA projects, far more than its share one might add. As a result, the area contains a wondrous display of all varieties of Moderne—Classical (sometimes called Fascist), WPA (straight lines), and Streamlined. Dams, schools, post offices, city halls, fire stations were built in this much maligned style and filled with paintings and sculptures by artists on relief. These still stand as monuments to nationalism based on need. They are usually ignored or considered fair game for demolition. Only recently have they been recognized as something more than an historical error.

The expressive devices of the architects of the First Bay Tradition may have been stimulated by local fantasy, but intellectually these architects participated in the climate of ideas which dominated American

Introduction

thought at the turn of the century. As evidenced in Frederick Jackson Turner's famous essay on "The Significance of the Frontier in American History" which he gave (significantly) at the Chicago fair of 1893, Americans were conscious that in the filling out of the continent, a turning point in American history had occurred. With the frontier closed, how would the old American virtues of individualism, resourcefulness, self-reliance, and democracy be sustained?

In this atmosphere of concern that all was not well, it was inevitable that a nostalgia for an earlier, simpler, more virtuous America would develop, even if that America had to be invented. The manifestations of this looking backward are clear in almost every area of American thought at the turn of the century. In fact, this thought was turned into action, as a movement grew to protect nature from the onslaught of progress. National, state and local parks were established so that Americans could symbolically return to the frontier, at least during weekends and summer vacations.

There were various offshoots of this back to the soil ethic one of which was the open-air school. By 1915, low spread-out single floor school buildings were being designed with no interior corridors and classrooms with entire walls composed of sliding or folding glass doors, which when open turned the class rooms into open porches.

An effect on architecture of this desire to return to nature was the emergence of the Shingle style of ancestral New England, the style which the Bay Region architects improvised upon. Indeed, their reversion to childhood, which we have previously noted, seems closely related to the return to the past for sustenance and fresh air. They found their happiest expression in the woodsy forms of the Arts and Crafts (in America the Craftsman) movement; not simply because redwood was at hand but because wood demanded craft, and craft meant a return to simpler virtues and individual honesty.

At the end of the 30s, new residential subdivisions, most of which were designed and built by developers, began to emerge in west San Francisco, down the Peninsula and in the hills behind Oakland. The houses in these subdivisions were packaged in a variety of styles ranging from the Colonial to the Monterey Colonial. In size these houses were modest, in livability (even for us today) they were as pleasant and functional as one would ask. A similar element of livability, informality and non-doctrinairism occurred in the school buildings of Ernest Kump, through his sensitive use of "warm" traditional materials, his open finger plans, and his general domestic forms and scale.

While urban sprawl was already gobbling up pear orchards before World War II, the fifteen years after 1945 witnessed an urbanization of the Peninsula and East Bay on a scale never before experienced. Urbanization or devastation? Thousands of acres of the most productive agricultural land in the nation were platted with tract housing. Acres of the Bay were filled in for domestic and commercial projects. Major freeways were built, and as they were projected further and further down the Bay and eastward beyond the Coastal Range, they drew new developments and new commercial centers like magnets. By the early 50s, the shopping center had become the towns' community centers, and by the 60s small shopping centers oriented around a supermarket were joined by large-scale, self-contained units centering on an open or enclosed mall and incorporating one or more major department stores. A number of architectural styles were employed, but most adhered more or less to the esthetics of the International style. Only in a few cases did the phenomenon of the shopping center inspire outstanding architecture. As ranch-house tracts continued to grow like fungus across the fertile land around San Francisco, Sacramento, and almost all the smaller cities, so in the 60s did the city centers—not outward but upward. San Francisco finally began to acquire a high-rise skyline, as did Oakland. All this was prestige packaging, but it was often defended in the verbiage of "urban renewal." Since the central city was "rotting" it behooved cities to meet the "urban crisis" by tearing down old buildings and eradicating social "problems" by building over them. While it cannot be denied that most central cities needed reform, it must be apparent by now that the results of urban renewal have been disappointing if not disastrous, in many cases cruelly displacing individuals and groups and needlessly destroying useful buildings, some of them of great historical and architectural significance.

Architecturally the Second Bay tradition continued, and the California ranch house, which in part was an outgrowth of the woodsy Bay Region houses of Wurster and others, became the popular mode, not only in California but eventually throughout the United States. In contrast, commercial and institutional buildings in northern California (and in the South as well) closely adhered to the Miesian aesthetics of the triumphant International Style. Few of these glass box commercial buildings can be looked upon today as really distinguished High Art buildings, but some, like S.O.M.'s John Hancock Building (1959), provide a much needed calm, a delicate neutrality to the urban street scene.

By the end of the 50s, the Second Bay tradition had, on the whole, become bland and dry. Its strength in its earlier years, like that of the First Bay tradition, was a direct outgrowth of its contrast and contradiction of urbane and vernacular forms and details. By 1960 these contrasts and contradictions had mellowed. A new vigorous synthesis was needed and this was supplied by a small group of Bay Area designers who came to the fore in the 60s, Charles Moore, William Turnbull, Richard Peters, George Homsey, and several others. Like their predecessors, these designers returned to the vernacular, in this case the California barn (a form utilized earlier in the late 40s by Joseph Esherick) and they turned the horizontal California ranch house on

Introduction

end to create a vertical cut out box with vertically connected interior spaces. They sheathed these elongated boxes in wood and contained their vertical volumes under ungainly shed roofs.

Once again an intricate play of contradiction and contrast took place, between the vernacular (some folk, some derived from the commercial builder) and a knowing and sophisticated awareness of Modern architecture and of architectural history. The monument of the Third Bay tradition is undeniably the condominium units at the Sea Ranch designed by Moore, Turnbull, and Lyndon in 1965. Here the conflict is not only apparent among the elements of the building but even more in the romantic and mysterious relationships which exist between this man-made object and the theatrical drama of its cliff side site.

With the exception of the cut-out box tradition and the all too slow emergence of BART (a rapid public transit system for the Bay Area), the decades of the 60s did not mark a major change from the 50s; freeways and urbanization continued unabated. The coastal strip from Santa Cruz to Carmel began to congeal together as a single urbanized area; Sacramento oozed out into its surrounding fertile farmland, and San Francisco sprouted an increased number of skyscrapers, some architecturally impressive such as the Bank of America Bldg. (1968), some openly advertising themselves like the pyramidal TransAmerica Bldg. (1972), but all of them creating physical and visual congestion. Work commenced on the first stages of the California Water project which was to bring the abundance of northern California water to the dry Southland. What all of this intensified urbanization and exploitation of the natural resources was doing in a negative way to the northern California environment began to be plain for all to see. From the days of the City Beautiful movement on, San Francisco had been the home of several pioneering efforts in local and regional planning and of organized groups of citizens, who had supported one or another of these planning efforts. In the 60s several groups emerged: The Planning and Conservation League and California Tomorrow, both of which were state-wide in their interests. These two planning organizations were joined by other environmental and conservation groups, notably the San Francisco based Sierra Club. By the early 70s these groups, taking advantage of an economic slump, were able to markedly slow down the pace of "development" and especially the exploitation of the land. Having partially succeeded in their initial goal, the planners, conservationists and environmentalists of northern California now face the difficult task of providing a positive planning and architectural program to rectify what has occurred and to maintain the tenuous balance between nature and man.

INTRODUCTION TO S. F. BAY — REGIONAL PLAN

PACIFIC RESOURCES INCORPORATED
Aerial Photographic Division

The San Francisco Bay area creates a powerful sense of place. Its extraordinary geographic clarity and the dominance of its physiography give vivid form to the concept of a San Francisco Bay Region. Its sheer extent, 140 miles north and south by 70 miles east and west, focuses attention and energy on a unifying regional network of communication and transportation. Beginning with the first European occupation, efforts at planning and developing such regional networks have accompanied settlement. In recent years this tendency has gained strength. Today the San Francisco Bay Area displays regional emphasis in planning and development quite unique among the major American metropolitan areas.

The Bay itself is the focus of the region. To the north, three parallel valleys open onto and define that edge of the Region. The eastern side is formed by the broad belt of mountains and intervening valleys that separate the Bay from the Central Valley of California. The Carquinas Straits cut through these hills and drain the great valley into the Bay. On the west two mountain-ridged peninsulas separate the Bay from the ocean: Marin to the north and San Francisco-San Mateo (the Peninsula) to the south. Between them the Golden Gate joins Bay and ocean. The long south arm of the Bay ends in the wide but rapidly tapering Santa Clara Valley. Taken as a whole it is geography so obvious in its structure that nearly every citizen and visitor sees it clearly in his mind's eye.

From the first, settlement has had a regional dimension as paths between the missions ringed the Bay. Only the breaks at the Golden Gate on the west and the Straits in the east interrupted the ring of roads the Padres laid out. With the end of the Mexican period, statehood in the U.S.A., and the beginning of the Gold Rush, the regional character of the Bay Area became somewhat eclipsed. As towns were founded, they tended to compete in a fever for speculative advantage. The sense of these late 19th century commercial feuds seems symbolized by the town named New York of the Pacific, located where Pittsburgh is now. Gold Rush prosperity passed the town by. It chose San Francisco as the regional capital, Oakland as transportation hub, and the north and south Bay valleys as market gardens. This general division of labor has held ever since except for the Santa Clara Valley which has become in the last generation a third great regional population and employment center.

The old roads between missions became highways, and steamship service crisscrossed the Bay. Railroads completed a network that served all the major centers, albeit with the aid of ferries such as the Atchison, Topeka and Santa Fe boats that terminated in a ferry pier in Richmond for that last leg to the city over water. The population increasingly used the area as a region. Suburbs developed. Employment scattered. Rich San Franciscans particularly used the whole area as their metropolis to exploit for summer houses, country estates, real estate, and commercial opportunities.

After the First World War, an extraordinary climate of business efficiency and engineering rationality triggered the first formal movements toward regional planning and development. Serious studies took place concerning such issues as rapid transit, highways, and various cross-Bay bridge possibilities. At the same time regional public works, particularly water supply, began to provide concrete experiences in area-wide thinking. This movement, led by Russell Van Nest Black and Frederick W. Dohrman, culminated in 1925 in a San Francisco based Regional Plan Association, then two years later in a draft plan and planning legislation.

Directly this effort came to little. The Plan Association went broke in the late 1920s. The whole movement was finally a disaster of the Depression. But indirectly it had a powerful effect. It provided an agenda for depression era public works that emphasized transportation connections and began the immensely expensive system that has allowed the automobile to take over from train and ferry. The monuments produced include the area's biggest: Golden Gate Bridge, the freeway connection north into Marin Co., the Bay Bridge and its connection through a tunnel in the Berkeley-Oakland hills to the valleys to the east, the Bayshore highway on the Peninsula, and many more.

The importance of regional public works planning seemed clear, and in the late 1930s the New Deal-sponsored National Resources Planning Board helped various governmental units begin planning. County-wide public works and land use planning began, particularly in San Mateo County. Though anti-New Deal forces killed the N.R.P.B. during the Second World War, the stage had been set for regional thinking. In the early 1950s two thrusts began.

One, for a regional rapid transit system, is covered in

detail in the next section. The other, for a regional planning authority as a first step toward regional government, saw light in the 1952 report of the San Francisco Bay Area Council. A decade later the state legislature established the Association of Bay Area Governments (A.B.A.G.) and serious planning began. The region includes the nine counties surrounding the Bay. Representatives of town, city, and county governments sit on the agency's board. A preliminary plan appeared in 1966 and a final regional plan was adopted by A.B.A.G. and its constituents in 1970.

In addition to transit and regional planning, the Bay itself became a major focus of regional concern. Fill of one sort or another, first to make farmland, but in the last century to make industrial sites, residential neighborhoods, shipping ports, and airports, had buried about half of the Bay's 700 square mile surface. Alarm over this led to a 1964 moratorium on fill and a permanent control in 1969. A new regional agency created by the state administered these controls. Now the Bay Conservation and Development Commission has halted most fill and controls most shoreline development.

Problems of air and water pollution have also led to regional agencies and, increasingly, regional solutions. The most recent of these area-wide efforts aims at openspace preservation. Beginning perhaps with A.B.A.G. openspace studies of 1961-62, a campaign is underway to create a regional openspace agency that will undertake a massive land preservation program. Already county, sub-regional, and federal agencies have begun an active expansion of their parkland holdings. In this campaign as in previous ones for Bay conservation, regional planning, and rapid transit, the name of planner T. J. Kent, Jr. stands out as a prime mover.

B.A.R.T. — BAY AREA RAPID TRANSIT DISTRICT

Of the many expressions of regional consciousness in the Bay Area none has attracted more interest worldwide than the ambitious decision to build a rapid transit system, the first new system in the U.S. in two generations. Although it was forecast 40 years ago, the first regional transportation plan was produced in 1956 by the Bay Area Rapid Transportation Commission, established in 1951 to study urban transportation needs. This plan called for 385 miles of rail rapid transit to service the five counties of San Francisco, Alameda, Contra Costa, Marin, and San Mateo. In 1962 Marin and San Mateo withdrew, and the other three counties authorized construction of a 75 mile system. The first construction contract was let in 1965, and the first section of the system, the Oakland-Fremont line, opened in 1972. According to present plans, the rest of the East Bay system and the San Francisco line will open in 1973.

A joint venture of three engineering firms, Parsons Brinkerhoff-Tudor-Bechtel, designed the system. They in turn hired 15 project architects, 8 landscape architects, and several industrial and graphics designers. Don Emmons served originally as Consulting Architect

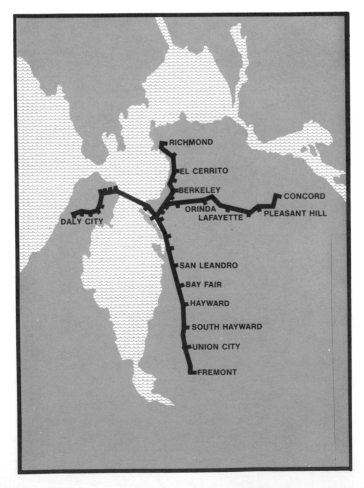

to develop the general architectural standards for the system and stations. He designed the award-winning structure for all the elevated sections of track. The overall station signing was designed by Ernest Born; miscellaneous graphics are by Tom Hisata. John Ely Burchard was the Visual Design Consultant to the Board. In 1966, Emmons was succeeded by Tallie B. Maule who has coordinated design efforts on the stations. The B.A.R.T. system received the H.U.D. Honor Award for "overall design excellence."

Some observers have felt that the contrast is too great between the super-comfortable trains designed by Sundberg-Ferar and the hard-edged stations designed to weather whatever storms of abuse the future may bring. Most of the stations are aerial or on-grade; subways have mezzanine concourses. When money was available, the interiors were enlivened with murals, mosaics, and super-graphics commissioned from prominent artists. Eventually all the stations will have works of art, but so far only the following have been installed on the Oakland-Fremont line:

MacArthur Station: Mosaic by Mark Adams
Lake Merritt Station: Plaster relief by William Mitchell
Coliseum Station: Mural by John Wastlhuber
San Leandro Station: Mural by Joseph Esherick
Union City Station: Mosaics by Jean Varda
Fremont Station: Mural by Tallie Maule

Some special landscaping design efforts embellish the right-of-way, particularly the linear park installed where the elevated train comes through Albany.

The visitor interested in touring the stations can buy a ticket to enter the system where he chooses, leave the train for a visit at each station, and return to his starting point without paying an additional fare.

Following is a list of stations by name, architect, and landscape architect. The map shows the whole system with the location of each station by name. Elsewhere in the guide the individual stations now open are located on section maps but are not credited in the text.

Stations	Project Architects	Landscape Architects
Test Track & Bldg.	Gerald M. McCue & Assoc.	Sasaki-Walker Assoc.
Embarcadero	Tallie B. Maule/Hertzka & Knowles Assoc.	—
Montgomery St.	Skidmore, Owings & Merrill	—
Powell St.	Skidmore, Owings & Merrill	—
Civic Center	Reid & Tarics	—
Van Ness	Reid & Tarics	—
Church St.	Reid & Tarics	—
Castro St.	Reid & Tarics	—
16th St. Mission	Hertzka & Knowles	Theodore Osmundson
24th St. Mission	Hertzka & Knowles	Theodore Osmundson
Glen Park	Corlett & Spackman/ Ernest Born	Douglas Bayliss
Balboa Park	Corlett & Spackman/ Ernest Born	Douglas Bayliss
Daly City	Gerald M. McCue & Assoc.	Theodore Osmundson
Richmond	Maher & Martens	Royston, Hanamoto, Beck & Abey
El Cerrito Del Norte	DeMars & Wells	Sasaki-Walker Assoc.
El Cerrito Plaza	DeMars & Wells	Royston, Hanamoto, Beck & Abey
North Berkeley	Kitchen & Hunt	Royston, Hanamoto, Beck & Abey
Berkeley	Maher & Martens	Royston, Hanamoto, Beck & Abey
Ashby	Maher & Martens	Royston, Hanamoto, Beck & Abey
MacArthur	Maher & Martens	Royston, Hanamoto, Beck & Abey
Concord	Gwathmey, Sellier & Crosby/Joseph Esherick & Assoc.	Anthony Guzzardo
Pleasant Hill	Gwathmey, Sellier & Crosby/Joseph Esherick & Assoc.	Anthony Guzzardo
Walnut Creek	Gwathmey, Sellier & Crosby/Joseph Esherick & Assoc.	Anthony Guzzardo
Lafayette	Gwathmey, Sellier & Crosby/Joseph Esherick & Assoc.	Anthony Guzzardo
Orinda	Gwathmey, Sellier & Crosby/Joseph Esherick & Assoc.	Anthony Guzzardo
Rockridge	Maher & Martens	Royston, Hanamoto Beck & Abey
19th St. Oakland	Gerald M. McCue & Assoc.	—
12th St. Oakland	Gerald M. McCue & Assoc.	—
Oakland West	Kitchen & Hunt	Robert Kitchen
Lake Merritt	Yuill-Thornton, Warner & Levikov	Douglas Bayliss
Fruitvale	Reynolds & Chamberlain/Neill Smith	Anthony Guzzardo
Coliseum	Reynolds & Chamberlain/Neill Smith	Anthony Guzzardo
San Leandro	Gwathmey, Sellier & Crosby/Joseph Esherick & Assoc.	Anthony Guzzardo
Bay Fair	Gwathmey, Sellier & Crosby/Joseph Esherick & Assoc.	Anthony Guzzardo
Hayward	Wurster, Bernardi & Emmons	Ralph Jones
South Hayward	Kitchen & Hunt	Robert Kitchen
Union City	Kitchen & Hunt	Robert Kitchen
Fremont	Kitchen & Hunt	Robert Kitchen

SF

SAN FRANCISCO

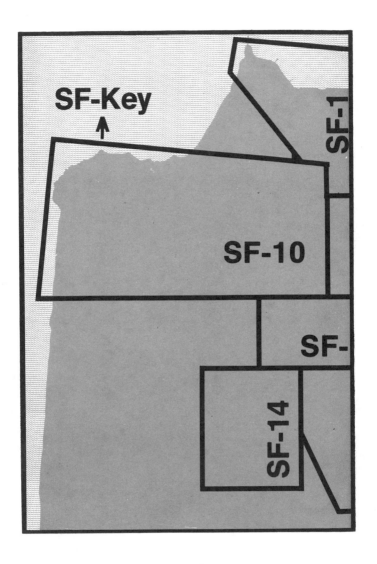

SF-Key

SF-1

SF-10

SF-

SF-14

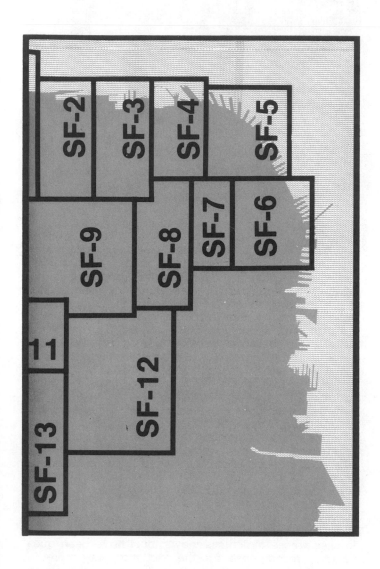

To look backward from present-day San Francisco—
"everybody's favorite city"—to the barren fog-swept
headlands that greeted Juan Bautista de Anza and
his little band of Spanish settlers in the spring of 1776,
requires an enormous leap of the imagination, or,
perhaps better, a trip to the still wild sections of the
Point Reyes peninsula, from whose forbidding beauty
one can begin to understand why the Indians shunned
the peninsula of San Francisco and the Spaniards considered it a hardship post. The topography that seems
so glamorous to us was only an obstacle made more
difficult by the scarcity of water and the almost total
absence of tree cover to give shelter from the biting
winds. While the Presidio and the Mission were settled
first, they generated only minimal supporting facilities
around them, and the first real residential settlement
occurred in 1834 around what is now Portsmouth
Square. By 1847, the population had grown to around
500, and Jasper O'Farrell had surveyed the gridiron
street plan north and south of Market as far west as
Hyde and out into the Bay to the east. Thus, the
framework was set on which the Gold Rush was to
impose a city overnight, forcing, with more enthusiasm than logic, the gridiron relentlessly over the hills
to sites whose matchless views must have been ques-
tionable recompense for the fact that they were inaccessible to horse and wagon. The push of development moved evenly westward through the latter half
of the century, so that by 1906, the area bounded by
Divisadero on the west, the Bay on the north and east,
and a rather undefined boundary south of the Mission, was fairly well settled with the closely packed
two and three-story wooden residential buildings still
evident today.

The "heights" of Pacific Heights and some grand avenues like Van Ness, South Van Ness, and Dolores,
were the choice sites for grand mansions, while the
fringes of Pacific Heights, what is now called the
Western Addition, and most of the Mission district

were built speculatively by builders using more or less standard plans, often doing whole blocks with slightly differing facades in much the same way as present-day builders.

The structure of downtown was much as it is, with major shopping around Union Square and business along Montgomery. The first few high-rise buildings had sprung up along Market and Montgomery around 1900. Concerns for planning the growing city prompted a citizen's group to commission a plan from Daniel Burnham in 1905. In the year before the earthquake, he sat in a cottage on Twin Peaks with a draftsman, producing a new City Beautiful image for San Francisco which was received with the ineffectual enthusiasm generally accorded such plans.

The earthquake of 1906 was more of a trauma than a turning point in the city's development. In spite of the plan Burnham had providentially produced just before, the drive to rebuild the shattered downtown was as impatient as the gold fever that had originally produced it, and things went back pretty much as they had been, with the addition of a good deal of steel and concrete stiffening.

Improved transportation and the push of population growth sent the city sprawling over the western dunes in the Twenties and Thirties in a more uniform and less interesting pattern made possible by the flat topography. Apart from the fertile eclectic imagery of the endless stucco facades, what is most characteristic is the density of these little boxes; only in the fancy subdivisions like St. Francis Woods, Forest Hills, and Seacliff do the houses become detached. Western San Francisco is not at all the visitor's image of hills, cable cars, and bay windows, but it is where about half of the city's population lives. Golden Gate Park—sand dunes turned Garden of Eden by persistent cultivation—is the chief reason that a visitor should venture that way.

Morley Baer: *Here Today*

Downtown and the hills which immediately surround it are San Francisco's image as well as where it began as a city; here the juxtaposition of hills and water, high- and low-rise, elegant and shack, and the compactness of it all combine to make a kind of urbanity that happens almost nowhere else in this country. The cityscape resulting from this combination is so rich and various that it would be wise not to take the listings of this guide as the limits of architectural interest. The rhythms of bay-windowed fronts or rectilinear backs of white wooden row houses marching over the hills are more satisfying than most high-rise facades. Seen from the surrounding hills, the baroque and gothic church towers of North Beach belie the insignificance of their architecture, providing vertical accents as effective as some of the great churches of Europe. The city is full of such happy accidents, where minor buildings fill major posts in the cityscape. So we urge you to walk, even at the pain of your leg muscles, enough to enjoy the surprises offered by the city's improbable conjunction of man and nature: the green of Angel Island seen at the end of a street, the cascade of little wooden houses tumbling down Telegraph Hill into the skyscraper canyon of lower Montgomery Street, or even the curiosities of ornament that adorn the ubiquitous bay windows.

Presidio Barracks

PRESIDIO & PRESIDIO HEIGHTS

Juan Bautista de Anza, commander of the first group of Spanish settlers, chose the site for the Presidio in the spring of 1776. It has remained a military base ever since, preserving the magnificent headlands of the Golden Gate in a nearly natural state. The only remaining trace of the Spanish is the commandant's adobe (SF 1/6), built into the present officers' club so that it is scarcely recognizable. But because the Presidio has been for years more a symbolic than an active post, it boasts a number of interesting pieces of 19th Century military construction, most notably Fort Point, one of the best preserved of pre-Civil War brick coast defense forts, and the only one west of the Mississippi. The old Station Hospital and barracks suggest that 19th Century military architecture was generally superior to 20th.

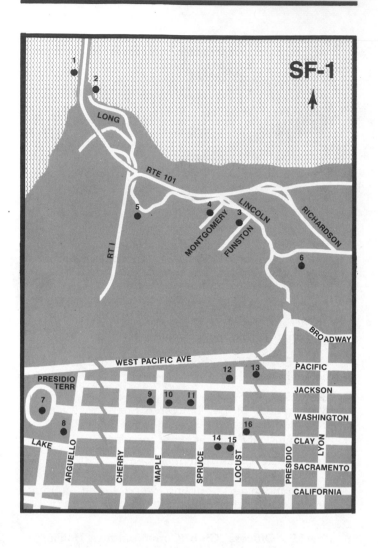

1. **Golden Gate Bridge** 1937; Irving Morrow, Consulting Architect. Joseph Strauss, Chief Engineer The 4200 foot clear span was until 1959 the longest in the world. The great achievement of placing tower foundations in the swirling currents of the Golden Gate, the superb setting, and the red color of the bridge make it one of the landmarks of bridge building. Moderne detailing remarkably adapted to heavy steel construction makes it an equally clear expression of its time.

2. **Fort Point**   1853; U.S. Army Engineers
   Just below the south bridge abutment—accessible from Long Avenue in the Presidio. Gradually being restored as a military museum.

3. **Old Station Hospital**   1857
   Funston Ave. S of Lincoln Ave.

   The first permanent building built by the U. S. Army here, its materials all came around the Horn. Beyond it to the south is an 1873 row of officers' houses.

4. **Barracks**   1895-1909
   Montgomery St. bet. Lincoln & Sheridan Aves. (W side of Main Parade Ground)

   One of the city's finest street facades.

5. **Presidio Religious Activities Center**   1902
   Lincoln Ave. E of Storey Ave.

   This handsome, rambling wood frame building would clearly not have survived on a more active post.

6. **Presidio Officers' Club (Commandant's House)**
   Moraga & Graham Sts., Presidio
   Originally c.1792; entirely built around and remodeled by the WPA in 1933.

7. **Presidio Terrace**
   Arguello Blvd. off end of Washington St.
   A remarkable collection of pretentious piles, the most remarkable being No. 7, an immense Hansel and Gretel cottage by W. R. Yelland, c.1930.

8. **Temple Emanu-El**   1926; Bakewell & Brown/Bernard Maybeck & G. A. Lansburgh, consulting Archts.
   Arguello Blvd. at Lake St.
   Chapel by Michael Goodman, 1938-40.
   Stained glass by Mark Adams, 1972-73.
   Sophisticated Arabo-Byzantine. The general massing and the courtyard are especially successful.

9. **Koshland Mansion**   1902; 3800 Washington St.
   The Petit Trianon transplanted—a nice foil for Mendelsohn across the street.

10. **House**   1952; Eric Mendelsohn
    3778 Washington St.

    A fine blend of Bay Region and International styles, with just a trace of early Mendelsohn streamlining in the rounded corner bay and port-hole windows.

11. **House**   1952; Joseph Esherick
    3700 Washington St.

    The Bay Region blending of informality and elegance is shown here in the unexpected but successful combination of barn siding and double-hung windows with delicate iron work and a formal entry.

12. **Roos House**   1909 & 1926; Bernard Maybeck
    3500 Jackson St.

    Maybeck's own brand of English Tudor lavished on a major house.

13. **Houses: 3300 Block of Pacific Avenue**
    2 Laurel St.   c.1945; remodeled by Clark & Beuttler
    3377 Pacific Ave.   c.1908; Julia Morgan
    3343 Pacific Ave.   1903; Albert Farr
    3333 Pacific Ave.   1902; Albert Farr
    3323 Pacific Ave.   1963; Joseph Esherick

    Less spectacular than the next block up the hill, this group continues the same high standard of brown shingle street facades.

14. **House** 1942; William W. Wurster
3655 Clay St.

15. **House** 1954; Wurster, Bernardi & Emmons
301 Locust St.
This one-story house with its irregular brown shingle exterior is an interesting contrast to the white brick urbanity of the one listed below, diagonally across the street.

16. **House** 1945; Wurster, Bernardi & Emmons
250 Locust St.

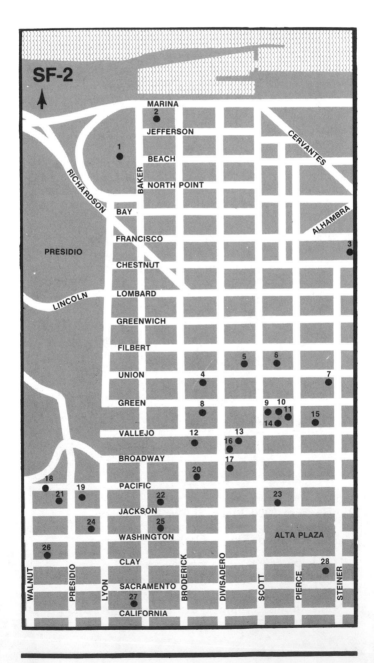

Pacific Hts.

Pacific Heights is a ridge running east and west along the city's northern flank from Van Ness Avenue to the Presidio. Annexed to the city as part of the Western Addition in the 1850s, it was settled sparsely in the 1860s, but remained an area of bare slopes and isolated houses until around 1890. Since then it has grown into the city's most stylish residential area, mixing grand mansions with more modest townhouses and increasing numbers of luxury apartment buildings.

North of Pacific Heights along the Bay stretches the Marina, most of which is built on land filled for the 1915 Panama-Pacific Exposition. The sole survivor of that Fair, the Palace of Fine Arts, stands at the western end of the area. The Marina was built up in the 20s and 30s in a uniform, rather bland version of Spanish Colonial Revival which gives it a stage-set quality unpunctuated by much in the way of architectural interest.

At its eastern end, Fort Mason juts into the Bay, again preserved as open space by the Army. Its wooded point was originally settled by several of San Francisco's most notable early citizens, including Colonel John C. Fremont, whose house was later razed for fortifications.

1. **Palace of Fine Arts** 1915; Bernard Maybeck
Baker St. at Beach St.

    Exploratorium open Wednesday through Sunday, 1 to 5 p.m. Until 1962 the crumbling stucco of the original building, built for the Panama-Pacific Exposition, gave eloquent if functionless expression to the mood of melancholy that Maybeck desired for his masterful stage set. Then, thanks largely to the generosity and persistence of Walter Johnson, who matched the funds raised by the city, the entire structure was rebuilt in concrete and is gradually acquiring uses within such as the Exploratorium, a theatre, and an art gallery.

2. **Double House (Dr. William Schiff)** 1937
Richard Neutra & Otto Winkler
2056-58 Jefferson St.

    A steel and glass facade fabricated of standard industrial sash members.

3. **Crocker Bank, Marina Branch** 1973
Wong, Brocchini & Associates
Chestnut St. bet. Steiner & Fillmore Sts.

4. **Rosstown - Townhouses** 1967; John L. Field
2600 Block of Union St., near Divisadero St.
Modern mannerist shingle style.

5. **Shingle House** 1890; A. C. Schweinfurth
Remodeled 1955; John Funk
2516 Union St.

6. **House** c.1872; 2460 Union St.
A Mansard-roofed house with paired dormers and center gambrel roof gable.

7. **St. Mary the Virgin Episcopal Church**   1891
2301 Union St.
Original architect unknown; remodeled by Warren Perry in 1953. An attractive shingle style church.

8. **House**   1939; William W. Wurster
2633 Green St.
A simple box with Moderne details, unusual for Wurster.

9. **House**   1938; Gardner Dailey
2750 Scott St.
Dailey was the most polished of the area's few pre-World War II practitioners of the International Style, but his houses never lost the regional informality of plan and massing.

10. **Two Houses**   1891 & 1895; Ernest Coxhead
2421 & 2423 Green St.
The quiet exterior of Coxhead's own house at 2421 conceals a marvelous interior, with a long, glazed entrance gallery on the west side running from a high-ceiling living room on the street to the dining rom on the rear garden. Upstairs the master bedroom extends into the high gable.

●11. **Casebolt House**   1865-66; 2727 Pierce St.
This noble Italianate pile is one of the oldest houses in Pacific Heights and was once the center of an extensive estate.

12. **House**   1952; Wurster, Bernardi & Emmons
2795 Vallejo St.

13. **House**   1938; John Ekin Dinwiddie
2660 Divisadero St.
Wood International Style with Moderne overtones in the angled, shadow box picture window.

14. **Warren Perry House**   1925; Warren Perry
2530 Vallejo St.

15. **House**   1968; John L. Field
2440 Vallejo St.

16. **Studio-Residence**   1941; Gardner Dailey
2674 Divisadero St.
Built for the then-director of the deYoung Museum, this International style box has one of the most spectacular Bay views possible.

17. **House**   1939; William W. Wurster
2560 Divisadero St.
One of Wurster's handsomest brick houses, on a commanding site at the top of Pacific Heights.

18. **Houses: 3200 Block of Pacific Ave.**
    3203   1901; rem. by Bruce Porter & Willis Polk
    3233   1909; Bernard Maybeck
    3235   William F. Knowles
   ●3232   1902; Ernest Coxhead—rem. 1959; John Funk

3234   1902; Ernest Coxhead
3236-40   William F. Knowles
3255   1910; rem. Willis Polk
3277   1913; Willis Polk

This steep block is one of the city's most harmonious. Only in New England or in the South does one expect to find such a group of fine houses; perhaps nowhere else can a group from this particular period be found. The mixture of elegance in detail with informality in materials and window arrangements is peculiarly San Franciscan.

19.   House   1912; Ernest Coxhead
3151 Pacific Ave.
The exigencies of hillside sites encouraged a remarkable freedom in plan and massing which, when combined with fine traditional detail, as in Coxhead's work, produced houses that were truly original without making a great point of it.

20.   2800 Block of Pacific Ave. & Raycliff Terr.
1 Raycliff   1951; Gardner Dailey
25 Raycliff   1959; Wurster, Bernardi & Emmons
55 Raycliff   1957; rem. by Germono Milono
75 Raycliff   1951; Joseph Esherick
2889 Pacific   1890?; Arthur Brown, Jr. (?)
2870 Pacific   1951; Wurster, Bernardi & Emmons
2830 Pacific   1910; Albert Farr
2820 Pacific   1912; Willis Polk
2810 Pacific   1910; Albert Farr
2800 Pacific   1899; Ernest Coxhead
A catolog of two generations of local domestic architecture, none of them outstanding examples, but interesting as a group.

21.   Double House   c.1900; Bruce Porter
21 & 23 Presidio Blvd.
A fine, double-bay-window, shingle facade.

22.   Howard House   1939; H. T. Howard
2944 Jackson St.
One of the best examples of the Streamlined Moderne style in the city.

23. Music and Art Institute (former residence) 1894
Willis Polk
2622 Jackson St.

Possibly Polk's first major commission this sandstone house has the rather heavy, spare classic detailing which he often used in his residential building.

● **24. Church of the New Jerusalem (Swedenborgian)**
1894; A. Page Brown
2107 Lyon St.

Joseph Worcester, the pastor who built this church, was the son of the founder of the New Jerusalem Church. Bruce Porter sketched the building, and Bernard Maybeck and A. C. Schweinfurth did the drawings in Brown's office. A descriptive leaflet is available within the church.

25. Engine Co. 23 - Firehouse (now residence) 1893
3022 Washington St.

San Francisco's only surviving Victorian fire house.

26. Osborn House 1895; Ernest Coxhead
3362 Clay St.

Another fine shingle-sheathed house.

27. Five Cottages 1882; William F. Lewis, builder
1805-1817 Baker St.

These Mansard-roofed cottages, by the builder William F. Lewis, are fine examples of early tract housing.

28. Seven Row Houses c.1875; 2637-2673 Clay St.

A group of beautifully restored and maintained two-story town houses in Italianate style.

Morley Baer: *Here Today*

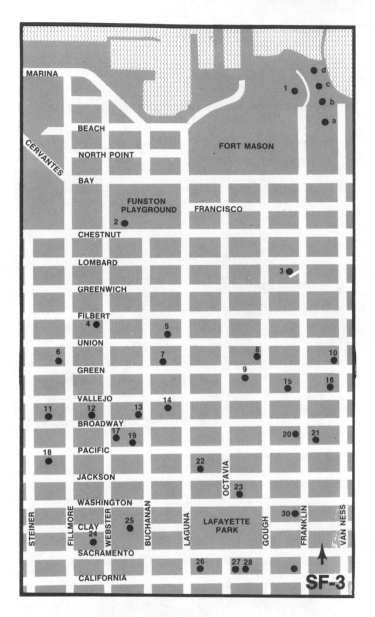

1. **Fort Mason**
   a. Officers' Club (orig. Brooks House with additions) 1855; rem. 1880s
   b. Quarters Two-part of Brooks House 1855
   c. Quarters Three-Moody House 1855
   d. Quarters Four-Haskell House 1855
   These buildings are off the end of Franklin St. The latter two have had a second story added.

2. **Marina Branch, S. F. Public Library** 1955
   Appleton & Wolfard
   Chestnut and Webster Sts.

   Typical of a series of pleasant, informal city libraries by this firm, this one has a prize-winning tapestry by Mark Adams in the reading room.

3. **Blackstone House** 1852
   11 Blackstone Court-off Franklin St. nr. Lombard St.

   A simple two-story cottage that is the rival of the Phelps House at 329 Divisadero for the title of the city's oldest intact house.

4. **Headquarters of the Vedanta Society** 1905
   Filbert and Webster Sts.

   Joseph A. Leonard
   A meeting of the mysterious East and the uninhibited West.

photo: California Historical Society

5. **Union Street Shops** 1870-80
   rem. 1965; Beverly Willis
   1980 Union St. and adjacent buildings

   In recent years, Union Street has been transformed from a sleepy convenience-shopping district to a busy specialty shop area, with a consequent refurbishing of a number of old buildings.

6. **St. Vincent de Paul Roman Catholic Church** 1916
   Shea & Lofquist
   Green & Fillmore Sts.

Frank Shea ranks as one of the few really interesting architects of Catholic buildings in an era when the Romans produced a great quantity of building and very little architecture. See also St. Anselm's in San Anselmo; St. Thomas Aquinas, Palo Alto; and St. Rose in Santa Rosa.

7. **Flats**   1875; 1950-80 Green St.

This early apartment building in Italianate style was moved so that its facades are now reversed; what shows on Green Street was the original back side.

8. **The Octagon—National Society of the Colonial Dames (former McElroy house)**   1857
2645 Gough St. (moved from across the street)
Rem. 1953; Warren Perry
Built according to the precepts of Orson Fowler, author of *A Home for All, or the Gravel Wall and Octagon Mode of Building* (1849). This is one of two surviving octagonal houses in San Francisco. (See 1067 Green Street.)

9. **House**   1940; William W. Wurster
1641 Green St.
Classic early Wurster—as straight a house as you could find anywhere, anytime.

10. **Holy Trinity Russian Orthodox Cathedral**   1909
1520 Green St.
Remarkable for being recognizable both as Russian and turn-of-the-century American.

11. **House**   1956; Campbell & Wong
2380 Broadway
Compared to its older neighbors, the seclusion of this house with its deep fenced entrance court is an interesting commentary on contemporary living.

12. **Convent of the Sacred Heart (former Flood Mansion)**   1916; Bliss & Faville
2222 Broadway
Elegant Spanish Renaissance revival.

13. **Apartment Building**   1973
Backen, Arrigoni & Ross
2000 Broadway

14. **Sarah Dix Hamlin School**   1965
Wurster, Bernardi & Emmons
2129 Vallejo St.
This concrete school still maintains the unadorned purity of the early work of this firm.
Next door at 2121 and 2127 Vallejo are a couple of interesting Queen Anne-Eastlake houses.

15. **House**   1875; Edmond M. Wharff
1737 Vallejo St.
A handsome free standing Mansard house, now a registered landmark, remodeled by William W. Wurster in 1941. 1737 across the street is a brick

apartment complex of great charm, reminiscent of a Norman village.

16.   **House**   1890; 1616 Vallejo St.
Queen Anne style.

●17.   **Bourn Mansion**   1894; Willis Polk
2550 Webster St.

Massive clinker-brick Georgian built for the president of the Spring Valley Water company, for whom Polk also did Filoli, a great estate down the Peninsula near Woodside.

18.   **House**   c.1855; 2475 Pacific Ave.

One of the oldest houses in Pacific Heights, although the entrance porch and false front are later, probably 1883.

19.   **Duplex**   c.1938; 2248-50 Pacific Ave.

A white stucco double house in Streamlined Moderne style.

20.   **Flats**   c.1910; 2413 Franklin St.

A graceful and well-maintained French Second Empire transplant, one of several in the city (see 1347 McAllister).

21.   **Double-Bay House**   1872
1782 Pacific Ave. at Franklin

One of the city's handsomest Italianate Victorians; impeccably maintained.

22.   **California Historical Society (former Whittier house)**   1894-96; E. R. Swain & N. J. Thorp
2090 Jackson St.

Fine detailing combined with powerful massing distinguish this house of specially imported brownstone. The period interiors are open without charge, Tues.-Sat., 9-5.

●23. Spreckels Mansion   1913
MacDonald & Applegarth
2935 Washington St.
A white plaster cast of the Grand Trianon.

24. Dental School of the University of the Pacific
1965; Skidmore, Owings & Merrill
2155 Webster St.
SOM did a master plan in 1962 for what had been
the Stanford University Medical School and Hospital. Two buildings were done by them, this and
the Research Building.

25. Presbyterian Medical Center
Webster to Buchanan Sts., bet. Sacramento and
Washington
Hospital   1972; Stone, Marraccini & Patterson
Medical Research Building   1963
Skidmore, Owings & Merrill
Medical Office Building   1973
Roger Owen Boyer & Assoc.
Old Stanford Hospital   1883
The last named building (slated for destruction)
is a rare survivor in San Francisco of Eastlake
done in brick. Across Webster St. from the Re-
search Bldg. is a fine group of false-front Italian-
ate houses of the 1870s.

26. Group of Italianate Houses   1870s
2018-20-22-26 California St.
A group of classic San Francisco townhouses.

27. Rathbone (Originally Atherton) House   1883
1990 California St.
This is a real test of the viewer's tolerance for
what used to be known as Victorian excesses.

28. House   1883; Sussman & Wormser
1976 California St.
One of the more full blown examples of the Stick-
Italianate style, it pales by comparison with its
neighbor above.

29. Haas-Lilienthal House   1886; 2007 Franklin St.

The Stick-Eastlake monument of the city, it demonstrates that whatever architecture has gained since the 1880s, it has certainly lost confidence.

NORTH WATERFRONT & RUSSIAN HILL

The North Waterfront is San Francisco at its most "native" and its most tourist side by side. The Sunday fishermen on the Municipal Wharf, the elderly Italians playing bocce ball next to the Maritime Museum, and the rest of the remarkable collection of humanity that seems to live in Aquatic Park could not be less involved with the streams of tourists flowing through Ghirardelli Square, the Cannery, and Fisherman's Wharf. Except for Fisherman's Wharf, the transformation of this area from working waterfront to tourist mecca is a product of the last ten years, starting with the remarkable Cost Plus Imports, which has expanded from one small loft building dealing in importers' leftovers to a world-wide operation with some 70,000 sq. ft. of retail space. Next came Ghirardelli Square, the

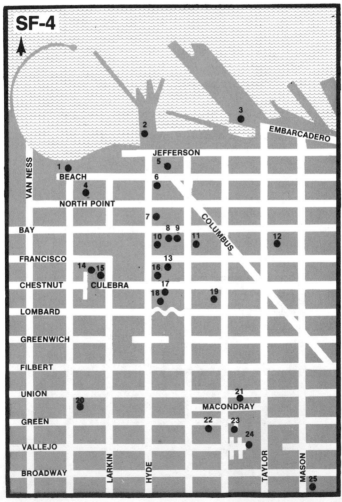

child of a truly enlightened developer, William M. Roth, who put the preservation of the old chocolate factory buildings and the quality of the new uses he put into them ahead of any return on his very sizable investment. Following in his footsteps, Leonard Martin in doing the Cannery has taken more of the same knocks with the same high goals, and both have set examples which are now being imitated all over the country.

Older and on a distinctly lower plane architecturally and commercially, but still enormously lively, is the area around Fisherman's Wharf. The best thing here is the carefully preserved remnant of the old crab-fishing fleet which ties up next to the restaurants on the Wharf and still sells its shrinking catch in a few over-the-counter market stalls.

1. **Maritime Museum**   1939; William Mooser, Sr. & Jr.
   Beach St. just W of Polk
   Open daily 10-5, admission free.
   Streamlined Moderne, nautical style, with some fine ship models and historical material inside. Murals by Hilire Hyler and Sargent Johnson.

2. **Hyde Street Pier & Victorian Park (San Francisco Maritime State Historical Monument)**
   Entrance at end of Hyde St. N of Jefferson
   State of California, Department of Beaches and Parks, open daily: 10-5, admission $.75, children $.25. The State is gradually gathering here a fascinating collection of old ships, consisting presently of the C. A. Thayer, a lumber schooner of 1895, the Wapama, a steam schooner of 1915, The Alma, an 1895 scow schooner, and the Eureka, a walking beam ferry of 1890 which operated on the Bay until 1957.

3. **Fisherman's Wharf: Crab Boats**
   Jefferson at Taylor St.

4. **Ghirardelli Square**   Polk, Larkin, Beach, Northpoint Block
   Originally Ghirardelli Chocolate Company, c.1860 to 1915. Buildings along Northpoint by William Mooser, 1893-1915

Rem. 1962-67; Wurster, Bernardi & Emmons
Landscaping by Lawrence Halprin & Assoc.
Fountain by Ruth Asawa
A wonderful jumble of brick buildings, the oldest
of which was still operating in 1962 with overhead
belt-driven machinery, has been lovingly transformed into a now famous complex of shops and
restaurants. A multi-level parking garage created
a series of terrace levels within the block, and
the architects added a series of new buildings on
the garage and along its north edge. The popularity of the whole attests to the success of its plan.

Morley Baer: *Here Today*

● **5. The Cannery**   c.1909; rem. 1968
Joseph Esherick & Assoc.
Leavenworth St. bet. Jefferson and Beach Sts.
Following in the footsteps of Ghirardelli Square,
this is a one-building version of the same idea.

6. Fromm and Sichel Headquarters   1973
Worley Wong, Ronald Brocchini & Assoc.
Hyde & Beach Sts.
Christian Brothers Wine Museum open to the pub-
lic.

7. Victorian Gothic House   1850-60; 2626 Hyde St.
Rem. by Thomas Church, 1954
A Gothic Revival house remodeled thoroughly
in the spirit of the original. The double stair case
and projecting wing have been added.

8. Terraced Houses   1937; William W. Wurster
757-763 Bay St.
765 Bay orig. 1850s, rem. several times, last in
1935 by William W. Wurster. A beautifully sited,
deceptively simple group.

9. **House**   1937; William W. Wurster
737 Bay St.

10. **Row of Cottages**   c.1900; Lucius Soloman, builder
2540-50 Hyde St.

11. **Studio**   1961; Clark & Beuttler
(Charles W. Moore, designer) 1961
2508 Leavenworth St.

12. **North Point Public Housing**   1950
Ernest Born & Henry Gutterson
Northpoint bet. Taylor & Mason Sts.
Well-planned and scaled concrete International style buildings with continuous access balconies.

13. **House**   1849; rem. 1854 & subs.; R. C. Ruskin
825 Francisco St.
One of the city's oldest surviving houses; its Italianate exterior appearance is the result of much later remodeling.

14. **Town Houses**   1963; Joseph Esherick & Assoc.
120-22, 126-28 Culebra Terr.

15. **House**   1951; Wurster, Bernardi & Emmons
2745 Larkin St.
This large town house is handled with a splendid disregard of formality. Its casual exterior covers an interior of great dignity and spatial interest, organized to take maximum advantage of the view.

16. **House**   1948; John Funk
998 Chestnut St.
The cubistic massing of this town house is especially appropriate to its spectacular site, giving it a compactness that, with its painted exterior, is close to older San Francisco houses.

17. **House**   1956; Henry Hill
66 Montclair Terr.
A long ribbon of glass ballooning out into a cantilevered semicircular bay gives a dramatic accent to an otherwise simple house.

18. **House**   1938; Gardner Dailey
65 Montclair Terr.

A fine example of late 30s Streamlined Moderne. The access to Montclair Terrace is from the famous twisting block of Lombard Street, whose lavish planting is maintained by the adjoining residents.

19. **San Francisco Art Institute** 1926; Bakewell and Brown. New wings; Paffard Keatinge Clay
Jones St. bet. Chestnut & Lombard Sts.

Two versions of exposed concrete, each highly successful in its way: the older, a stripped Spanish Colonial Revival with a handsome courtyard; the newer, Corbusian **beton brut** handled with great authority, both designed to take the hard use their art student occupants give them.

20. **Alhambra Theater** 1930; Miller & Pflueger
Polk St. bet. Union & Green Sts.
Moorish Movie House at its best.

21. **Macondray Lane**
Bet. Union & Green Sts. from Leavenworth to Taylor St.

A two-block pedestrian street on the steep north face of Russian Hill. This should make you want to move right in, unless both your soul and your feet are flat.

22. **1000 Block of Green Street**
Bet. Leavenworth & Jones Sts.
1088   Former Firehouse 1907
1085   Apartments: Joseph Esherick 1966
1067   Fusier Octagon House 1857-58. Mansard roof and cupola added in 1880s.
1055   Italianate House 1866. Rem. by Julia Morgan 1916
1045   Queen Anne House
1039-41-43   Italianate Flats 1880s (moved here after 1906)
1033   1880s Italianate Houses.
A rare group of survivors of the 1906 earthquake and fire, which virtually razed this part of the city.

23. Summit Apartments   1965; Smith, Barker, Hanssen
999 Green St.

The powerful architecture of its base emphasizes
the overwhelming difference in scale between
the tower and its neighbors, dramatizing a conflict that contemporary architecture does not seem
to be able to handle as gracefully as the eclectic
20s and 30s in the neighboring towers.

24. 1000 Block of Vallejo Street
Accessible by ramps (designed by Willis Polk)
from Jones St.

Town Houses: 1, 3, 5 & 7 Russian Hill Pl.   1915-16;
Willis Polk

Town Houses: 1085 & 1740-42 Vallejo St.   1915-16;
Charles McCall

Marshall Houses: 1034 & 1036 Vallejo St. 1884. A
third, 1038, was demolished for a never built high
rise project.

House: 1045 Vallejo St., 40-42 Florence St. 1860.
Rem. c.1916; Willis Polk

Shingle House: 1023 Vallejo St. 1917; Julia Morgan

Polk House: 1013-15-17-19 Vallejo St. 1892; Willis
Polk

Identifiable from anywhere to the south and east
as a spot of green on the otherwise solidly built-
up hillside, the top of Russian Hill is one of the
choicest residential enclaves in the city, epito-
mizing that peculiarly San Francisco paradox of
upper class unpretentiousness. Originally it was
almost entirely owned by the Livermore family and
was developed by them with Willis Polk as architect for many of the houses. Polk himself lived at
1013-17.

27. Public Housing for the Elderly   1969
John Bolles & Assoc.
990 Pacific Ave.

SF-5　Telegraph Hill

Telegraph Hill was the inland terminus for the first West Coast telegraph originating at Point Lobos, which signaled the arrival of ships off the Golden Gate. Where Coit Tower now stands was a semaphore which could be seen from downtown. A small hill made even more abrupt by quarrying around its north and east sides, it is the home of bohemians rich and poor who enjoy some of the city's best views and most fog-free weather. Most of the buildings range from unpretentious to downright shacks, remarkable chiefly for the ways they cling precariously to precipitous slopes. Anyone who fails to venture up, or preferably down, the steep streets is missing San Francisco's most unique and magical living environment.

The Bay originally extended into the hollow between Telegraph and Russian Hills; hence the name North Beach for the city's Italian district, still happily full of the sounds and smells of Italy. Superb delicatessens, coffee houses, restaurants, and most of the city's night spots keep the area around Broadway and Columbus seething with life day and night. Columbus Ave. is the spine of North Beach, and where it termin-

Morley Baer: *Here Today*

ates at Montgomery, you are suddenly out of Italy and in downtown.

1. **Western States Bankcard Assn.**　1969
   Arthur Gensler & Assoc.
   100 Northpoint St.
   A handsome low-rise concrete office building.

2. **Northpoint**　1967; Wurster, Bernardi & Emmons
   2211 Stockton St.

3. **Office Building (formerly Old Telegraph Hill Neighborhood Association)** 1908-09
   Bernard Maybeck, Addits. 1913 & 1928
   1736 Stockton St.

   This neighborhood association was founded by Alice Griffith, a pioneer figure in San Francisco social work. Now remodeled into shops, offices, and apartments, the building has an interior court with balcony access to the second floor.

4. **Residence**　1942; Gardner Dailey
   275 Telegraph Hill Blvd.

5. **Flats**　1941; Gardner Dailey
   351 Filbert St.
   The classic San Francisco dwelling of wood with bay-windows and slab sides restated in modern terms with the addition of balconies.

6. **Coit Tower**   1934; Arthur Brown, Jr.
   Top of Telegraph Hill (reached via Lombard St.)
   Given to the city by Lillie Coit in memory of her
   husband, the tower has WPA murals depicting
   California life around its base and offers a superb
   view of the city.

7. **Apartment House**   1937; J. S. Malloch
   1360 Montgomery St.
   An unusual contractor-built early Moderne building with exterior murals.

8. **Darrell Place and Napier Lane**
   Two pedestrian streets off the Filbert steps which
   have changed little since the Gold Rush days.
   60 Darrell St. at the end of the upper one is a
   house and sculptor's studio by George Rockrise,
   1958; 228 Filbert St. dates from 1873.

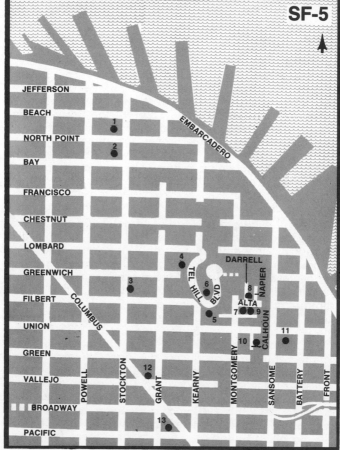

9. **House**   1852; 31 Alta Street

10. **Kahn House**   1939; Richard Neutra
    66 Calhoun Terr.
    A building by Neutra in the line of the Lovell
    Health House in Los Angeles, this was originally
    painted white. Across the street at 9 Calhoun is a
    cottage of the 1850s that is one of the city's oldest.

11. **The Ice Houses #1 and #2**   1914
    rem. 1970; Wurster Bernardi & Emmons
    1265 Battery & 151 Union Sts.

    Two handsome old brick warehouses remodeled as interior furnishing showrooms. This area below Telegraph hill has most of the surviving old waterfront warehouses of the city.

12. **St. Francis of Assisi**   orig. 1866; rest. 1907
    610 Vallejo St.

    Severely damaged in the 1906 earthquake, this church was rebuilt faithfully to its early Gothic revival design.

13. **R. Matteuchi Jeweler's Shop & Street Clock**   1907-09
    229 Columbus Ave.

    A rare and still (as of this writing) intact example of turn-of-the-century shop design.

DOWNTOWN

San Francisco's downtown was built out into the Bay from the original village settlement of Yerba Buena along what is now Grant Avenue. From Montgomery Street east, most of the east/west streets were originally wharves along which the ships of the Forty-Niners docked, were abandoned, and eventually became' buildings from which the prows sometimes emerged. The center of the first settlement was at Portsmouth Square extending south along Dupont (now Grant) to the Mission Road, which angled off southward to Mission Dolores, giving its skew axis to the streets from Market south.

The Bay, the hills and Market Street have contained and defined downtown since the Gold Rush thrust urbanity on the city overnight. Within this area, the business center along Montgomery Street and the shopping center around Union Square have shifted remarkably little since they were first established in the 1850s, maintaining a vitality rivaled by few United States cities. Most of the buildings and businesses were wiped out by the earthquake and fire of 1906, but returned as soon as possible to their old locations. The post-fire rebuilding produced the base of low-to-medium-rise loft buildings that until the skyscraper boom of the 1960-70 decade provided most of the rental space. Until the 1960s, a few survivors of the earthquake, like the noble old Mills Building, and under half a dozen skyscrapers of the 20s to early 30s were downtown's only big office buildings, but somehow these few combined to give an animated skyline and a feeling of intense urbanity. This has been so intensified by the new upthrust that cries of Manhattanization are heard and high-rise growth has become a major political issue, but even without public opposition, the office boom has probably spent itself for some time to come.

It is expressive of the temperament of its inhabitants that the city has produced many pleasant buildings, few distinguished ones, and fewer still outright "dogs," and that both business and shopping districts have many examples of tasteful small-scale rehabilitation overshadowed by the new scale of towers in a way that keeps the older scale as base and produces a San Francisco "feel" that visitors always seem to note. Above all, downtown, even at its most mundane, is jerked into another level by the vistas at the ends of the streets: Twin Peaks at the end of Market, Telegraph Hill at the end of Montgomery, the Bay Bridge at the end of California; and almost any collection of towers would look fabulous seen from across the Bay at sunset.

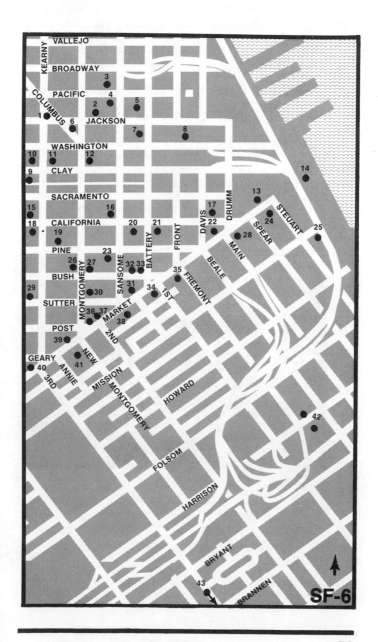

1. **Columbus Tower**   1905; Field & Kohlberg
   Rem. 1959; Henrik Bull
   Columbus & Kearny Sts.

2. **Jackson Square**
   Jackson St. bet. Montgomery & Sansome Sts. and adjacent to Montgomery St., Hotaling Pl. & Washington St.
   Note especially the following:
   - 470 Jackson   Solari Bldg. East-Larco's Bldg. 1852
   - 432 Jackson   Yeon Building 1906
   - 463 Jackson   Hotaling Annex West c.1860
   - 451 Jackson   Hotaling Building 1866
   - 445 Jackson   Hotaling Annex East c.1860
   - 441 Jackson   Medico-Dental Building 1861
   - 415-31 Jackson   Ghirardelli Building 1853
   - 732 Montgomery *Golden Era* Bldg. (now Knoll Showroom) 1852; rem. Florence Knoll
   - 728-730 Montgomery   Genella Bldg.-Belli Annex 1853-54
   - 722 Montgomery   Belli Bldg.-Langerman's Bldg. 1851
   - 804 Montgomery   Bank of Lucas, Turner & Co. 1853-54
   - 530 Washington Burr Building 1859-60

   The city's first officially designated Historic District, this is the only group of downtown business buildings to survive the 1906 earthquake and fire. Restored as a center for furniture and fabric showrooms, it has successfully (with a few exceptions) withstood new building pressures, even serving as the nucleus and inspiration for the now quite widespread practice of restoring old brick loft buildings for modern shop and office space.

3. **Musto Plaza**   1970
   Bull, Field, Volkman & Stockwell
   350 Pacific Ave.
   A handsome warehouse rehabilitation.

4. **Brick Commercial Building**   c.1907
   315-319 Pacific Ave.
   One of the earlier restorations in this area, this displays some of the most elegant brickwork of all.

5. **Jackson Place**   1907; rem. 1964; Lloyd Flood
   Mid. block bet. Washington & Jackson, Sansome
   & Battery Sts.

6. **Old Fugazi Bank Building (later Bank of Italy, Transamerica Bldg.)**   1911; Field & Kohlberg
   4 Columbus Ave. at Montgomery St.

   A gleaming white terra cotta flatiron with elegant
   Classic-Revival ornament.

Morley Baer: *Here Today*

7. **U. S. Customs House**   1906-11; Eames & Young
   555 Battery St.

8. **Golden Gateway Redevelopment Project**
   Battery St. to the Embarcadero bet. Broadway &
   Clay Sts.

   Urban Renewal Plan 1957; Skidmore, Owings &
   Merrill. Competition for Design and Development
   1959; won by Wurster, Bernardi & Emmons, Inc.,
   and DeMars & Reay. Phase One Residential De-
   velopment 1961-63; Master Plan, Garages, Point
   Towers and Town Houses along Jackson Street—
   Wurster, Bernardi & Emmons, Inc., and DeMars &
   Reay; Town Houses along Washington Street—
   Anshen & Allen. Landscape Architect: Sasaki,
   Walker Assoc.

   The city's architecturally undistinguished and colorfully inefficient produce market was urban-re-
   newed into this model image of upper-middle
   class downtown just at the high tide of the renewal wave. A little too neat to be real, it does fit
   reasonably well into the city fabric in spite of the
   still unresolved joint between its second story
   plazas and the ground floor sidewalks around.

   Alcoa Building   1964; Skidmore, Owings & Merrill
   1 Maritime Plaza

   Architects for the garage and rooftop buildings;
   Wurster, Bernardi & Emmons. Landscape Archi-
   tects: Sasaki, Walker Assoc. Sculpture by Marino
   Marini, Henry Moore, Charles O. Perry, and Jan
   Peter Stern. Fountain by Robert Woodward.

photo: Morley Baer

Embarcadero Center 1971-; John Portman & Assoc. Battery St. to the Embarcadero bet. Clay and Sacramento Sts.

> **Security Pacific Bank Bldg.** 1971
> 1 Embarcadero Center
> Sculpture by Willi Gutman
> **Levi Strauss Bldg.** 1973; 2 Embarcadero Center
> **Hyatt Hotel** 1972; 3 Embarcadero Center
> (projected at 60 stories)
> The office towers are larger versions of Portman's Peachtree Center office slabs in Atlanta. The hotel contains one of the great interior spaces of the city.

Ferry Park 1971; Lawrence Halprin & Assoc. and Mario Ciampi
Market St. at the Embarcadero
Fountain by Armand Vallaincourt.
Equestrian statue of Juan Bautista de Anza.
The fountain has been so celebrated in local controversy that only the first-time viewer can have anything fresh to say about it. A space is hereby provided for the purpose.

9. **Old U. S. Sub-Treasury** 1877; 608 Commercial St.
   What remains is the ground floor of the old building which was dynamited during the 1906 fire.

10. **Portsmouth Square** 1960
    Royston, Hanamoto & Mayes
    Kearny St. bet. Washington & Clay Sts.
    The first buildings of the village of Yerba Buena were built around this square, now the major open space of Chinatown and used with the orderly intensity that only non-Anglo-Saxons seem able to achieve.

11. **Chinese Cultural and Trade Center and Holiday Inn** 1971
Clement Chen and John Carl Warnecke & Assoc.
750 Kearny St.

A piece of spot redevelopment on the site of the old Hall of Justice. This is a hotel with token culture in the base.

12. **Transamerica Pyramid** 1972
William Pereira & Assoc.
600 Montgomery St.

Dropped here by some invaders from Outer Los Angeles, it may not go away; in fact, it has even produced a skeletal twin on Mount Sutro. The two are best seen from across the Bay.

13. **Market Street Beautification Project** 1971-74
Mario Ciampi, Lawrence Halprin & Assoc., John Carl Warnecke & Assoc.
Market St. from the Embarcadero to Twin Peaks

In a remarkable outpouring of civic interest, the voters of San Francisco passed a 24.5 million dollar bond issue in 1968 to realize one of the unfulfilled opportunities among the world's great streets. If private improvements match the public, the street at pedestrian level may at last rival the glittering image it has at night from the top of Twin Peaks.

14. **Ferry Building** 1894; A. Page Brown
Market St. at the Embarcadero

Now walled-off behind the freeway, this is a forlorn symbol of the days when the city had a perfect transportation pattern, with trans-bay commuters arriving by water directly to the city's heart and fanning out easily to their destinations. A revival of commuter ferries may bring it back to life.

15. **Hartford Building** 1964
Skidmore, Owings & Merrill
650 California St.

A 33-story, pre-cast-concrete-clad tower immediately adjacent to and designed in conjunction with St. Mary's Rectory.

16. **Bank of California**   1908; Bliss & Faville; **Office Tower**   1967; Anshen & Allen
400 California St.
The tower was carefully related in scale and materials to the magnificent Corinthian temple banking hall.

17. **Union Bank Building**   1972
Welton Becket & Assoc.
50 California St.
The building at 100 California across Davis Street was also done by Becket in 1959.

18. **International Building**   1962; Anshen & Allen
601 California St.

● 19. **Bank of America World Headquarters Building**
1970-71; Wurster, Bernardi & Emmons, Inc., and Skidmore, Owings & Merrill, with Pietro Belluschi as design consultant
555 California St. at Kearny St.
Sculpture by Masayuki Nagare.
The 52-story carnelian granite-clad tower with its undulating wall is the largest object in the downtown skyline. It is connected to the three-level bank pavilion by a plaza with a concourse below which cuts through the middle of the block.

20. **Bank of Montreal**   1971
Hugh Stubbins-Rex Allen Partnership
333 California St.
Snappy interior of the chrome and plastic school.

● 21. **Industrial Indemnity (orig. John Hancock) Building**   1959; Skidmore, Owings & Merrill
255 California St. at Battery St.
A granite-clad reinforced-concrete bearing wall is supported on sculptured concrete piers, which provide a street-level arcade. The executive offices are unusually placed on the second floor with a private garden.

22. **Mutual Benefit Life Building**   1970
Welton Becket & Assoc.
1 California St.

23. **Pacific Stock Exchange**   1927; Timothy Pflueger
301 Pine St.
A strange combination of Classic Revival and early Moderne. Sculpture by Ralph Stackpole.

24. **Southern Pacific Building**   1915; Bliss & Faville
1 Market St.
One Market Plaza 1972-4; Welton Becket & Assoc.

25. **Audiffred Building**   1889
11-21 Mission St. at the Embarcadero
A lonely mansard roofed survivor of the 19th Century waterfront.

Morley Baer: *Here Today*

26. **Russ Building**   1928; George Kelham
    235 Montgomery St.
    A mildly Gothic skyscraper; from 1928 to 1964 the city's tallest building.

27. **Mills Building**   1892; Burnham & Root
    220 Montgomery St.
    Mills Tower   1907; Willis Polk
    220 Bush St.
    The Chicago School's only surviving contribution to the cityscape, this noble pile weathered the earthquake of 1906 with interior fire damage. Now the city's oldest large office building and still one of the best.

28. **Pacific Gas & Electric Co. Buildings**
    1925; Miller & Pflueger
    245 Market St.
    1971; Hertzka & Knowles
    77 Beale St.

29. **Hallidie Building**   1917; Willis Polk
    130 Sutter St.

Morley Baer: *Here Today*

The legendary all-glass facade was a highly successful effort on Polk's part to produce a low budget—fast construction building. Originally blue and gold for the client, the University of California, and with a plain glass curtain at ground level.

30. French Bank of California   1972; Michel Marx
130 Montgomery St.

A small *tour de force* interior in the best French white-and-chrome manner.

31. Crown Zellerbach Building   1959; Hertzka & Knowles and Skidmore, Owings & Merrill
1 Bush St. at Market St.

Plaza and Wells Fargo Bank (orig. American Trust Co.),   1959; Skidmore, Owings & Merrill.
Fountain   1959; David Tollerton.
Mechanics Monument   1899; Douglas Tilden
Market & Battery Sts.

As new buildings go higher and downtown becomes denser, the graciousness of the Crown Zellerbach complex becomes even more remarkable than when it ushered in the office building boom of the 1960s.

32. 130 Bush Street Building   1910
George Applegarth
A small delight in a narrow place.

33. Shell Building   1930; George Kelham
100 Bush St.
A Zig-zag Moderne skyscraper.

34. Office Building   1973
John Carl Warnecke & Assoc.
525 Market St.

35. Metropolitan Life Building   1973
Skidmore, Owings & Merrill
425 Fremont St.

36. Wells Fargo Building   1966; John Graham & Co.
44 Montgomery St.

37. **Hobart Building**   1914; Willis Polk & Co.
582 Market St.

38. **Standard Oil of California Building**   1966
Hertzka & Knowles
555 Market St.

39. **Aetna Life Building and Crocker Plaza**   1970
Welton Becket & Assoc.
600 Market St.

40. **Citizens Federal Savings Building (former Old Mutual Bldg.)**   1902; William Curlett; Addition 1964;
Clark & Beuttler
700 Market St.

41. **Garden Court of the Palace Hotel**   1909
Trowbridge & Livingston
New Montgomery St. at Market St.
The pre-1906 Palace was a bay-windowed pile of about the same size as today's, with a famous open galleried court the full height of the building. The great glass-domed dining court is the only distinguished feature of its successor.

42. **Pacific Telephone Co., Main Offices**   1924
Timothy Pflueger
140 New Montgomery St.
Inspired by Eliel Saarinen's second prize design for the Chicago Tribune Tower Competition, this tower is a solid block when seen from the north and a hollow L from the south.

43. **Pacific Telephone Co. Equipment Bldg.**   1972
McCue, Boone & Tomsick
611 Folsom St.
Careful control of environment was the primary concern in the design of this building which houses complex and delicate equipment. The program resulted in the unusual windowless skin of aluminum panels interrupted only by glazed indentations where personnel circulation and lunch rooms occur.

44. **Pacific Telephone Co.**   1970
J. C. Warnecke & Assoc.
633 Folsom St.

● **45. Sailors' Union of the Pacific**   1950
William Gladstone Merchant
450 Harrison St.

Union Oil Building   1940; Lewis P. Hobart
425 First St.

A Streamlined Moderne pair right next to the Bay Bridge approach. The first building is nautical in flavor while the second exemplifies the transformation of a building into a sign which is an inescapable landmark for those crossing the bridge.

Between Second and Third Sts., just south of the bridge approach, is a ramshackle but lively little loop known as South Park, only surviving remnant of the once fashionable residential development of Rincon Hill, the knoll from which the Bay Bridge springs. The Park was laid out in a small-scale reminiscence of London by George Gordon, an English developer, in 1854.

46. Southern Pacific Terminal   1915
Charles Whittlesey
Third and Townsend Sts.

Once the land gateway to the city, this now forlorn Mission Revival station faces an uncertain future, as do most of its kind.

NOB HILL - UNION SQUARE - CHINATOWN

Much of the magic that draws streams of tourists to San Francisco is contained in the small area defined by Nob Hill and Chinatown on the north and east, Market Street on the south, and Jones Street on the west. At its heart, around Union Square, is one of the most stable and attractive downtown shopping areas in the United States. Nob Hill with its hotels, clubs, and luxury apartments manages to maintain the same image of glamour and high life that it must have had before 1906 when its top was the exclusive province of the railroad and gold rush millionaires; and Chinatown, thanks more to the enduring propensity of the Chinese for street life than the veneer of chinoiserie that has been laid on its buildings, supplies the proper exotic note.

Nob Hill was too steep to be readily accessible and hence remained a barrier to the expansion of downtown until the invention of the cable car in 1873, just in time to make available for the Floods, Crockers, Stanfords et. al. a magnificent series of commanding sites for their palaces. With the passing of the palace

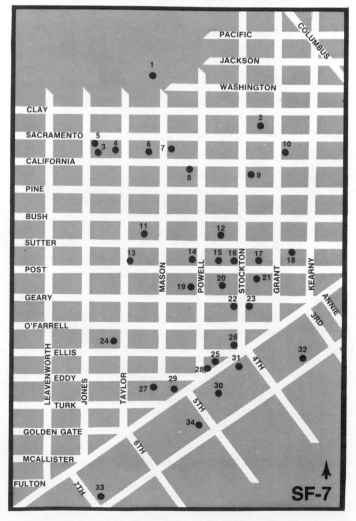

photo: California Historical Society

era in the holocaust of 1906, major institutions and hotels took their place, happily maintaining at their center the best of the palaces, that of James P. Flood, reincarnated with additions by Willis Polk as the Pacific Union Club. It carries on a noble dialogue of red and white with the Fairmont, which was virtually complete when it was gutted in 1906, but Dorothy Draper later more than made up for that disaster with her splendid lobby. On the other side of the Pacific Union Club, the site of Collis Huntington's Italian Renaissance palace is graced by an urbane park with a replica of the Tartarughe Fountain at its center, and on the site of the Crocker's French Renaissance chateau is Grace Cathedral.

1. **Cable Car Barn and Power House**   1887
   1390 Washington St.

   Although it is well off the top of the hill, it seems appropriate to list this source of power for the conqueror of Nob Hill with the buildings it made possible. Worth a visit by all who wonder what makes the things go.

2. **Donaldina Cameron House (Presbyterian Mission)**
   1907; Julia Morgan
   920 Sacramento St.

   A simple, utilitarian box built of clinker brick.

3. **Grace Cathedral (Episcopal)**   1928; Lewis P. Hobart. Completed 1965; Wiehe, Frick & Cruse
   A remarkable piece of poured-in-place concrete
   work, if less successful as Gothic architecture.
   The doors at east front are casts of the Ghiberti
   doors on the Baptistry in Florence.

4. **Cathedral House**   1911; Austin Whittlesey
   1055 Taylor St.
   The oldest and most authentically Gothic in feeling of the Cathedral's buildings.

5. **Cathedral School for Boys**   1965
   Rockrise & Watson
   1275 Sacramento St.
   Neatly fitted into its cramped site, this concrete
   school makes an architectural feature of its roof-
   top play area.

Note the stripped French-Second-Empire apartment
house at 1036 Sacramento across the street. Down Sacramento at 1202 Leavenworth is another interesting
shingle apartment house. Up Taylor at 1110, a diminutive Italianate cottage built by Flood for his coachman.

6. **Pacific Union Club**   1886; Augustus Laver
   Rem. and wings added 1907; Willis Polk
   1000 California St.
   The then-fashionable brownstone had to be imported from the East at vast expense. To those
   fortunate enough to penetrate within, the dining
   room in the west wing presents the quintessence of
   a great club room. Polk's work also included add-
   ing windows in the attic story and suppressing
   an awkward tower over the entrance.

7. **Fairmont Hotel**   1906; Reid Brothers
   California and Mason Sts.
   A turn-of-the-century Renaissance Revival building and one of a fast-dwindling number of hotels
   which deserve the adjective "grand"—on this side
   at least. The additions on Powell (Mario Gaidano,
   1962) are contemporary anywhere-hotel.

The Mark Hopkins Hotel (Weeks & Day, 1927) rises on the site of that gentleman's Victorian Folly, and in 1936 was given by Timothy Pflueger its celebrated roof-top cocktail lounge, the great-granddaddy of a now numberless progeny. Across the street at 1001 California is an elegant French Baroque apartment house, and just down Mason at 831-49 are four townhouses by Willis Polk (1917). At 1021 California is a superb townhouse done by Col. George Schasty in 1911. The garage next door (Anshen & Allen, 1956), is a careful effort to minimize the impact of this unsympathetic use.

8. Stanford Court Hotel   1912
California St. at Powell St.

Remodeled from apartment house to hotel by Curtis & Davis, 1972.

Down California Street, a turn south at Joice Alley brings one to a flight of steps down to Pine Street that is one of those magic pieces of small-scale urban design that work best because they are least premeditated. Threatened by a high-rise development, they may not survive much longer. Another genial anachronism is the Dennis T. Sullivan Memorial Fire Chief's home at 870 Bush St.

9. Old Metropolitan Life Building   1909; 1930
LeBrun Brothers; Timothy Pflueger
600 Stockton St.

Garden by Thomas Church
Gleaming terra-cotta Roman Revival, probably not long for this world now that Metropolitan is moving out.

Chinatown stubbornly refuses to degenerate into a simple tourist trap because the Chinese refuse to give up their crowded former (and in places continuing) ghetto for the rest of the city that is no longer closed to them. At the north end, around Grant and Jackson, the food stores are as authentically exotic as one could ask. A few unmodernized shops such as Sang Wo at 867 Grant and Tin Bar Tong at 947 Grant recall what the street must have been in the old days of the China Trade, and some of the older self-conscious pieces of chinoiserie such as the old Telephone Exchange of 1909 at 743 Washington, and the row of buildings on the west side of Waverly Place of the same period, contribute to the life the Chinese themselves so effectively give to Grant Avenue and the adjoining streets by using them as their living room. Even though tasteless modernizing in the most garish super-Chinese has taken a heavy toll over the past few years, the whole thing somehow works, especially on a foggy night.

10. **Old St. Mary's Church**   1853-54
    Craine & England. Restored 1969; Welsh & Carey
    California at Grant St.

    Rectory (Paulist Center of the West)   1964
    Skidmore, Owings & Merrill
    660 California St.

    St. Mary's has burned twice—in 1906 and 1969—but each time has been faithfully rebuilt along its original lines. The Rectory has a small chapel with stained glass and Stations of the Cross by Mark Adams. Across the street, the garage-top St. Mary's Square (Ekbo, Royston & Williams, 1960) contains Beniamino Bufano's stainless steel and granite statue of Sun Yat-Sen.

photo: Morley Baer

11. **Women's Athletic Club**   1915; Bliss and Faville
    640 Sutter St.

● 12. **Medical-Dental Office Building**   1930
    Timothy Pflueger
    450 Sutter St.

    Remarkably simple massing for its time and an undulating terra cotta and glass wall make this the best and most original of Pflueger's many contributions to downtown San Francisco. The lobby is an Art-Deco period piece mixed with a pre-Colombian theme.

13. **Bohemian Club**   1930; Lewis P. Hobart
    624 Taylor St.

    A tasteful brick building for San Francisco's establishment bohemians.

14. **United Air Lines Ticket Office**   1971
    Arthur Gensler & Assoc.
    Powell and Post Sts.

15. **Quantas Building** 1972
Skidmore, Owings & Merrill
350 Post St.

16. **Regency Hyatt Hotel** 1972
Skidmore, Owings & Merrill
Post & Stockton Sts.

    A 140-foot height limit on this side of Union Square placed the tower at the Sutter Street end of the site. The triangular front pavilion holds the Post Street building line while opening a plaza on Stockton, expressing this double role in its two facades. The fountain of baker's clay cast in bronze by Ruth Asawa is a panorama of city life.

17. **Gump's** 250 Post St.

    A legendary store that boasts consistently superb window displays.

18. **Streeter & Quarles West** 1970
Robert Middelstadt & Monte S. Bell
271 Sutter St.

    A swinging sporting goods store for sporting swingers.

19. **St. Francis Hotel** 1904 & 1908; Bliss & Faville. Tower 1972; Williams Pereira Assoc.
Union Square & Powell St.

20. **Union Square** Powell, Post, Stockton & Geary Sts.
Dewey Memorial 1901; Robert I. Aitken and Newton Thorp
Underground Parking Garage 1942; Timothy Pflueger
The first of all under-park parking garages, on top of which beats the heart of downtown.

21. **Helga Howie Boutique (originally V. C. Morris Store)** 1949; Frank Lloyd Wright
140 Maiden Lane

    This small store is one of Wright's most deceptively simple lessons in the mastery of space: a cube with blank walls, a skylit roof, and a spiral ramp within make a magical setting that was most appropriate to the fine glass and china originally sold here.

22. **I. Magnin & Co.** 1946; Timothy Pflueger
Stockton & Geary Sts.

The smooth marble block with slightly projected windows proved so apt an expression for this famous store that the same design was used in Seattle.

23. **City of Paris by Liberty House** 1900; Clinton Day
Stockton & Geary Sts.

Given a welcome refurbishing and a new lease on life by its new occupant, the interior of the grand old store was modeled closely on the Parisian department stores of the turn-of-the-century.

24. **San Francisco Hilton** 1964; William Tabler.
Tower 1971; John Carl Warnecke & Assoc.
Taylor & O'Farrell Sts.

● 25. **Sommer & Kaufman Shoe Store** 1929
Kem Weber & A. F. Roller
838 Market St.

A battered (after some insensitive remodeling) remnant of what was a classic piece of early Moderne shop design. The building which houses Cable Car Clothiers on the corner of Powell and Ellis is another interesting example of the same style.

26. **Great Western Savings & Loan** 1973
Skidmore, Owings & Merrill
Stockton & Ellis Sts.

27. **Hallidie Plaza Building** 1973
Skidmore, Owings & Merrill
Eddy St. & Hallidie Plaza

28. **Flood Building** 1905; Albert Pissis
870 Market St.

29. **Powell Plaza** Powell, Eddy & Market Sts.
Plaza 1973; Mario Ciampi, Lawrence Halprin & Assoc., John Warnecke & Assoc.

30. **The Emporium** 1909; Albert Pissis
835 Market St.

Downtown's largest department store. A great

central dome skylight typical of the period is so blandly treated as not to count for much in the vast interior.

31. Pacific Building   1908; C. F. Whittlesey Co.
821 Market at Fourth St.

An early reinforced concrete building remarkable for its Sullivanesque terra cotta ornament and for its landscaped interior court, whose walls are handsome enough to have been a facade in a later, simpler era.

32. St. Patrick's Church, Facade   1872; **Interior**   1907
756 Mission St.

The handsome brick facade survived the earthquake; the interior that went with it, alas, did not.

33. Main Post Office and Federal Court House   1905
James Knox Taylor
Seventh at Mission St.

Heavy-handed but handsome turn of the century neo-baroque. The interiors are unusually lavish.

34. Old U. S. Mint   1870; A. B. Mullet
Fifth & Mission Sts.

A battered veteran of decades of neglect, now due for restoration as a monetary museum. Much of the silver from the Comstock Lode was coined here. The style is Tuscan Doric, drier than Mullet's more ornate Second Empire work in Washington and St. Louis.

WESTERN ADDITION

Before 1906, Van Ness was San Francisco's grand avenue. With widely spaced stately homes, it looked much like the great residential streets of many other 19th century American cities. Its width and accessibility made it a natural choice when the Army Engineers were looking for a line of defense against the fire, and so they dynamited both sides from Market Street to the Bay. From this blow the street recovered to become first a temporary replacement for downtown shopping and then the original auto row of the city, with the palaces of Packard and Cadillac replacing the earlier great houses. The descent of the automobile from these heights has brought the street down with it, and now it is nothing but another seedy traffic-clogged thoroughfare, lined with auto dealers and motels, a monument to today's automobile world.

Its one truly grand moment is provided by the Civic Center, as fine a monument to the City Beautiful movement of the early 1900s as you can find in this country. A competition was held in 1912 to replace the monstrosity at the corner of Van Ness Ave. and Market St. which collapsed in the earthquake. The site chosen was a compromise between the older site and the site proposed by Daniel Burnham in his 1905 plan. The winning plan by Bakewell and Brown was carried on with rare consistency through the 1930s.

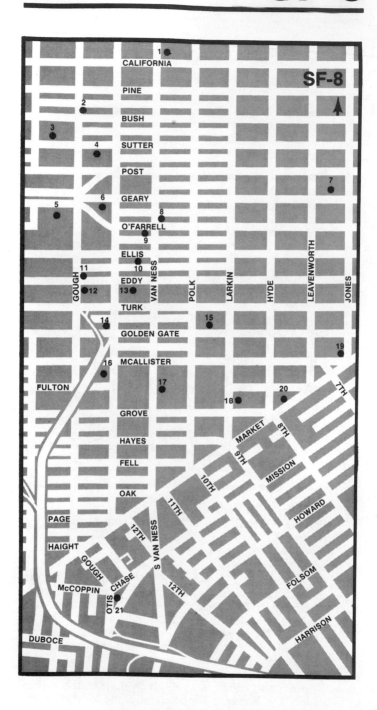

1. **Bank of America Auto Center Branch** 1969
   Smith, Barker, Hanssen
   1640 Van Ness Ave.

   The most interesting elevation at this exposed concrete drive-in bank is around the corner on California Street.

2. **Trinity Church** 1893; A. Page Brown
1668 Bush at Gough St.

A squat square stone Gothic Revival church; the tower is open into the nave.

3. **Thomas Payne House** c.1880; William Curlett
1409 Sutter St.

A candle-snuffer corner tower distinguishes this Stick-Eastlake house.

4. **American National Red Cross Building** 1950
Gardner Dailey
1550 Sutter St.

Chaste International style enlivened by one of the early examples of designed form board texture and some Bay Region touches like small-paned glass.

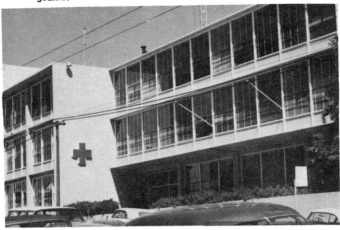

5. **St. Mary's Cathedral** 1971
Pietro Belluschi, Pier Luigi Nervi, and McSweeney, Ryan & Lee
Geary at Gough St.

In 1960, after this site had been renewed with a supermarket, a fire completely destroyed the old cathedral on Van Ness. A quickly arranged trade demolished the year-old market, giving the Archdiocese a suitably prominent site in exchange for its Van Ness property. Four 190-foot hyperbolic paraboloids roof the 2500 seat space over a base which contains meeting rooms, a rectory, a convent, and to the south, a parochial high school. The stained glass is by Gyorgy Kepes, the baldochino by Richard Lippold, and the organ is designed by Father Robert F. Hayburn.

6. **First Unitarian Church** 1888. **Administrative Bldgs. and Church School** 1970; Callister, Payne & Rosse
Franklin & Geary Sts.
Organ by Robert Noehren

The new concrete and redwood buildings form a remarkably harmonious group with the old stone Romanesque Revival church.

7. **Islam Temple**   1917; T. Patterson Ross
   650 Geary St.
   A little bit of old Islam in San Francisco.

8. **Cadillac Showroom**   1921; Weeks & Day
   1000 Van Ness Ave.

9. **Chrysler (orig., Earle C. Anthony Packard) Show-room**   1928; Bernard Maybeck
   901 Van Ness Ave.
   This noble space, designed for cars of another era, is fortunately still in use. The interior with its elaborate coffered ceiling was originally lighted by immense pendants and lights in the column capitals.

10. **Redevelopment Agency Building**   1970
    John Bolles & Assoc.
    939 Ellis St.

11. **Family Service Agency**   1928; Bernard Maybeck
    1010 Gough St. at Eddy St.
    Maybeck's personal stamp is evident here in the handling of such elements as the spiral fire escape in its slot, the fenestration on the west facade, and the fence motif.

12. **St. Paul's Lutheran Church** 1894; A. J. Kraft
999 Eddy St.
A steel engraving of Chartres executed in wood and stucco.

13. **F. D. Stadmuller House** 1880; P. Schmidt
819 Eddy St.
A large and well-maintained Italianate House. Several more are at 946, 948-54, 962 and 964 Eddy Street.

14. **House** 1876; 807 Franklin St.
Italianate style.

15. **Federal Office Building** 1959; Albert F. Roller, Stone Marraccini & Patterson & John Carl Warnecke
450 Golden Gate Ave.
The new scale of the Federal Government. Fortunately, kept a block away from the old Civic Center.

16. **California State Bar Association** 1962
Hertzka & Knowles
601 McAllister St.

17. **San Francisco Civic Center**
Franklin & McAllister to Market & Hayes Sts.
● **City Hall** 1915 (competition 1912); Bakewell & Brown
Civic Auditorium 1913; John Galen Howard, Fred Mayer & John Reid, Jr. Rem. 1964; Wurster, Bernardi & Emmons and Skidmore, Owings & Merrill
Public Library 1916 (competition 1915); George Kelham
State Office Building 1926; Bliss & Faville
Opera House and Veterans Auditorium 1932; Brown & Landsburgh
S. F. Museum of Art & Bookstore rem. in Veterans Building 1971-72; Robinson & Mills
Federal Office Building 1936; Bakewell & Brown
The design of San Francisco's Civic Center is largely the result of competitions. Its focal point and finest building is the City Hall, which suc-

ceeds so far beyond most such 20th century efforts at Renaissance grandeur that it invites comparison with its models. The dome, both inside and out, is especially fine.

18. **Planning Commission Offices (former Visitor's Information Booth)** 1941; 100 Larkin St.
   Streamlined Moderne sitting in the middle of classic grandeur.

● 19. **Hibernia Bank** 1892; Albert Pissis
   1 Jones St. at McAllister & Market Sts.
   Early and rather up-tight Neo-Classic with a dome at the corner.

20. **Fox Plaza** 1967; Victor Gruen & Assoc.
   Market, Grove & Larkin Sts.
   A multi-use complex on the site of the greatest of the old movie palaces; the high-rise has apartments over offices, the low block has a shopping arcade with a fountain by Ruth Asawa.

21. **Old Juvenile Court and Detention Home** 1914
   Louis Christian Mullgardt
   150 Otis St.
   High rise Spanish Colonial Revival with Mullgardt's special touch in the remarkably contemporary wall articulation.

The Western Addition added to the city by the original charter of 1851, but it was not opened for development until the 1870s and 80s. Although the Addition actually included Pacific Heights, the term is now taken to refer only to the area south of California and west to Divisadero, then the city boundary. Before redevelopment it was a catalog of exuberant, if run-down, late 19th century speculative housing which had gone from upper middle-class houses to flats to ghetto in the period from 1906 to 1950. What was a substantial Japanese settlement before World War II wiped out by relocation, but returned afterward to find a small place in a then largely black area. Shown by a survey in the early 50s to have the highest incidence of substandard housing in the city, it was a natural candidate for renewal. A master plan prepared by Vernon DeMars provided the desired east-west expressway and sited new high-rise residential buildings on the high land. This plan became a credo for locating such buildings in the cityscape until challenged by the recent anti high-rise outcry. Typically for the time, the redevelopment process swept the heart of the area clean, replacing black slum with upper middle-class high rise. The second phase, surrounding the first, has followed a more circumspect course, with community participation in varying degrees, smaller scale projects, scattered site public housing, and a substantial amount of preservation and rehabilitation. The result, while understandably rough around the edges, is well worth study, especially after you understand that fully as much human frustration can be contained in a quaint Victorian house in genial, tolerant San Francisco as in a brick walk-up in central Harlem. Area A-1 had almost no examples of how to rebuild the modern city; A-2 has some. Around the two areas which dominate the Western Addition are a few fine remnants of the earlier exuberance.

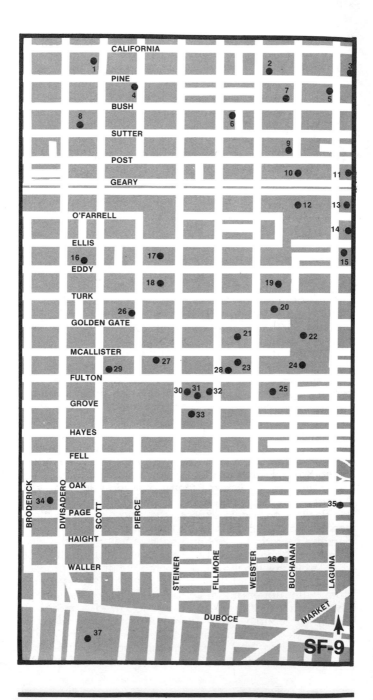

1. **Ortman-Shumate House**   1870; 1901 Scott St.
   Still in the original owner's family, this fine Italianate house is one of the very few in the city that conserves its spacious grounds and carriage house.

2. **Berges House**   1884; 1900 Webster St.
   An elegant Italianate with interesting blind windows on the Pine St. facade.

3. **Public Housing**   1972; Chan-Rader & Assoc. 1880 Pine St.
   Exposed concrete high rise with the currently fashionable angularities.

4. **Mary Ann Crocker Old Ladies Home**   1890
   A. Page Brown
   A long, low, undulating-shingled building, beautifully detailed and very unusual for San Francisco. It has been stripped of its projecting parapets.

5. **Row houses**   1887-90; 1801-45 Laguna St.
   Even Stick-Eastlake speculative housing had a high respect for the unity of the street.

6. **Row houses**   c.1874; 2115-25 Bush St.
   Cottage Row (in center of block). A beautifully simple group of Italianate false fronts.

7. **Stanyan House**   c.1852; 2006 Bush St.
   Stanyan Flats   c.1885; 2000-2012 Bush St.
   One of the oldest houses in the area. Its large lot was developed into rental housing by the original owners.

8. **Unity Hospital (originally Maimonides Health Center)**   1950
   Eric Mendelshon & Michael Gallis. Rem. 1953; Hertzka & Knowles
   2356 Sutter St.
   Designed for the chronically ill, this once elegant building was remodeled by moving the glass line out to fill in the balconies when the original scheme failed.

9. **Nihonmachi (Japanese redevelopment project)**
   Master Plan: Okamoto-Liskamm with Van Bourg/Nakamura & Assoc.
   Toho Building   1972; Rai Okamoto and Assoc. Post & Buchanan Sts.

10. **Japanese Cultural and Trade Center**   1968
    Minoru Yamasaki and Van Bourg/Nakamura & Assoc.
    Peace Pagoda   Dr. Yoshiro Taniguchi
    Fillmore to Laguna bet. Post & Buchanan Sts.
    Neater, more overtly oriental, and far less interesting than the collection of little shops in Victorian houses which it replaced. The opposite side of Post St. still maintains some of the old flavor, with a fine Japanese market and the remarkable Soko Hardware Co. on the corner of Buchanan.

11. **The Sequoias—San Francisco** 1969
Stone, Marraccini & Patterson
1400 Geary St.
A 25-story 300 unit precast concrete-clad retirement community.

12. **St. Francis Square** 1961; Marquis & Stoller
Geary bet. Webster & Laguna Sts.
Most successful architecturally and socially of A-1's housing projects, this 299 unit moderate-priced co-op was financed by the ILWU under an FHA 221-d-3 program.

photo: Karl Riek

13. **Laguna/O'Farrell Apts.** 1964; Jones & Emmons
66 Cleary Court

14. **Laguna Heights** 1963; Claude Oakland
Ellis and Laguna Sts. (N side)
Two in-town Eichler projects.

15. **Western Park Apts.** 1971; Thomas Hsieh
Laguna & Ellis Sts. (S side)

16. **Old St. Patrick's Church** 1854; 1822 Eddy St.
Moved and remodeled in 1873 and 1891, originally from lower Market St.; the city's oldest frame church.

The following are typically block-size two and three-story wood frame apartment and town-house projects which exemplify the scale of A-2 renewal. Around them are many examples of rehabilitated older housing.

17. **Marcus Garvey Square** 1971; Whisler-Patri Assoc.
Pierce-Ellis-Steiner-Eddy Sts.

18. **Martin Luther King Square** 1970
Kaplan & McLaughlin
Pierce-Eddy-Steiner-Turk Sts.

19. **Malcolm X Square** 1973; Whisler-Patri Assoc.
Webster-Eddy-Buchanan-Turk Sts.

20. **Thomas Paine Square**   1971; McGuire & Catough
    Webster-Turk-Laguna-Golden Gate Sts.

21. **Prince Hall Apartments**   1971
    Kennard & Silvers
    Fillmore-Golden Gate-Webster-McAllister Sts.

22. **Frederick Douglass Haynes Gardens**   1973
    Marquis & Stoller
    Golden Gate-Laguna-McAllister Sts.

23. **Friendship Village**   1971; Buckley & Sazevich
    Fillmore-McAllister-Webster-Fulton Sts.

24. **Loren Miller Homes**   1972; Wasserman & Herman
    McAllister-Laguna-Fulton Sts.

25. **Banneker Homes**   1970; Joseph Esherick & Assoc.
    Landscape Architect - Lawrence Halprin & Assoc.
    Webster-Fulton-Buchanan-Grove Sts.

26. **Andreozzi House**   c.1886; N. Andreozzi
    1016 Pierce St.
    Heavily ornamented Stick style.

27. **French Second Empire Apartments**   c.1900
    1347 McAllister St.
    Elegant French Neo-Baroque; note also 1376-92
    across the street—a Queen Anne row.

28. **Westerfield House**   1889; Henry Geilfuss
    1198 Fulton St.
    A huge towered and bracketed Queen Anne pile
    built for a noted baker. Diagonally across the
    street at 1201 is a house by A. Page Brown.

29. **Old Holy Virgin Russian Orthodox Cathedral** 1880
    858-64 Fulton St.
    Originally built for another denomination, this
    Gothic Revival church was taken over by the
    Russians in the 1930s.

30. **French-American Bilingual School (former Probert
    House)**   1894. Additions   1971; Beebe & Hersey
    940 Grove St.
    Eastlake with a hint of Colonial Revival.

31. **Koster House**   c.1895; 926 Grove St.
A potpourri of late 19th century styles.

32. **House**   1895; 820 Fillmore St.
Late Queen Anne style.

33. **House**   c.1880; 975 Grove St.

34. **Phelps House**   c.1850; 329 Divisadero St.
Probably the oldest intact house in the city, this charming simple Gothic Revival farmhouse is now buried in the middle of the block and visible only from Oak St. It was prefabricated in New Orleans and shipped around the Horn.

Morley Baer: Here Today

35. **Dietle House**   1885; Henry Geilfuss
294 Page at Laguna St.
One of the handsomest Stick style houses in the city. An elaborately ornamented Eastlake-Queen Anne town house.

● 36. **Nightingale House**   1882; 201 Buchanan St.
Another Stick-Eastlake masterpiece. This is more rural looking with its gable roof and tower.

37. **St. Francis (Franklin) Hospital**   1970
Stone, Maraccini & Patterson
Castro & Duboce Sts.

RICHMOND — GOLDEN GATE PARK

The area between the Presidio and Golden Gate Park, known as the Richmond, was almost undeveloped until the second decade of the 1900s. Naturally a flat area of wind-and-fog swept dunes, like all of western San Francisco it awaited the pressure of population and the flowering of Golden Gate Park to become a pleasant but architecturally undistinguished middle-class residential area. It is composed almost entirely single-family row houses of the 1910-1930 period, with flats and low-rise apartments along the main arteries, like Geary, Clement, and California, the first two also providing the major strip shopping facilities for the area. Here and there the shops show that this area has some concentrations of European immigrants, notably French, Russians, and Germans, which give it a far more interesting flavor than its buildings would indicate. At the western end are several spectacular headlands overlooking the Pacific and the Golden Gate; the site of Comstock Lode engineer Adolf Sutro's mansion, the site of several incarnations of the Cliff House, Sutro's great Baths which flourished in the late 19th Century, and finally Lincoln Park, which contains the replica of the French Palace of the Legion of Honor which Alma de Bretteville Spreckels gave to the city as an art museum. Between Lincoln Park and the Presidio lies the area's most fashionable section, Seacliff, developed by Mark Daniels between 1912 and 1915, largely independently of the prevailing gridiron, to take advantage of the spectacular views of the Golden Gate.

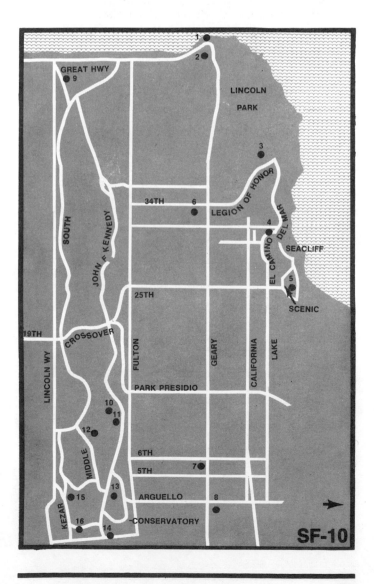

1. **Cliff House Site**
   Point Lobos Ave. (western end of Geary St.)
   Original 1863, burned in 1894, rebuilt as Victorian Folly by Adolf Sutro, burned again in 1907, present structure 1908.

   Sutro Baths Site 1000 Point Lobos Ave.
   Site of 6 indoor salt water pools, seats for 7000 spectators, conservatories lined with palms, Egyptian relics, and all the trappings of a Victorian glass palace dedicated to recreation. Demolished in 1969 for a still unrealized housing development.

2. **Sutro Heights** Point Lobos Ave.
   Now dotted with decaying plaster statuary and gone to seed, this promontory was the site of Sutro's mansion. The forlorn kiosk is a memento of days when the public was invited to the gardens of the Comstock Lode millionaire.

3. **California Palace of the Legion of Honor** 1916
   George A. Applegarth
   Lincoln Park (access from 34th Ave. & Clement St. or El Camino del Mar)
   Open daily 10-5, admission free.
   Primarily European painting of the 16th to 20th centuries. The Achenbach Foundation is one of the country's best print collections.

4. **House** 1963; Joseph Esherick & Assoc.
   895 El Camino del Mar at 32nd Ave.
   A shingle box with the later Esherick syncopated window rhythms. Across the street at 850 is a Wurster, Bernardi & Emmons house of 1958.

5. **Houses** 1915; Willis Polk
   9, 25 and 45 Scenic Wy.
   Polk's stucco residences are characterized by boldly modeled classical detailing set, in the Spanish manner, against plane surfaces.

6. **House** 1913; Willis Polk
   726-34th Ave.
   A small shingle house with unusual fenestration and a rear courtyard.

7. **French Convalescent Hospital and Medical Building** 1970-71; Paffard Keatinge Clay
   Geary Blvd. at 6th Ave.
   Monumentally scaled exposed concrete frames with glass infill.

8. **Roosevelt Junior High School** 1934
   Miller & Pfleuger
   460 Arguello Blvd.
   Marvelous constructivist brickwork, highly reminiscent of Dutch Expressionist buildings of the late teens and twenties. One of San Francisco's very few pieces of distinguished school architecture.

GOLDEN GATE PARK

Like the rest of the western half of the San Francisco peninsula, Golden Gate Park was simply a mass of shifting sand dunes until trial and error, water and fertilizer, laboriously transformed it into its present lushness, largely under the aegis of John McLaren, its supervisor from 1887 to 1942. The site was selected in 1869 after Frederick Law Olmstead had recommended setting aside substantial park areas in the City. The original plan was drawn by William Hammond Hall, the first supervisor, in 1871, but how to anchor the dunes and transform them into reasonable soil remained a problem until McLaren's day. In its entirety, the Park is one of the finest and best-used pieces of late 19th Century romantic park design in the country. The recurring fog and mild climate enable it to stand today's heavy use better than parks elsewhere, so that visitors find it hard to believe that its green lawns are trampled every weekend by thousands of happy users, active and passive. All the traditional park recreation facilities are provided plus a few unusual ones like the polo field, site not only of polo games but of several great be-ins and rallies, and the Japanese Tea Garden, probably the park's most visited feature. Most road maps show all of the Park's major elements adequately, so this guide will only list the important architectural features.

9. **Murphy Windmill**   1905
   SW cor. of Park nr. Lincoln St. & the Great Highway
   Originally built, as was the now stripped North Windmill, to pump well water to irrigate the Park.

10. **Japanese Tea Garden**   1893-4
   Music Concourse at NW cor.
   Originally part of the 1894 California Midwinter International Exposition.

11. **M. H. deYoung Memorial Museum** 1916; Louis Christian Mullgardt. Remod. by Arthur Brown, Jr. Brundage Collection of Oriental Art 1965; Gardner Dailey & Assoc.
Music Concourse, N side

    Open daily 10-5; admission free
    Originally modeled at deYoung's insistence on Mullgardt's Court of the Ages for the Panama-Pacific exposition of 1915, the building was denuded of its elaborate churriguresque stucco ornament because of earthquake danger.

12. **California Academy of Sciences**
North American Hall, Steinhardt Aquarium and African Hall 1915-31; Lewis P. Hobart
Hall of Science & Morrison Planetarium 1951 Weihe, Frick & Kruse
Cowell Hall 1968; Milton Pflueger
Whale Fountain 1939; Robert Howard
Open daily 10-5; admission $.50

13. **Conservatory** 1875; Lord & Burnham. Greenhouse Manufacturers, Irvington, New York
John F. Kennedy Dr.

    Prefabricated and shipped around the Horn for James Lick, it was bought for the city after his death in 1876 and finally erected in 1878. One of the finest surviving Victorian glass Follies.

photo: California Historical Society

14. **Park Headquarters (former McLaren Lodge)** 1895
    E. R. Swain
    John F. Kennedy Dr. nr. Stanyan
    Stripped, tile-roofed Richardsonian Romanesque.

15. **Children's House** 1885; Percy & Hamilton
    Carousel
    Nr. South & Kezar Drs.
    The Children's House is another example of Richardsonian Romanesque; the Carousel was originally built by Spillman in North Tonawanda, New York, in 1912, and was first used at the 1939 Fair on Treasure Island.

16. **Alvord Lake Bridge** 1889; Ernest Ransome
    Under Kezar Dr.
    The first reinforced concrete bridge in the U. S., distinguished more by its cast in place stalactites than its use of the new material.

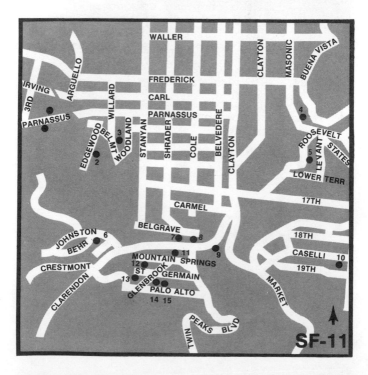

Around the fringes of Mount Sutro and Twin Peaks is an interesting collection of residential backwaters with some spectacular views, the price for which is a considerable amount of wind and fog. Twin Peaks Blvd. offers a full 360° panorama of the city including an axial view down Market St. that should be seen both day and night.

The lower eastern slopes of this cluster of hills are sheltered from the west wind and fog and were built up earlier, although they were inaccessible enough to escape intensive development until the last two decades.

1. **University of California Medical Center**
   Parnassus Ave. bet. Arguello St. & 4th Ave.
   a. **Health Sciences Instruction & Research Units 1 & 2** 1961-67; Reid, Rockwell, Banwell & Tarics
   (Behind Moffit Hospital to the S)
   Two square clear-span towers linked by vertical circulation. The labs are surrounded by perimeter corridors; utility ducts run outside of the building wall.
   b. **Surge Research Lab** 1966; Marquis & Stoller
   c. **Outpatients Clinic Building & Parking Structure** 1972; Reid & Tarics
   The older buildings of the Medical Center are uniformly undistinguished and most of the newer ones are visible only by turning up the road behind the original group.

2. **House** 1911; Louis Christian Mullgardt
   226 Edgewood Ave.
   Edgewood is a charming brick-paved, tree-lined street with many interesting houses. The rear elevation of this one has a high battered stucco foundation surmounted by a glass gallery facing the view.

3. **House** 1936; Richard Neutra
   90 Woodland Ave.

4. **House** 1910; Bernard Maybeck
   1526 Masonic Ave.

Morley Baer: *Here Today*

Even here, in one of his modest shingle houses, Maybeck's work stands out from the typical houses of the period which line the street.

5. **House**   c.1910; 439 Roosevelt Wy.
   Possibly the only Corinthian-columned bungalow around.

6. **U. C. Medical School Married Student Housing**
   1959; Clark & Beuttler and George Rockrise
   Johnstone Dr.

7. **House**   1955; Anshen & Allen
   2 Clarendon Ave.

8. **Cottage**   1917; Bernard Maybeck
   196 Twin Peaks Blvd.

9. **House**   1950; Malone & Hooper
   49 Twin Peaks Blvd.

10. **Alfred Clarke Mansion (Nobby Clark's Folly)**
    1892; 250 Douglas
    An enormous Queen-Anne pile with corner candle-snuffer domes.

11. **Moffitt House**   c.1920-40; 30 Mountain Spring Ave.
    A fascinating rambling brick structure built gradually by its owner.

12. **House**   1958; George Rockrise
    150 St. Germain

13. **House**   1948; John Funk
    2 Glenbrook Ave.

14. **House**   1959; Campbell & Wong
    175 Palo Alto Ave.

15. **House**   1959; Charles Warren Callister
    176 Palo Alto Ave.

The wind and fog-swept upper reaches of Twin Peaks have an interesting collection of 40s and 50s houses, several of which are listed above.

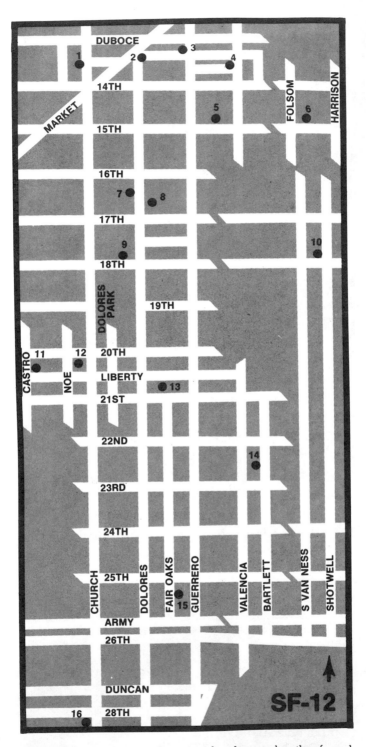

The Mission location was wisely chosen by the founding padres for their church and settlement as the sunniest and most sheltered area of the northern peninsula. It was the recreation area of the early city, gradually becoming built up in the 1870s and 80s, with very substantial houses, most of which have either disappeared or been divided into apartments. Mission Street is the commercial spine of this very self-contained and heavily Spanish speaking area. The handsomest part of the area is along palm-lined Dolores, with the Mission itself, Dolores Park, and a fair number of the surviving Victorian mansions. The hills to the west were built up around the turn of the century with smaller working class speculative houses, which now form the most interesting supply of older middle-income housing in the city, and so have become something of a melting pot, combining older blue-collar and younger middle class families of all races.

1. **St. Francis Lutheran Church (orig. St. Angsar)**
   1905-07; 152 Church St. at Reservoir St.
   Austere brick Gothic Revival, built for a Danish seamen's congregation.

2. **California Volunteers Memorial** 1903
   Douglas Tilden, sculptor
   Dolores at Market St.
   The city's finest equestrian sculpture, nobly sited at the head of Dolores, but now overwhelmed by auto and supermarket signs.

3. **Row houses** c.1878; 120, 122, 126 Guerrero St.
   A superb and well maintained group of classic San Francisco Italianate townhouses with bay window false fronts.

4. **Levi Strauss Factory and Playground;** Original building, 1906; playground and restoration, 1970; Howard Friedman & Assoc.
   250 Valencia St.

5. **Valencia Gardens** 1943
   Wurster, Bernardi & Emmons/Harry Thomsen
   Sculpture by Beniamino Bufano
   15th St. bet. Guerrero & Valencia Sts.
   One of the landmarks of public housing design, this has only recently begun to show signs of vandalism and neglect.

6. **Far West Laboratory for Educational Research and Development** rem. 1972
   Esherick, Homsey, Dodge & Davis
   Folsom at 15th St.
   A brick warehouse gutted and re-filled as a government sponsored center for research in inner city educational problems.

7. **Mission San Francisco de Asis (Mission Dolores)**
   1782, rest. 1920; Willis Polk
   1321 16th St.
   The city's most venerable and famous building; its humble scale is dramatized by the monster next door. The padres chose this site as the least unfriendly on what was regarded for the next 70 years or so as a barren, fog-swept peninsula, largely unfit for human habitation.

8. **Notre Dame School**   1907; 347 Dolores St.
   This handsome mansarded structure replaced one destroyed in the fire of 1906 (this was its southernmost penetration) whose elaborate iron gates remain.

9. **Mission High School**   1926; John Reid, Jr.
   18th & Dolores
   Appropriately enough, the best of the city's Spanish-Colonial Revival schools.

10. **St. Charles School**   c.1875
    3250 18th St. at Shotwell St.
    A rare, surviving 19th century frame school house.

11. **Houses**   1961 & 1963; George Homsey
    4067 & 4069 20th St.
    Contemporary versions of the San Francisco row house on a very steep site.

12. **Row houses**   1898; Fernando Nelson, builder
    725-733 Castro St.
    Four Stick-Eastlake style houses by a speculative builder.

13. **Houses**   1870 & 1878; 109 & 159 Liberty St.
    Two Italianate town houses.

14. **Gompers High School**   1939; Masden & Hurd
    Barlett bet. 22nd & 23rd Sts.
    The best view of this fine piece of Streamlined Moderne is from Valencia. For another school of the same style see the George Washington School, 1935, by Miller & Pflueger, at 32nd Ave. & Anza St.

15. **Holy Innocents Episcopal Church**   1890 (Porch 1913); Ernest Coxhead
    455 Fair Oaks St.
    A remnant, now half hidden, of early undulating shingle Coxhead. Fair Oaks also boasts a number of interesting Stick-style houses.

16. St. Paul's Roman Catholic Church 1890
Church St. at 20th St.

> Stone twin towered Gothic Revival, straight from a steel engraving of the period, with an interesting iron columned interior.

Two architecturally unfulfilled but attractive open spaces at the southern end of the Mission are worth mentioning: Bernal Park and Holly Park. Remote from the rest of the city, Potrero Hill is another agreeable and unpretentious backwater without much in the way of architectural interest.

Along Third Street south of Potrero Hill are an interesting Streamlined-Moderne lift bridge (late 1930s) across the Islais Creek Channel and the South San Francisco Opera House of 1888 at Newcomb Ave. and Mendell St., a wooden Eastlake hall which did a flourishing theatrical business in this surprising location. Just beyond it at 5075 3rd St. is a brick and concrete library of 1969 by John Bolles & Assoc.

The Hunter's Point Naval Shipyard projects into the Bay to the east with its major landmark an enormous crane, one of two in the country capable of lifting a battleship gun turret.

On the southern edge of the city, between Sunnydale and Velasco Aves. north of Schwerin St. is Geneva Terrace, an Eichler high and low rise housing project of 1965 by Claude Oakland.

DIAMOND HEIGHTS

Diamond Heights is a steep and windy ridge just south of Twin Peaks which remained undeveloped long after the rest of the City because of its austere weather and the fact that it had originally been platted in the standard gridiron plan, which here finally met its limit; many of the lots were both inaccessible and unbuildable. On these grounds it was declared a Redevelopment Area in the 1950s, even though it was open land. Vernon DeMars did a street plan which followed the contours and a competition was held for the first phase development in 1961. Of the winning design by Cohen and Leverson, which was to have high rise towers on the hilltop and north slopes, only one group of townhouses was built. Single family houses by Eichler and others gradually filled the western slopes; an elementary school, shopping center, and several churches were built by the early 60s, and recently in another building spurt, most of the remaining sites have been built up with townhouses, apartments and more single family housing. South and west of Diamond Heights, Glen Canyon Park and Playground forms a remarkably wild and secluded stretch of open space in the center of the City.

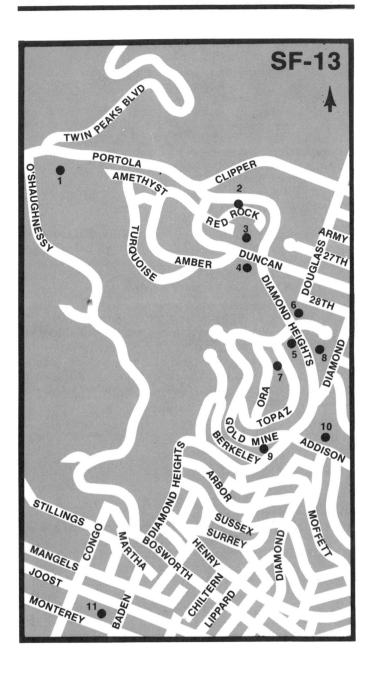

SF-13

1. **Diamond Heights High School** 1972
   Reid & Tarics Assoc.
   O'Shaunessy Blvd. & Portola Dr.
   This low, stepped back concrete complex promises
   to be the City's first architecturally distinguished
   high school in many years.

2. **Red Rock Hill Town Houses** 1962
   Cohen & Leverson
   Diamond Heights Blvd. & Duncan St.

3. **Diamond Heights Village** 1972; Red Rock Wy.

4. **St. Nicholas Syrian Antiochian Orthodox Church**
   1963; William F. Hempel
   Diamond Heights Blvd. & Duncan St.

5. **St. Aidan's Episcopal Church** 1963
   Skidmore, Owings & Merrill
   101 Goldmine Dr.
   An irregular hexagon of white stucco with an interior lit by a hidden clerestory and windows in the manner of the southwest missions. The mural painting is by Mark Adams.

6. **Village Square** 1972; Morris Lorbach
   E side Diamond Heights Blvd. bet. Duncan & Valley

7. **Gold Mine Hill** 1967; Fisher-Friedman Assoc.
   Gold Mine Dr. & Ora Wy.

8. **Vista del Monte** 1971; Smith, Barker, Hanssen
   E side Diamond Heights Blvd. S of Gold Mine Dr.

9. **Glenridge** 1969; Clement Chen & Assoc.
   Diamond Heights Blvd. & Berkeley Wy.

10. **Engine Co. No. 7, Firehouse** 1963
    Rockrise & Watson
    80 Digby St.

11. **Conservatory** 1917; Frank Merrill
    236 Monterey Blvd.
    This remarkable wood and glass conical roofed building was built, along with an observatory tower behind, by the inventor-owner.

The Sunset is remarkable chiefly for the blocks of stucco row houses produced by builder Henry Doelger in the 1930s, best seen in the Avenues of the middle 30s. They must have been made with a set of giant cookie cutters: one Spanish Colonial, one French Mansard, and so on. Immaculately kept and landscaped, they make a naive but lively street. Among them are occasional bits of Moderne commercial development and schools, and even an occasional Moderne house, such as the double house at 26th Avenue and Kirkham. Stern Grove, in the midst of the Sunset, is a eucalyptus-filled ravine where free concerts are held in the summer. It contains a charming gambling casino of the 1890s called the Trocadero Inn which was restored in the 1930s under the direction of Bernard Maybeck as a recreation building for the park. Along the Great Highway is a further sprinkling of Moderne, and architect Ernest Born's own simple redwood house of 1951, at 2020 Great Highway.

South of the Sunset is the Fleishhacker Zoo of 1951 by Lewis Hobart, the architecturally undistinguished campus of San Francisco State University, largely done by the State of California Division of Architecture, and Park Merced, a Metropolitan Life development of 1951 by Angus McSweeny, L. Shultz, and Thomsen & Wilson. At 994 Brotherhood Way just west of 19th Avenue is the Holy Trinity Greek Orthodox Church of 1964 by Reid, Rockwell, Banwell & Tarics.

The trolley tunnel completed in 1917 opened the area west of Twin Peaks to development, but the two most interesting subdivisions of the area actually preceded the tunnel by a few years: St. Francis Wood, planned by Frederick Law Olmstead, Jr. and John Galen Howard in 1912, and Forest Hills, laid out by Mark Daniels in 1915. Both have streets aligned with the contours and free-standing houses with generous land-scaping, unlike the older hilly parts of the city. St. Francis Woods, in particular, with its white houses, planting strips along the streets and fountain-inter-sections reflects the influence of the City Beautiful movement. The foggy weather helps keep the planting almost too verdant to be true.

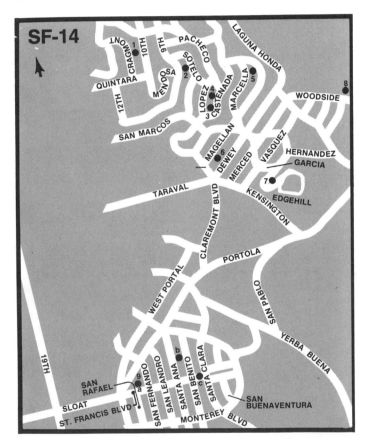

1. **House** 1939; William W. Wurster
   30 Cragmont Ave.

   Fine vintage Wurster, also visible from below on 10th Ave.

2. **House** 1919; Bernard Maybeck
   51 Sotelo St.

   A long, informal cottage with its main wing per-pendicular to the street. A pulpit-like balcony dominates the street facade.

3. House   1916; Bernard Maybeck
270 Castenada St. at Lopez St.

A shingled house whose corbelled corner bay window and the eave treatment of the living room wing might have been merely quaint in other hands than Maybeck's.

4. House   1915; Glenn Allen
35 Lopez Ave.

A heavy lidded, stucco box with wonderful Sullivanesque ornament. In the area there are a number of Prairie style houses, most based upon Wright's 1906 Ladies Home Journal theme. Three of these may be seen at 343 Montalvo Ave., and at 770 & 780 4th Ave. All were built between 1910 & 1918.

5. House   1921; S. Heiman
1 Marcella at Magellan St.

Pointed Mother Goose upon a pointed site.

6. Forest Hills Club House   1919; Bernard Maybeck
381 Magellan St.

Built by volunteers from the area, its lofty meeting room has a great exposed beam ceiling.

7. House   1970; Baken, Arrigoni & Ross
111 Edgehill Wy.

A tautly-stretched shingle and glass exterior wrapped around a series of wood and concrete platforms.

8. Woodside Gardens Housing for the Elderly   1968
Smith, Barker, Hanssen; Landscape Arch., Lawrence Halprin & Assoc.
255 Woodside Ave.

Concrete high rise interestingly massed and sited among the eucalyptus.

9. **St. Francis Woods** 1912
Frederick Law Olmstead, Jr. & John Galen Howard
  a. **Gates at St. Francis Blvd. & Portola Dr.** 1912
John Galen Howard
  b. **Terrace & Fountains on St. Francis Blvd.** 1913
Henry Gutterson
  c. **Model Houses** 44 San Benito St. 1913; Louis
Christian Mullgardt. 50 & 58 San Benito St. 1914-
15; Henry Gutterson

The tasteful Spanish Colonial Revival style of the models has been maintained to a remarkable degree by architectural controls, demonstrating the virtues and limitations of such enforced uniformity.

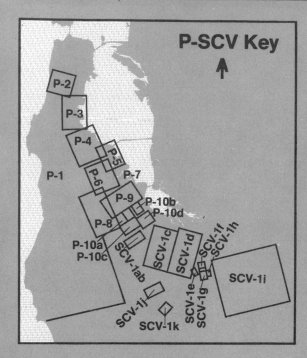

P-SCV Key

↑

P-2

P-3

P-4

P-5

P-1

P-6

P-7

P-9

P-10b

P-10d

P-8

P-10a

SCV-1c

SCV-1d

SCV-1f

SCV-1h

P-10c

SCV-1ab

SCV-1i

SCV-1j

SCV-1e

SCV-1g

SCV-1k

PENINSULA

P

P   **Introduction**

The Peninsula, a great northward pointing arm with San Francisco at its fist, divides the Bay from the Pacific Ocean. Its clearly defined geography and the pathways it defined have determined its urban development, and in large measure its architecture. It extends from Palo Alto or thereabouts at the edge of the Santa Clara Valley northwards about thirty-five miles to the Golden Gate. San Francisco occupies only the northernmost five or six miles, and is usually considered separately. The remaining 30 miles, with its skein of parallel roads and railways and its now continuous chain of towns, is the Peninsula.

Geographically, a ridge of mountains, the Santa Cruz Range, dominates. On the west side it drops through rolling foothills to a bluff above the Pacific. But on the east a more gradual alluvial slope ends in a plain of tidal flats and marshes. This side offered a pathway to Mission Dolores and later San Francisco, a level route but for the one obstacle of the San Bruno mountains which cross it just south of the present city-county line.

Development on the Peninsula followed a very clear historical sequence. First, in the late 18th century, came the road connecting Mission Santa Clara and Pueblo San Jose (see Santa Clara Valley) with Mission Dolores (see San Francisco). A mission outpost appeared halfway between at what is now San Mateo. Then at the end of the Spanish era and on into the Mexican period of the first half of the 19th century, a series of land grants dedicated the plain, marshes, and large parts of the foothills to great Ranches. They quickly gave way to American style farms, big and small, purchased outright or taken over by squatting. The Gold Rush was on, San Francisco burgeoned, and the Peninsula began to supply it with meat, butter, truck crops, and timber. A stagecoach route down the mission road, El Camino Real, generated stops every few miles, and these, in turn, formed the nuclei for towns.

About the time the Civil War ended, a new railroad connected San Francisco and San Jose. This sparked the first flow of wealthy people to the Peninsula to build estates. Actually a few rich gentlemen farmers preceded them. Hillsborough, Burlingame, Belmont, Atherton, even Saratoga in the Santa Clara Valley, became sites of great country houses, and often very creditable architecture and garden art.

After the turn of the century a new pattern began. Good white collar folk began to occupy modest subdivisions around the railroad depots. The 1906 earthquake and fire greatly accelerated this. By the 1920s the Peninsula had become a chief suburban appendage to the City. The Bayshore highway, later freeway, carved out a new route paralleling El Camino Real and the railway. Cars began to dominate movement.

Then, after the Second World War, development really took off, and this time it was not just bedroom dwellings for San Francisco workers. Industry, especially the aero-space-military-industrial combine, chose the Peninsula as the site for tens of thousands of new jobs. Shopping followed. Now the easily built-up area has been developed nearly solidly over the whole thirty miles. It retains its clear structure, a chain of towns along the path, in which are sprinkled a considerable number of Northern California's treasures of architectural and environmental art.

PACIFICA AND COASTSIDE SAN MATEO COUNTY

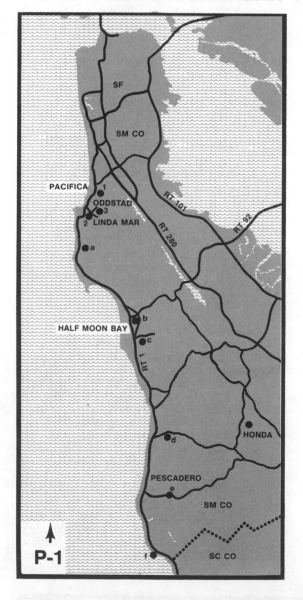

High mountains and cold fog have held back from the Peninsula's Coastside the urban development that has sprawled down the Bayshore. Only in the very north, a stub of freeway, about four miles of Route 1 south from Daly City, has opened the coast. Here a group of old settlements, places like Sharp Park, Vallemar, Rockaway Beach, San Pedro Terrace, and Linda Mar, have been collected into a confederated town called Pacifica. A few monuments peak out from the sprawl.

1. **Oceana High School**   1963; Mario Ciampi
   401 Paloma Ave.

   From under the gnarly cypresses near the row of old cottages that line Paloma Ave., a big crescent of curtain-walled classrooms encircling a square space-framed gym can be seen. Not great architecture perhaps, but a striking, other-worldly feeling of contrast.

2. **Francisco Sanchez Adobe**   1846
   Linda Mar at SW cor. Adobe Dr.

   This neatly restored adobe uses the foundations of an outpost of Mission Dolores built about 1780. The 1953 rebuilding effort, and its maintenance as a state historical monument, succeed in recreating a fragment of Alta California amidst the sprawl. Worth a stop.

3. **St. Peter's Roman Catholic Church**   1964
   Mario Ciampi
   700 Oddstad Wy.

   A round hall walled in glass, under a huge, wriggly, concrete umbrella, most typical of its time.

Pacifica represents the limit of intense sprawl. From Pt. San Pedro to Pt. Ano Nuevo the coastside landscape preserves the look of early California settlement. Since first explored by Gaspar de Portola in 1768, it has been occupied by ranchers and farmers who in more recent times have devoted themselves to raising flowers, Brussels sprouts, and pumpkins. This makes a fall visit particularly photogenic. The lack of well-developed highways through the hills from the Bay side has so far discouraged large scale development so that the patterns of small towns and farm clusters in valleys are still legible. The edge of the ocean is gently scalloped with moderate stretches of public beaches and punctuated by the lighthouses of Montara, built in 1887 (a), and Pigeon Pt., 1872. The beaches commemorate an enlightened county openspace purchase of the 1930s. Most have since been turned over to the state.

Half Moon Bay, the oldest town in San Mateo County, was settled in 1840. The early adobe buildings have vanished, but the first wooden house, built by James Johnston in 1853 in the style of a New England saltbox, stands, empty and weather-beaten, in a field near Higgins Rd. and Main St. (c). The Community Methodist Church, 1872, in Victorian Gothic Revival style, at Johnson and Miramontes Sts., is the principal architectural work (b). Nearby is a Victorian Gothic cottage with lace verge boards at 596 Purisima. Around the corner at 527 Main St. is the first store in the area, built in 1872. Its neighbor, 535-537, is another typical false front, commercial building of the period. The whole street was the scene of a community "paint-in" in 1970 which colored it up in a pleasant, fashionable way. A freeway from San Mateo currently inches its way across the pass above Half Moon Bay. Already it has triggered much speculation and some tract house development.

About 5 miles south is the valley of San Gregorio Creek whose crossroads town features a general store and post office building with a Spanish Colonial Revival stuccoed front, and San Gregorio House, a well-proportioned wooden inn with second story balcony, c.1850, which served hunters, fishermen, and farmers of the area (d).

The next town is Pescadero, a short distance inland, whose North St., the old main street, has several simple, rectangular, columned porches and gabled roofs. On Pescadero Creek Road is a more elaborate version of this house style with its porch along the long side and scrollwork brackets. The Pescadero Community Church, 1868, on San Gregorio St. is a simplified Victorian Gothic Revival building whose wooden boards are scored to simulate stone. St. Anthony's Church,

1870, on North St., has more elaborate detail and a doll house scale which exactly suits the miniature cypress allée leading to it.

DALY CITY, COLMA

The arbitrary line that slices off the City and County of San Francisco from the rest of the Peninsula has, in the opinion of local historian Frank Stanger, "no respect for ordinary human conventions, but cuts boldly across streets and property lines, and even through people's bedrooms. On the Bay side of the Peninsula it bisects Visitacion Valley diagonally, leaving the north portion of it in San Francisco and the south in San Mateo County. The people in the Valley are divided for political purposes, but in other ways act as one community. Over the hill to the south is the [then, not now] unincorporated community of Brisbane."

To the west the line crosses the historic gateway through which El Camino Real entered the City. From there it passes over the still largely open Pacific headlands—thanks to two golfcourses—and tumbles down the steep bluffs to the ocean below.

Perhaps the towns closest to the City hold little of interest for serious viewers of architecture and environmental design. They are ordinary, even ugly places, to many eyes. Yet each is very strongly just what it is: Brisbane, a home-made workingman's bedroom community; Colma, the graveyard marble orchard *par excellence;* and Daly City, a sprawled, contemporary, moderate income suburb.

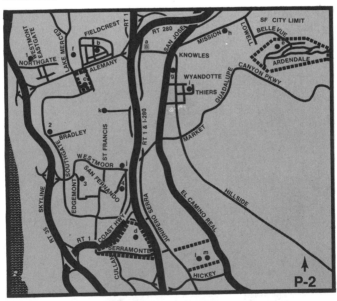

On the rolling, usually fog-shrouded highlands above the Pacific, against the southern boundary of San Francisco itself, Daly City has played a sequence of roles determined by its dominant neighbor. First market garden, dairy and across-the-line-from-the-police fun town, in 1906 and again in the late 1940s, it sheltered an exodus from the City. The earthquake converted much of John Daly's farm and the truck gardens of his neighbors into a tent city. The present bedroom suburb grew from the mass migrations of middle American families after World War II. Today, Daly City, the proverbial suburb, stands where only a generation ago WPA writers found, "fields and slopes . . . covered with . . . lettuce, artichokes, Brussels sprouts, pansies, marigolds, and violets."

The town centers on the historic land gate to San Francisco used successively by the colonial trail, El Camino Real, called Mission Street from Daly north, the railroad, the Interstate freeway system, and, most recently, the Bay Area Rapid Transit District. BART has its western and present Peninsula terminus at 400 Knowles Avenue designed by McCue, Boone & Tomsick, 1972 (a). One day, if politics permits, the rapid transit system may extend farther down the Peninsula toward San Francisco International Airport and beyond, following the same historic path as the road and railroad.

This area offers a striking example of post-World War II suburban design in the vast subdivision called Westlake built by Henry Dolger, developer of the Sunset District in San Francisco. Extending from the city limits south to Serramonte, from the Pacific bluffs to Interstate 280, and forming the major part of Daly City, it coherently obeys traditional community design principles. It has, for instance, elementary school centered, through traffic free, residential neighborhood units, an articulated park and recreational openspace system, and a town center complex of shopping, community and high school facilities just like the textbooks say it should. The sector about the Westlake Elementary School, Mario Ciampi, 1955, 80 Fieldcrest Drive (b), bounded by the city limits, I-280, Alemany and Lake Merced Boulevards, illustrates the faithful use of the neighborhood unit idea. Westlake Shopping Center, Henry Dolger designer, 1950-60, 375 South Mayfair Avenue, *is* the community center (c).

Incidently, this shopping center provides a splendid example of the transitional form between strip commercial development and the modern enclosed mall center. Nearby Mission Street and most of El Camino Real all the way down the Peninsula to San Jose perfectly illustrate strip development. Also nearby, the Serramonte Center by Welton Becket, 1967, north of Serramonte Boulevard (d), offers in contrast the most up-to-date type of shopping center layout. It has a totally enclosed, air-conditioned, pedestrian mall embellished with a great indoor fountain that spouts water from a fancy fixture twenty feet high on the ceiling.

East of Westlake, and east of the historic center of Daly City, lies another characteristic bit of post-World War II residential development: the zigzag necklace of little stucco row houses that loop diagonally up the north face of the San Bruno Mountains on South Hill, Ardendale, and Alto Vista streets (e). Movies and still photographs have made these a familiar image. Still farther to the east in Daly City lies the immense Cow Palace or State Livestock Exhibit Pavilion, State Architect, 1941, south side of Beneva Avenue, enter opposite Santos Street (f), still the Bay Area's major exhibition and indoor sports facility, but a particularly graceless work of architecture.

1. **Olympia Primary School** 1954; Mario Ciampi; addition 1957
   200 Northgate Ave.
   Humble concrete block and steel sash construction, and a neat courtyard plan exemplify the straightforward functionalism of its time.

2. **Vista Mar Elementary School** 1959
   Mario Ciampi. Lawrence Halprin, lands. arch.
   725 Southgate Ave. at northeast corner of Bradley Dr.
   A wiggly, folded plate roof on a hollow circle plan make this a uniquely imageable schoolhouse. Vista Mar won a number of design awards.

3. **Westmoor High School** 1958; Mario Ciampi. Lawrence Halprin, landscape architect.
   131 Westmoor Ave. at Edgemont Dr.
   An ambitious period piece of polychromed structural steelwork, boldly sited on high ground exposed fully to the ravages of the salt-laden fog.

Mario Ciampi designed most of the public buildings in Daly City during its growth years. These structures form the focal points in the sea of Dolger designed houses with their curious, ranch-house-on-top-of-a-garage stock plans made up with endlessly varied pop facades in all sorts of nice pastel shades. Serious students may want to track down the rest of Ciampi's Daly City work: Fernando Riviera Elementary School, 1960, 101 Lake Merced Blvd. (g); War Memorial Community Center, 1950, 6655 Mission Street (h); Vista Grande Elementary School, 1953, northeast corner Wyandotte/Avenue and Thiers Street, a neat bit of barrel shell construction (i); Garden Village Elementary School, 1956, 208 Garden Lane (j); and Pauline Margaret Brown Elementary School, 1957, 305 Eastmoor Avenue (k). Taken together in their setting, and seen in the nearly constant fog of Daly City, these works of Ciampi form a memorable episode.

4. Hope Lutheran Church 1955; Mario Corbett (original church only)
Cor. San Fernando Wy. & Sullivan Ave.
A handsomely detailed gem of Bay Area Style woodsy church building, partly compromised by an ungainly newer church school structure.

Once the name Colma identified the area in Daly City around where San Pedro Road forks off from the El Camino Real. Now it designates a unique incorporated town of almost a million graves and only a few hundred living, breathing citizens. Beginning in 1887 with Holy Cross Cemetery, the potato farms along the County Road and the railroad became graveyards. Just before the end of the century San Francisco passed an ordinance banning any further burials within the city limits. By 1904 ten cemeteries existed. Later Colma incorporated within a carefully drawn line that made local government resemble nothing so much as a cemetery committee.

In contrast to the rich collections of monuments which grace many late Nineteenth Century cemeteries in the East and Midwest, Colma offers little for the architecture and sculpture buff. Local stone cutters used ordinary stock designs for almost all of the markers. The Tevis tomb by John Galen Howard, c.1912, at the end of Myrtle Street in Cypress Lawn provides a sweet bit of nostalgia (l). From the same period is a Willis Polk tomb for the Naphthalys family done in a solid Roman-Renaissance Revival Style and also located in Cypress Lawn Cemetery (m).

The little working class settlement called Brisbane began as a real estate speculation on the northeast slope of the mountains facing the City. The first sub-division took place the year after the Bayshore line of the Southern Pacific opened on a path roughly paralleling the old San Bruno toll road, now visible in somewhat straightened out form in the path of Old Bayshore Blvd. Several promoters tried selling the lots. Nothing clicked, though, until about 1930. Then Brisbane's very cheap lots became choice sites for a Depression-born wave of do-it-yourself workingmen. This tradition has continued. But the town's image has gained a certain corporate gloss with the opening on its doorstep of the Crocker Industrial Park which runs to the northwest in the little Guadalupe Valley.

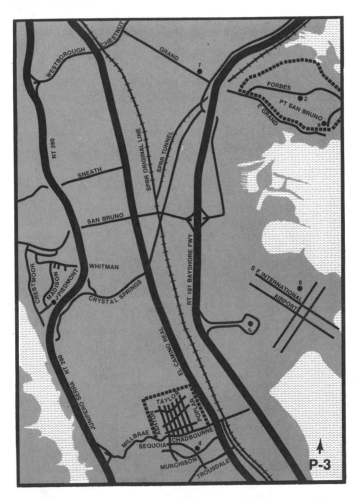

Between the ridge down the middle of the Peninsula and the marshes and sloughs of Bayside, from San Bruno Mountain on the north to an arbitrary survey-or's line that runs east-west through present-day Hillsborough and Burlingame, lay the great Spanish, then Mexican, cattle ranch called Buri Buri. After California joined the Union, much of it became the famous Miller-Lux spread that put steaks on the tables of post Gold Rush San Francisco. Throughout most of the nineteenth century three or four stage stops along El Camino Real and a few ranch buildings marred the open landscape. Only toward the turn of the century did industry and modest housing tracts begin the urbanization process. The earthquake brought refugees of course, and many stayed; but it was not until after World War II that development really took off. Even then little ambitious design was attempted. Though the airport now makes it a gateway to the region, travelers will find few monuments to visit here. Perhaps only those concerned with the everyday building of working men and women will find the area worth exploring.

SOUTH SAN FRANCISCO

The sign you see on the mountainside says it like it is, "South San Francisco: The Industrial City." It started in 1891 when Swift and Co. bought a piece of the Miller-Lux ranch on which to build a meatpacking plant. Armour and others followed almost immediately. A town to house and service the workers was platted in 1892. Paint and chemicals, steel and shipyards started up. By the time of World War I the town was complete with schools, churches, hospital, business district and civic center, in addition to the industrial area, port, and a variety of residential areas, many distinct ethnic identities.

"South San Francisco is an *industrial* suburb of San Francisco," wrote Peninsula historian Frank Stanger, "in the same sense that other towns on the Peninsula are *residential* suburbs." Swift picked it because it was a beef production headquarters already. Today the town remains almost as it was in the early years of the century except where the Bayshore Freeway slices through and where the old port and embarcadero have been leveled and filled for new industrial expansion.

1. **Civic Center—City Hall**   1920; Coffee and Werner. **Carnegie Library**   1914, addition 1941
   400 Grand Ave.
   City Hall follows a Classic Revival mold, the library is less easy to pinpoint.

2. **Cabot, Cabot & Forbes Industrial Park**   1965 Wilsey, Ham & Blair, engineers. Sasaki, Walker, Lackey, landscape architects and planners. Aristides Demetrios, sculptor.
   Access from East Grand Avenue, take Forbes Boulevard to Point San Bruno Boulevard to reach sculpture (a).
   A textbook example of modern industrial park planning embellished with Demetrios' heroic abstraction. The developer, Cabot, Cabot & Forbes, built much of Boston's famed Route 128 industrial area.

SAN BRUNO

A stage stop in the ranchland where the San Bruno toll road along the Bayshore from San Francisco joined the El Camino Real, its urbanization did not begin until the 1890s with the construction of the racetrack named for Rancho Buri Buri heir Torribio Tanfarán. Arrival of the electric railway from San Mateo in 1903 coincided with the first residential subdivision. Quake victims offered "free camping space" provided the first wave of settlement. In World War I the U.S. Navy took over Tanforan track—the name had become corrupted—and then vastly expanded the base as World War II began. The open space thus preserved until recent times explains the present landscape of new shopping centers, tract housing and freeway interchanges so close to the City.

3. **Crestmoor High School** 1962; Reid, Rockwell, Banwell & Tarics Assoc.
   300 Piedmont Ave.

   Practically inaccessible and almost invisible in its freeway-buried little valley, Crestmoor is the northernmost of a series of pacesetting high schools built from 1956 to 1962 for the San Mateo Union School District. The others, Mills High School in Millbrae (Millbrae 4) and Aragon and Hillsdale High Schools in San Mateo (San Mateo 22 and 23), are far easier to get at. A visit to any one will explain the concepts.

MILLBRAE

In 1860 Gold Rush "bonanza king" Darius Ogden Mills bought the 1500 acre, oldest son's share of the Buri Buri. Six years later he completed the huge great mansard-roofed mansion that stood until 1954 amid extensive lawns shaded with Himalayan cedars and set about with cast-iron shepherd-maidens posing with baskets of flowers. It was the first great estate house on the Peninsula, herald of an era, but nothing is left now. Its site is marked by a group of banal apartment buildings at Ogden and Murchison Drives on the Millbrae-Burlingame line.

During the Civil War, Mills sold the San Francisco and San Jose Railroad a right-of-way through his estate and in the deal got a station built near the southeast corner of Millbrae Avenue and California Drive in stripped Queen Anne style. Encouraged by the commuting potential town building efforts began in 1889, but not much happened until after the earthquake. Only in the 1920s did a characteristic commuter village emerge on the gridiron blocks off Hillcrest Blvd. west of Poplar Ave. designed largely in a vernacular version of the Spanish Colonial Revival style. After the depression and World War II development hiatus, most of the remaining land including the hundreds of acres still left in the Mills estate became swiftly built up.

● **4.**   **Mills High School**   1958; John L. Reid & Partners
400 Murchison Dr.

A major California monument in the New Brutal-
ism style along with the three other buildings in
the series done by Reid and his partners for the
San Mateo Union School District. This building
displays the characteristic vocabulary of industrial materials, construction· methods and architectural forms. Easy to see, especially from the
north along Millbrae Ave., it is marked by black
color steel Vierendal frames against immense,
gray rectangles of cladding. [See also Crestmoor
(San Bruno 3) and Aragon and Hillsdale (San
Mateo 22 and 23).]

Busiest area airport, San Francisco International stands
on the site the city government selected for a flying
field in 1927 after studying eight alternatives on the
Peninsula and one in the East Bay—Oakland located
its airport at the latter site. The wisdom of the choice
is confirmed by the fact that the location has adapted
smoothly to continuous changes in demand and technology over nearly half a century. Current terminal
expansion started in 1960 following long-range plans
by associated architects John Carl Warnecke and
Dreyfuss & Blackford. The United Airline maintenance
base on the north end of the field is the largest single
Bay Area industrial employer.

photo: Morley Baer

5.   **United Airlines Hanger**   1955
Skidmore, Owings & Merrill

On field just north of approach road to terminal.
An articulated structure of shapely concrete columns, cantilevered steel plate girders, and hung
sheet metal cladding generally attributed to the
hand of SOM partner Myron Goldsmith.

6.   **American Airlines Hanger**   1971; Conklin & Ros-
sant. Lev Zetlin, Assoc., engineer.
On field northwest and across runways from terminal.

Immense hyperbolic-parabolas of stressed-skin
sheet metal cantilever from a central structure to
make possible this inventive solution to the jumbo-
jet shelter problem.

HILLSBOROUGH, BURLINGAME, SAN MATEO

These three Peninsula towns present a tightly inter-woven story. San Mateo became the first Spanish set-tlement between San Jose and San Francisco when the friars made it an important farming outpost of Mission Dolores. The eighteenth century mission building stood just across El Camino Real from the present St. Matthew's Episcopal church (19). In 1846 Mexican Governor Pico granted Rancho San Mateo to Cayetano Areñas who in turn sold it to San Francisco entrepreneur W. D. M. Howard in the early 1850s.

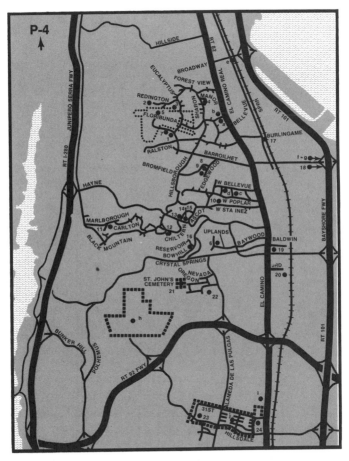

Howard's land became the development center for the three present towns, Hillsborough, Burlingame and San Mateo. The settlements began to take on their present character at the turn of the century: great estates in Hillsborough, and, at first, modest commuter colonies in Burlingame and San Mateo, then in the last three decades increasing industry and commerce. Now all three are largely built up in their own way so that any new endeavors require destruction of old buildings and gardens. Still many of the estates remain to give the area some worthy architectural monuments, and their heritage seems in part to have continued to the present a tradition of serious garden and building art.

"To prevent its rich country estates from being drawn
into the growing cities of San Mateo and Burlingame,"
Hillsborough incorporated in 1910. This defensive move
worked. As its founders hoped, the town exists today
as a private preserve for large homes, albeit a bit
diminished from its turn of the century splendor. It
remains a place of tasteful, native oak and bay tree
studded landscapes sheltering big houses, free from
any hint of commerce, industry, or even such plebian
amenities as parks and sidewalks. Predictably such a
town contains its share of fine domestic architecture.
Hillsborough has passed through three cycles of development beginning with William Davis Merry Howard's purchase of Rancho San Mateo in the middle of
the Nineteenth Century. Though Howard died young,
his descendants prospered and multiplied. His wife re-
married twice and family pressures began to fragment the immense ranch. In the 1890s the second
round of development began with construction of five
"cottages," actually generous country houses, designed
by A. Page Brown of San Francisco for a speculative
market. These were located along the El Camino Real
between Floribunda and Bellevue. Three remain (a).
The Burlingame Country Club was organized in one
of these cottages in 1893. The communal life of this era,
even its gentile politics, centered on the Club. In 1894,
for instance, the members passed the hat for money
to build the handsome Burlingame railroad station
(Burlingame 17). This structure served as town hall for
the then unincorporated area, and as a species of social center as carriages full of children came to meet
the top-hatted capitalist patriarchs returning from the
City on the afternoon train. Next door, centered on
present Park Street, the Club members laid out their
polo field. The people admitted to this world built
opulent mansions sited handsomely in great parks. A
few remain (2, 3, 4, 5, and 6 are examples).

After World War I, with the appearance of the progressive income tax and the changing personal economics of a burgeoning affluent class, most of the
big estates were subdivided into mini-estates. This
process accelerated even more after the Second World
War. Now Hillsborough presents a landscape of me-
ticulously groomed plots of but a few acres each on
which curiously plain houses have been built. By and
large the oaks and bay trees catch the eye rather
than the architecture. Perhaps only the prolific William
Wilson Wurster achieved an architecture appropriate
to the new era of diminished affluence (8, 9, 12, 14,
and 15).

After Hillsborough was incorporated the original Howard manse, the ornate but homely "El Cerrito" moved
to a new site, became the town's all-purpose civic
center, school, library, town hall, police station and
firehouse. The present city hall complex replaced it in
1930 (b). Located outside the estate area at the one
point where the town line touches the county road,
El Camino Real, it sits across Floribunda from the A.
Page Brown cottages. This building offers an interest-

ing twist by providing in one compound for not only the usual city hall functions but also a house for the police chief and apartments for the firemen and their families. Since then but one architecturally noteworthy public building, the North School complex (1), has appeared in Hillsborough.

1. **North School complex**　1950, Ernest J. Kump; additions 1952 and 1956
   Eucalyptus Ave. south of New Place Rd.
   A classic Kump Module elementary school which demonstrates the faultless expandability of this design prototype. On the same site are **Halfway House Recreation Center** 1957; Ernest J. Kump and **William H. Crocker Junior High School**　1959 and 1965; Ernest J. Kump

Among the remaining grand estates are:

2. **Joseph D. Grant Mansion, "Strawberry Hill."**
   1910; Lewis Hobart
   End of Redington Rd. (Note: this house is not accessible or visible from the public road.)
   A fine, small, stripped Italian Renaissance palace complete with parapet sculptures set in the most lovingly maintained grounds imaginable. A beautiful testament to Hobart's talent as both an architect and landscape designer.

3. **George T. Cameron Mansion, "Rosecourt"**　1913;
   Lewis Hobart
   815 Eucalyptus Ave.
   Another handsome Hobart design and one that can be glimpsed from the road. The entry gate frames the principal facade.

4. **George Newhall, Sr. Mansion, "La Dolphin"**
   1914; Lewis Hobart
   1760 Manor Drive

5. **William H. Crocker Mansion, "New Place"** 1910 or 1911; Lewis Hobart. Bruce Porter, landscape architect. Additions and remodeling, 1954; John Lord King
   End of New Place Rd.

   Set in what must be one of the Peninsula's finest man-made landscapes, the middle of the Burlingame Country Club, the house and its interiors give some clue as to how it was then. The remodeling had best not be discussed, but the basic fabric of this mansion and the preceding three give ample evidence of Lewis Hobart's power in the then fashionable Renaissance Revival idiom.

6. **Crystal Springs School for Girls; former Charles Templeton Crocker Mansion, "The Uplands"** 1913; Willis J. Polk
   400 Uplands Dr.

   Boldly sited on a knoll at a bend in San Mateo Creek, this is one of Hillsborough's better landmarks. The grounds once included most of the land between El Cerrito and Crystal Springs Roads plus the hill to the west where the little F. L. Wright house (16) is hidden. Look back from there for a nice view of the Uplands. Polk's design, in the Roman-Renaissance Revival style, has Ionic first story with a ballustraded attic surmounted by a second, set back attic.

In the recent third wave of development, a number of well known designers have contributed their talents, though Wurster's work is by far the most prevalent. Yet even more ubiquitous in the contemporary Hillsborough scene is the garden design of the prominent San Francisco architect, Thomas Church. Few of his designs, unfortunately, can be identified here because of privacy considerations. Occasional garden tours occur during which it is possible to see gardens by Church and others.

7. **House** 1972; David Robinson
   25 New Place Rd.
   A stylish recent work.

8. **Henderson House**   1932; William W. Wurster
   711 Bromfield Rd.
   Wurster's spare, neo-Regency *par excellence*. Look into the inviting entry court, glimpse the garden facade from the road.

9. **G. Pope, Jr. House**   1936; William W. Wurster
   735 Bromfield Rd.

10. **Coxhead House**   1903; Ernest Coxhead
    120 West Santa Inez
    A high, shingled fence on the front property line practically hides this Shingle Style villa from view. Only its gables and artistically disposed roof shakes show. Coxhead built this house for himself during the first wave of mini-estate development.

Nearby, and actually over the line in San Mateo not Hillsborough, are several interesting houses of the period when the great estates were first being broken up and developed. An early example of the type is the charming Ernest Coxhead design at 134 West Poplar Ave. with its row of gables and twin porches facing the street (c). A later one, also just over the line in San Mateo, is the W. W. Wurster design of 1940 at 231 Bellevue (d).

11. **House**   1952; Richard Neutra
    1430 Carlton Rd.
    A fine, perfectly characteristic, early 1950s work by this Southern California leader of the International Style.

12. **House**   1952; Remodeled by Wurster, Bernardi & Emmons.
    877 Chiltern Rd.
    Originally, and still, mostly, an eclectic house of the 1920s.

13. **House**   1956; Germano Milano and Mario Ciampi
    760 Chiltern Rd.
    Standard, one-story Bay Region contemporary vernacular knowingly handled to make an elegant large house.

14. **Henning House**   1937; William W. Wurster
    751 Chiltern Rd.
    Restrained, understated, formal yet freely composed fenestration, irreplaceable twelve-inch-wide shiplap redwood siding deceptively hidden under light gray paint, perfectly complimentary garden design, and other typical features make this a splendidly typical Wurster house.

15. **Dinkelspeil House**   1940; William W. Wurster
    301 Ascot Rd.

16. **House**   1941; Frank Lloyd Wright
    101 Reservoir Rd.
    A neat little decorated, late thirties, triangular-grid Wright house. The famous homebuilder Jo-

seph Eichler once lived here before he began constructing houses; he claims the experience is what turned him on to homebuilding and led him to leave the wholesale food business.

The landed gentry of what would become Hillsborough actually established Burlingame first by using the name for their country club and then their privately built railroad station (17). Predictably, as commuting took hold, massively reinforced by the refugees from the 1906 earthquake and fire, districts within walking distance of the Peninsula train stations were subdivided and developed in small homes. The first plat for such a development in Burlingame was filed in 1898 covering the gridiron blocks just south of the station. A mile and a quarter up the line, Ansel Easton in 1905 platted another early subdivision just in time for the flood of refugees. He built himself a railroad station in 1911 to make permanent the flagstop established earlier. Once called Easton Station, it is now called Broadway (e) for the street that connects it to the El Camino Real. Streets like this and Burlingame Ave. which connect stations to the main highway invariably became the principal shopping streets of the Peninsula towns during the railroad commuting era. The two-centered town thus created incorporated as Burlingame in 1908. In the areas around the two stations, blocks of 1910 to 1920 vintage bungalows attest to this fact. During the Twenties, the town spread north onto part of the Mills estate and around the edge of Hillsborough well up into the hills. It was a period of explosive growth; Burlingame offered the perfect suburban image for that era. As a consequence the last three decades have had much less effect on the appearance of Burlingame. Though it has a small and appropriately dismal looking industrial district on bayfill, it is free of massive shopping centers, freeway interchanges and sprawled tract housing.

● **17. Burlingame Station, Southern Pacific Railroad**
1894; George H. Howard and J. B. Matthews
Burlingame Ave. and California Dr.

"This first permanent building in the Mission Revival Style of architecture," reads the plaque announcing that it is a registered California Historical Landmark, "used 18th Century roof tiles from the Mission San Antonio de Padua at Jolon and the Mission Dolores Asistencia at San Mateo." The principal architect was a son of W. D. M. Howard, purchaser of Rancho San Mateo and first American settler.

The Peninsula's largest city claims to be its oldest. On March 27, 1776, Father Pedro Font, chaplain of the Anza expedition, crossed and named San Mateo Creek. Later when Mission Dolores needed to establish a farming outpost because San Francisco was so barren, and needed a wayside hospice halfway down El Camino Real to San Jose, they chose this place. During the era of the ranchos and the earliest of the large estates, it became a major stagecoach stop. Reputedly the original halfway house stage stop became part of the fabric of the Mills Memorial Hospital nurses' home. By the 1860s San Mateo had developed into a "business district" in the middle of farm country. It even boasted a waterfront and shipping industry located where the Creek became a tidal slough. Then the railroad arrived in 1863. It accelerated development. Soon a first plat was filed covering some sixteen blocks around the depot. Remains of this early building can still be seen in the few "gothik" houses along Delaware Street, for instance, number 45 South Delaware (f).

As San Mateo grew it became a center for retail trade and commerce, for education and religion. It remains that today. The older areas blend easily into the adjoining parts of Hillsborough and Burlingame (see Hillsborough 10). A period of explosive growth finally hit the town after World War II. Then housing tracts, shopping centers, freeways, and giant educational plants appeared in the southern part of the city to give San Mateo its present form (21, 22, and 23).

18. **Woodlake Residential Community**　1965
    Wurster, Bernardi & Emmons. Lawrence Halprin, landscape architect
    S side Peninsula Ave. bet. N Humboldt & N Delaware Sts.
    A large—nearly a thousand unit—apartment community fitted out with all the trappings such as tennis, swim and health clubs, putting greens, etc. The design represents one of the first and still on of the best Planned Unit Developments (PUDs) in the Bay Region. Though the architecture looks dull, the energetic landscaping more than makes up for it.

19. **St. Matthew's Episcopal Church**　1909; Willis J. Polk.　1957; expanded by M. Pflueger
    El Camino Real and Baldwin Ave.
    The always versatile Polk this time produced a very correct Gothic village church. Pflueger daringly cut it in half to insert a carefully matched new section so the nave would seat 160 additional worshipers.

20. **St. Matthew's Roman Catholic Church**　1899
    3rd Ave. at South Ellsworth Ave.
    Brick, Roman-Renaissance Revival style basilica of a sort rarely seen west of the Mississippi.

21. **Parrott family Tomb**　1885
    Northeast corner of St. John's Cemetery, enter from Oregon Ave.
    A perfectly sited Roman-Renaissance fragment.

22. **Aragon High School**　1960
    Reid, Rockwell, Banwell & Tarics
    900 Alameda de las Pulgas.

23. Hillsdale High School 1956
John Lyon Reid & Partners
Del Monte Street between 31st Ave. and Hillsdale Blvd.

Hillsdale was the first and Aragon next to the last in the remarkable series of New Brutalist Style high schools executed by Reid and his various partners between 1956 and 1962 for the San Mateo Union High School district. Architectural critic Allan Temko wrote of one of these buildings, "Confronting a suburb littered with TV aerials, the school asserts its own disciplined ideal of rational order in a technological age." Yet he concluded, "the fundamental hermetic quality," of the structure, "will remain, hemmed-in, troglodytic, a dream of technocracy, as if the year were already 1984." Temko and others have attributed much of the expert industrial vocabulary used in these buildings to engineer partner, Alexander Tarics.

Other components of the San Mateo educational plant have fared worse architecturally. Once, for instance, the College of San Mateo, the region's pioneer junior college, found quarters in the lovely ex-US Merchant Marine Academy built out on Coyote Point at the beginning of World War II to the designs of Gardner Dailey. A few of the lesser structures remain primarily as units of the Junior Museum established there since the area became a park(g). The College, meanwhile, has moved up into the foothills above the town along the new Route 92 Freeway in what must be one of Northern California's most pompous yet empty formalist compositions, J. C. Warnecke & Assoc., 1965; West Hillsdale Blvd. N of Rt. 92 (h).

As the automobile became more and more dominant, the old centers in the San Mateo-Burlingame area held on remarkably well. From the old area near the railroad stations south, some strip commercial development occurred during the 1930s. The Streamlined Moderne style dog and cat hospital of 1933 at 2600 El Camino Real represents an especially choice piece from this period (i). The post-World War II era saw the perfection of the shopping center and south San Mateo gained its focus then with the construction of the Hillsdale Center (24).

24. Hillsdale Shopping Center 1954-67 in stages;
Welton Beckett & Assoc.
El Camino Real at 31st Ave.

This early center went through a classic series of design modifications and expansions so that it presents a textbook on the evolution of the shopping center. The earliest parts were frontage stores of the type characteristic of the 1940s. The major part of the center was built around an internal pedestrian mall, in its time it was a pioneer in this direction and it retains a certain design quality that, though dated, makes shopping here very pleasant. The most recent modifications introduced at Hillsdale are the double deck parking structures which promise good things in terms of reducing the normal expanse of asphalted parking lots.

Behind the center, in the area bounded by Hillsdale and 31st Ave. up to the Alameda de las Pulgas, lies an interesting bit of Radburn type residential site planning that dates from the immediate post-World War II period (j). Few recent tracts provide such quiet amenity.

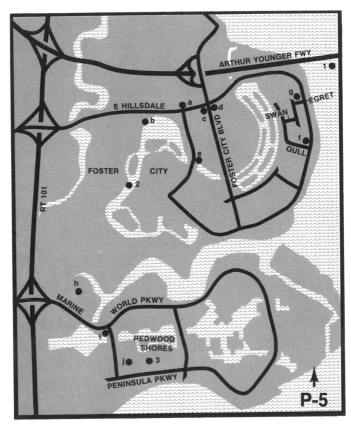

FOSTER CITY

Some eight square miles of tidal mudflats east of the Bayshore Freeway have been transformed over the last decade into two comprehensively planned, largely residential subdivisions of the type we have come to call "new towns." Foster City, the largest and by far most complete, occupies a previously farmed island between San Mateo Slough, now called Marina Lagoon, and Belmont Slough, an area that is just south of Route 92 and the San Mateo Bridge approach. Next to Foster City, on the south side of Belmont Slough and extending to Steinberger Slough, lies the presently aborted town called Redwood Shores. Famous designers participated in the early stages of both towns, and a few distinctive contemporary works were built before economics banalized or halted the building programs. However, the simple fact of their being new towns makes them both worth a visit for people concerned with housing and urban development.

1. **San Mateo Toll Bridge** 1968; California State Division of Bay Toll Crossings, engineers; William Stephen Allen, consulting architect
   State Rt. 92 connecting Younger Fwy. in San Mateo with West Jackson St. in Hayward on the E. side of the Bay.

   Close to the San Mateo shore a graceful, high level steel girder arches over the main shipping channel to connect the miles of causeway on concrete pilings that cross the Bay. The extraordinary thinness of the steel girder span comes from the orthotropic design which makes possible a reduction in the depth of the structure by using the road surface itself to carry a major share of the load. The sensitive design of this bridge vindicates the vigorous campaign on behalf of better bridge esthetics triggered by the awkward and ugly Richmond to San Rafael Bridge built some years earlier.

2. **Foster City** 1961 and continuing; Wilsey and Ham, engineers and land planners. Ruth and Krushkov, city planners. T. Y. Lin, engineers for bridge design. James Levorsen, architect for street furniture.

   Access from East Hillsdale Blvd. interchange on the Bayshore Fwy. Rt. 101, or Foster City Blvd. interchange on the Arthur Younger Fwy. Rt. 92. The buildings and places listed below are arranged along a looped pathway that offers a suggested automobile tour for the visitor.

   a. **Foster and Wells Fargo buildings** 1962
   Edward D. Stone
   1015 East Hillsdale Blvd. near Shell Blvd.

   A pleasant fragment of what was to be a grand, monumental composition formed by the two completed structures flanking a never-built high-rise office tower and the back of the plaza. A site model of Foster City as originally envisioned sits near the stairs in the lobby of the Foster building, or at least it did when last checked. The streets, parks, and landforms are pretty much as shown on the model; the buildings, especially the high-risers, are all imaginary.

   b. **Central Park** 1969
   Royston, Hanamoto, Beck & Abey
   East Hillsdale Blvd. between Shell and Edgewater Blvds.

   A stylish bit of decorative greenspace overlooking the widest stretch of the lagoon formed in part by a small slough that crossed the island. This was enlarged, carefully shaped, and used as a main element in the storm drainage system for Foster City. It makes a well used amenity with the help of many access beaches and a fleet of small boats.

c. **Public Safety Building** 1972; Mario Gaidano
East Hillsdale Blvd. at Foster City Blvd.

An improbable bit of late 1960s Philadelphia style brickwork.

d. **Commodore Apartments** 1962; Edward Durrell Stone
Foster City Blvd. between East Hillsdale Blvd. and Balclutha Dr.

Low budget Stone classicism, one of the first structures in town.

e. **Bridges,** a total of four   1961; T. Y. Lin, engineer. Lawrence Lackey, consulting architect.
East Hillsdale Blvd. (2), Foster City and Shell Blvds.

Ambitious efforts to integrate lighting and separated footpath with a high arched roadway bridge that will offer sufficient clearance for small sailboats.

f. **Port-O-Call shopping center** 1964
East Hillsdale Blvd. at Gull Ave.

First, and so far only, commercial center in Foster City. Across the street a pleasant surprise: the Hillbarn Players legitimate theater.

g. **Group of houses** 1965; Claude Oakland. Joseph Eichler, builder.
1001-1083 Egret St.

A characteristic work of this enlightened builder and his most frequently employed designer.

Complete the tour loop by following Gull Avenue to Beach Park Boulevard. Here a large block of Kaufman and Broad condominium townhouses mark the corner where a right turn to Foster City Boulevard will return the visitor to the starting area. On the way a recent neighborhood convenience shopping center at Marlin Avenue and the new Junior High School between Tarpon and Swordfish streets offers a glimpse of things still to come in the Foster City design palette. On the Boulevard between Bounty and Polynesia Drives the Franciscan apartments nicely represent the pop, eclectic revival style that has turned out more successful in the market place than the town's clean Stone beginnings.

3. **Redwood Shores**
   First plan: 1959; The Architects Collaborative (Cambridge, Mass., Walter Gropius senior partner) Alvin Zelver, planner.
   Second plan: 1964; Dean, Austin, Williams, landscape architects.
   Third plan: 1968; Leslie Salt Company staff.
   Daniel, Mann, Johnson, Mendenhall, architects and engineers for the city and the improvement district.
   Access from Bayshore Freeway Route 101 at Ralston Avenue (Marine World) interchange.
   The Leslie Salt Company, largest private owner of San Francisco Bay wetlands—they use them as evaporating pans in the large scale production of salt from seawater—decided in the 1960s to begin urbanizing its vast holdings. Dogged by a long drawn out period of planning and waiting for governmental approvals, they had just begun house sales when the feds slapped an embargo on them against approval of FHA loans. The government was worried about earthquake hazard. Earthquakes tend to turn filled ground into a soft liquid that swallows up whole buildings without a trace. When the embargo was lifted, the momentum had vanished and town building halted.

   h. Marine World 1968; Mario Gaidano
   Marine World Parkway.
   A 1960s style commercial amusement park.

   i. Sales Pavilion 1968; William Hedley. Royston, Hanamoto & Beck, landscape architects.
   Marine World Parkway.
   A jewel of pole framing and contemporary shingle work. Look at the Redwood Shores housing through the slit space of the balcony.

   j. Original townhouse development 1969
   Stanley Schwartz, developer.
   A distinguished speculative housing development design.

Rancho de las Pulgas, or flea ranch, which ran from San Mateo Creek on the north to San Francisquito Creek, and from the Crystal Springs Valley to Bayside, covered the largest area of any Peninsula land grant. It belonged to the Arguello family who, through the able advocacy of the Puerto Rican Mezas, avoided losing it to squatters or through the land title court tests that characterized the period of Americanization. All of the Bayshore towns from San Mateo south to Palo Alto lie within its boundaries. The two northernmost of these, Belmont and San Carlos, began as baronial focal points: the latter as the headquarters of the Rancho, the former as the estate of the Peninsula's most colorful early American tycoon. Both towns were slow to develop, though after World War I both became increasingly built-up bedroom suburbs.

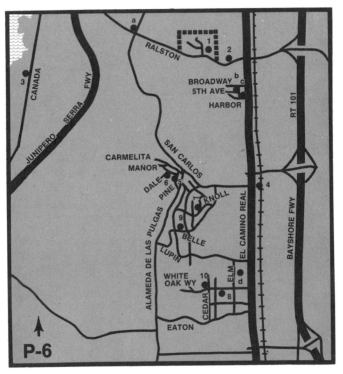

Comstock Lode multi-millionaire, financial genius and gambler, William Chapman Ralston, bought Italian Count Lussetti Cipriana's house and land in the valley called Cañada del Diablo which he in turn had purchased from the Arguellos. Ralston enlarged and transformed it into the Peninsula's most extravagant showplace (1). Only a few years before, it had been nothing but open ranchland with a single stagestop where El Camino Real crossed the mouth of the canyon. After a decade came financial crisis, talk of scandal, and Ralston's body found floating in the Bay. A sequence of new owners took over. Soon only the area immediately around the main house, the present College of Notre Dame, remained. The rest had been subdivided, first for a series of asylums and sanitoriums along Ralston Avenue—a row of these remain—then later for housing. By now sprawl covers Belmont, joining it seamlessly to San Mateo on the north and San Carlos to the south.

1. **Ralston Hall, College of Notre Dame** 1855; original Cipriana house. 1865-75; vastly enlarged by John P. Gaynor
   College of Notre Dame Campus, Ralston Ave. at Notre Dame Ave.

Morley Baer: *Here Today*

Wm. C. Ralston, a flamboyant, immensely rich Gold Rush figure, employed architect Gaynor, the man he would also employ to do the Palace Hotel in the city, and an army of skilled workmen, to convert Count Cipriani's modest house into the Peninsula's most splendid mansion. In its brief day, formal dinner for 100 became commonplace and by 1868 it accommodated 120 weekend houseguests.

Gertrude Atherton, of the family for whom the nearby town was named, called it, "an immense, rambling, French-looking structure." But its real glory appeared inside. There the edifice developed a three-layered space in plan consisting, first, of well-lit foyers, enclosed verandas and morning rooms in the outer layer, then a belt of drawing and sitting rooms which gave · finally onto the great rooms of state, the stairhall, the ballroom and the baronial diningroom. Moving partitions, immense sliding doors, and single-hung wall panels that disappeared upward one layer to the next. In style and decor it is best described as high Victorian-Mansard-French, freely redone in fine woods. The interiors have largely survived in fine fashion. The College deserves special thanks for the loving care with which they maintain this treasure of Northern California's unfortunately limited architectural patrimony. Some of the nearby, new campus buildings, the dorms of 1968 by Hollis and Logue, for instance, exhibit the same close concern.

2. **Woodmont Apartments** 1967;
   Backen, Arrigoni & Ross
   1050 Ralston Ave.
   A cascade of white stucco walls and green composition roofs on the hillside above the road. It
   looks quite chic, almost as though it were just
   imported from Switzerland, excepting only the
   lack of brute concretework.

Little about Belmont's expansive postwar residential
growth merits special attention in this guide. Three
churches, two new and one old, may be of interest.
Church of the Holy Cross, 1964; Reid, Rockwell, Banwell & Tarics, 900 Alameda de las Pulgas (a) sports
Bay Region trelliswork across a small-scale Byzantine
Stucco form; Church of the Good Shepherd, 1964; Clark
& Beuttler, 1300 5th Street (b); and Belmont's first
church, the Chapel of the Good Shepherd, 1865, 1336
5th Street (c).

Above the urbanized strip of Bayside Peninsula, along
the line of the San Andreas Fault, lies a beautiful valley, since 1863 a main link in San Francisco's water
supply. First Pilarcito reservoir, then San Andreas,
Upper Crystal Springs and finally in 1887-1890 Lower
Crystal Springs reservoir with its pioneering poured
concrete dam across the San Mateo Creek filled the
valley floor. Even after the City socialized the privately owned Spring Valley Water Company in 1930,
and completed the ambitious Hetch Hetchy project
that brought water from Yosemite Park in the Sierras
in 1934, these lakes and their watershed remained
key parts of the system. That explains the fact that
no development mars the slopes seen so spectacularly
from the new I-280 Freeway.

3. **Pulgas Water Temple** 1938; S. F. Water Dept.,
   Public Utilities Comm.
   Canada Rd., west side, above San Carlos halfway
   between Rt. 92 and Edgewood Rd.
   Opening of a cross-bay aquaduct that tapped the
   ground water supplies of Pleasanton and Sunol
   in Alameda County received the kind of monumental celebration apparently only possible in
   America during the City Beautiful movement and
   the parallel ascendency of the Roman-Rennais-
   sance Revival Style.

SAN CARLOS
The Arguello family ranch house once stood about two
blocks northwest of the San Carlos City Hall near the
present corner of Magnolia and Cedar Streets. Long
after sovereignty passed from Mexico to the United
States the area remained primarily grazing land. The
railroad passed through in 1863, but until 1887 no
regular stop existed here. That year construction

started on a station (4) and a first subdivision plat was filed. Still nothing. By 1903 all of fourteen families had moved here. The house at 520 Elm Street designed and built by W. G. Kraeger is one of these first fourteen (d). Even the earthquake did not start anything. Development began only after World War I. Then in the 1920s San Carlos became the Peninsula's fastest growing community. Even during the depression decade of the 1930s, population trebled.

Little remains from before the First War, and little built since makes news, although reduced versions of the characteristic Peninsula development cycles do exist. From the estate era there is the Brittan layout (5 and 6), from the period of the mini-estates a couple of noteworthy dwellings present themselves (7 and 8), and from the flowering of public building after the Second World War the predictable finger-plan schoolhouses (9 and 10).

4. **San Carlos Chamber of Commerce, former San Carlos Station, Southern Pacific Railroad** 1888
   El Camino Real opposite San Carlos Ave.
   A humble bit of Richardsonian Romanesque made from the same pretty sandstone as the first elements of the Stanford University campus.

5. **Nathaniel Brittan House** c.1870; 40 Pine St.
   A large house in a mixture of Shingle Style and half-timber.

6. **Nathaniel Brittan "Party House"** 1872
   James A. Adams
   125 Dole Ave.
   Multi-faceted multi-gabled redwood folly surmounted by an octagonal lantern, built to cope with its owner's riotous life-style.

7. **Timby House** 1941; William W. Wurster
   621 Knoll Dr.
   One of those basic Wurster's in a lovely garden.

8. **Watson House** 1909; Louis Christian Mullgardt
   1557 White Oak Wy.
   Hidden behind a new ranchburger, a nice cottage in Mullgardt's typically personal idiom.

9. **Brittan Acres Elementary School** 1952
   John Lyon Reid & Partners
   Belle and Tamarack Aves.
   Classic, one-story finger plan, wood construction, exposed piping on the outside offers a nice early Brutalist touch.

10. **White Oaks Elementary School** 1945 Ernest J. Kump, addition 1948. 1953; annex, John Carl Warnecke.
    White Oak Way and Cedar St.
    Here Kump constructed a prototype of his later, much used module. This time he built it of steel with a flat roof.

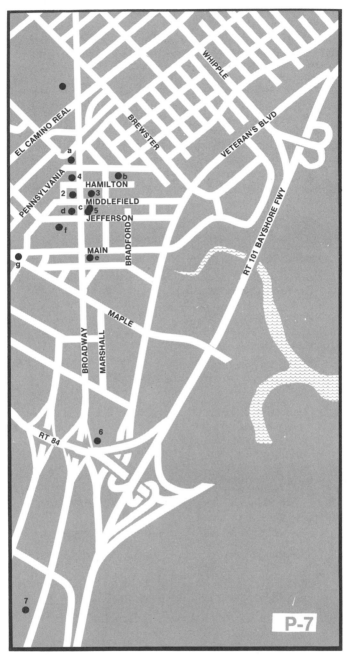

The head of tidewater on Redwood Creek, the point nearest the Woodside redwood forests at which logs could be floated on the Bay for the journey to the City became a natural place for a town. Near this point, too, El Camino Real and later the railroad crossed the Creek. The magic tidewater mark became the center for the Peninsula's first town worthy of the name.

S. M. Mezes, Esquire, attorney for the Arguello clan in their fight to secure their title to the Rancho de las Pulgas, made the first plat for a town here. He wanted to call it, naturally enough, Mezesville. It did not stick. But he is to blame for the curious angular relationship between the streets of downtown Redwood City and the El Camino Real which sets most of the Peninsula's street geometry.

Oldest of the string of towns along the El Camino Real, Redwood City naturally became the seat of the San Mateo County government when it was formed in 1856. By 1858 people began calling the town by its final name, and in 1867 they incorporated it. The new name, Redwood City, celebrated economic facts. This was the main lumber mill center and shipping point for the industry that built and rebuilt San Francisco as the city expanded, burned and reconstructed itself. The forests were gone by the end of the third quarter of the Nineteenth Century, but the mills hung on for another fifty years. Now all that is gone and the town functions mainly as a government center.

Little remains of the old Redwood City but the street grid oriented to now mostly filled-in Redwood Slough and two old houses, the Lathrop house (4) and a house on Main Street (e). More remains from the turn of the century when its governmental role began to be more important than lumbering (3 and 5). The center of town continued to grow importantly in the 1920s (1 and 2), but soon suburban sprawl began to engulf everything and reduce the importance of old centers like this. This trend still continues.

1. **Sequoia Union High School** 1924, music building 1928, library 1939; Coffee & Werner
   Broadway between El Camino Real and Brewster
   Once the estate of Moses Hopkins, Mark's brother, this, the first of the Peninsula's big union high schools, preserved much of the estate including, originally, some of the buildings. Now these are all gone; only some of the rich specimen plantings remain. The half century old, rambling Spanish Colonial Revival plant looks almost as though it had really been here for centuries. It makes a nice contrast with the new buildings of the San Mateo Union High School district in San Mateo (22, 23), Millbrae (4), and San Bruno (3).

Redwood City's central area clusters around the long since filled place where Redwod Creek interrupted Broadway. About six blocks northwest of this point Broadway met El Camino and in 1868 was crossed by the railroad. The present station, a simple colonnaded pavilion, was built in 1909 (a). The business and government district runs south from here.

2. **Fox (Sequoia) Theater block** 1927
   2200 block of Broadway
   Small town movie palace of the 1920s in a vaguely Gothic style perhaps touched by the Art Deco.

3. **San Mateo County Court House** 1904, rebuilt 1906-08. Addition 1939; Glen Allen
Middlefield Rd., Hamilton St., Broadway and Marshall St.

Homegrown variation on Roman-Renaissance Style themes, exterior detail includes a colossal order with American eagle capitals. The real joy comes inside. Here a fine rotunda opens up to a stained glass dome decorated in patriotic motifs. On the Broadway side the building connects to a new block of equal or greater size designed in the PWA Moderne fashion, and actually built with PWA money. Nearby, between Hamilton and Winslow Streets, the new San Mateo County Government (administration) Center and Hall of Justice rather dumbly face each other across a mall on a closed block of Bradford Street (b). The latest buildings prove that the course of architecture need not be onward and upward.

4. **Benjamin G. Lathrop House** 1860
627 Hamilton St.

A fine Victorian Gothic Revival Style dwelling from Redwood City's first decade, the oldest house left in town.

5. **Bank of San Mateo building**   1909
2000-2002 Broadway

Two story, stucco, French Baroque-like design with much generous classical detail. See also the Fitzpatrick block next door at 2010 (c) and the building across Broadway on the northwest corner with the inventive redwood heraldly emblazoned on its corner-facing cartouche (d).

Other downtown bits that may perhaps be worthy of note include the Diller building, 726 Main Street, the oldest commercial building in town (e); the city government complex consisting of firehouse, police station, Chamber of Commerce, city hall, library, and post office, all clustered around the corner of Jefferson Avenue and Middlefield Road (f); and an anachronistic old house, c.1860, at 1018 Main Street (g).

6. **Redwood City Municipal Services Center**   1970;
Daniel, Mann, Johnson, Mendenhall
1400 Broadway

Perfectly well done, vernacular, Miesian design.

7. **Ampex Corporation office building**   1959
John Carl Warnecke & Assoc.
401 Broadway

Rectangular donut plan two story office pavilion that recalls Ed Stone's designs of the 1950s. Surely detailed, nicely kept up. Obviously intended as one unit in a planned R & D campus that never seems to have been realized. Walk into the slightly formal garden between this building and the cafeteria opposite to get a real feel for the design of the time.

WOODSIDE, PORTOLA VALLEY

Lumbering began during the Mexican era in the interior valley above the Rancho de las Pulgas, now Atherton and Menlo Park. This area became the Rancho Cañada Raymundo in one of the very last of the old, pre-American land grants. The Gold Rush triggered a frantic building boom in San Francisco. This in turn tremendously stimulated lumbering. In and around Woodside the industry grew from two small mills in 1848 to eight bigger ones in 1853. These operations quickly stripped the area of virgin redwood. By the 1860s cutting had been forced to move over the ridge to the Pacific slopes. In a few more years lumbering here was all but dead.

The beginning of the Woodside community was marked by the opening of Dr. R. O. Tripp's first store in the fall of 1851, the only store at the time between San Francisco and Santa Clara. His second building, which still stands (2), from the time of its opening in 1854, was the place to go for supplies and refreshments for the entire lumbering area which at its peak employed as

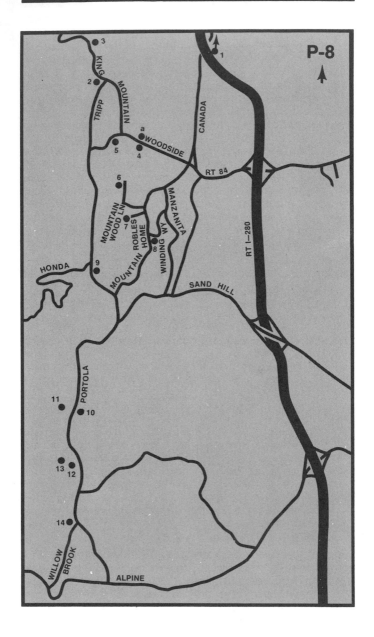

many as a thousand lumberjacks. For 50 years, with the exception of one of Grover Cleveland's terms, it served as the district's post office as well as dispensary of food and liquor.

By the turn of the century Woodside, now cut over completely, became estate land with the founding of such showplaces as the Josselyn (3) and Folger (5) mansions. Like the other Peninsula estate communities, the 1920s brought to Woodside a shift to smaller places typified by the familiar villas designed by Wurster to be set in gardens designed by Church (6, 8). Estate building and some subdivision activity began in this period to penetrate into the heretofore undeveloped

Portola Valley. Some few community buildings came with the big estates such as Polk's neat little church (10); most appeared only in the post-World War II period. (4, 11, 12, 13 and a). But this architecture, nice enough in itself, makes little impression. Though the great trees are gone, dense second growth timber and strong foothill landforms in this beautiful valley dominate the works of man.

1. **William B. Bourn Estate, "Filoli"** 1916; Willis J. Polk. Bruce Porter and Chesely Bonestell, landscape arch's.

   Entrance to the grounds off Cañada Rd. near Edgehill (Note: these grounds are not open to public.)

   Bourne, who inherited a Mother Lode gold mine and ran the Spring Valley Water Company (see Crystal Springs Valley), employed Polk to build a great house. Once again that amazingly versatile architect rose to the challenge, and, working in yet another revival style, produced a sumptuous Tidewater Virginia Georgian Colonial design. His collaborators fittingly completed it with acres of beautiful gardens.

2. **Dr. R. O. Tripp's Woodside Store** 1854
   Kings Mountain Rd. at S.W. corner of Tripp Rd.

   Dr. Tripp's historic store reigned for more than a generation as commercial, entertainment and communications center of the Woodside logging district. Now it serves as a county historical monument and museum set in a fetching second-growth redwood landscape. Dr. Tripp's house is across the street at 3301 Tripp Rd.

3. **Charles Josselyn House** 1906; Clarence Tantau
   400 Kings Mountain Rd.

   Attractive one story villa composed of Renaissance and Baroque elements. Two wide eaved, gabled projecting pavilions joined by an Ionic pergola enclose a fine formal patio.

4. **Woodside Community Church** 1891; original building. 1960; new building, Wurster, Bernardi and Emmons. Stained glass designed by Mark Adams.
   3154 Woodside Rd.

P-8 Portola

A simple, square cornered "village church" to which a far larger, more seriously artless second village church has been connected by a cloister formed of new Sunday school rooms.

Across the street there is a rather miscellaneous, incrementally built cluster of school rooms called the Woodside School, constructed between 1947 and 1969 to the designs of at least three local firms, Clark & Beuttler; Delph Johnson, Poole and Storm; and Kingsford Jones (a).

5. **James A. Folger Mansion**   1905; A. Page Brown
3860 Woodside (no public access)

   A turn-of-the-century pile which defies stylistic pigeonholing; grandly scaled, full of stucco baroque, but with expansive hip roofs and Secessionist chimneys.

6. **Reid Dennie House**   1963
Joseph Esherick & Assoc.
222 Mountain Wood Ln.

   Nice, artless, creamcolored, board-and-batten Wurster-like farmhouse at the end of a pretty drive up Mountain Wood Lane.

7. **Jackling House**   1925; George Washington Smith
Robles Rd. at 400 Mountain Home Rd., actually at the end of Robles which was once the drive for this house.

   A major Spanish Colonial Revival villa set in the remains of a once great estate.

8. **Shuman House**   1949
Wurster, Bernardi and Emmons
607 Mountain Home Rd. at SE cor. Winding Wy.

   Elegant, rambling late Wurster style ranch house in unusual light colored oiled vertical wood siding. The almost inevitable Church garden, visible over the hedge, is worth looking at.

9. **Charles Brown Adobe**   1839-46
2000 Portola Rd., actually set well back in a private estate, the roof at least is clearly visible to the east from the public road at a point 500 feet north of California Historical Marker #478.

   In all probability the oldest building in San Mateo County, the Brown adobe has been carefully restored and looks very authentic now.

10. **Our Lady of the Wayside Roman Catholic Church**
c.1920
930 Portola Rd.

11. **Valley United Presbyterian Church**   1965; Inwood and Hoover
945 Portola Rd.

    Lots of tough, boulder filled concrete dominated by a steep timber A-frame roof give this church an ambitious interior.

by a steep timber A-frame roof give this church
an ambitious interior.

12. **Christ Episcopal Church** 1957; Clark & Beuttler
    815 Portola Rd.
    Simple, woodsy structure with a high pitched roof.

13. **Portola School** 1955, addition 1957; Callister and
    Rosse
    765 Portola Rd.
    Multicolored, wood-frame finger plan bunched
    behind the still preserved little red schoolhouse.

14. **The Sequoias Retirement Homes** 1961; Skidmore,
    Owings & Merrill
    501 Portola Rd.
    A big, campus-like group of stucco pavilions with
    hip roofs all connected together and attached to
    various central services by many, many covered
    walks. Much admired, 1964 HUD award.

ATHERTON, MENLO PARK

By the early 1860s, on two adjoining pieces of the
Rancho de las Pulgas, three men began building estates, the names of which would remain as the two
southernmost towns in San Mateo County. J. D. Oliver
and D. C. Glynn, brothers-in-law fresh from Menlough,
County, Calway, Ireland, bought 1700 acres, built adjoining houses, and over their shared entrance drive
erected a three-arched gate emblazoned "Menlo Park."
Naturally enough, ten years later when the railroad
arrived, the stop here became the Menlo Park Station.
Soon the first subdivision took place in the settlement
of Menlo Park, and the town was on its way into being.
The settlement and the station became the center
around which all the country estates south of Redwood
City grouped. The first of those, laid out in 1860 for
Faxon Dean Atherton covered nearly a square mile
between what are now Atherton and Valparaiso
Streets. This wealthy, cultured and traveled man, and
his house, set the tone for the area throughout the
last half of the Nineteenth Century. Remains of the life
style still exist. His novelist daughter-in-law, Gertrude

photo: Bancroft Library

Linden Towers

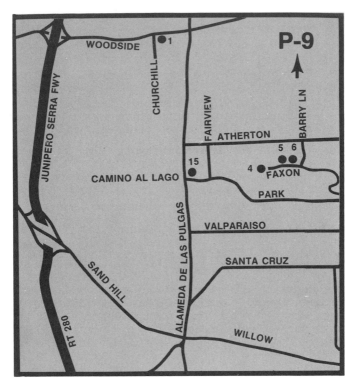

Atherton, described life there in loving detail as a series of long summer afternoons spent with neighbors "on the wide verandah, sewing, embroidering, exchanging recipes, gossiping. I often wondered," she wrote, "if life anywhere else in the whole wide world were as dull."

Other estates followed. Perhaps the grandest, certainly the most obstentatious began in 1878 for Virginia City mining tycoon James L. Flood. Called Linden Towers, this remarkable, turreted extravaganza, stylistically, High Victorian Wedding Cake, lasted until 1934 when it was auctioned off piece by piece because no one could afford to run it any longer. It stood in what is now Flood Circle in the middle of Linden Park subdivision for mini-estates (a).

The history of Atherton town in many ways parallels that of its twin, Hillsborough, to the north. It came into being in just the same way—an incorporation designed to prevent assimilation of the estate people and their lands by the *hoi polloi* of Menlo Park. Again the defensive strategy worked; Atherton remains a totally residential, upper class community.

Architecturally it went through a somewhat less articulate development sequence than Hillsborough though the same three stages were evident: vast country estate-farm enterprises, then immense and sumptuous showplaces for the post-Gold Rush millionaires, and finally subdivision into mini-estates for the affluent mass. Little remains here of the first two phases (3, 8,

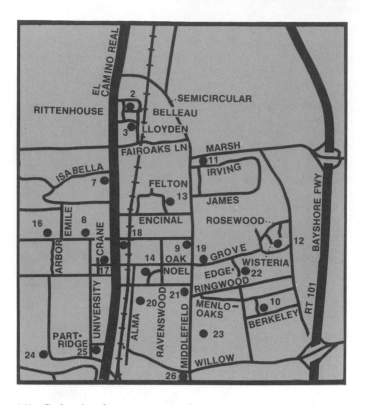

10). Only the last stage perhaps matches some of the fine designs to be seen in its twin to the north. Atherton does have its quota of nice Wurster and their contemporaries (2, 4, 5, 6, 11, 12, 13).

With the end of the Mexican era, the district around Menlo Park rapidly changed from grazing land to American style farms. Then as soon as the railroad appeared settlement began. For some years the population continued to have a heavy Irish bias. Roman Catholic institutions provide much of the district's most attractive architecture (16, 19, 23). During World War I a huge military camp sprang up. It housed 45,000 men at a time, who learned to fire artillery in the rolling hills near the present western limits of the town. Since then Menlo Park has gradually been transformed into one of the major Peninsula cities, mainly residential in character though it does house a few major institutions and employers, most notably the Stanford Research Institute.

After an abortive attempt to incorporate way back in the 1870s, it was not until 1923 and 1927 respectively that Atherton and Menlo Park became independent cities. Now the two towns coexist neatly with the fancy houses in one and the lesser things in the other. Functionally, however, they remain one community, and are treated as such in this guide.

1. **Woodside High School** 1957; Ernest J. Kump
   Woodside Rd. at the southeast corner of Churchill Ave.

Actually just outside the town line of Atherton in an unincorporated area, this is another in the series of pure Kump Module educational buildings, and it too is nicely colored, offering such delights as electric blue structural steelwork.

The next group of entries comprises houses of various sizes, ages and styles, from mansions to cottages, from 1860 to nearly the present moment, delicate vernacular Victorian Gothic to self conscious contemporary forms.

2. **Lyman House** c.1942; Wurster & Bernardi
Selby Ln. at Osborn Ave.

This house represents the ultimate in artless modesty of design. Its influence may be seen in the early Joseph Eichler development along Dawn Dr. and Sunnymount Ave. in Sunnyvale (c).

3. **George A. Davis House** 1940; Mark Daniels
11 Rittenhouse Rd.

A medium size streamline Moderne Style house. Daniels handled the idiom here as well or better than anyone anywhere else on the Peninsula.

4. **Joseph R. Coryell Carriage House** c.1900
Willis J. Polk
48 Lloyden Dr.

Handsome, rambling Mission Revival design set in authentically planted grounds. Again in this house Polk demonstrates his amazing versatility and mastery of the Styles, and at the same time a delicacy that civilizes the awkward Mission motifs. Actually this structure was but the first phase of an ambitious estate plan; the rest was never completed.

5. **House** 1927; George Washington Smith. Later additions by William W. Wurster and others
99 Faxon Rd. (This house is on a private drive at the end of Faxon and is not visible from the public road.)

The most accomplished of the very few Northern California works of Santa Barbara's acknowledged master of the Spanish Colonial Revival style. The house and fine grounds can be only glimpsed through the gate off the cul-de-sac on Faxon Road.

6. **House** 1957; George Rockrise
98 Barry Ln. at Faxon Rd.
A mixture of traditional Bay Region, Japanesey and 1950s contemporary ideas in a nice big house.

7. **Joseph Eichler House** 1958; Anshen & Allen
72 Barry Ln.
A contemporary design characteristic of its time, memorable because of the dominating aquamarine blue standing seam metal roof.

8. **Capt. James W. Watkins House** c.1860
25 Isabella Ave.
Sweet, early Victorian Gothic Revival prefab made in Connecticut and shipped 'round the Horn to here. Perhaps the oldest house to be seen in the area.

9. **Douglas Hall, Menlo School; former Payne Mansion** 1906, rebuilt 1910; William Curlett
Valparaiso St.
Nicely preserved though heavily used 56 room mansion in the Roman-Renaissance Revival Style.

10. **House** c.1905; Frank S. Van Trees
400 Middlefield Rd.
Ave.
At first sight it looks like a classical revival design, but on a closer look all sorts of discrepancies show up—the asymmetry of the entrance, for instance, and the curiously missing columns. All in all a pleasantly homely attempt at grandeur.

11. **Peninsula School of Creative Education; former Coleman Mansion** 1882
Peninsula Wy. and Berkeley Ave.
Grand Italianate pile with sweeping verandas, now somewhat worn by heavy use as a prep school. Some of the new structures on the school grounds merit a glance.

12. **House** 1953; Anshen & Allen
19 Irving Ave.
A vintage work by this firm.

13. **House** 1954; Frank Lloyd Wright
83 Wisteria Wy.
Beautiful, beautifully made, beautifully kept, landscaped and maintained late Wright house in his standard red brick and redwood.

14. **William Corbus House**   1939
    William W. Wurster
    239 Felton Dr.
    Ordinary and nice, standard Wurster windows which seem almost totally uncomposed, board walls, deceptive plainess.

15. **Edgar Mills House**   c.1880
    1040 Noel Dr.
    Rather ordinary Italianate house of the period now shelters an antique shop that serves luncheon.

The remaining entries, mostly public and institutional buildings, quite predictably occur mainly on the Menlo Park side of the town line. Atherton's pure residential character means that it gives room to little besides houses; even the town hall masquerades as a ranch house and the railroad station as an early 20th Century garden gazebo (b).

16. **Los Lomitos Elementary School**   1946
    Ernest J. Kump
    299 Alameda de las Pulgas
    Early, and classic, Kump modules.

17. **Convent of the Sacred Heart**   1898, rebuilt after 1906; J. J. Devlin
    1100 Valparaiso Ave.
    Red brick, Mansard Style main building with a nice strong Roman Baroque porch in cut stone. Lovely grounds, lusher by far than Devlin's seminary (23), include rows of squatty palms and strategically placed, immense, branching oaks, all soft dark green to go elegantly with the soft dark red of the building.

18. **Russian Orthodox Church, former Episcopal Church of the Holy Trinity**   1886
    1220 Crane St.
    Modest little Stick Style building.

19. Chamber of Commerce offices, former Menlo Park Station of the Southern Pacific Railroad   c.1880
1100 Merrill St.

Cute Eastlake Style depot, a perfect set for a western movie and just the sort of building for which preservation is both practical and wonderfully civilized.

Morley Baer: *Here Today*

20. Church of the Nativity (Roman Catholic)   1872
210 Oak Grove Ave.

First Catholic church in Menlo Park, a Catholic community from the first. As fine a wooden, Victorian Gothic Revival Style building as you can see in the West. Well cared for.

21. Menlo Park Civic Center   1963 to 1970
Kingsford Jones
Between Alma & Laurel Sts. between Ravenswood Ave. & Burgess Park

An ambitious civic exercise combining on one campus separate buildings in a matched, contemporary residential style for city administration, city council chambers, public library, recreation center, etc.

22. Conference building, Stanford Research Institute
1971; Skidmore, Owings & Merrill
333 Ravenswood Ave.

A refined but thoroughly enjoyable quadrangle set about a fine, European feeling court. This is the only artistically distinguished building in the extensive miscellany of the SRI campus, once a military hospital site.

23. **Laurel Elementary School**   1945-50; Ernest J. Kump
95 Edge Rd.
Yet another nice finger-plan of the author's usual modules.

24. **St. Patrick's Seminary**   1898, rebuilt 1908
J. J. Devlin
Middlefield Rd. bet Ringwood & Santa Monica.
A large, bold complex in the French Second Empire Style, relieved with some Romanesque detail. Grander in scale but not nearly so felicitously sited as Devlin's nearby convent (16). Curious wooden stable stands close by the main building.

25.- **Allied Arts Guild,** old barns 1885; Pedro de Lemos and Gardner Dailey. 1927; some later additions
Arbor & Cambridge St.
A delightful 1920s period piece in the Spanish Colonial Revival Style. Reservations needed for lunch, but with them you transport yourself back to the heyday of the American Arts and Crafts Movement.

26. **Peninsula Volunteers Retirement Apartments**
1961; Skidmore, Owings & Merrill
817 Partridge Dr.
Homey looking, two story, wood apartment cloister—the human side of SOM.

photo: Morley Baer

27. **Sunset Magazine Headquarters**   1962; Higgins & Root/Cliff May. 1963; Clark & Stromquist/Cliff May
West side Middlefield Rd. at Willow
The apotheosis of the Bay Region and Peninsula life style, and what could be more fitting?

The youngest major settlement on the Peninsula, and northernmost Santa Clara County town, Palo Alto epitomizes the affluent, space-age, but humane culture associated with contemporary Bay Area life. Moral sentiment started Palo Alto. After founding his famous university, Leland Stanford caused the town to appear because neither neighboring Menlo Park nor Mayfield would outlaw saloons and booze. Prohibition is long gone. What remains is the suburban university town *par excellence*, one that displays a fine range of twentieth century themes in environmental design and architecture.

Timothy Hopkins, son of Stanford's business associate Mark Hopkins, bought 700 acres across El Camino Real from the new campus, and platted the town in 1889 under the name University City—a name Stanford later made him give up. Hopkins renamed it Palo Alto (tall tree) for the area's chief landmark, a 1000 year-old, twin trunk redwood that had been named more than a hundred years earlier by the Portola expedition. (It stood on the county and town line just where El Camino and the railroad crossed San Francisquito Creek. The first trunk fell in a storm about the time the campus was started. The second remained until 1968.) Earlier this land and the land of the campus and other nearby places had been part of a Spanish land grant called Rancho Rinconada de San Francisquito.

Somewhat to the south on another part of the same Rancho a place called Mayfield Farms had become by the 1850s a stage stop, five years later a post office, and in 1867 a town, Mayfield. Palo Alto swallowed it in 1925, but its outline remains in the distinctive grid of streets named for Civil War generals tucked between California Ave. and Page Mill Expwy. between El Camino Real and the Southern Pacific tracks. To the west across El Camino Real, north of California Ave., lies the College Terrace subdivision, c.1890, with streets named for colleges. In Mayfield proper nothing much remains from the old days. But in College Terrace the Griffis cottage at 1181 College St. c.1890, suggests the modest dwellings that once made up Mayfield.

In 1885 Jane and Leland Stanford founded the university as a memorial to their only son who had died shortly before. The campus they built remains one of the architectural treasures of Northern California (the next section of this guide covers it). For the first half century, the town Hopkins founded across El Camino grew up in a concentrated fashion around the original plat. It remains one of the Bay Area's richest architectural landscapes (see Palo Alto Central Area).

In the 1920s a brief surge of development well to the east in the area now part of unincorporated East Palo Alto saw a unique utopian community flourish momentarily. Runnymeade, brain child of Charles Weeks, aimed at a self-sufficient life style based on tiny, homestead-like, family chicken farms under the motto "one acre and independence." Little remains now but a street name out East University Ave. and a curiously widely-spaced street grid. Recently the area has become a black ghetto where once again utopian movements have sprung up, including one that seeks to rename East Palo Alto after the Kenyan capital, Nairobi.

After World War II Palo Alto entered a new growth cycle triggered partly by the precedent breaking Stanford Industrial Park on university owned land (see Stanford Industrial Park). The newer south side of town offers many textbook examples of the kind of environmental design that characterizes the good life on the sunset coast. In recent years this environmental concern created unique public openspace reserves: Foothills Park, a largely undeveloped preserve several miles to the west out Page Mill Rd. (only open to Palo Alto residents); and a wildlife and recreation area at Sand Point and Mayfield Slough at the Bayshore end of Embarcadero Rd.

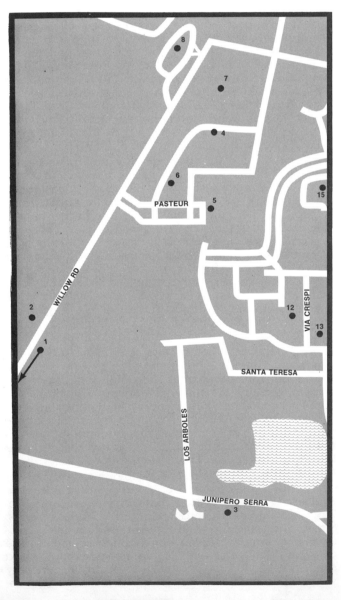

With a prescient confidence that they were establishing one of the world's great universities, Leland Stanford and his wife employed the finest talents of the time to design the campus. The great landscape architect Frederick Law Olmsted did the site plan, and it was he who created the extraordinary planning concept embodied in the Quadrangle (10). Shopley, Rutan and Coolidge, the Boston architectural firm that had inherited the practice of H. H. Richardson, carried out the first round of buildings within the Olmsted plan. Charles Allerton Coolidge of that firm actually did this work which included, in addition to the Quadrangle, Encina Hall (26), the Museum (15), and the Memorial Church (11).

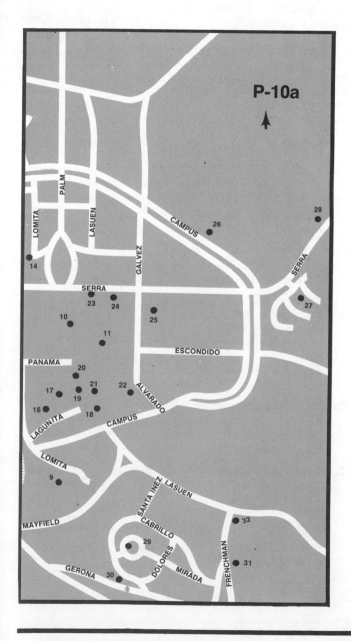

The initial wave of campus building continued through the first two decades of the twentieth century. Halfway along, the 1906 earthquake struck down a number of the original buildings. These were soon rebuilt. During the 20s, 30s and 40s little development took place except for the Hoover Institution on War, Revolution and Peace (25). In the middle 1950s a new cycle of expansion began when, with the help of the Ford Foundation, Stanford undertook seriously to become a world class university. White Plaza and the buildings surrounding it (20, 21, 22,) and the palatial Stanford Hospital (5) number among the more interesting architectural expressions of recent expansion. This burst of building activity has yet to cease: as this guide goes to press, a new law school complex is about to begin.

Stanford's original grant endowed the university with vast land holdings. Most of this resource has been used for the campus itself or remains open. (Just now much of the open area is dotted with huge parabolic radio astronomy antennas giving the golden hills of the back campus a curiously futuristic quality.) Some of the Stanford land has been devoted to residential subdivisions in which dwelling sites are leased to faculty members following a precedent common among eastern Ivy League schools like Princeton. A few interesting houses appear here (30, 31, 32, 33). But a far more inventive use appears in the powerful entrepreneurial spirit which has surfaced in recent times and led to leasing land to income producing commercial and industrial enterprises. These include professional offices grouped near the hospital (6 and 7), a regional shopping center (8), and the nationally known Stanford Industrial Park (q.v.).

A visitor and guide service is located at the left (east) side of the main entrance to the Quadrangle.

1. **Stanford Linear Accelerator**   1968
   2575 Sand Hill Rd.

   An immense non-building two miles long built to machine-tool tolerances. I-80 freeway goes right over the accelerator structure. It is easily seen from the road, but best seen from the air.

2. **Oak Creek Apartments** 1969; John Carl Warnecke
   1700-1815 Willow Rd.

   Thoughtful site planning on a partially wooded creek bank makes this project.

3. **Center for Advanced Study in Behavioral Sciences**
   1954; Wurster, Bernardi & Emmons; Thomas D. Church, land. arch't.
   Junipero Serra Blvd.

   The perfect scholars' ivory tower built in mainstream Bay Region style and set in sensitively enhanced nature.

4. **The Barn, Cafeteria (former Riding Stables)** c.1870
    rem. 1966; Off Quarry Rd.
    The last remains of the Stanfords' stock ranch that
    became the campus. The interior has been re-
    modeled as cafeterias and shops.

5. **Stanford University Hospital** 1959
    Edward Durrell Stone
    300 Pasteur Dr.
    By far Stone's most ambitious design in the Bay
    area, done at the apogee of his decorated, yet
    stripped classical style. One wonders how such a
    pretty hospital functions.

6. **Medical Plaza** 1959
    Wurster, Bernardi & Emmons; Lawrence Halprin,
    land. arch't.

7. **Stanford Children's Hospital** 1969
    Stone, Marraccini & Patterson
    520 Willow Rd.
    Another demonstration that Foothill College started
    a Bay Region style version suitable for institution-
    al buildings. This is the site of Ms. Lindheim's
    important functional studies of children's hospital
    design.

8. **Stanford Shopping Center** 1957; Welton Beckett
    El Camino Real at SW cor. Willow Rd.
    Undistinguished architecturally but a landmark in
    campus development.

9. **The Knoll** 1918; Louis Christian Mullgardt
    Lomita Dr.
    Built as a president's house, it now shelters aca-
    demic functions behind its pink and battered
    walls.

●10. **Quadrangle** 1891; Shepley, Rutan & Coolidge;
    Frederick Law Olmsted, land. arch't.
    Serra St. at end of Palm Dr.
    These warm yellow sandstone buildings, whose
    marvelously organized red tile roofs shelter broad
    connecting arcades, exhibit a westernized Richard-
    sonian Romanesque style touched by Mediter-
    ranean motifs with results perfectly attuned to site
    and climate. One of the few great university com-
    plex design concepts of all time: a variety of spec-
    ial purpose and generalized educational struc-
    tures plugged into a two-level circulation grid. The
    materials and some of the stylistic ideas form the
    architectural vocabulary for much of the rest of
    the campus. The planning concept remains unex-
    ploited here though much used recently in the East
    and in Europe.

11. **Memorial Church** 1903, rebuilt after the earthquake 1913; Charles Allerton Coolidge, C. E. Hodges
Located in the Quadrangle at the back (south) opposite the main entrance.
Centerpiece of the composition and main monument to the Stanfords, its artwork and design help make this eclectic favorite. The university guide service map explains it all.

12. **Physics Lecture Hall** 1957; Gardner Dailey
W of Quadrangle across Lomita Dr.

13. **Herrin Hall and Herrin Labs** 1967
Milton D. Pflueger
NW cor. Serra St. & Lomita Dr.

14. **Chemistry Building** 1902; C. E. Hodges
Lomita Dr. next to Herrin (13)

15. **Museum** 1892; Shepley, Rutan & Coolidge
Lomita Dr. at SW cor. Campus Dr.
The museum and the chemistry building use the materials vocabulary of the Quads in much more pedestrian isolated structures. The museum has railroad rails buried in the masonry to strengthen it.

16. **Faculty Club and Plaza** 1965
Edward Page. Thomas D. Church, land arch't.
Bet. Santa Theresa St. & Lagunita Dr.
The tree shaded open space makes this place special.

17. **Tresidder Memorial Union** 1962
Spencer, Lee & Busse
Bet. Santa Theresa St. and Lagunita Dr.

18. **Dinkelspiel Memorial Music Auditorium** 1957
Milton T. Pflueger, Spencer & Ambrose
Lasuen St. at end of Lagunita Dr.

19. White Memorial Plaza   1964; Thomas D. Church
Space formerly occupied by Lasuen St. bet. Old
Union (20) & Store (21)

This public space is one of the few accessible
works of Bay Region style garden design pioneer
Church. Fountain by Aristides Demetrios.

20. Old Student Union   1915; Charles T. Whittlesley
W side White Memorial Plaza

One of the first buildings to break with design tradition set by the Quadrangle, it nevertheless
looks picturesquely Mediterranean and pleasant.

21. Post Office and Book Store   1960
John Carl Warnecke
E side White Memorial Plaza

Another version, or fragment of a version, of Foothill College, this design seems very much at home
in this milieu.

**22. Stanford Center for Research and Development in
Education**   1972; Skidmore, Owings & Merrill
Alvarado Row at end of Galvez St.

A new note in brut concrete.

23. Art Gallery   1917; Bakewell & Brown
Serra St. just E of Quadrangle

**24. Hoover Institution on War, Revolution and Peace
(Hoover Tower)**   1941; Bakewell & Brown
Serra St.

A major popular landmark in a round-headed
Moderne style that looks vaguely like the late
work of Bertram Goodhue.

25. Encina Hall   1891; Shepley, Rutan & Coolidge
Serra St.

Originally the university's dormitory for men, recently university administration offices. Devasta-
ted by fire in 1972.

26. Roscoe Maples Pavilion   1969
John Carl Warnecke
Campus Dr.

A field house design that depends upon formally
articulated banks of bleachers.

27. **Married Student housing**   1959 Wurster, Bernardi & Emmons; 1964 & 1966; Campbell & Wong
Off Campus Dr.
Low-rise by Wurster, Bernardi & Emmons; high-rise by Campbell & Wong

28. **School Construction Systems Development (SCSD) Pilot Unit, now Stanford Employees Credit Union**
1964; Ezra Ehrenkrantz. Structural system design by Inland Steel, Robertson Ward, architect
770 Pampas Ln.
This jewel-like pavilion, assembled from factory-made pieces, was chosen by English critic Reyner Banham to exemplify one of the two poles that characterized recent architecture in California. (He chose Moore's Condominium at Sea Ranch for the other pole.)

29. **Hoover House**   1919; Arthur B. Clark & Birge Clark
Cabrillo Ave.
A large Mission Revival villa composed of undecorated cubelike concrete elements that show considerable affinity to the Southern California work of Irving Gill.

30. **House**   1953; Aaron Green
553 Gerona Rd.
Green is a graduate of Taliesin and was for some years F. L. Wright's Bay Area representative.

31. **House**   1939; Ernest Born
745 Frenchmans Rd.
International style dwelling in horizontal wood siding instead of white plaster.

●32. **House**   1937; Frank Lloyd Wright
737 Frenchmans Rd.
One of Wright's first hexagonal grid houses, it features the plan organization that became characteristic for the next twenty years—living spaces pivoted about a central chimney mass in or behind which lay a high, skylit kitchen. The small lot and the landform conspire to prevent Wright's usually subtle siting (see for contrast his other nearby houses in Hillsborough and Atherton).

Downtown Palo Alto memorializes Hopkins' original plat even though the business buildings on the main drag, University Ave., have been torn down once or twice since the beginning. Originally the strip between El Camino Real and Middlefield Rd. was composed of typical late 19th century falsefront wood store buildings. Mainly in the 1920s these were replaced by a continuous facade of Spanish Colonial Revival commercial structures, many of which remain today (see (2) Ramona St.). In the last thirty years some of these have given way to more modern isolated buildings, but because most of the commercial activity has grown up elsewhere downtown, Palo Alto retains a strong Twenties flavor.

Nearby residential areas offer a fine catalog of styles characteristic of the half century between 1890 and 1940. The original plat which ran from El Camino to Middlefield Rd. and from Hawthorne to Addison has largely gone the way of the business area with a second and third wave of development replacing the original late 19th century building. Only a few houses and a church or two remain (7 & 8). Additions extended Palo Alto north to San Francisquito Creek and east to Embarcadero Rd. in the early years of this century. In the 1920s and 1930s further extensions brought the town to the line of present Oregon Expressway. These twentieth century additions contain a fine display of the eclectic styles of the time. This period saw the beginning of a park-like civic center in the Rinconada Park area near the intersection of Embarcadero and Middlefield Roads.

1. **Palo Alto Station, Southern Pacific Railroad**   1941
   Mitchell Ln. & SP tracks

   The Streamline Moderne style of this station must have complemented perfectly the Southern Pacific streamliner trains of the early 1940s.

2. **500 block of Ramona St.**   1929
   Birge Clark and Pedro de Lemos
   500-544 on W side & 533-589 on E side of Ramona

   A fine bit of commercial stage setting in the then-approved Spanish Colonial Revival style; not Santa Barbara, but impressive for Northern California. A major component of the composition, the Ramona Hotel at the southeast corner of University, has disappeared to make way for the recent and undistinguished Crocker Bank. What remains has some nice touches: patios, courtyard tearooms, and picturesque details.

   There are other nice bits of downtown in the various revival styles, and the contemporary Union Bank by Ernest J. Kump, 1971, at 400 University (d).

3. **Varsity Theater block**   c.1930
   498 University Ave.

   An undecorated miniature of the Fox Arlington Theater in Santa Barbara—Spanishy, ambitious

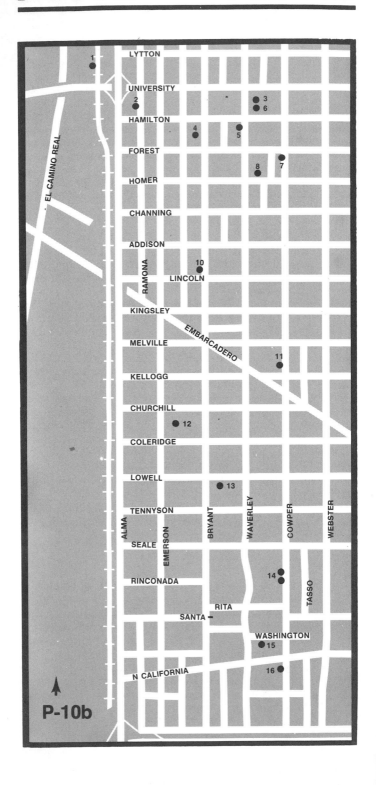

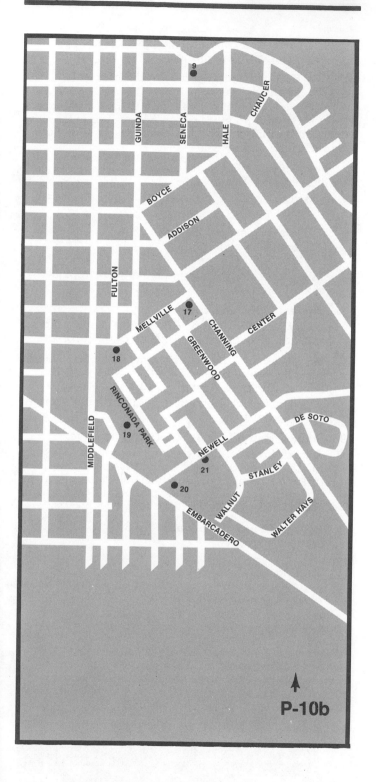

P-10b

for Northern California, complete with open air pedestrian shopping lane.

4. **City Hall**   1970; Edward Durrell Stone
250 Hamilton Ave.
Compare with the previous city hall by Nichols (19). Behind the city hall on Forest Ave is the new main public library by Spencer, Lee & Busse, 1970, (e).

5. **Post Office**   1932; Birge Clark
380 Hamilton St.
Spanish Colonial Revival again, but somewhat denuded.

6. **All Saints Episcopal Church**   1968
William Garwood
555 Waverly St.
This rather bombastic concrete work replaced a modest, shingle, village church.

7. **House**   1894; 706 Cowper St.
Boldly scaled Queen Anne villa abounding in spindlework and other varieties of gingerbread.

8. **St. Thomas Aquinas Roman Catholic Church**
1902; Shea and Shea
NE cor. Homer & Waverly Sts.
Wooden Gothic Revival, too late to be Victorian, but of that ilk.

9. **Squires House**   1905; 900 University Ave.
A local favorite, now designated a state historical landmark and possibly saved. A rather free Renaissance Revival style which, because of its imposing Ionic porch and pediment, gets called "Greek Revival."

10. **Kellogg House, "Sunbonnet"**   1899
Bernard Maybeck
1061 Bryant St.
The big gambrel roof that comes down over the second floor like a bonnet gives this distinctive early Maybeck its nickname.

This area, once known as "Professorville," abounds with comfortable looking turn of the century villas. Many are brown shingled Bay Region houses, for instance, at 1005 Bryant St. just up the street from Maybeck's Sunbonnet house is the Frank Angell residence of 1892 (f). Others cluster nearby on Lincoln, Kingsley, Melville, Waverley, and Ramona as well as Bryant.

11. **Pettigrew House**   1925; George Washington Smith
1336 Cowper St. N of Kellogg Ave.

A fine example of a Spanish Colonial Revival house by this Santa Barbara architect.

12. **Mendenhall House**   1937; William W. Wurster
1570 Emerson St. S of Churchill

A Moderne house in white painted redwood.

13. **Haehl House**   c.1910; John Hudson Thomas
1680 Bryant St.

Typical stucco box with Secessionist detail, the only Thomas house in this part of the Bay area.

14. **The Misses Stern's houses**   1930; Birge Clark
1950 and 1990 Cowper St.

Two large complementary Spanish Colonial Revival dwellings, handsomely sited and planted as a single composition. Obvious affinities to the G. W. Smith design down the street (11).

15. **House**   1934; Carr Jones
2101 Waverley St.

One of the always fascinating Mr. Jones' most original compositions. Designed and built with the extraordinary loving care that makes him first and finest in the Cinderella style, in this case almost transforming it into some dimly remembered European farmhouse vernacular. See other Carr Jones works in Berkeley and Piedmont.

16. **Raas House**   1939; William W. Wurster
2240 Cowper St.

This time a work in Wurster's personal style of the time, a mode that combined elegance and refinement with artlessness and unprecedented details.

17. **Palo Alto Military Academy (orig. Miss Harker's School)**   1903; Coxhead & Coxhead
    814 Melville Ave.

    By the time this guide gets into your hands, this nice Shingle style school seems destined to have gone the way of most such buildings: be torn down as either a site for small homes or a commercial or industrial complex that services them.

18. **Lucie Stern Community Center**   1935; Birge Clark
    Middlefield Rd. at SE cor. Melville Ave.

    This streamlined Spanish Colonial Revival theater and arts center set a high standard for Palo Alto's public buildings. It both symbolizes a public focus of community life and remains compatibly residential in scale and motives. For years afterward this standard prevailed. Then came the new city hall (4); the tradition had broken.

19. **Rinconada Park**   1953; Eckbo, Royston & Williams
    N cor. Middlefield & Embarcadero Rds. intersection

    An important community focus, once town center, graced by great oaks and felicitous new planting.

20. **City Hall, now Cultural Center**   1953
    Leslie Nichols
    Embarcadero Ave. & SE cor. Newell Ave.

    A gracious example of public architecture derived from ranch house themes complete to a heavy, wood shake roof. Originally built as a city hall, Palo Alto's explosive growth coupled with this site's off center location conspired to make that use short lived. Now an integral part of the Rinconada Park culture complex.

21. **Library**   1959; Edward Durrell Stone
    1213 Newell Ave.

    Proof that this architect can do appropriate looking and ingratiating work. Stone takes much the same set of materials and forms used in the somewhat earlier city hall next door (20), and composes them somewhat more formally. The happy result is a distinguished branch library, formerly a main library, for Palo Alto.

STANFORD INDUSTRIAL PARK

Stanford University's enterprising exploitation of its vast land holdings has generated a unique center of light, R&D industrial and commercial development, a model among industrial parks, and the envy of other communities anxious for clean and beautiful tax rateables. As a work of environmental design, the park depends more on lease restrictions governing ground coverage, building setbacks, and landscaping standards than on any direct, overall design. Planner L. J. Fourcroy and landscape architect Thomas D. Church consulted on the layout and the set of restrictions. The park was begun in 1959 and development continues. The buildings offer little more architecturally than stock plan industrial buildings anywhere else. Only a very few stand out.

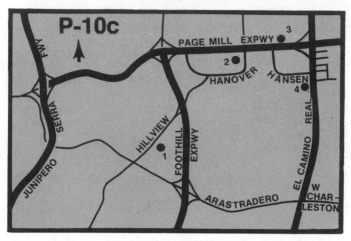

1. **Syntex Corporation Campus: Administration Building and first labs** 1960; Clark, Stromquist. **New labs and master plan** 1972; McCue, Boone, Tomsick
   3401 Hillview Ave.

   The newest building in this complex looks more authoritative than the older ones, but the most engaging part of this complex, a set of temporary structures around a spaceframe shaded court, has disappeared to make way for the new construction.

2. **Hewlett Packard Corporation Headquarters** 1970
   Clark, Stromquist, Sandstrom
   1501 Page Mill Rd.

3. **Alza Corporation Building** 1970
   McCue, Boone, Tomsick
   950 Page Mill Rd.

   Brick infilled steel frame adds an unexpected touch of plastic interest to this solidly done International style skeleton frame building. Hanging all those brick *brise-soleil* in midair troubles some purists.

photo: Jeremiah Bragstad

4. **Varian Associates, now Hewlett Packard**   1953
   Eric Mendelsohn & Michael Gallis
   El Camino Real at Hansen Wy.
   An undistinguished gable roofed loft structure, but it has Mendelsohn's name on it.

PALO ALTO SOUTH SIDE

The south side of Palo Alto from Page Mill Rd. and the Oregon Expwy. south to the city limits became urbanized only recently. The area is characterized by well designed middle income tract housing and supporting neighborhood facilities. It is larded with Eichler subdivisions including two of his best known (1 & 4). For more of the Joe Eichler story see Sunnyvale and the Lucas Valley and Terra Linda areas of Marin County.

1. **Fairmeadows subdivision**   1952; Anshen & Allen.
   Also some houses by Jones & Emmons
   Bet. Meadow Dr. & E Charleston Rd. E of Alma St.

photo: Joshua Freiwald

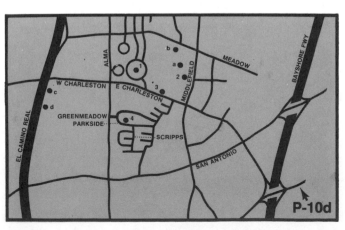

This subdivision with its curious concentric circle street layout must be Eichler's most photographed work. Environmentally it does not have the quality of the less formalized designs like Greenmeadows across E. Charleston Rd. to the south.

Next to Fairmeadows on the east, J. Pearce Mitchell Park (a) and a complex of community facilities clustered around it includes some worthy architecture. Taken as a whole the complex offers evidence on the continuing delights of Peninsula life lavishly supported, as it so often is, by well designed public works.

2. **Mitchell Park Branch Library** 1959
   Edward Durrell Stone
   3700 Middlefield Rd.

   Stone at his most congenial; very much a twin to his other Palo Alto library (Palo Alto Central Area, 21)

3. **Palo Alto Unitarian Church** 1959
   Joseph Esherick & Assoc.
   505 E. Charleston Rd.

   A contemporary version of rural vernacular in old California, unprepossessing but pleasant.

Other facilities around the park include Wilbur Ray Lyman Junior High, two elementary schools, Mitchell Park Community Center, and several churches other than the above listed Unitarian building. These include the flamboyant Covenant Presbyterian Church on Meadow Dr. (b)

4. **Greenmeadows subdivision** 1953
   Anshen & Allen; Jones & Emmons; Claude Oakland
   Bet. E. Charleston Rd. & San Antonio Rd. E of Alma St. & Central Expwy.

   The central recreation facility and childcare center is at Parkside Dr. and Scripps Ave. reached most easily from Alma St. by going E on Greenmeadow St.

   Joe Eichler's own favorite among his dozens of Peninsula and Santa Clara County tracts. The houses represent various translations of the vernacular Bay Region and ranch house styles into a very acceptable mass produced, yet varied spec house design.

El Camino Real W of Mitchell Park Greenmeadows area displays some choice roadside design. Among these are two large motel complexes that date back before the national chains had homogenized stock plans for such facilities: Rickey's Studio Inn, first part 1951 with many later additions and modifications, by Ernest J. Kump originally, 4219 El Camino Real on a large superbloc site on the southeast corner of W Charleston Rd. (c); and Dinah's Motor Hotel, 1957, Campbell & Wong, practically next door at 4269 El Camino (d). A more recent tidbit of roadside design appears up the street toward the center of town in The Record Store, 1971, by Whistler-Patri at 3159 El Camino Real, a zoomy, toplit, wooden cube (e).

SCV

STA CLARA VALLEY

SCV   Introduction

Santa Clara Valley, "the garden valley of heart's delight," perhaps the finest orchard land in the world, has shifted in the last generation from growing apricots and prunes to growing people. Nowhere has more productive soil been paved over, more beautiful agricultural landscape transformed into endless tract houses, strip commercial development and wirescape—a garden demolished. Yet in its place has emerged a new garden for people. Santa Clara Valley now shelters hundreds of thousands of working people and their families. It provides them with nearly every imaginable service close at hand. And it blesses them, as it did the prunes, with a particularly salubrious climate only lately somewhat blemished by nitrous oxide emissions, etc.

Santa Clara Valley denotes a broad alluvial plain formed by a whole system of small streams which flow north into the bay where the plain joins an equally broad area of tidal flats. In clear weather, mountains are visible from almost any point in the valley. To the east bare brown foothills merge into the chapparal covered peaks of the Mount Hamilton Range of observatory fame. The other side of the valley is defined by the green and wooded Santa Cruz Mountains which slant across from northwest to southeast. Originally oak studded grassland covered the valley floor. Capt. George Vancouver, seeing it for the first time in 1792, wrote that it looked like "a park which had been planted with true old English oak."

The name comes not from a river but from the first European settlement in the area, Mission Santa Clara de Asis, 1777, the seventh in date of founding among the chain of twenty-one missions in Alta California. Almost simultaneously the Spanish viceroy in Mexico City commissioned settlement of Pueblo San Jose facing the mission from the opposite bank of the usually dry Guadalupe River. This was California's first town as distinguished from military bases and missions.

For three quarters of a century the valley served the tallow and hide economy of pre-Gold Rush California. Then in the 1850s the market caused by a growing population, plus the fortuitous discovery that artesian well water underlay the whole valley, turned it overnight into a vast garden. It produced three foot long carrots weighing 40 pounds, tomatoes more than two feet in diameter, immense vegetables of every sort, huge wheat yields and fruit crops. In the 1860s orchards of prunes, apricots, plums, walnuts, pears and cherries began to dominate. Sun dried Santa Clara fruit entered world markets. Spring blossom time brought thousands of visitors. Starting in February with the almond blossoms, and extending on into April, the flowering trees turned the valley white as though covered by snow.

Settlement in the 1850s was restricted to the little, still sleepy town of San Jose, to the mission which the Jesuits were converting to a university, some stage stops on El Camino Real as it ran from San Jose toward the Peninsula and San Francisco and in the other direction up the valley toward Gilroy to the south, and two tiny water mill settlements, Los Gatos and Saratoga. The stage stops became marketing and fruit processing towns especially after the railroad reached San Jose in 1864. That town became the urban focus for the whole valley. Here architecture began to flourish and by the 70s some traces of civic design appeared. Still, as late as 1940, this was an agricultural not an urban landscape.

The change hit. The population of Santa Clara County exploded from 175,000 in 1940 to more than a million thirty years later. Subdivisions of speculative tract houses filled most of the central and western valley in a triangle from Palo Alto and Los Altos in the northwest east to Santa Clara and San Jose and south or southeast to Saratoga and Los Gatos. To the north of this area a great industrial district spread out in another triangle from Palo Alto to San Jose to Milpitas on the road up the East Bayshore. All of this occurred at a very low density, leapfrogging over holdout orchardists, so that today the million people spread out over an immense area. Bypassed groves and truck gardens can be found in even the most densely urbanized parts of the valley. Economically and socially a single spread-out city has emerged on the order of Los Angeles; but politically, again much like the megalopolis of the south, it is fragmented into incomprehensible patterns of small and large incorporated places and special districts interspersed with much county territory. A planner's nightmare!

LOS ALTOS HILLS

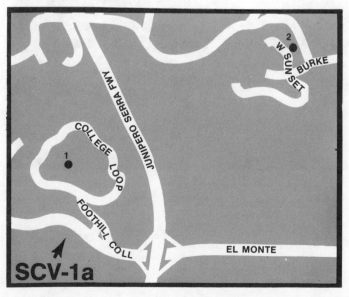

Los Altos Hills, a recent, automobile age, upper-middle-class, almost exurban, residential suburb offers a felicitous natural environment but little notable environmental design or architecture. It is, however, the home of one of Northern California's chief landmarks of contemporary design, Foothill College. Don't miss it!

1. **Foothill College**   1962; Ernest J. Kump, Masten & Hurd, assoc. arch't.; Sasaki, Walker & Assoc., land arch.
   12345 S. El Monte Ave.

   The perfect California design of its era. The Foothill College motifs: great, overhanging, double-pitched, wood-shake roofs; buttress-like exposed concrete columns (they *do* take the horizontal earthquake loads); simple walls of glass, redwood and brick; clusters of detached pavilions that play variations on these themes while they are all set about in a verdant, sculptured green landscape. These motifs have been repeated elsewhere numberless times by Kump and hordes of imitators (see San Jose Civic Center (c) and Stanford (7) for nearby examples, respectively, of both.) No matter the familiarity of the images, the original retains its power. And it is a power that seems to bridge the worlds of high art—the critics gave it many awards—and public taste—the people have clearly taken Foothill to their hearts.

photo: Karl Riek

2. **Eurich House**   1939; Richard Neutra
   13081 W Sunset Dr.

   White painted plaster forms sparingly embellished with silver colored woodwork make this look perfectly characteristic of what it is: a bit of 1930s International style imported from Southern California.

The small triangle of blocks bounded by Edith Ave. on the north, San Antonio Rd. on the east and Fremont Ave. on the southwest contains the central district of Los Altos, such as it is. This area and the crescent of streets just across Fremont were the site of the first urbanization. Here remain a handful of respectable buildings from the 1900s and 1910s.

Since the end of World War II the same forces that have urbanized so much of the rest of the Peninsula and Santa Clara Valley have pretty well filled up Los Altos. It has joined the ranks of developed, upper-middle-class, bedroom towns, though one still happily marked by a few remaining apricot archards.

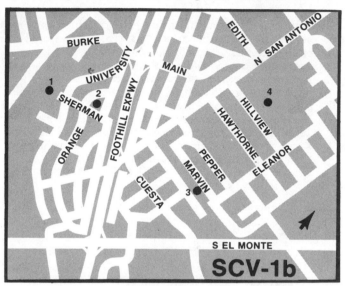

1. **House** c.1905; 500 University Ave.

   A fine, wide Craftsman Shingle style house facing the street. It sports a strongly modeled facade and shingled barge boards.

2. **Foothill Congregational Church (orig. Christ Episcopal Church)** 1917; Ernest Coxhead
   461 Orange Ave.

Little cloister of steep-roofed church and parish buildings around a court, the front wall of which was added later. Full of nice Coxhead tricks like the waist high windows in the church hall to maintain its weensy scale.

3. **Johnson/Stafford houses, "three houses in an orchard"** 1939
   Richard Neutra, Otto Winkler Assoc.
   180 & 184 Marvin Ave. & guesthouse behind 184
   Unusual group of tiny International style cottages in redwood.

4. **Los Altos Civic Center** 1960; Ernest J. Kump
   1 N San Antonio Rd.
   Four separate buildings set out carefully to preserve the trees in an old apricot orchard. The city pridefully maintains the orchard, planting new trees as the old ones die, to keep intact this happy link with a recent rural past. The four buildings house the city hall, police department, youth center, and public library. All use the handsome standardized module Kump devised during the 1950s for schoolhouse construction. They demonstrate the adaptability of an elegant forerunner in the systems building movement.

MOUNTAIN VIEW, SUNNYVALE AND CUPERTINO

The towns of northwestern Santa Clara Valley—Mountain View, Sunnyvale and Cupertino—which stretch from Palo Alto and Los Altos on the west to old Santa Clara on the east, provide Northern California with its little Los Angeles. But for the fact that the remains of orchards are prunes not oranges, the stereotype seems complete: a grid of freeways two to four miles apart overlaid on an agricultural landscape squared-off in a mile and half-mile checkerboard of wide, commercially developed, arterial streets. Within the squares, tract house subdivisions, schools, and neighborhood parks occur with mechanical regularity.

Little remains of the rural past. The few efforts at preservation have mainly failed as in the case of Sunnyvale's mid-19th Century Murphy house, a farmstead given to the city, made centerpiece in an historical park, then destroyed by fire, vandalism and disinterest. A few scattered farm houses still exist awaiting the bulldozer, but none seem to stand out architecturally.

Downtown Sunnyvale and Mountain View started life as stagecoach stops on the El Camino Real. When the railroad came along running parallel to the road, and simultaneously the orchard boom took hold, both became fruit marketing and canning towns. A few bits remain, some big rambling cannery structures along the tracks (the area's one significant architectural work, Wurster's Schuckl building (6) is part of one of these), and some traces of the old downtowns. Even downtown in Sunnyvale has largely disappeared thanks to the Bay Region's first officially complete and closed out urban renewal project (a).

Today these towns hold interest mainly for those concerned with the overall patterns of urbanization during the 50s and 60s. The Cherry Chase district noted below (b & c), however banal the tract house design, typifies this interest. As elsewhere in Northern California, an occasional suburban school, commercial or industrial building offers a welcome but random architectural focus.

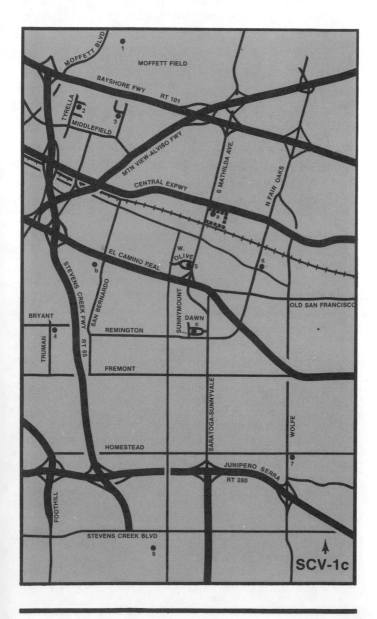

1. **Moffett Field Dirigible Hangers** 1933, 1942
   Moffett Naval Air Station

   Three immense dirigible hangers form the largest man-made landmark in the Southbay area. On a clear day they can be seen from Mt. Tam in Marin County or Grizzly Peak Blvd. in the Berkeley Hills. The Navy constructed the big one on the west side of the field to house the giant zeppelins it favored in the early 1930s. The slightly smaller pair to the east docked anti-submarine blimps during World War II.

2. **Tyrella Gardens Apartments** 1971
   Robert Mittelstadt
   449 Tyrella Ave.

   A spare, International style design for moderate rent apartments and townhouses organized on a highly original site plan.

3. **Fairchild Camera and Instrument Building** 1968
   Simpson, Stratta & Assoc.
   464 Ellis St.

   Straightforward prism of glass and rusty Corten steelwork much articulated.

4. **Chester F. Awalt High School** 1961
   Ernest J. Kump
   SE cor. Truman & Bryant Sts., Mountain View

   Standard Kump modules organized into a big, brown, wooden, finger plan—a textbook school design.

The Cherry Chase neighborhood in Sunnyvale, bounded by El Camino Real, West Fremont, Stevens Creek Freeway and the Saratoga-Sunnyvale Rd., offers a typical example of the sprawl that swallowed the orchards. The early L type shopping center at the southwest corner of San Bernardino and El Camino marks an entrance to the area, and it gives a clear picture of the primitive stage of neighborhood shopping center design (b). The spec-built houses that carpet the surrounding blocks include one architectural curiosity, the first houses built by Joe Eichler. The flat and mono-pitch roofs along Dawn Dr. and Sunnymont Ave. (c) mark out this pioneering development. At this point in time, the relationship between Eichler's tract house designs and the Bay Region style work exemplified in the artless-appearing houses of William W. Wurster and others during the 1930s and 40s seems clear. Compare the Dawn Dr. and Sunnymont houses with the Lyman house, 1941, by Wurster & Bernardi, Selby Ln. at Osborn Ave. in Atherton.

5. **Sunnyvale Civic Center: City Hall** 1958; Milton Pflueger; **Public Library** 1960; Milton Pflueger; **Municipal Court** 1967; William Hedley; **Public Safety Center** 1971; Goodwin L. Steinberg
Civic Center Way & Olive Ave.

   This building group, which also includes some carefully related designs for neighboring private office and utility buildings, expresses serious concern for a carefully controlled material and form palette at the price of banality.

6. **California Growers & Canners (orig. Schuckl Canning Company Office Building)** 1942
William W. Wurster
100 S Fair Oaks Ave. NE of intersection with Evelyn Ave., almost under the Fair Oaks overpass across the SP tracks, Sunnyvale

   Brutally buried under the new overpass, its urban setting in a once small town at the exposed corner of the great fruit canning works can only be imagined today. Nevertheless, roughsawn, brown-stained redwood siding looks perpetually new set off by trim painted a pale salmon color. A classic marriage of Bay Region and International style motifs, and Wurster's masterpiece among his non-residential work.

7. **Hewlett-Packard Warehouse, formerly Varian Assoc.** 1967
Rockrise, Odermatt Mountjoy & Amis
11000 Wolfe Rd. at SE cor. of Homestead Rd., Cupertino

   Round-cornered, glass and concrete block enclosure, nice small office element, stylistically more 70s than 60s.

8. **De Anza College** 1968; Ernest J. Kump; Masten & Hurd. Royston, Hanamoto, Beck & Abey land. arch'ts.
21250 Stevens Creek Blvd. at intersection with Stevens Creek Freeway, Cupertino

   The same designers and the same clients as Foothill (Los Altos Hills 1) produced here another campus of equal distinction. If it does not hold quite the same high place in recent California architectural history, it is only because it came later and depended more on previous users of the site, the Charles Baldwin estate, "Beaulieu," designed by Willis Polk, c.1902. The architectural vocabulary seems somewhat historicist and certainly more sentimental than at Foothill. But for many people the preserved bits of gardens, gazebos and buildings enriches the environment and makes it a particularly civilized monument in the generally anti-historical sprawl of the Santa Clara Valley.

EASTERN SUNNYVALE, SANTA CLARA AND WESTERN SAN JOSE

Between the centers of Sunnyvale and the city of Santa Clara, a four mile wide belt of modern industrial plants and housing tracts has largely replaced the orchards and flat truck gardens. Except for Santa Clara itself where the inner area goes back to mission days, this development simply continues the patterns that characterize western Sunnyvale, Mountain View, and Cupertino. Around the Mission a little town coalesced of which the remaining relic is an adobe of c.1792 (a) at 3260 The Alameda. As stated on the plaque registering it as State Landmark no. 249, it was ". . . one of several continuous rows of dwellings for Indian families of the Mission." It is now the Santa Clara Women's

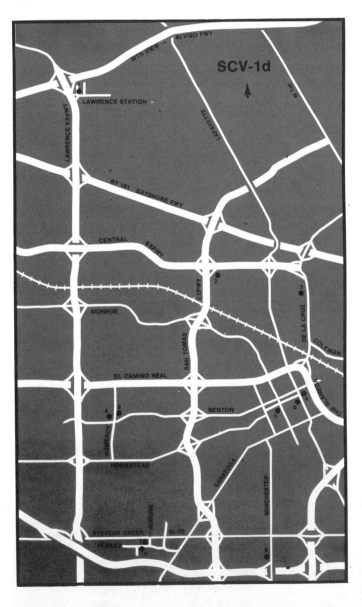

Club. The Mission, rebuilt time and again as first flood then earthquake and fire destroyed it, stood on the present University of Santa Clara campus (b). In recent years an urban renewal project has bulldozed away much of the central area (c). Outside the old town a few modern industrial, commercial and multi-family residential structures offer a bit of architectural interest to relieve the landscape of sprawl.

1. **GRT Building**   1970; Brown, McCurdy, Neary
   1265 Lawrence Station Rd.

   Stylish, long, low building composed of office and lab modules clad in purplish-brownish-redish-rusty Corten steel.

photo: Jeremiah Bragstad

2. **Memorex Corporation Headquarters**   1971
   Leland King. Royston, Hanamoto, Beck & Abey, land arch't.
   San Tomas Expwy. at SE cor. Central Expwy.

   A space age looking industrial campus of crystal-line white and black buildings in a rich green landscape of lawns, trees and fountains. One of the most effective of the many corporate spreads in the Peninsula-Santa Clara Valley area.

3. **Container Corporation of America Administration Building**   1967; Skidmore, Owings & Merrill
   2800 de la Cruz Blvd.

   One-story glass pavilion that starts out comfortably Miesian but ends improbably in a massive up-curved sweep of roof overhang.

4. **Pomeroy West**   1965
   Claude Oakland. Sasaki, Walker & Assoc., land. arch't.
   NW cor. Pomeroy Ave. & Benton St.

5. **Pomeroy Green**   1963
   Claude Oakland. Sasaki, Walker & Assoc, land.
   arch't.
   NE cor. Pomeroy Ave. & Benton St.

   These two tracts were among the pioneering town-
   touse developments that triggered the wave of
   planned unit, high density, attached housing that
   had by the 1970s all but captured the mass housing market in California. Starting in the 1950s,
   architects advocated such solutions in place of
   the sprawl of single family detached housing.
   These twin projects, thanks to the enlightened
   sponsorship of Joe Eichler, helped make the architects' dreams prevail.

6. **Brookdale Apartments**   1968; Wong & Brocchini
   222 Auburn Wy.

   A more careful than average, recent garden apartment group. A stock plan basic building, this
   time in rough sawn siding and bright aluminum
   sash, flip-flopped to make twin building group-
   ings around a common green.

7. **Meridian Park office and shopping center**   1972
   Frank L. Hope Assoc.
   4300-4400 Stevens Creek Blvd.

   An arrestingly up-to-date group of diagonally
   sided, wooden commercial structures decorated
   with big super graphics.

8. **Winchester House**   1884-1922; who knows?
   Winchester Blvd. at NE cor. of intersection with
   Stevens Creek Frwy.

   An Eastlake-Queen Anne shingle pile turned
   tourist attraction. Local history has it that Widow
   Winchester (her husband invented the gun) believed she would live as long as she kept building. The front of the house (late on the tour) contains some very elaborate but unfinished Eastlake
   interiors and some magnificent windows in Tiffany's "spider web" pattern.

SAN JOSE, HANCHETT PARK AND THE ALAMEDA

What could be more natural than that California's
first ceremonial way should connect the state's oldest
European settlement with the mission just three miles
away across the Guadalupe River. At its height, three
continuous lines of willow trees enclosed its two broad
carriageways. Later grand houses lined the Alameda
and the first wave of subdivision development adjoined
it. The willows have died. Other trees replaced them.
Most of these have gone too. The grand houses are no
more. They have been replaced with meaner but more
democratic things like motels, small offices, and apartment blocks. But in the blocks just to the west, some of
the old subdivisions remain unchanged, a rich collection of bungalow styles.

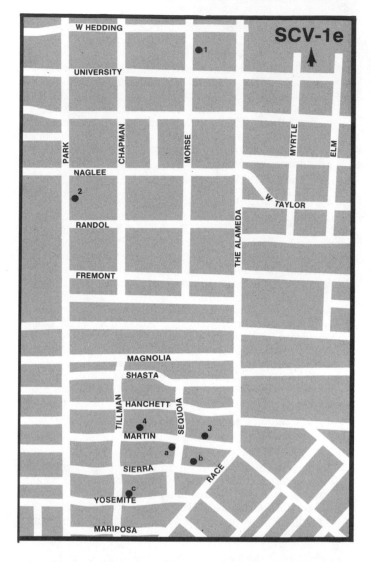

1. **Stevens House**   1926; Louis Christian Mullgardt
   838 Morse St.

   Half-timbered, rambling bungalow, if that is possible at this late date, and Mullgardt's only Southbay work. (See Berkeley and Piedmont for his more characteristic houses.)

2. **Rosicrucian Park**   1927 through 1972; mostly by Earle Lewis
1342 Naglee Ave.

World headquarters of the Ancient, Mystical Order of Rosae Crucis occupies a block square landscaped park crowded with properly Old Empire Egyptian looking buildings, some more so than others. They contain offices, classrooms and museums. The most authoritatively Egyptian style structure, the main museum, open to the public, contains some nice artifacts, educational displays, and a real live plaster mockup of an Old Empire tomb wired for sound.

The Hanchett Residence Park, bounded by the Alameda, Hester, Park and Race Sts., was developed c.1910-20 by T. S. Montgomery & Sons, and laid out by landscape architect John McLaren. As an up-to-the-minute subdivision, it boasted stores, saloons, laundries on the main street, different varieties of trees lining each residential street, modern septic tanks, circulating water, electric street lights, concrete sidewalks, gutters, and curbs. Architecturally it is the home of the bungalow, modest in scale but boastful in decoration. Most of the houses were, according to a real estate brochure of the time, to be designed by the local firm of Wolfe & McKenzie. The ones listed here were published by the firm of Wolfe & Wolfe. The heavily Wrightian Arts and Crafts persuasion of these small buildings should be viewed with a tolerance for the local translation.

3. **Bungalow**   c.1910; Wolfe & Wolfe
1163 Martin St.

Carefully lifted from the Prairie School context, this little house with elegant Arts and Crafts windows is the best local example of what happens when a minor talent meets a major movement. At 1208 Martin (a), 1151 Sierra (b), and 1299 Yosemite (c) are other less lavish designs in the same style by the same firm.

4. **Bungalow group**   c.1910
1225, 1233, 1241, 1249, and 1257 Martin St.

Five choice variations on the bungalow theme, as nice a group as you will find in Northern California.

SAN JOSE CIVIC CENTER

Government in Santa Clara County has tended to suburbanize along with everything else. The City of San Jose moved its city hall from the historic location of nearly two centuries out north on 1st St. back in 1959, following the County lead. Together they built an ambitious superblock civic center (a). At this point local government occupies nearly two dozen structures in the area bounded by N 1st, W Mission, Guadalupe Pkwy. and Route 17 Frwy. None of them stands out architecturally and taken together they do not really jell as a campus. Nevertheless it represents a big effort and the results do offer a catalog of everyday office and public building styles of the 50s and 60s.

Out N 1st St. two office buildings seem worthy of passing note. The George S. Nolte building, 1969, by Claude Oakland, at 1731, a small, discreet, one floor structure made of wood, glass and exposed bar joists looks reminiscent of the 1950s (b). Across the street at 1720 N 1st, the California Water Service Company Headquarters of 1964 by Ernest J. Kump, landscaped by Royston, Hanamoto, Mayes & Beck, uses the motifs of Foothill College (see Los Altos Hills 1) to make a nice looking office layout (c).

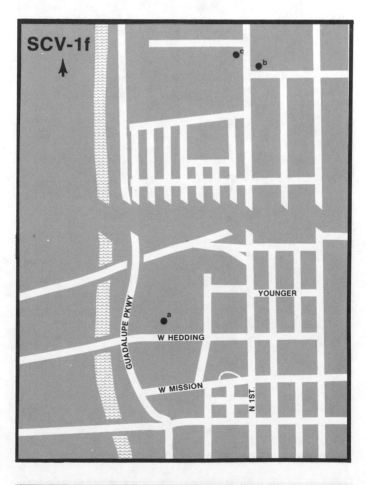

SAN JOSE CENTRAL AREA

As the oldest secular settlement in California, San Jose deserves more veneration than it usually gets. Nowadays, mention San Jose and most people think only of sprawl. Actually, for most of its two centuries San Jose was a fairly concentrated town set in an open landscape. Today a concentration of interesting architecture within the few blocks of its central area symbolizes this.

The 18th century pueblo emerged around an open space still called the Plaza (16). Though for nearly a

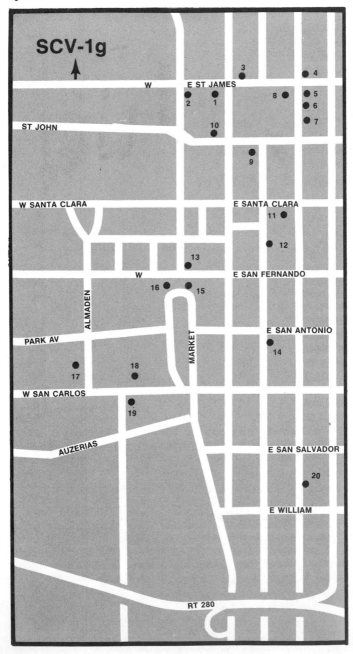

hundred years its growth was exceedingly slow, it had its moments, After statehood, for instance, the first legislature, "the legislature of a thousand drinks," met here in San Jose. No buildings remain from that first century, only place names and street patterns.

The real burst of growth in San Jose followed on the agricultural boom in the Valley, the boom caused by the gold-diggers' appetite and the discovery of water. (Fountain Alley, downtown between 1st and 2nd Sts. commemorates one of the first artesian wells, dug accidently and drained by a ditch along the line of this valley.) The city visible today dates from these times. Its chief monument is St. James Park, focus of the expanded city of the 1860s onward, a park laid out by ex-Yale professor Chester Smith Lyman, an immigrant to the land of heart's delight.

In the confident era of the orchard boom, San Jose went shopping for appropriate styles with which to dress its public buildings. In this spirit a remarkable collection of structures was built around St. James Park. Preserved through the center city stagnation that sprawl induced, this precinct presents an architectural zoo unrivaled in the Bay Area as a catalog of styles and an example of urban continuity by contrast. Those interested in the historic quest for the proper expression of civic monumentality should take a walk around the Park, cross St. John St., and go south on Market to where contemporary San Jose is rising from the dust of urban renewal around the old Plaza.

1. **Santa Clara County Court House**   1866; N 1st St.
   A handsome, vigorously detailed Neo-Classical building that lost its dome in an earthquake but fortunately survived the movement of the county headquarters out to the new civic center.

2. **Superior Court Building**   1964; Ernest J. Kump
   W St. James St. at cor. of N 1st
   This rather bland, contemporary brick building offers a nice contrast as well as a breathing space to its neighbor, the old court house.

3. **Classical Revival Building, now Gospel Lighthouse**
   c.1870; 43 E St. James St.

4. **Sainte Claire Apartments**   1895; A. Page Brown
   65 E St. James St.

   A medley of Spanish, Mudejar, and Prairie in brick by the architect of the San Francisco Ferry Building.

5. **Scottish Rite Temple**   c.1900; N 3rd & E St. James

6. **First Unitarian Church**   1891; G. W. Page
   160 N 3rd St.

7. **Eagles Club (orig. Methodist Church)**   c.1900
   140 N 3rd St.

   Although these three buildings come from the bargain basement of the turn-of-the-century emporium of styles, they have a uniformity of scale that contributes much to the harmony of the park. The curious interior of the Unitarian Church repays a visit.

8. **St. James Community Center**   1967
   Higgins & Root
   St. James Park

   A modest, contemporary contribution, sensibly scaled for its location in the middle of the park.

9. **Trinity Episcopal Church**   1863
   N 2nd & E St. John Sts.

   Wooden Victorian Gothic Revival church with a particularly fine display of interior carpentry—worth a visit. One James W. Hammond, a sea captain and member of the parish, supervised the construction that included windows brought 'round the Horn.' In 1875 the original church was cut in half and moved around to permit expansion into a cross plan. Office and parish house are recent, and in the case of the newest work, very unfortunate additions that add nothing to the charm of this oldest church remaining in San Jose.

10. United States Post Office 1933; Ralph Wyckoff
N 1st St. at cor. of W St. John

One of several well designed Spanish Colonial Revival post offices by this architect.

11. Century Block c.1890
60-78 E Santa Clara St.

Largest and most vigorous late Victorian business block in downtown. It characteristically houses the I.O.O.F. Hall on the upper floors.

12. Letitia Building 1890
66-72 S 1st St.

Another fine Victorian business building, this one in Romanesque Revival style.

13. St. Joseph's Roman Catholic Church 1877
Hoffman & Clinch
Market St. NE cor. of San Fernando

Huge Neo-Classical thing with a monumental interior that looks as though it had truly been made in Rome. The story of St. Joseph's through the 19th century tells of one tragic fire after another which destroyed a succession of buildings until this one. In 1875 Father Congiato selected Brian Clinch to design the church because he was "a thorough student of the Greek and Roman literature and of all art forms . . . He read a selection from the New Testament in the Greek text each day," according to the account published in the parish bulletin.

14. Y. W. C. A. Building 1918; Julia Morgan
S 2nd St. at NE cor. of San Antonio St.

Another in Miss Morgan's chain of somewhat Renaissance style, somewhat Mediterranean structures for the Women's Y.

15. San Jose Art Museum (orig. U. S. Post Office, then Main Library) 1892, 1937 & 1971
Market St., SW cor. of San Fernando

A Richardson Romanesque structure with proportions just a shade too spindly to do the style justice. The most significant fact about this building is the public will to preserve it. Through two total changes of function and consequent extensive re-modelings it remains an object lesson in civic responsibility. In practically any other American city but San Jose this nice monument would be long gone.

16. **Plaza and Park Center Urban Renewal Project** 1777, renewal started 1957
Roughly Market to Guadelupe River, Santa Clara to San Carlos St.

The parklike space in the middle of Market St. between San Fernando and San Carlos Sts. marks the middle of the original pueblo and the seat of the town government for nearly two centuries. The city hall was only moved when the new civic center was built. The area between the Plaza and the Guadalupe River to the west underwent the federal bulldozer through the decade of the 1960s. Now a new kind of downtown has begun to emerge. It looks a lot like the Civic Center on N 1st in the sense that it is a collection of stylish but isolate buildings set well apart in an automobile landscape of parking lots and arterial streets, only the least bit softened by specimen tree plantings. The main complete part of the renewal project is the financial center which contains the Wells Fargo Building of 1971 by Skidmore, Owings & Merrill (a), and the Park Center Plaza dominated by the Bank of America tower designed by Victor Gruen Assoc. and completed in 1972 (b).

17. **San Jose Community Theater**   1972; William Wesley Peters, chief arch't.; Taliesin Fellowship, Frank Lloyd Wright Fdn., & Aaron Green, assoc'd arch. 255 Almaden Blvd.

Pink-brown stucco confection decorated with gold anodized aluminum, it displays an obvious affinity with Wright's Marin Co. Civic Center. The interior includes some surprises: a giant balcony bridging the orchestra and free of the back wall, continental seating in the longest rows ever, and a tricky ceiling that hinges down to make a small theater out of the big one.

18. **San Jose Civic Auditorium**   1934
William Binder & E. M. Curtis
145 W San Carlos St.

Big Spanish Colonial Revival pile of a building
that meets the street in a nice, human scaled colonnade. Like the other monuments of downtown
San Jose, this expression of the taste of the 1930s
gains meaning from the whole.

19. **San Jose Public Library**   1971; Norton S. Curtis
180 W San Carlos St.

What a fitting climax to the architectural zoo!

20. **Queen Anne-Eastlake house**   c.1880; 418 S 3rd St.

SAN JOSE STATE UNIVERSITY AREA

In 1870 the State of California moved its one and only
state normal school from San Francisco to the purer
climate of San Jose. That move started the big campus
that now houses the State University just a few blocks
from the "hundred percent corner" downtown. The
zone immediately around the campus grew up in the
late 19th and early 20th centuries as a genteel residential area largely serving the school. Later, as it became one of the largest units in the State College system (College became University only in 1972), it ruthlessly expanded into the residential blocks. Now an urban renewal project has joined in to force additional
change by "connecting" the campus to the Plaza (San
Jose Central Area 16) four blocks to the west along San
Antonio St. Urban designers Rockrise & Odermatt are
at work on this San Antonio Mall project.

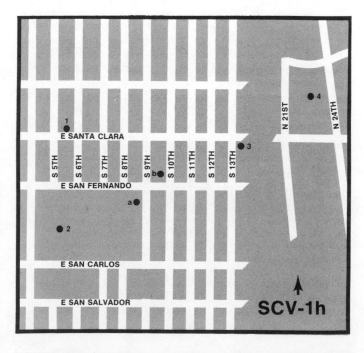

1. **First Methodist Church** 1906; James C. Newsom
24 N 5th St.
The outstanding example in the Bay area of the Mission Revival style used in a religious building.

2. **Morris Daley Hall, San Jose State** 1909
Walter Parker, State Arch.
This building, the focal point in the westernmost quadrangle of the campus, represents the one and only highpoint of architecture on this campus. Most of the extant structures come from the hand of the State Architect. Like the other campuses in the State College system, this offers convincing testimony to the banality of most bureaucratically produced architecture. In recent years, in an effort to change directions, State College work has been given to architects in private practice. If the works on this campus fairly measure the effects of this shift, it looks as if it pushed the private practitioners too far toward expressionism for its own sake. See, for instance, the parking garage of 1970 by Callister & Payne at the corner of San Fernando and 9th (a), or the new Student Union (1972) by Ernest J. Kump diagonally across 9th St. (b).

3. **House, now ΣΧ fraternity house** 1904
Bernard Maybeck
62 S 13th St.

Perhaps the rarity of houses like this suggests something about the social standing of a normal school at the turn of the century in contrast to the universities at Berkeley and Palo Alto.

4. San Jose High School   1952, add'n 1961
Ernest J. Kump
245 N 24th St. nr. Julian St.
Very large finger-plan school that has held up very well.

EAST SAN JOSE

East of San Jose the land slopes up, at first gradually, then sharply toward the Bay area's highest point, Copernicus Peak in the Mt. Hamilton range. Topography, water problems, poorer soil on this side of town meant cheaper land, and cheaper land meant poorer people, the wrong side of the tracks. But the mountains made important things possible like Alum Rock Park (1) and Lick Observatory on Mt. Hamilton (2). And recently land scarcity, coupled with a broader affluence, has begun to change the social image of East San Jose—witness Eastridge Shopping Center (3), the Bay region's newest and fanciest.

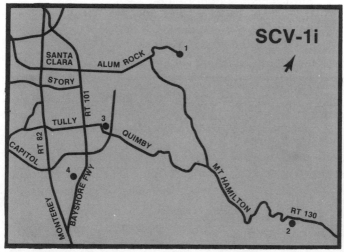

1. Alum Rock Park   1872, various later additions & changes
End of Alum Rock Ave., also accessible from Penitencia Creek Ave.

First major park in the Santa Clara Valley, it covers about 400 acres surrounding the natural mineral springs in the Upper Penitencia Creek Canyon. Tree-lined, ceremonial Alum Rock Ave., built at the time the park was opened, remains a still impressive shadow of its former elegance. In the 1890s a steam railroad, later electrified, connected the park to downtown San Jose. By then a complete spa had evolved on the canyon floor including plunge, bathhouse, hotel, cafes and casino. Now only ruins in a picnic ground mark this. Famous city beautiful era planner Charles Mulford Robinson had a hand in these improvements.

2. **Lick Observatory**   1877, many later additions
Mt. Hamilton Rd., 18 miles of switchbacks above Alum Rock Ave.

Perhaps the Bay region's finest monument to late 19th century technology and science, the fortress-like main building houses founding astronomer Lick's magnificent 36'' refracting telescope as well as exhibits and other wonders. Daily tours for visitors.

3. **Eastridge Shopping Center**   1971; Avner Naggar
Tully & Quimby Rds.

Newest, most innovative enclosed mall regional shopping center in Northern California and among the largest anywhere. Inside, its three levels of shopping breaks precedent. Outside its location on the suburban fringe, and on the wrong side of the tracks, breaks an even more rigid taboo of shopping planning.

4. **Coyote River Park**
Rt. 101, access from Hellyer Ave.

Nearly ten miles of linear park and percolation basin form a green spine for the most recent direction of urbanization in the Santa Clara Valley.

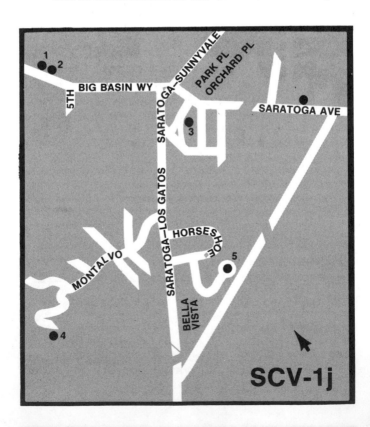

Saratoga started out as McCartheysville built around an 1851 grist mill. Twelve years later C. W. Healy laid out the first town plat. As the 19th century closed, the town changed its image and became the southernmost of the Peninsula's grand estate districts, an outpost of the Hillsborough and Atherton world to the north. But it did this on a much more modest scale than its kin up the Peninsula.

Today some fragments remain from its first incarnation (1 & 2), and a couple of fine monuments of the estate era still exist (4 & 5). Beginning in the 1920s the interstices in these earlier patterns have filled up with pleasant but architecturally undistinguished upper-middle-class suburban development. The Eldridge Spencer designed Sheldon P. Patterson Memorial Library of 1927 at 14410 Oak St. (a) shows how civilized concrete block and steel sash become in the hands of a sensitive eclectic designer—shades of late Maybeck. The library echos nicely the well mannered civic tradition set by Julia Morgan's 1916 clubhouse (3).

1. **Erwin T. King House**   1876; 14605 Big Basin Wy.
   A Carpenter Gothic house from the days when Saratoga milled grain.

2. **Pettis Livery Stable**   1898; 14605 Big Basin Wy.

3. **Saratoga Foothill Clubhouse**   1916; Julia Morgan Park Pl.

   Another worthy, warm and woodsy Shingle style women's club by California's great woman architect.

4. **Senator James D. Phelan Mansion, "Montalvo"**
   1912; William and Alexander Curlett with E. C. Gottschalk; John McLaren, land arch't.
   End of Montalvo Rd. off Saratoga-Los Gatos Rd.
   A more-or-less Renaissance Revival grand villa set in splendid grounds laid out by the redoubtable John (Golden Gate Park) McLaren himself. The ladies of the Montalvo Association keep it open as a landscape park, arboretum and art center, a civic labor of great responsibility and sensitivity.

5. **Blaney Villa**   1914; Willis Polk
   20021 Bella Vista Ct., at end of the cul-de-sac
   A rambling complicated design with Renaissance and Mediterranean motifs, towers and projecting wings offering yet another episode in the extraordinarily varied palette of Polk's talent. Trees, pink stucco, modern revisions and the loss of most of its grounds cannot diminish the architect's genius.

6. **St. Andrew's Episcopal Church**   1963
   Warren B. Heid. Stained glass by Mark Adams
   13601 Saratoga Ave.

7.   Camp Swig Multi-Use Building   1967
Henrik Bull
6 mi. up Big Basin Wy. from the main crossroads
in Saratoga
Auditorium, crafts, music, drama, and a library for
a Jewish summer camp huddle comfortably under
this friendly wooden tent.

LOS GATOS

The name comes from the Mexican era Rancho Rinconada de los Gatos—wildcat corner ranch—but the
town, like neighboring Saratoga, started as a grist
mill settlement. Unlike it, though, Los Gatos remained
more commercial and middle-class by virtue of its location astride the main route out of the Valley across
the mountains to Santa Cruz. A fragment of the mill
era remains (6). Later, as redwood lumber poured down
out of the mountains, a prosperous little town emerged.
Bits of this remain too (1 & 2).

Later Los Gatos became a suburb like everyplace else
in the Valley. The freeway sliced up Los Gatos canyon to cleave the town in two. Through annexation,
the town spread out northeastwardly to join San Jose
in seamless sprawl. Now the off-center has been partly

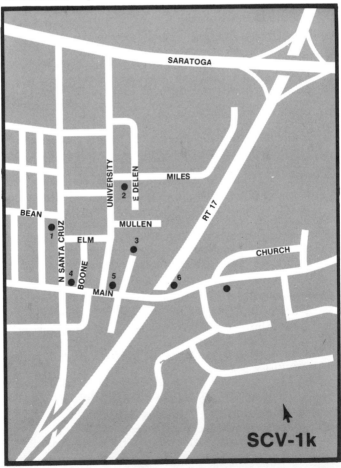

saved and picturesquely modernized. Old Town Shopping Center epitomizes these changes (3).

1. **House, now Little Village Chapel of Peace Funeral Home** c.1890; 123 Santa Cruz Ave.

   A prosperous new use has preserved this Queen Anne style dwelling.

2. **House** c.1890; 128 University Ave.

   Queen Anne style.

3. **Old Town Shopping Center, formerly Los Gatos High School** c.1925; remodeled in 1966 by Frank Laulainen
   University Ave.

   Originally a stripped Spanish Colonial Revival stucco schoolhouse, now reconstructed to work neatly as a shopping center in the woodsy contemporary style. The result is a complex and pleasant design curiously recalling the Monterey Colonial Revival. It makes a shopping center of great character though no architectural purity—a sort of suburban Ghirardelli Square.

4. **Bank Building** c.1930; 198 Main St.
   Moderne style.

5. **Fretwell Building** c.1890
   NE cor. Main & University Sts.

   A rare, but tiny, stone Romanesque Revival commercial block, more Furnessian than Richardsonian.

6. **Forbes Flour Mill** 1854
   Below Mill St. buried behind the buildings on Main, Mill & Church Sts.

   A real live mid-19th century stone ruin, and a registered state historical landmark.

7. **Los Gatos Civic Center** 1967
   Stickney & Hull. Sasaki/Walker, land. arch't.
   110 E Main St.

   A curiously planned and scaled set of miniature International style pavilions. A prize-winner, but what is it doing here?

NEW ALMADEN

New Almaden explains itself by its name as the major mercury production center of its time. No longer worked, it was the first major mining enterprise in California. Production began in the 1820s. Demand for mercury in gold mining made it a boom town after the middle of the century. Now a gently decaying backwater, a few old buildings along the main street testify to former glory. Among these are the mine superintendent's house, appropriately named Casa Grande, of 1854, and the Wells Fargo building, now a museum, of about the same time. Ruins of the old brick mercury smelting ovens and stills lie on the hillside to the north. The 1920s saw an attempt to make New Almaden into a resort. It failed, and a special brand of exurbanite lives here now.

M

Marin County conjures up a succession of images from bare, rolling highlands with superb fogscape to picturesque former fishing villages that recall the Riviera. In between are the older suburban communities whose insulation is gradually being worn away by rapacious development. Historically Marinites have set their faces against urbanism preferring the land-oriented pursuits of ranching, dairy farming, and lumbering. During the Mexican rule the county was carved up into land grants whose central settlements, Sausalito, San Rafael, Bolinas, and Tomales became the first towns after California's admission to the union in 1850. In 1875 the North Pacific Coast Railroad, owned by San Francisco entrepreneur Peter Donahue, began a run from Sausalito to Tomales which served the coastal farming and lumbering communities. Although a commercial failure, it was responsible for suburbanizing Marin by seeding the communities of Sausalito, Corte Madera, Kentfield, Ross, San Anselmo, and San Rafael with commuters. By 1884 a line from San Rafael to Tiburon opened up the other side of Richardson Bay. The completion of the Golden Gate Bridge in 1937 and the Richmond-San Rafael Bridge in 1956 made the territory as accessible as any other in the Bay Area as shown by the nearly 75% increase in population of the post-World War II boom decade of 1950-60. This surge of development has substantially altered the character of Marin. The shaved hills along U.S. 101 with their crowns of undistinguished housing are sad to see, but the older communities and the recent, well-planned valley developments have the quality of Arcadian retreat that is Marin's strongest image. Route 1 from the Bay to the Ocean side sweeps the mind clear of the man-made world as the panorama of coastal scenery unfolds. The road gradually descends to sea level at Stinson Beach, first settled by Capt. Alfred Easkoot about 1876. On the way are three arresting structures, dramatically sited against the hillside, designed and built by Valentino Agnoli, a former student of Bruce Goff, in 1968, '69, and '72. They are best described as handcrafted, technological fantasies strongly reflecting Goff's design philosophy. On the southwestern side of the road where Panoramic meets Route 1 is a shingled bungalow of 1915 designed by G. Albert Landsberg, chiefly known as the creator of opulent movie palaces.

Along the shore is Sea Drift, a privately owned sand spit where a number of houses by famous architects have been built. Since the area is not open to the public they are not listed here. Further north is the town of Bolinas, a ship-building center in the 1880s later to become a favorite summer residence community. One of the buildings that makes entering town a pleasant experience is the Calvary Presbyterian Church, 1877, in Victorian Gothic Rev. style. Some wooden, false-fronted commercial buildings and shanties complete the town's commercial center; the old residential area is a picturesque collection of Shingle Style and Chalet variants around the cove. On the mesa above is an arrested subdivision now sprinkled with a *Whole Earth Catalogue* of do-it-yourself house plans for shingled boxes and domes, mostly built from the late 1950s to the present.

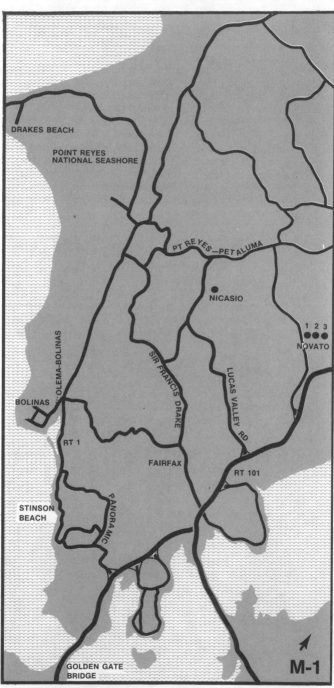

Leaving Bolinas the road north follows the North Shore Railroad line through the towns of Olema, Pt. Reyes Station, Marshall, and Tomales, built as agricultural shipping stations to supply San Francisco with the bounty of Marin. Most have moments of "main street" featuring commercial buildings of Victorian Gothic or Mission Revival style. In Tomales, Our Lady of the Assumption Church is a rather elaborate Victorian Gothic building of 1860.

Stretching from Bolinas northwest along the ocean is a geological mystery, Point Reyes National Seashore. According to the latest learned opinion this land mass drifted up from somewhere around the Santa Barbara coast eons ago to anchor itself on the Marin Coast. The unlearned can take comfort in the notion that Northern California possesses this beautiful stretch of Southern California coast. The town of Inverness, an early summer residence community, is located at the entrance to the park. Sir Francis Drake Blvd. leads to Pt. Reyes Light Station and to Drake's Bay where the Drakes' Beach Facilities, designed by Wong & Brocchini in 1967, houses offices and an interesting museum.

Valentino Agnoli House

Sausalito M-2

William A. Richardson was an English sailor, who planned the first townsite in San Francisco in 1835. A short time later he was granted the Rancho Sausalito as the dowry of his Mexican bride. The land was held intact from 1838 to 1869 when one thousand acres of it was purchased by the Sausalito Land and Ferry Co. which subdivided the property as a speculative development served by its ferry line from San Francisco. The North Pacific Coast Railroad assumed the ferry in 1875, and commuter settlement began.

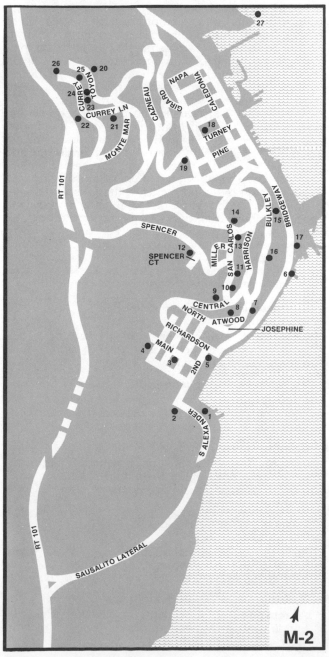

Until 1941, when the ferry and railroad lines were discontinued, Sausalito was the major entrance for the ever-growing number of commuters to southern Marin County. The post-war building boom had less effect on Sausalito proper than on the less built-up areas of Marin, but the community has grown to its very limits.

The trip from San Francisco to Sausalito is one of the most glamorous passages between a major city and a suburban community in the United States today. The broad sweep of Bay and Ocean seen from the Golden Gate Bridge is complemented by the great bare headlands, fortunately preserved from development by government ownership. Visitation Point provides a magic view of San Francisco as well as an overview of Ft. Baker in the sheltered cove of Horse-shoe Bay. The Fort, purchased in 1866 as Lime Point Military Reservation, was named Fort Baker in 1897, and can be visited by taking the marked road off the Sausalito Lateral turnoff from the freeway. Its simple, turn of the century, Classic Revival buildings are set with military regularity around the parade ground giving a pattern book image of military settlements of the period. Back on the road to Sausalito the traveler is taken through a series of cuts in the hills to a shore-line drive where the view of the hillside dotted with houses and the water dotted with boats strongly re-calls such Mediterranean towns as Positano. However, the sleepy-fishing-village image of pre-World War II has been replaced by a composite one of a commuter-tourist-boatsman community which makes a weekend tour by car a frustrating experience.

1. **Dickinson House**   1890; Willis Polk
   26 Alexander Ave.
   One of the earliest houses in the area, this box with a waterside porch has shingle siding done appropriately in permanent waves.

2. **Victorian Gothic cottage**   late 1860s; 215 South St.
   Another early arrival in the neighborhood, this house, reputedly brought around the Horn, was added to with former ships' cabins.

3. **Schuller House**   1899; 603 Main St.
   The builder-owner of this essential "salt box" house had both enthusiasm and talent for carving ornamental detail. The doorway with its Goth-icky decoration is notable.

4. **Cottage**   1874; Griswold
   639 Main St.
   Just up the street is another carpenter's dream house with an elaborate combination of forms held together visually by icicled verge boards.

5. **Valhalla**   c.1870; 201 Bridgeway
   A restaurant in one form or another since its building, this social landmark has a splendid view of San Francisco and the Bay.

6. **Ondine's** c.1897; 558 Bridgeway
The San Francisco Yacht Club which moved to Sausalito in 1878 has made the town a major recreational center for the Bay Area. It was originally housed in this restaurant building. Next door is a small, picturesque building, now Scoma's, which was formerly a launch rental service used from 1917-1937 by the Sausalito Land and Ferry Co.

7. **House** 1950; Joseph Esherick
60 Atwood Ave.
The foundations of a castle started by William Randolph Hearst form the base and determine the plan of this notable house, visible only from below on Bridgeway.

8. **House** 1939; Gardner Dailey
39 Atwood Ave.
This crisply detailed house seems younger than it is, especially in the use of a metal flue and exposed mill frame, elements that have since become widely used in residential architecture.

9. **Sausalito Woman's Club** 1913; Julia Morgan
Central Ave. at San Carlos Ave.
This carefully designed, shingled building has a strong utilitarian character softened by exotic landscaping. Its environmental quality recalls an older, more secluded village.

10. **House** 1948; Wurster, Bernardi & Emmons
42 San Carlos Ave.
Across the street this quietly inconspicuous house makes an harmonious neighbor.

11. **Villa Veneta** 1893; remodeled by Willis Polk c.1908
16 San Carlos Ave.
This boldly detailed house for Capt. J. H. Kilgrif, makes a bow to Venice through its Venetian Gothic windows.

12. **House** 1955; John Carl Warnecke
2 Spencer Ct.
The deck, visible from below, is the dominant element of this design which appears like a great tree house.

13. **Christ Church** 1882; **Guild Hall** 1889; **Memorial Porch** 1912
Santa Rosa St. & San Carlos Ave.
This church which began in Carpenter Gothic style has, through careful alterations, become the harmonious Shingle Style building we see today.

14. **Christ Church Parish Hall** 1967; Henrik Bull
Santa Rosa St. & San Carlos Ave.
A post and beam Bay Region Style building with Maybeckian overtones which complements the building it serves.

15. **House** c.1900; 140 Bulkley Ave.
This architectural curiosity evolved from a water tank to a simple but striking tower residence.

16. **St. John's Presbyterian Church** 1905
Coxhead & Coxhead
100 Bulkley Ave.
Ernest Coxhead's last Shingle Style church has an unusually stark interior culminating in a clerestoried pyramidal tower. Its entrance arch is truly groovy.

17. **Sausalito Square**
From St. John's Church there is a fine bird's eye view of this square with its improbable elephant lamp posts and pleasant fountain set in a foursome of palm trees. Its small scale is sadly dominated by the large scale parking lots nearby although it is nicely framed by the surrounding buildings, particularly the Mission Revival Hotel of c. 1910. Perhaps the best thing one could wish for this part of Sausalito is that the automobile could magically disappear.

18. **Silva House** c.1900; Turney & Bonita Sts.
A Colonial Revival house with elegant balcony and wood detail, unique in Sausalito.

19. **Gardner House** 1869; Cazneau St. & Girard Ave.
Sausalito's oldest house in its original state and a typical Victorian Gothic cottage design of the period with central gable, verge board of lace icicles, and split-columned porch.

20. **House** 1956; 66 Toyon Lane
A good example of Bay Region design of the 1950s with Japanese overtones.

21. House

Curry Lane has a fine collection of houses that present the Bay Region Post and Beam style of the 1950s in variations.

21. **House** 1958; John Funk
139 Curry Lane

22. **House** 1955; John Hoops
227 Curry Lane

23. **House** 1953; Roger Lee
244 Curry Lane

24. **House** 1953; Charles Warren Callister
250 Curry Lane

25. **House** 1956; John Hoops
260 Curry Lane

26. **House** 1958; Henrik Bull
290 Curry Lane

27. **Sausalito Houseboats**
Sausalito's floating suburb, a collection of largely do-it-yourself dream boats. For years this bohemian community has withstood onslaughts by both tourists and the constabulary concerned with sewer problems.

MARIN CITY, just N of Sausalito off Rt. 101
Marin City Plan 1958; Demars & Reay; Land. Arch't., Lawrence Halprin; Public Housing, John Carl Warnecke & Assoc., Aaron Green
The city came into existence as a community of temporary wartime housing for workers in the nearby Marin Shipyards. The population high was about 6,000, down now to about 1,600. It is a totally "redeveloped" city, built first directly by the Federal Government, then torn down and rebuilt with such federal aids as urban renewal, public housing, 221(d)3, etc. The federally-aided low-rent public housing project has 300 units on 32 acres. Multistory cast-in-place concrete units in the hills by Aaron Green **(1)**; lower, single story wooden structures by Warnecke **(2)** on the plain; and pole-frame construction, one and two story relocation dwellings on the hillside by Demars & Reay **(3)**. The **Manzanita Neighborhood Center** on Drake Rd. was designed by Karl Treffinger in 1968.

Before the 1870s the Tiburon peninsula, to which Belvedere was connected by a narrow strip of land, was a stretch of barren, rolling terrain belonging to John Reed's Rancho Corte Madera del Presidio. From 1875-1890 the Union Fish Company, the only industry ever to touch its shores, occupied a stretch of land on what is now West Shore Road on the Southeast coast of Belvedere. In 1884 Peter Donahue completed his San Francisco & North Pacific Railroad from San Rafael to Tiburon where it terminated at the ferry landing for San Francisco. The station, 1920 Paradise Dr., company store and shops were constructed near the landing, and housing for the workmen was built. Some of these simple wooden cottages stand on Mar West near Esperanza St. (a). Tiburon Town or Shark Town, as it was known in translation, was a rough and ready place frequented by fishermen and railroad men, a contrast to the well-behaved commuter-resident and tourist population of today. Main St. has even undergone a major face-lifting, beginning in 1955, sponsored by paint magnate Fred Zelinsky, which by doctoring some 20th century buildings has created a usable past suitable for tourist consumption. The waterfront restaurants whose back decks look over the Corinthian Yacht Harbor to San Francisco are euphoric places. The harbor was first a haven for houseboats called "arks" which began to come in the 1880s bringing summer residents and mooring for the winter in the sheltered cove reached by a floodgate through the spit now covered by Beach Road. These floating domiciles which became increasingly elaborate toward the turn of the century began to be beached around 1910, and slowly vanished from the scene. Some recognizable arks can be seen at 88 and 104 Main St. (b), and 27 and 52 Beach (c). The latter incorporates a ship cabin from the side-wheeler *China*.

About the time that the arks were cruising around Belvedere, gracefully served by merchants who rowed out to provision them, the institution which had the major effect on the residential character of Belvedere was founded. This was the Belvedere Land Co., established in 1890 with title to the peninsula. The present offices of the company (d) built in 1905 and the cottages (e) built in 1906 are handsome Shingle Style buildings designed by Albert Farr. The first contribution the company made to the environment was the planting of pine and eucalyptus trees among the scrub oaks that were native to the land. The results of this forestation supplemented by the extensive but informal landscaping of the houses have created the kind of paradise that Americans associate with the Riviera. Besides the vegetation, another strong resemblance is in the pattern of narrow, winding streets, connected by vertical lanes, that ring the peninsula. The first wave of buildings, from 1890 to about 1910, strongly reflects the Shingle Style of the eastern seaboard with variations by local architects like Willis Polk and Albert Farr. The post-war building grows out of this tradition almost untouched by the International Style. The Belvedere Lagoon is a showcase of architecture by practically every leading architect in the

Bay Area, but unfortunately its view side is to the
water so that there is no clear way to mark the individual works. General views from the hills are about
the best you can do unless you have a boat handy
in which to go out on the Lagoon. In fact, many of the
notable houses on the peninsula itself can only be
seen from the water; those listed are selected for their
accessibility as well as architectural interest.

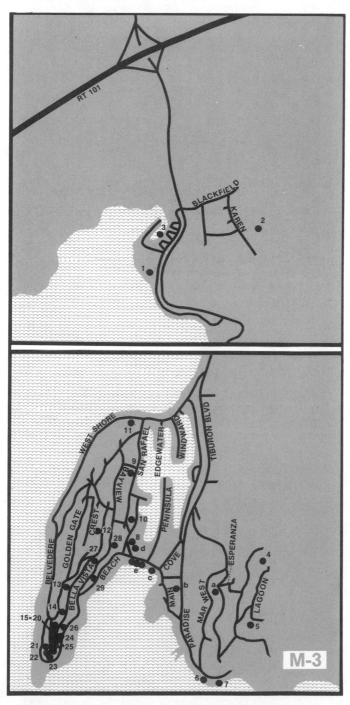

1. **Hilarita Reed Lyford Res.**   1874; now Audubon Society
   376 Tiburon Blvd.
   A bracketed Italianate villa built for the daughter of the owner of the Rancho Corte Madera del Presidio, this house was fortunately preserved by its removal from Strawberry Point to this site. It was restored by John Lord King in 1957 and now serves as headquarters for the Audubon Society.

photo: Morley Baer

2. **Bel Air School**   1956; John Lyon Reid; 1959 addit., Callister, Payne & Rosse
   259 Karen Way
   A good example of the California finger-plan school of the 1950s.

3. **Cove Apts.**   1965; John Lord King
   Tiburon Blvd. north of city limits
   A 16 acre tract containing 284 units, a clubhouse, indoor and outdoor pools, saunas, and a tidal pond, these straightforward, woodsy buildings are among the most direct and appealing spec housing in the Bay Area.

4. **Old St. Hilary's Church**   1888
   Above intersection of Alemany & Esperanza Sts.
   A humble, Carpenter-Gothic church, said to have been designed by its rector, the Rev. Hugh Lagan. It is now the Landmarks Society Museum, surrounded by a wild flower preserve, and the principal visual landmark on the hillside.

5. **House**   1969; Quinn & Oda
   Ridge Rd.
   Another visual landmark on the hillside designed in the cut-out box style of the 1960s.

6. **House**   1970; Fisher-Friedman
   2028 Paradise Dr.
   A shingled pavilion floating just above the waters of the Bay; the best view of it is from the cardboard Riviera villa just south.

7. Hygeia Tower c.1890; 2036 Paradise Dr.

All that came of Dr. Benjamin Lyford's utopian concept for the all-around healthy community. As the husband of Hilarita Reed, the good doctor was blessed with extensive land holdings around the southern end of the Tiburon peninsula on which he laid out a contour street plan with lots to be sold to clean-living people. Significantly there were few sales and no building. The street pattern was a contribution to the area whose lucky inhabitants have a splendid view of the Bay looking due south to San Francisco whose Pacific Heights ridge looks like a pork loin roast neatly carved by its north-south streets.

8. Belvedere Town Square

The Shingle Style in one form or another gives this place an harmonious context. Notable buildings are: The Belvedere Land Co., 1905; the Cottages and apt. house by Albert Farr 1906, across the street; and the Town Square Apts., 1955, by Shubart & Friedman.

9. First Church of Christ Scientist 1952
Charles Warren Callister
San Raphael Ave.

The spearhead plan of the fine wood and concrete church is echoed in every detail of the building and its landscaping so that it seems the most natural consequence of the shape of the site.

10. Community Hall c.1890; Albert Farr
Bayview & San Raphael Ave.

This somewhat English-Half-Timber style building is a former Presbyterian Church which, minus its tower and spire, was moved from Laurel and Bayview about 1950.

Still and all, Belvedere and Tiburon are rare examples of communities that make historic preservation work.

11. Moffitt Res. c.1900; enlarged 1914 by Willis Polk
8 West Shore Rd.

If you think this house would be more at home in San Francisco's Pacific Heights you're right! It once stood at 1818 Broadway and, when slated for destruction in 1962, was sliced in half and barged across the Bay.

12. **House**   1962; Joseph Esherick
    11 Crest Rd.
    An elegant house in the middle period Bay Region Shingle style.

13. **Pomander Walk and Woodwardia Lane**
    Pedestrian paths criss-cross Belvedere, and one could spend a happy day just exploring them. These two seemed particularly entrancing.

14. **House**   c.1900; 304 Golden Gate Ave.
    A fine Shingle Style house consisting of three gabled boxes cut and interlocked. It strongly suggests the hand of Albert Farr.

15. **Peterson House**   1903; Clarence Ward
    332 Golden Gate Ave.
    A Shingle Style house with a small bay window intricately set in an arched opening on the facade.

16. **House**   1904; Albert Farr
    334 Golden Gate Ave.
    A large, Tudor style, half-timbered house which commands the hillside and is one of the chief sights of Belvedere's north-western flank.

17. **Holmes House**   1905; Daniel McLean, Contractor
    340 Golden Gate Ave.
    Also visible from Bella Vista below, the gambrel-roofed, shingled house has strong affinities with the Shingle Style of the eastern seaboard.

18. **Moore House**   1895; remodeled by W. Polk 1906
    416 Golden Gate Ave.
    Originally a cottage, this many gabled, half timbered house has retained a doll house scale.

19. **Rey House**   1893; Willis Polk
    428 Golden Gate Ave.
    A stucco house with strong, simple classic lines and a Mediterranean tone, it has a skylight and open trellis work over the upper windows to provide maximum light for the third floor studio.

20. Blanding House c.1900; 440 Golden Gate Ave.
The original manor house in Classic Revival style of the Gordon Blanding estate which covered the southern tip of the peninsula. It shares an incomparable view of the Bay with a stucco Mediterranean style house called the "organ house" because a wing of it is given to a concert room featuring a large organ. The house was built in the 1890s and supposedly remodeled by Polk in 1906. Other buildings which belonged to the estate are the shingled carriage house at 333 Belvedere and the gardener's house at 343 Belvedere.

21. House 1967; Callister & Payne
455 Belvedere Ave.
A quietly handsome house by a firm that has contributed much to the fame of Bay Region architecture; it is very well designed for its site.

22. House 1972
John Field/Bull Field/Volkmann/Stockwell
6 Blanding Lane
A combination of polygonal volumes gives this house a very sculptural form.

23. House 1972; Callister & Payne
End of Blanding Lane
A very large shingled house which reflects the character of some of the older houses on the peninsula. It stands on the site of the recently demolished Mediterranean villa designed for George Blanding by Julia Morgan.

24. Maillard House c.1895; 251 Beach Rd.
Designed by its owner this multi-storied house has a fine corner tower and graceful encircling porch typical of west coast Queen Anne Style. Also visible from Bella Vista.

25. House c.1930; 499 Bella Vista
A Swiss-fairy-tale house very lovingly done.

House 1892; 460 Bella Vista
It may be truly said of this house that it has a Queen Anne front and a Mary Ann behind.

26. House c.1900; 207 Bayview Ave.
A composite style house, largely Colonial Revival, with elaborate fenestration and a remarkable Chinese bird house.

27. House 1971; Rodney Friedman
230 Bayview Ave.
A bold, stylish house designed by the architect for himself and best seen from the town below.

28. House 1894; D. A. McLean
140 Bayview Ave.
A Mother Goose style work designed by the contractor who worked on many of Belvedere's early houses for his family.

The first and only real commercial operation ever to occupy Mill Valley was a saw mill built on Cascade Creek by John Reed, owner after 1834 of the Rancho Corte Madera del Presidio from whose redwood-filled canyons he supplied lumber to the San Francisco Presidio. Adjoining his property to the south was the

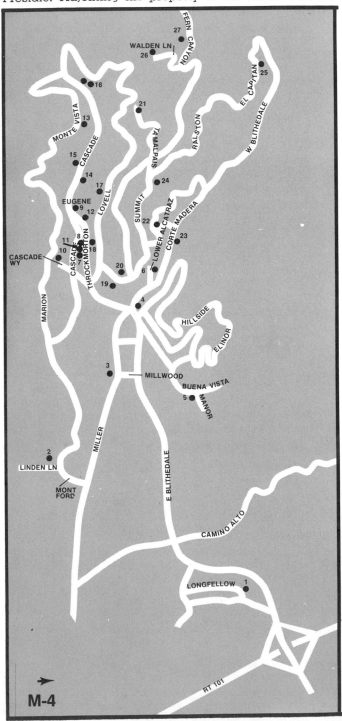

Rancho Sausalito, 19,000 acres owned by William Richardson and administered by Samuel Throckmorton. After Richardson's death, financial reverses forced Throckmorton to mortgage 15,000 acres. After his death in 1887 these were acquired by a group of San Franciscans who formed the Tamalpais Land and Dairy Co. Michael M. O'Shaughnessy was hired to survey and plat the land creating a town called Eastland after Joseph G. Eastland, head of the group. The next step was to plug the town into the North Pacific Coast Railroad by building a spur line south to Almonte on the San Rafael-Sausalito line. Once this was accomplished, the town was set to go and in fact did when some 3,000 people purchased lots at public auction in 1890.

Later that year the name was changed to Mill Valley. Most of these first property owners built summer homes, but with the coming of electric rail service in 1903 the commuting time became short enough to encourage year-round living. In fact, it took as short a time to get from San Francisco to Mill Valley by ferry and rail then is it does now by automobile. This ease of access which has brought a steadily growing population has not substantially changed Mill Valley's atmosphere of rustic seclusion. The long approach over the flatland is cluttered with random development and occupied by a somewhat transient population which is not community oriented. This influx has brought too many cars to crowd the town center and overburden the narrow canyon roads. But it is in the heart of the redwood canyons, in the dense green shade of the great trees, that Mill Valley's original aspect of quiet retreat is most apparent. Many of the buildings would be insignificant in another setting, but given the quality of the place they have a special interest. It is one of the best places in the Bay Area to see fine unarchitected architecture usually in the vernacular wood styles. Some suggested drives are indicated on the map by dotted lines.

1. **Two houses**   1959; Raphael Soriano
   20 & 24 Longfellow Rd.
   A pair of houses tucked into the hillside below street level which show Soriano's Southern California International Style aesthetic.

2. **Homestead Valley**   1968; Wong & Brocchini
   120 Linden Lane
   This award winning public housing project for the elderly has a pleasant, human scale.

3. **Apts.**   1970; John O'Brien Armstrong
   Miller Ave. at Millwood
   Yet another variation in the mannered box style of the 1960s, these apartments are designed with more originality than usual.

4. Marin Outdoor Art Center   1905
Bernard Maybeck
Buena Vista & Blithedale Ave.
Few architects have been more adept than Maybeck at effects of such simple directness as this projection of trusses through the roof to express the structure outside as well as in.

5. Tennis Club   1966; John Field
Buena Vista at Manor Dr.
A simple, shingled structure that blends well with the older buildings of Mill Valley.

6. Cottage   c.1900; 19 Lower Alcatraz Pl.
A summer cottage with a strong "folk" character and a highly unlikely Japanese fence.

● **7. Mill Valley Library**   1969
Wurster, Bernardi & Emmons
Throckmorton at Elma St.
A pleasant unpretentious design for a public building which fits well with the town and with its wooded site.

8. Harvey Klyce House   1900
501 Throckmorton Ave.
Mill Valley's talented builder built this Shingle Style house for himself.

9. House   1955; Roger Lee
41 Eugene St.
A typical Bay Region Style house from the 1950s and a perfect foil for a matchless site.

10. Three cottages   c.1900;
35, 37, 39 Cascade Way
Cascade Way ends in the Dipsea Trail Steps. Perched on its narrow shoulder are three wee cottages which epitomize the summer shanty origins of much of Mill Valley. The upper and lower ones are constructed of interlocking timbers like the Lincoln Log toy sets.

11. House   c.1925; 84 Cascade Ave.
The almost edible gingerbread house that Hansel and Gretel found in the heart of the forest.

12. House   1893; 146 Cascade Ave.
An eastern Shingle Style farm house that followed Horace Greeley's advice.

13. House   1960; Marquis & Stoller
410 Monte Vista Ave.
A representative design of this prominent Bay Area firm.

14. Washington House   c.1895; Willis Polk
276 Cascade Ave.
Heavy remodeling has made this house of more interest to the student of Polk than the architectural sightseer.

15. House   1971; Wm. W. Kirsch
265 Cascade Ave.

Not so much a work of architecture as a showcase for a collection of art windows salvaged from older buildings.

16. Two houses   1969; Daniel Lieberman
881 & 861 Lovell Ave.

A highly personal blend of technology and folk sources, these houses have a strong affinity with the work of such futuristic designers as John Lautner and Bruce Goff.

17. House   1970; Wm. W. Kirsch
215 Lovell Ave.

A fusion of the mannered box style of the '60s and the Mother Goose style of the '20s.

18. House   c.1895; Harvey Klyce
167 Lovell Ave.

Basically the work of Klyce but remodeled with great empathy by its architect owner who added such apparently original features as the round window near the entrance.

19. Evans House   1907; L. C. Mullgardt
100 Summit Ave.

A vertical composition with a dramatically canti-levered porch best seen from below. The house is a variation on the bungalow style by one of its most original masters.

20. Coffin House   1893; Emil John
15 Tamalpais Ave.

A Queen Anne style house designed to look like a ferry boat. Although Alonzo Coffin owned a pattern shop in San Francisco, the house is dis-tinguished more for its inventive shingle work.

21. House   1971; Ivan Poujatine
400 Tamalpais Ave.

A contemporary design which shows an imag-inative use of old timbers.

22. Lovell White House   c.1890; 95 Magee Ave.

The most striking feature of this simple redwood box crowned with an octagonal turret is its grace-fully arched, shingled veranda. It was built for the director of the Tamalpais Land and Dairy Co. who clearly wished to survey all he mastered.

23. Billings House   1891; 160 Corte Madera Ave.

This large woodsy house appropriately called Redwood Lodge bespeaks the perfect summer, country residence.

● **24. Green-Johnston House**   1961, Marquis & Stoller; Landscaping by Lawrence Halprin.
366 Summit Ave.

A well-sited house in the middle Bay Region man-ner originally designed as a double residence.

25. Ralston L. White Memorial Retreat   c.1912
Willis Polk
2 El Capitan Ave.
Unlike many of Polk's designs this house has no strong stylistic commitment. Notable for its very large windows and porch openings, it was intended to be covered with vines at the wish of the client.

26. Pence House   1962; Marquis & Stoller
4 Walden Lane
A most dramatically sited house composed of two hipped-roof pavilions.

photo: Karl Riek

27. House   1966; Pafford Clay
25 Fern Canyon Rd.
Appropriately called the Tamalpais Pavilion, it was designed by the architect for himself and strongly suggests a large concrete moon-viewing platform.

A loop drive from West Blithedale Ave. on Bigelow to Hillside, Elinor and back down again on Oakdale is recommended for those who are interested in the vernacular Shingle Style houses of the area. Apparently anonymous, most of them are dignified by careful proportions and fine detail.

CORTE MADERA, 2 mi. N of Mill Valley, off Rt. 101

Marin County Branch Library   1971
Smith, Barker & Hanssen
707 Meadowsweet Dr.
Winner of the 1972 Plywood Association Design Award this branch library has the appearance of several wooden boxes cut out and fitted together to express its plan. It sits gracefully on a eucalyptus studded slope and complements the older, Shingle Style building above it.

Golden West Savings and Loan   1971
M/L/T/W—Wm. Turnbull & Assoc.
Corte Madera Shopping Center, Tamalpais Dr. & Madera Blvd.
A zoomie bank interior with super-graphics by Barbara Stauffacher.

Kentfield M-5

In 1902 the North Shore Railroad published an illustrated pamphlet extolling the charms of the area it served. It pictured gracious resort hotels, substantial homes, and vistas of the verdant countryside around. The substantial homes have multiplied, the hotels have vanished, and the rural delights of open meadowlands and wooded glens remain only in public parks and private estates. Still in the older sections of Ross and San Anselmo the qualities of exclusive suburban retreat are as evident as they were in 1902. The brochure describes Ross as "the very paradise of a residential district convenient to San Francisco and sheltered under the huge lee of the great Tamalpais range. Its climate is much superior to that of much-lauded Santa Barbara." Further it points out that San Anselmo's crossroads location where three valleys come together makes it possible for the resident to choose the elevation or orientation he desires. After seventy years there is little choice left.

The first stop across the now developed plains is Kentfield, former estate of Albert Kent who purchased the large tract from a Ross Valley pioneer named William Murray about 1870. His house at 200 Woodland Rd., built in 1872 in Victorian style was remodeled in 1916 by Bliss & Faville. The following listings are only a few of the many fine designs in the area, most of which are impossible to see from a public road.

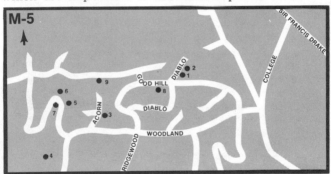

1. **House**   1949; Fred & Lois Langhurst
   100 Diablo Dr.

2. **House**   1949; Charles Warren Callister
   106 Diablo Dr.
   Two fine designs strongly influenced by F. L. Wright.

3. **Esherick House**   1951; Joseph Esherick
   30 Acorn Way
   An outstanding example of the early work of this architect with a barnlike simplicity which recalls vernacular architecture of early California.

4. **House**   1959; Jack Hillmer
   75 Upland Rd.
   A cantilevered deck roofs the carport of this remarkable house, framed with a triangular grid of beams supporting the roof in a single plane over both one and two story areas.

5, 6, 7. 3 Houses: 436 Woodland Ave. 1970; 444 Woodland Ave. 1950; 445 Woodland Ave. 1963; Joseph Esherick & Assoc.

These houses exhibit a range in design concepts of this famous Bay Area firm from early to recent work.

8. House 1949-58; Henry Hill
329 Goodhill Rd.

A lavish house by one of the major designers of the 1950s which takes maximum advantage of its site.

9. House 1947; Hilmer & Callister
405 Goodhill Rd.

Although only a fragment is visible it is worth glimpsing the triangular plan of this house with its great pointed prow and trees projecting through the roof.

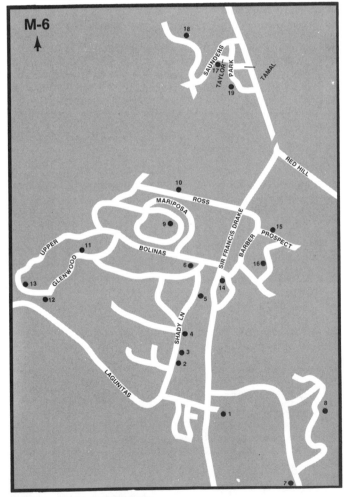

ROSS, SAN ANSELMO

At the intersection of Sir Francis Drake Blvd. and Lagunitas Rd. is the Civic Center of Ross whose buildings, set around Ross Common, have an appropriate suburban, residential character. The Marin Art and Garden Center preserves as an office the Victorian Gothic carriage house of 1865 **(1)** of the original Worn estate.

Shady Lane is one of the perfect environmental moments of Old Ross, a carefully created country lane without curbs or sidewalks, lined with close-set trees. Two impressive houses from earlier days are the great Shingle Style house, c.1905 **(2)** on the east side after the intersection of Upper Ames Ave. and its neighbor at 34 Shady Lane in the Queen Anne-Eastlake Style, c.1874 **(3)**. Further north on the same side near the intersection of Southwood Ave. is a house designed by Donald Olsen in 1966 **(4)** and at 72 Shady Lane is the latest development of the Shingle Style by Marquis & Stoller, 1972 **(5)**. Shady Lane ends at Bolinas Ave. where St. Anselm's Catholic Church stands, a personal translation of the late Shingle Style into a half-timbered structure by Frank Shea, 1907 **(6)**.

7. **Quisiana**   1900; 131 Laurel Grove Ave.
   A late flowering of the Queen Anne style in free form on a huge scale.

8. **Hopps House**   1906; Bernard Maybeck
   Winding Way nr. Canyon Rd.
   One of Maybeck's great houses in his shingled chalet style.

9. **San Francisco Theological Seminary:**   Chapel 1897; Montgomery Hall   1892; Wright & Saunders Bolinas & Richmond
   Looming up like a castle on the Rhine, this complex of buildings is one of the enduring landmarks of the area. The two buildings listed are fine examples of Richardson Romanesque, and the lovely grounds were landscaped by Wm. Penn Mott, then Park Superintendent for Oakland.

10. **John R. Little Residences**   1970; Albert & Abend
    108 Ross Ave.
    A well-designed complex of redwood townhouses for student families.

11. **House** c.1900; Glenwood Ave.
The striking similarity between this house and 73 Winship make it almost certainly the design of Maxwell Bugbee.

12. **House** 1896; John White
Glenwood at Upper Rd.
A fine Shingle Style house by an architect closely associated with Bernard Maybeck.

13. **House** 1900; John White
Upper Rd.
A large house with a strong Shingle Style character translated into half-timber construction.

14. **Bugbee House** 1890; Maxwell Bugbee
73 Winship Rd.
Bugbee's fondness for bulbous form is evident in this house he built for himself.

15. **House** 1908; Julia Morgan
15 Prospect Ave.
A carefully crafted house with a simple, rustic character.

16. **House** 1904; Coxhead & Coxhead
160 Prospect Ave.
An unassuming design whose visual interest is concentrated in an elegant entrance composition. It is slightly altered by a second story bedroom addition.

17. **House** c.1890; 206 Saunders Ave.
A prime piece of Victorian Chinoiserie.

18. **Breck House** 1910; Maxwell Bugbee
100 Alder Ave.
The most romantic shingled tower anywhere belongs to this boldly detailed house with an innovative interior prompted by the owner's interest in the Eskimos. It is hard to understand it from the outside but it was known as the "igloo house."

19. House

19. **House** 1893; Coxhead & Coxhead
96 Park Dr.
A restrained Shingle Style house appropriately chosen by the North Shore Railroad for use in its brochure of 1902 as an example of the stately manor presiding over the open countryside.

Mission San Rafael was founded by Fr. Vicente Serra in 1817, chiefly as a sanatorium for the Indian wards of the church who became ill in considerable numbers in foggy San Francisco. The Secularization Act of 1833 closed down the Mission forcing the sale of about 22,000 acres of land to one Timothy Murphy. The farm village of which he became mayor prospered and, with the coming of the railroad, was the transportation and commercial center of Marin County. The original mission buildings became building materials for the growing town; the mission church was altered to the point of being a modern structure. In fact, most of the old buildings of San Rafael have fared poorly with only bits and pieces left to give an idea of the old town. One exception is the Ira Cook guest house, now the Marin County Historical Society Museum, an elaborate Victorian Gothic cottage of 1879 at 1125 B St. **(1)**.

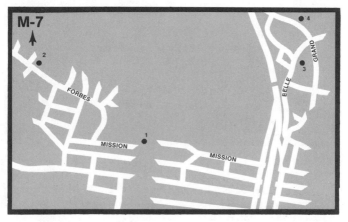

2. **House**   c.1889; Newsom & Newsom
230 Forbes Ave.

A charming example of the Newsom's work complete with lions reclining on the moon gate porch entrance.

3. **The Dominican Convent:** main building 1889; James Chisholm
1520 Grand Ave.

This imposing Italianate structure with Mansard roof is the original building of this oldest Catholic College for Women in California. Around 1920 the college acquired two residences for dormitories; Meadowlands, 1888, Olive and Palm, a rambling Shingle Style building with white painted trim; Edgehill, 1882, a Queen Anne Rev. with Classical detail. The new Library was designed in 1964 by Shubart & Friedman.

Morley Baer: *Here Today*

4. **House** c.1905; John Ralston Hamilton
1644 Grand Ave.

A highly sophisticated design by a little known Bay Area architect which shows the influence of Ernest Coxhead.

SANTA VENETIA

1. **Marin County Civic Center** 1957-1972; Frank L. Wright; Aaron Green, associated architect; William Wesley Peters, Taliesin Associated Architects

This futuristic palace is the most dramatically sited building in the Bay Area and one of the most impressive of Wright's late works. The master plan was submitted in 1957. The first phase of construction on the Administration Building was completed in 1962, after Wright's death. It houses the county's administrative, financial, and physical development departments as well as the main branch of the County Library. The Hall of Justice, occupied in 1969, is a wing attached to the north end of the Administration Building. The courts, law agencies, offices of the County Clerk and Recorder and the Public Social Services Dept. are located here. Together they bridge three hills. Three arched drive-through entrances separate main public access from traffic to the jail. The Veteran's Memorial Auditorium, a separate building, was completed in 1972. The Post Office Building at the foot of the entrance drive is the only building by Wright ever to be commissioned by the United States Government.

2. **Rodef Sholom Temple**   1962; Marquis & Stoller
170 N. San Pedro Rd., Santa Venetia

A chaste base with an expressionistic super-structure.

3. **Venetia Oaks**   1970; Campbell & Wong; Royston, Hanamoto, Beck & Abey, Land Arch.
263 N. San Pedro Rd.

Winner of a 1971 HUD Award for Public Housing for the Elderly.

MARINWOOD, TERRA LINDA

Terra Linda was one of the first valleys along U.S. 101 to be developed starting in the mid-1950s. It is now a typical suburban, satellite city whose edges are blurred with those of San Rafael.

1. **Commerce Clearing House Headquarters Building**
1968; Marquis & Stoller
Quail Hill Rd.
An imposing building in brut-concrete style prominently sited on the hilltop. It is the first increment of an 84 acre professional park and residential community.

2. **Northgate Dental Clinic**   1968
Smith, Barker, Hanssen
920 Northgate Dr.
Basically a box visually strengthened by an impressive constructivist veneer.

3. **Eichler Homes**   1955; Anshen & Allen
Manuel Freitas Prkwy. between Las Gallinas & Las Ovejas Aves.
The original development of Terra Linda which has aged nicely.

4. **The Meadows**   1965; Welton Beckett
910 Lea Dr.
A planned unit development, pleasantly sited. The general proportions of the buildings with shallow-pitched roofs and second story balconies recall the Monterey Colonial Style.
Lucas Valley

5. **Lucas Valley Eichler Homes**   1963-; Claude Oakland & Assoc.; Land. Arch't., Royston, Hanamoto, Mayes & Beck
Lucas Valley Rd. bet. Huckleberry & Idleberry Rds.
The most praiseworthy example of speculative housing development in Marin County. The sensitive and sensible residents have managed to purchase the hill above to preserve its beautiful setting.

NICASIO

The center of the Rancho Nicasio, granted in 1835, became a town about 1850 when it boasted a 22 room hotel (now gone), a blacksmith's shop, grocery store, livery stable, boarding house and race track. The square was set aside about 1870 when Nicasio had hopes of becoming the county seat. It still provides a perfect 19th century rural scene for those who wish to suspend reality for a while and believe that exurbia is far away. The principal landmark on the square is Our Lady of Loretto Church, 1867, in simplified Victorian Gothic Rev. Style. Just outside town on San Geronimo Rd. is the Nicasio School, 1871, a little red school house in Victorian Gothic, beautifully maintained. From here the trip to Olema or Pt. Reyes Station is a matchless Marin experience.

St. Vincent's School   c.1920; end of St. Vincent Dr.
This romantic vision from the freeway at the end
of an alley of great eucalyptus trees makes it
clear that among the styles to take root in California the Spanish Colonial Revival was one of
the most appropriate to the land. The buildings
are strongly Churrigueresque and set in gardens
reminiscent of old Seville.

Morley Baer: *Here Today*

NOVATO

An old agricultural center which burgeoned and
sprawled in the 1950s and '60s. Most of the old buildings are gone, but Novato has kept one notable example as its City Hall, the former Presbyterian Church
of 1889, Victorian Gothic, at Delong Ave. and Sherman **(1)**. The latest in civic buildings is represented by
the Library, 1971; Marquis & Stoller; at 1720 Novato
Blvd. **(2)**

3. Bahia   1968; Callister & Payne
3 mi. no. of Novato Blvd. on Pt. Reyes-Petaluma
Rd.

A well-designed, planned unit development
around an artificial lagoon for water oriented
recreation. The condominiums are designed in
the woodsy style typical of this firm.

EAST BAY

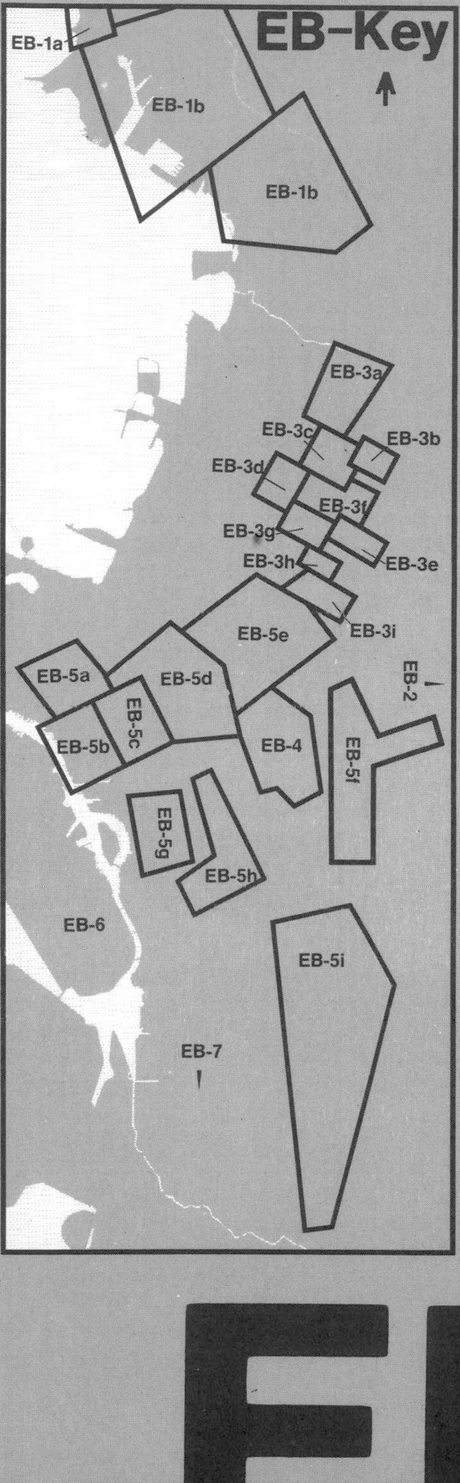

EB-Key

EB-1a
EB-1b
EB-1b

EB-3a
EB-3c
EB-3b
EB-3d
EB-3f
EB-3g
EB-3h
EB-3e
EB-3i
EB-2
EB-5e
EB-5a
EB-5d
EB-5c
EB-5b
EB-4
EB-5f
EB-5g
EB-5h
EB-6
EB-5i
EB-7

EB

EAST BAY INTRODUCTION

The East Bay is geographically defined by the Bay shore on the west, Carquinas Straits on the north, and on the east by a range of coastal hills much of which has successfully been incorporated into the East Bay Regional Parks system. Its dominating feature is Mt. Diablo (3,849 ft.). Southward the chain of rippling brown hills continues, punctuated by dark green canyons, and climaxes at Mission Peak (2,517 ft.) whose grassy brown sides subside into the plains of San Clara County where Mt. Hamilton (4,209) provides a southern boundary point. The communities of the East Bay developed naturally along a transportation network which first served to connect the missions at Santa Clara and San Jose in the south with the Spanish-Mexican settlements which extended northward to Richmond. The ranchos with their vast acreage owned by a single family were more than agricultural holdings; they functioned also as basic units of civil government with clusters of adobe buildings serving the family enterprises somewhat like the civic centers of today. After the American annexation of California in 1847 they posed a problem for the Yankee settlers eager for land, and in the 1850s were gradually broken up through sales to private individuals or illegally by squatters. In most cases their headquarters became the centers of development for the new towns forming in the East Bay area. In the 1850s as the gold rush fever subsided and disillusioned miners sought a more stable way of life, settlements devoted to lumbering and agriculture prospered. Most were laid out in blocks or lots after a degree of economic viability insured some permanence; gridiron platting, synonomous with urban order in this period, was generally imposed on the new towns even in outright defiance of the terrain.

In the decade of the 1860s, railroad fever succeeded gold rush fever providing the rising East Bay population with a network of rails which culminated in the western terminus of the transcontinental system at Oakland. Development reached a new peak after the San Francisco earthquake and fire of 1906, when a substantial number of settlers displaced from the city chose to remain across the Bay; but by far the greatest surge of population came during World War II when hundreds of thousands came to work in the wartime industries concentrated in the area from Richmond to San Lorenzo. Though wartime population pressure taxed the housing resources of the urban centers, it was in the post-war period that the building boom, both industrial and residential, began to devour the open country replacing fields, orchards, dairy farms, and truck gardens with industrial complexes, housing tracts, and shopping centers. Freeways replaced the railroads, serving both old and new areas as people chose the relative freedom of the individual automobile in greater and greater numbers. Beside the freeways new housing tracts littered the landscape; the housing market, generally steady through the post-war

Introduction

decades, has been most active recently in the Fremont district. The latest transportation system to serve the East Bay area is the Bay Area Rapid Transit system designed to provide efficient linkage for the urban and suburban communities and so decrease the pressures to build more freeways and devour more open space.

Opposite San Francisco are the principal cities of Alameda County: Albany, Berkeley, Emeryville, Piedmont, Oakland, Alameda, and San Leandro which make up the long urbanized shelf of the East Bay. This shelf, averaging three miles in width, backs up to a range of high hills whose upper reaches from north to south support the automobile-based communities of El Cerrito, Kensington, the Berkeley hills, Montclair, and the highlands of Oakland bounded by the East Bay Regional Parks. The older parts of these communities, first developed in the 1920s, have a generally eclectic architectural character. The recent parts, often because of the terrain, display the now familiar Bay region house of wood, simply detailed, whose most notable feature is a deck or series of decks pulled out like trays to overhang the precipitous slopes below and provide an indoor-outdoor living area oriented to a Bay view. The landscape in which these houses are set is entirely man-made, judging by early photographs which show a rippling, treeless terrain like that behind Fremont today. Early hill-dwellers like the dairy farmers of Piedmont planted hedgerows of eucalyptus trees as windbreaks for their fields, but major forestation began in the first decade of the 20th century when real estate entrepreneurs Frank C. Havens and F. M. "Borax" Smith seeded enough eucalyptus trees to shade the hills from Berkeley south to Mills College. Joaquin Miller, the "Poet of the Sierras," and his friends are credited with planting some 75,000 eucalyptus, pines, cypresses, and acacias in his 80 acre homestead, now a city park. However, little of this transformation and subsequent settlement would have been feasible had not Anthony Chabot dammed up the waters of the Temescal Creek in 1870 to provide a reservoir for the area and a water system for the East Bay.

The development of the flatlands was quite different. Settlement hugged the shore stretching along a stagecoach line which, after 1852, ran north and south along what is now San Pablo Ave. A freight and ferry service called Jacob's Landing became the town of Ocean View, now West Berkeley, laid out in the usual gridiron pattern. Similar settlements in Oakland were Clinton and San Antonio Parks which merged to form Brooklyn, annexed by Oakland in 1872. The network of horsecar lines gave way to steam lines which in the 1890s became an electrically powered rapid transit system put together by F. M. "Borax" Smith who intended it to serve the cause of selling parcels of land by the simple means of providing buyers with transportation. The resulting real estate boom was the first stage of the urbanization that has merged the flatland cities into one continuous strip of low-density commercial and residential development.

In contrast to most Bay Region towns which had gentle beginnings as farming, lumbering, crossroads and trading centers, Richmond began life as a railroad and factory town. In 1900 the Santa Fe Railroad started things by laying its tracks on a causeway across the mudflats and sloughs that would become the Richmond flatland, through a tunnel under the Potrero Hills to a transcontinental terminal at Ferry Point. A year later Standard Oil began a huge refinery on the north slope of the Potrero. Two towns started, East Yard on the slope between the refinery and the tunnel, and Richmond on the flats along the west end of the present main drag, MacDonald Avenue. (A. S. MacDonald sold the Santa Fe its land and platted Richmond.) The towns combined, incorporated, and expanded east toward the mainland hills in 1905.

Industry prospered. Four decades of aggressive port development made Richmond the number two harbor on the Pacific Coast by the 1940s. Available space, harbor facilities, natural geography, and supporting

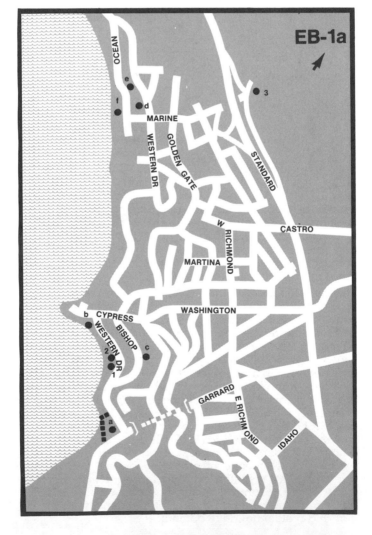

industrial base made Richmond an "arsenal of democracy" in World War II. The West Coast assembly plant which Ford had opened in 1931 became the Richmond Tank Depot. Starting in 1940, Henry Kaiser's Todd-California Company built four mammoth shipyards and, practically overnight, was launching a ship a day. Scores of other war plants boomed. Together they employed 130,000 war workers. Population soared. In three years it quadrupled from less than 25,000 people to about 100,000. From 1941 to about 1943 about 25,000 emergency dwellings were constructed. Today, thirty years later, derelict shipyard cranes mark the inner harbor skyline seen from Route 17, silent reminders of Richmond's brief glory.

The War transformed Richmond. For a few brief years a vast, incredibly busy, boom town sprawled across the flatland and the filled-in sloughs from the Potrero to the San Pablo corridor below the Mira Vista Hills of El Cerrito. After the war much of it was abandoned. Kaiser closed up. Ford moved to Milpitas. The newly affluent white working housing attracted low income people. Blacks from the South who came during the war to work the shipyards had no place else to go. Yet a remarkable optimism prevailed, symbolized first by the ambitious civic center built at the war's close (4) and later by a notable sequence of housing and renewal projects that have refashioned much of the boom town area (5, 6, 7, 8, 9).

Recently the oldest part of the town, once East Yard now called Point Richmond, on the saddle of the Potrero Hills, has become an "in" place to live, eat, and shop. Old houses, stores, restaurants, and churches have been painted up and otherwise revived make an oasis looking down on a landscape of refineries, rail yards and deserted harbor works. A generation ago people crossed the saddle and started building on the Bay side. To get there take Garrard Boulevard through the tunnel to Western Drive. (A tiny, thoughtfully placed park, Keller Beach (a), on the water's edge at this intersection offers a rest stop, a place to picnic, and a smashing view of the City across the Bay.

● 1. **House** 1939; R. M. Schindler
125 Western Dr.

A rare design by a famous Southern California architect, the walls of this small house were originally sheathed in roofing felt held in place by horizontal wood strips.

2. **House** 1935; W. W. Wurster
215 Western Dr.

All things considered, possibly the finest of the small Wurster houses of the 1930s. Only the fact that the walls are made of concrete unit masonry instead of wood detracts from the classic Bay Region quality of this pair of pavilions set in a beachfront eucalyptus grove. To see it best, look into the board fenced yard from the extreme northwest corner.

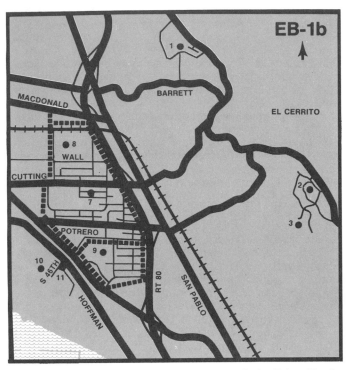

Nearby at 111 Western Dr. is a neat little John Funk-designed house of 1942 (b), and visible to the north from in front of the Wurster house is a white, Harvard-box style residence by Donald Olsen built in 1957 (c). The address of the Olsen house is 221 Bishop, but from that street only the plywood, double-barrel-vault carport is visible.

Western Dr. is discontinuous. In the next section at 331 there is a brand new, zoomie teepee-shaped house shingled in shiny scales of black plastic designed by

Walter T. Brooks (1971) (d), next door at 339 a characteristically modest Bay Region house of 1950 by Serge Chermayeff with a 1966 addition by Ernest Born (e). One house below the last segment of Western Dr. deserves note: a fine, weensy, Wrightian fancy by Olaf

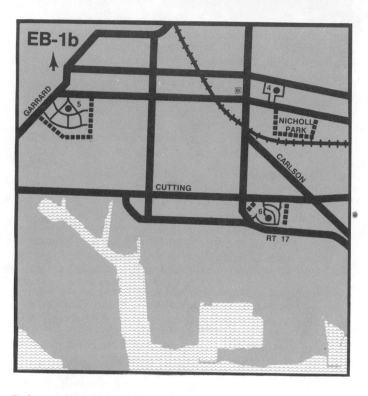

Dolstrand at 612 Marine Ave., completed in 1969 (f).

3. Chevron Research Laboratory Bldg. 1967
McCue, Boone, Tomsick
Standard Dr. inside the Standard Oil Refinery gate.
Across the freeway approach to the Richmond-San Rafael Bridge from Point Richmond, this six-story concrete structure stands out against the chemistry set clutter of the refinery. The building is a 1968 A.I.A. Honor Award design that derives its articulate form by expressing the laboratory services on the exterior of the building.

photo: Morley Baer

Back in Point Richmond, bits of old East Yard remain, now refurbished, in the area around the triangular village square (i). A block up West Richmond Street, the town's first two churches still stand next to each other, the shingled Our Lady of Mercy, and the midwestern-looking brick First Methodist (truly first, built in 1906) (j). An early group of railroad workers' houses, two block-long facing rows of cottages on Idaho Street across the tracks from the square, have mostly survived 70-odd years of remodeling (k).

4. **Civic Center** 1947-49; Milton Pflueger
Richard H. Vaughn, landscape arch.
Barrett & Nevin Sts., 25th to 27th Sts.

A monument to post-war confidence in the most perfectly characteristic style of the time. View the axial composition from Nevin St., walk up the middle under the City Hall to Barrett, turn left and visit the ingratiating art gallery and teaching center.

5. **Atchison Village** 1941-42
S of MacDonald Ave. bet. Garrard & 2nd Sts.

This World War II housing project offers an object lesson in the meaning of housing quality. It demonstrates that environmental concern and tender, loving care can make the difference between decent housing and a slum.

This beautifully preserved emergency housing serves to introduce the next four entries. Taken together, they provide an instructive passage in the design of government-aided project housing and one of the few successes in the otherwise pretty sorry history of urban renewal in Northern California. Serious students will want to examine the Richmond accomplishment.

6. **Easter Hill Village** 1954; DeMars & Hardison
Lawrence Halprin, landscape arch.
Bet. Cutting & Hoffman Blvds., 25th to 28th Sts.

A widely honored public housing project built on the ruins of a hill Kaiser demolished to make fill for his shipyards. The rock-strewn site design gives special character to the plan. This project, in which the architects tried hard to avoid the project look, earned epithets like "planned chaos" and made some view DeMars' work as anti-architecture. Twenty years of hard use show—be prepared.

7. **IB Project** 1957; DeMars & Hardison
Cutting Blvd. to Fall St., 45th to 49th Sts.

As an experiment to test the possibilities for in-fill renewal housing on land made vacant by clearing barracks-type emergency housing, the city built this little project without federal aid. As such, it represents a milestone in local concern and environmental responsibility. The developer who built it, Barrett Construction Company, employed the same architects who had done Easter Hill (6). They carried their ideas about planned chaos a step farther. Note the occasional pre-war house that has been saved and incorporated into the plan. These are all owner-occupied dwellings even though some are attached row houses.

8. **Potrero Urban Renewal Project** 1960-; Phase 1 & 2, Hardison & DeMars; Phase 3, Hardison & Komatsu; John F. Kennedy Park, Osmundson & Staley; other landscaping by Royston, Hanamoto, Beck & Abey

    Most of this area has been developed in various types of single-family, owner-occupied housing by various designers and builders except for the large site devoted to the high school. On one tract of Potrero project land, Barrett Construction Company and its architects continued the effort to produce a low-cost, vernacular, in-fill residential architecture. Note especially the block between 45th and 49th (1) across Cutting Blvd. from the Pilot Project (7).

9. **Eastshore Park Renewal Project** 1952-71 Hardison & DeMars

    Another area of wartime barracks-type housing cleared and mostly developed in single-family, owner-occupied dwellings. The main public open space of the renewal area, Eastshore Park from which the project gets its name, has been nicely developed by landscape architects, Royston, Hanamoto, Beck & Abey, 1970 (m). A rather interesting subsidized project built by the Marimont Foundation lies in this area. Designed by Hardison & Komatsu, it is called Crescent Park and was completed in 1970 (n).

10. **University of California Richmond Field Station** 1968; Marquis & Stoller; **Materials Testing Lab.** 1965; Skidmore, Owings & Merrill

    The great S.O.M. testing lab looms up from the trees to mark this satellite of the Berkeley campus.

11. **Stauffer Chemical Company Office Bldg.** 1961 Gerald McCue; Sasaki, Walker, landscape arch. 1200 S 47th St.

    Foursquare concrete and glass structure which exhibits the high quality of McCue's youthful work.

EL CERRITO

El Cerrito occupies the eastern edge of the Mexican land grant given Don Francisco Castro about 1823. The rancho covered all of the Richmond peninsula from the Berkeley Hills, then called Mira Vista, on the east, to the Potrero Hills at Point Richmond on the west, between the Peralta grant at what is now the Alameda County line and Pinole to the north where the Martinez rancho began.

The adobe built by Don Francisco was enlarged to fourteen rooms by his son, Don Victor, who turned it into the center of a developing agricultural-commercial settlement which later became the town of El Cerrito, the "little hill," whose namesake lies to the south in

Albany. The adobe suffered many transformations including that of auto trailer court and no longer exists. El Cerrito has become a low density, residential community whose homes spread evenly across the flatland and up over the hills. It merges with Albany, a former embarcadero for ferries to San Francisco, incorporated in 1908 in Alameda County.

12. Mira Vista Elementary School 1951
J. C. Warnecke
Mira Vista Dr. & Hazel St.
Beautiful siting and long-linked gable roofs distinguish this much published school.

13. House 1955; Donald Olsen
1366 Brewster Dr.
The clear articulation of frame and glass accented by a sculptural stairway is appropriate to the wooded site.

14. House 1949-55; Roger Lee
8300 Buckingham Dr.
A large house typical of Bay Region design of the 1950s with spectacular site and view. It is best seen from the intersection of Contra Costa and King Drive.

15. First Unitarian Church 1961
Wurster, Bernardi & Emmons
1 Lawson Rd.
A large church in the Post-and-Beam style originated by this firm. The pulpit and candlesticks were designed by Nancy Genn.

ALBANY (not mapped)
House 1960; George Homsey
899 Hillside
A prototype house of the Bay Region style of the 1960s; essentially a vertical box cut apart and reassembled.

HERCULES

On the San Pablo Bay between Richmond and the Carquinas Straits is the town of Hercules, founded in 1869 to make dynamite for the gold miners. It has been a manufacturing center for explosives ever since. There is nothing here of great architectural interest, but those whose nostalgia for the 19th century embraces its typical company town will find pleasure in this almost military composition of simple white frame houses dotted over the hillside. It is also the starting place for the beautiful Franklin Canyon Rd. which goes eastward toward Martinez.

VALLEJO

At the first convention of the legislature of the future state of California in 1848, General Mariano Vallejo, Senator from Sonoma, offered his land on the Carquinez Straits as the site of the new capital. With the land he offered money to build the town and the capitol. By 1853, Vallejo's failure to produce the statehouse caused the legislators to move to Benicia instead. Consequently the town owes more to the location of the Mare Island Navy Yard, established in 1854, and to the acquisition of the rail terminus for the Sacramento Valley than to the good general, who left only his name.

In the railroad-run decade of the 1870s, great things were forecast for Vallejo—principally that it would surpass Oakland—but this also was false prophecy. By 1880 the place had settled for 6,000 souls. It was this modest town that experienced the stunning World War II invasion of shipyard workers who were housed in every available place including virtual cities built overnight, like Chabot Terrace, Wurster & Bernardi, 1942, which provided 3,000 units of housing but no schools.

Post-war abandonment ensued leaving downtown pretty much worn out. Like so many Bay area boom towns, Vallejo turned to urban renewal. The result: a lot of clearance and a brave plan with a new business district and waterfront park, Marina Vista, designed by Royston, Hanamoto, Beck & Abey, in 1967. The designers tried to unify the new building with set-backs and two-story colonades, but the individual building architects resisted. In the resulting mish-mash one notices first the most assertively individual building, the Redwood Bank, 1971, by Smith, Barker, Hanssen,

at 303 Sacramento St., a nice enough piece of contemporary design, but a confounding of the urban design idea. The main contemporary civic monument is the John F. Kennedy Memorial Library, 1970, by Marquis & Stoller/Beland & Gianelli, at Santa Clara and Georgia Sts.

The hill east of downtown, roughly bounded by Sonoma, Capitol, El Dorado, and Georgia Sts., is a residential remnant of old Vallejo. At 639 Georgia St. is a slightly remodeled Victorian Gothic cottage, c.1870. Just beyond it at 705 is a typically complicated Eastlake exercise of the 1890s. A drive around the hill reveals other interesting examples of late 19th and early 20th century design. Of particular note is the Victorian Gothic house at 918 Sutter St., which displays in its scale and jigsawed decorative detail a delicacy more typical of its eastern counterparts.

At 110 Admiral Callahan Lane (on the east side of Hwy. 80) is a two-story clapboard house, c.1860, which is part Greek Revival, part Italianate. Next to the house is a characteristic Wood California tank and well house.

LAFAYETTE
ORINDA

Behind the ridge that separates the shore communities from the valley to the east lie the commuter towns of Contra Costa County: Orinda, Lafayette, Walnut Creek and Concord. As recently as World War II they were rural settlements reached by the Caldecott Tunnel begun in 1933. Now the interstate freeway system connects them with Oakland and San Francisco through two new tunnels, and subdivisions and shopping centers have largely replaced the walnut groves and orchards. The heavily wooded hills of the older residential areas of Orinda and Lafayette hide many fine houses from the eyes of the tourist. One which can be seen from the road is a house which Charles Moore designed for himself at 33 Monte Vista Rd. in Orinda, in 1962 **(1)**. This deceptively simple white frame box with hip roof and sliding barn doors has the kind of intricately compartmentalized interior associated with the work of this architect. In the original plan it was to be one of four pavilions set formally around a courtyard.

photo: Morley Baer

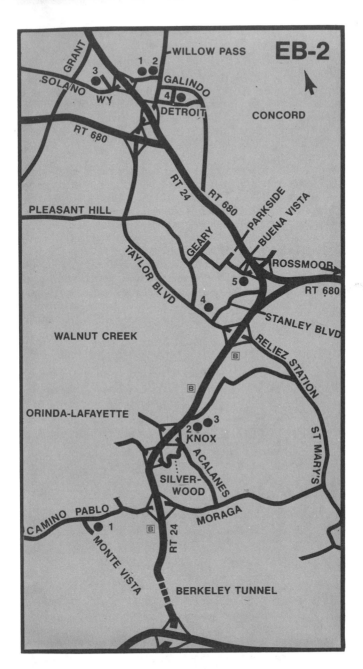

Eastward in Lafayette is the Lafayette-Orinda United Presbyterian Church on Knox Dr., designed by Rockwell & Banwell in 1966 with stained glass windows by Mark Adams **(2)**. Prominently set on the hillside, the formidable exterior of this church is matched by an interior of uncommon strength whose roof truss is clearly articulated by handsome joinery.

Nearby is a residential development with a number of houses by the prolific firm of Ian McKinley & Assoc. Nos. 59, 63. 65, 71, 72, 76, 79, 80, 83, 95 & 99 are notable. They were designed from 1961-63 **(3)**.

photo: Harrington-Olsen

Acalanes Union High School, 1200 Pleasant Hill Rd. in Walnut Creek was designed by Franklin & Kump with additions which spanned a period from 1939-1955 **(4)**. It stands as both prototype and pinnacle in the evolution of the one-story, modular, open-plan California High School: a model that changed design around the world. With Carmel High School, this complex represents Ernest Kump's pivotal contribution to the type. The many additions—only the western tier of classrooms, the library, and the small gym were in the original—demonstrate the perfect flexibility of the planning concept. Details and materials reflect the Southern Californian International Style of the 1930s. Their unaffected quality shines out today. A remarkable school board and maintenance staff have creatively polychromed the buildings, and achieved an almost Japanese perfection in the courtyards.

Trinity Lutheran Church, Belluschi/Skidmore, Owings & Merrill; 1956, stands at 2317 Buena Vista, a short distance off Rt. 680 **(5)**. It is a well-done hall church with indirect day-lighting and a handsome organ.

6. Rossmoor Leisure World 1960-65;
Callister & Payne
Rossmoor Pkwy. at Tice Valley Blvd.
One of the largest and most famous retirement communities in California. Not open to the public.

7. Tice Valley Elementary and High School 1964
John Lyon Reid & Assoc.
Tice Valley Rd. at Rossmoor Pkwy.

CONCORD
This rapidly sprawling residential community with thriving manufacturing and shipping industries still contains two moments of its early past: **(1)** Don Salvio Pacheco Adobe, 1835, on the Central Plaza; **(2)** Fernando Pacheco Adobe, 1834, 3119 Grant at Solano St. The first is a two-story adobe now much altered; the second was reconstructed in 1941 and is the perfect picture of the earth-bound adobe in a still rural setting. Both were built by the family who originally settled the area.

3. **Concord Civic Center: Administration and Municipal Court Bldgs.** 1966: Ernest J. Kump. **Library** 1959; Donald Powers Smith. **Recreation Building** 1963; R. W. Ratcliff. W. Willow Pass Rd. bet. Parkside and Esperanza.

4. **Taxco** 1970; John Field/Field, Bull, Volkman & Stockwell
Laguna & Detroit Ave.
140 units of white stucco housing in contemporary Mediterranean style whose well-designed site plan creates courtyard spaces for the units.

MARTINEZ

Martinez was named for Ignacio Martinez, retired Comandante of the San Francisco Presidio, whose agent, Col. William Smith, laid it out in 1847. In 1850 it became the seat of Contra Costa County because of its location on the Suison Bay. It quickly developed important fishing, canning, and oil industries. The Civic Center contains some good examples of WPA Moderne, and a notable Courthouse of 1901.

The major monument is the John Muir House, c.1860, 2 miles south of Martinez near the junction of Alhambra Ave. & Highway 4. It is a two story Italianate house. Nearby in the park is the two story Vicente Martinez adobe, built in 1849.

The towns of Pittsburgh and Antioch, both begun in 1849, are the locations of large industrial plants strung along the waterfront area of the Sacramento River Delta. Pittsburgh has the more colorful history, having been laid out by William Tecumseh Sherman and named, with considerable shortsightedness, The City of New York of the Pacific by the Yankee soldiers who first settled there. It became Pittsburgh because of the Pittsburgh Coal Co. established there about 10 years later. Until recently it possessed a remarkably substantial central business district built up in the first decades of the 20th century, but the area is scheduled for demolition as part of a major urban renewal project. Both towns are more interesting from a sociological rather than an architectural point of view, being examples of abandonment by the affluent classes who have fled to the newer housing developments of central Contra Costa Co.

BRENTWOOD

On the north side of Marsh Creek Rd. about 4 miles south of Brentwood is a lonely monument picturesquely sited in a valley with a backdrop of mountains. It is the John Marsh house, built in 1856, by Thomas Boyd. The house is a large Gothic Revival building with a square Italianate tower.

DANVILLE

Danville entered history in 1852 with the arrival of Daniel Inman who named it after Danville, Ky. It was the center of an important wheat producing area but is now converting to asphalt as the San Ramon Valley develops. The center of town has some pleasant commercial buildings from the turn of the century and a hotel whose owner has made good use of the wreckage of nearby older houses by reassembling their bits and pieces around the backside of the hotel.

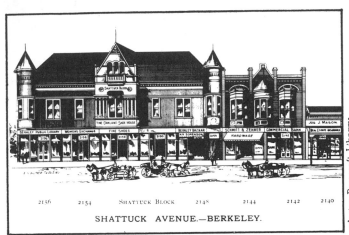

photo: Bancroft Library

SHATTUCK AVENUE.—BERKELEY.

The city of Berkeley developed out of two separate and distinct communities: the flatland settlement of Ocean View oriented to Oakland and the Bay, and the hillside community oriented to the university. The latter community began in 1859, when the Rev. Henry Durant, founder of the College of California, and an academic committee purchased a 160 acre tract for the future location of the College, then in downtown Oakland. Feeling that urban bustle was out of concert with academic pursuits, the group sought and found in the hills to the north the ideal, arcadian setting. To partially finance the purchase, a townsite of one acre lots was platted in the usual gridiron plan and settlement began. One of the first pieces of business of the new institution was the appointment of a Naming and Planning Committee which recommended a system of north-south "streets" named for famous American scientists and east-west "ways" named for famous men of letters. After many proposals, the town was finally named after Bishop George Berkeley whose line "Westward the course of empire takes its way" seemed sufficiently stirring to the founding fathers. In 1866 Frederick Law Olmsted was hired to plan the campus and the surrounding area. He proposed winding streets unconnected by cross streets with lots grouped in five sub-areas around open recreation and social spaces. However, the only feature which survived the relentless march of the gridiron scheme is University Ave., the central axis he drew in line with the Golden Gate.

In 1878 Berkeley was incorporated with the town of Ocean View. The large strip of open fields that separated the communities was gradually filled in by steady residential-commercial development, but unlike Oakland, Berkeley has avoided metropolitan ambitions. In 1916 a piecemeal zoning ordinance with eight zoning classifications permitted 20% of the owners of frontage to determine by petition the character of the rest of the block. Since more than 90% of the buildings were single family residences the natural tendency of like to choose like meant that Berkeley has called itself "the City of Homes" ever since.

Berkeley

The northwestern area of Berkeley from El Cerrito south to Eunice St. is laid out in a series of contour streets converging at the Arlington Circle, bisected by Marin Ave. which then climbs straight to the top of the ridge. The older homes date from the turn of the century when the area was rolling meadowland. Residential sections like Thousand Oaks and Cragmont, planned by Mark Daniels in 1905, developed with houses set on moderate-sized lots. Although there has been a steady infilling of houses to the present day the dominant architectural character is eclectic.

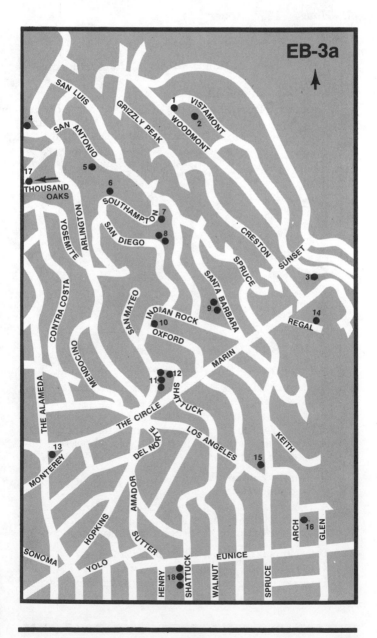

EB-3a

1. **House** 1968; Richard C. Peters
   541 Woodmont

2. **House** 1968; Richard C. Peters
   574 Vistamont
   Two houses which show the contemporary interest in the theme and variation of the vertical "box."

3. **House** 1954; Joseph Esherick
   2727 Marin Ave.
   Flattened gable roofs with broad, over-hanging eaves give this house a Japanese look, often seen in the Bay Region Post and Beam Style of the 1950s.

4. **House** 1957; Roger Lee
   1801 San Antonio Ave.
   Typical Bay Region design of the 1950s.

5. **John H. Spring House** 1913-14; John Hudson Thomas
   1960 San Antonio Ave.
   Thomas' personal version of the classical, Beaux Arts house; the result is closer to Wagner and the Viennese than to McKim, Mead and White.

6. **Jeralemon House** 1923; Bernard Maybeck
   168 Southampton
   Built immediately after the 1923 fire, this house of semi-fireproof materials has an interesting plan in which the entrance is a "hyphen" between the house and a studio.

7. **Nachtreib House** Warren Perry
   111 Southampton
   A personalized Spanish-Colonial Revival design; next door at 117 is another impressive Spanish-Colonial design with a complex interlocking roof.

8. **Two Houses** 1952 & 1956; Donald Olsen
   771 & 775 San Diego Rd.
   Two early designs by an untypical Bay Region architect. 771 is the architect's own house.

9. **Jones House**   1914; Carr Jones
   822 Santa Barbara
   Hagopion House   1916; Carr Jones
   830 Santa Barbara
   The first and second houses designed by this architect, a student of Maybeck. Both represent an interesting adaptation of the Swiss Chalet style with basement walls battered for earthquake-proofing and windows framed in horizontal bands.

10. **Fleager House**   c.1911; John Hudson Thomas
    915 Indian Rock Rd.

11. **Pratt Houses**   1911; John Hudson Thomas
    800 Shattuck Ave. at Indian Rock Rd.; 959 Indian Rock Rd.; 961 Indian Rock Rd.
    These three houses are excellent examples of Thomas' design during the period when his work comes closest to that of the Austrian Secessionists.

12. **Little house**   1914; Purcell & Elmslie
    832 Shattuck Ave.
    The only work on the west coast by this well known midwestern Prairie firm; this small cottage was doubled in size after it was built.

13. **Firehouse No. 4**   1962; Robert W. Ratcliff
    Alameda at Marin
    Although made of concrete, this is really a circus tent used as a firehouse.

14. **House**   1968; Donald Olsen
    861 Regal Rd.
    A stark, simple exterior with a spatially dynamic interior.

15. **House**   1914; T. C. Peterson
    1104 Spruce St.
    Although designed by an architect who had recently arrived from the east, this is one of the best local examples of a large house done in the California Craftsman Style.

16. **Schneider-Kroeber House** 1907; Bernard Maybeck
1326 Arch St.
Maybeck's largest house in the Swiss Chalet Style with scroll-sawn balconies and broad, gracefully bracketed eaves.

17. **House** c.1936; 1855 Thousand Oaks
A two-story Moderne house close to the International Style.

18. **Flagg Houses** 1901-1906; Bernard Maybeck
1200, 1208, 1210 Shattuck Ave.
These three houses are variations on the Swiss Chalet theme. 1200 is perhaps the most interesting for its combination of board-and-batten with shingle siding and elegant eave brackets. 1208 was originally a one-story library-study, and 1210, built for a daughter, is a variation with a pronounced vertical emphasis.

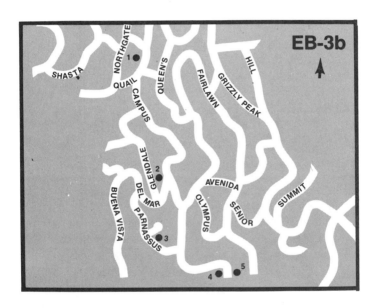

1. **House** 1939; John Funk
1212 Campus Dr.
1939 is a startling date for this timeless modern house.

2. **House** 1963; Richard C. Peters/Peter Dodge
141 Del Mar Ave.
A white box cantilevered over a hillside. The interior spaces open to a court which functions as a light well for a somewhat sunless site.

3. **House** 1939; Gardner Dailey
95 Parnassus Way
A good example of Dailey's design in the late phase of the Streamlined Moderne.

4. **House** 1963; Moore, Lyndon, Turnbull, Whittaker
   1590 Campus Dr.
   A Berkeley-little-boxes-on-stilts-on-the-hillside design by the firm that made them famous. The
   house was not completed as designed.

5. **House** 1968; James Alcorn
   1589 Campus Dr.
   A clean, vertical box design.

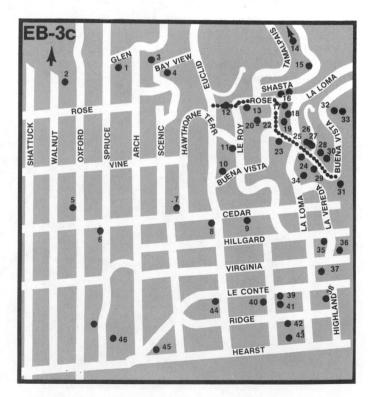

1. **Dempstor House** 1907;
   2204 Glen at Spruce
   This imposing structure designed by its owner of
   heavy timbers, was one of many built after the
   earthquake which used a framing system designed to resist seismic forces.

2. **Napoleon Bonaparte Byrne House**   1868;
   1301 Oxford St.
   This considerably altered Bracketed Italianate villa is the oldest house of architectural distinction in Berkeley.

3. **House**   c.1924; Henry H. Gutterson
   1321 Bayview Pl.
   Yet another Berkeley Swiss Chalet enlivened by folk-derived stenciled designs.

4. **Senger House**   1907; Bernard Maybeck
   1324 Bay View Pl.
   What appears to be the main entrance of this house was actually designed for ceremonial occasions only. The real front door opens directly onto a public sidewalk while the major part of the house turns its back to the street and faces a large private garden.

5. **Boudrow House**   c.1893; 1536 Oxford St.
   Fate has happily preserved this large house in Queen Anne-Eastlake Style as a welcome moment on an otherwise drably modernized street.

6. **Hillside Club**   1924; Mark White
   2286 Cedar St.
   Although no longer a cultural symbol this building by Maybeck's brother-in-law recalls the quiet aura of Berkeley's golden age.

7. **Van Deusen House** 1938; William Wilson Wurster
1598 Hawthorne Terr.
A deliberately unpretentious design typical of Wurster's early work. It sits very discreetly on its corner site.

8. **Foulds House** 1928; Henry H. Gutterson
1600 Euclid
This house is the best expression of Gutterson's personal mode: an unassuming but distinctive combination of elements from the California adobe and the Swiss Chalet. The corner bench at Euclid and Cedar is a rare example of a design contribution to the amenity of the street.

9. **House** c.1925; 2532 Cedar St.
Pueblo Revival with a pinch of the Midwestern Prairie style.

10. **Kennedy House** 1923; Bernard Maybeck
Euclid Ave. and Buena Vista Way
Spanish tile and stucco blend with Gothic detail in this colorful double residence linked by a bridge. The split gable roof, replaced after the fire, originally terminated in trellis work and provided a skylight which ran the length of the ridge.

11. **House** c.1930; Carr Jones
1500 Le Roy Ave.
A story-book house in a convincing, if fanciful, vernacular.

12. **Rose Walk** Bernard Maybeck, 1913; Henry Gutterson, 1925-36
North Berkeley's perfectly planned environment compressed into one block. Maybeck designed the walk with its concrete retaining walls in 1913, and it was built with neighborhood contributions. Somewhat later it was acquired by Mr. and Mrs. Frank Gray who, after the 1923 fire, hired Henry Gutterson to design one and two family houses on its north side. These were designed in consultation with Maybeck and are ingeniously sited to provide private spaces and a general air of gracious living on a small scale. The south side houses came later; the final house at the LeRoy Ave. end was finished in 1936.
Despite the 1923 fire which swept over the ridge, claiming most of the area's houses, the north-of-campus-neighborhood remains one of the city's richest architectural provinces. It was the home of architects such as Bernard Maybeck, Ernest Coxhead, and John Galen Howard, members of a small but special group whose buildings, constructed for the most part during the first 30 years of the 20th century, have achieved lasting fame for their freshness of planning and use of natural materials. These men were also active in the Hillside Club whose members, given to aesthetic and literary as well as social pursuits, were

so keenly aware of its culture-defining role that they offered design counsel to the neighborhood for house and garden, encouraging a simplicity of decor and a preference for the William Morris tradition of handcrafted art. This concern extended to a concept of neighborhood planning which insisted on streets following the contours of the hills and supported the landscaping of public and private property.

A walk following the dotted line on the map should give the visitor a composite picture of pre- and post-fire Berkeley.

13. **Howard House**   1912; John Galen Howard
1401 Le Roy Ave.
Designed in an "L" shape to follow the lot line, this long, horizontal, shingled house shows the degree to which the style of an eastern establishment architect was influenced by western informality. Julia Morgan added a library wing in 1927 so skillfully integrated that it seems part of the original design.

14. **Rowell House**   c.1914; John Hudson Thomas
149 Tamalpais Rd.
Thomas' great house in the Craftsman Style expresses a personal handling of masonry and half-timber.

15. **House**   c.1910; Bernard Maybeck
2465 Shasta Rd.
Once a cottage on the edge of a canyon, Maybeck "Chalet-ed" it into an imposing house of three stories on the canyon side. The two porches on the road have typical Maybeckian wood joinery.

●16. **House**   1959; Warren Callister
2625 Rose St.
House   1958; Warren Callister
2637 Rose St.
Two houses by an influential Bay Area architect. The upper one presents a formal, closed aspect to the street while the lower one is nearly submerged in the hillside. They are more visible from Shasta Rd.

17. **Warren Gregory House** 1903-06; John Galen Howard
1459 Greenwood Terr.

Designed as a country retreat from San Francisco, this house was enlarged after the 1906 earthquake for year-round living, but conserves a rustic character. For 20 years it has been the home of William Wilson Wurster, famous Bay Region architect and former Dean of the College of Environmental Design, who subdivided the property on the flat meadowland opposite the house into seven sites around a grassy common. The architects of the Greenwood Common houses, though not all of the same school, held compatible design philosophies which insured a harmonious relation of place and part.

20. (7) House

18. **Two cottages** 1955; Wurster, Bernardi and Emmons

19. **House** c.1950; Winfield Scott Wellington
1471 Greenwood Terr.

20. **No. 1**   1955; Donald Olsen
No. 3   1954; Joseph Esherick
No. 4   1954; Harwell Hamilton Harris
No. 7   c.1920; R. M. Schindler
No. 8   1953; Howard Moise
No. 9   1954; Henry Hill
No. 10 1952; John Funk

21. **Gregory House** 1908; Bernard Maybeck
1476 Greenwood Terr.

A restrained and elegant box whose roof line echoes the slope on which it perches. The handcrafted, somewhat whimsical aspect of the houses up Buena Vista Way is absent here.

22. **House** 1912; John Galen Howard
1486 Greenwood Terr.
Howard's essay in the Maybeckian Craftsman mode.

23. **Jackson House** 1939; Michael Goodman
2626 Buena Vista Way
A characteristic stripped-down Regency design of the 1930s.

Over the crossroads of La Loma and Buena Vista hangs an imaginary sign saying "Abandon 20th century hang-ups, all ye who enter here!" This is Maybeck country, a land of invention coupling experimental materials and craft tradition. The houses listed below present a vocabulary of Maybeck's design ideas from cutaway eaves as in 2704, to the use of "bubblecrete"—dipped sacks for siding as in 2711, to steep-pitched, shingle roofs, polychromy, and industrial sash in 2733. Maybeck lived in 2711, and designed some of the other houses for members of his family and close friends. Far from being a pure designer he did a large part of the construction himself and particularly enjoyed handfinishing the interiors.

● **24.** **Mathewson "Studio"-House**   1916; Bernard Maybeck
2704 Buena Vista Way

25. **Bernard Maybeck "Sack" House**   1924;
2711 Buena Vista Way

26. **House**   1968; Felix Rosenthal
2717 Buena Vista Way
This house takes its place comfortably between Maybecks, harmonizing by the use of shingle siding and simply expressed post and beam system.

27. **Tufts House**   1931; Bernard Maybeck
2733 Buena Vista Way

28. **Wallen House**   1925; Bernard Maybeck
2751 Buena Vista Way

29. **Gannon House**   1924; Bernard Maybeck
2780 Buena Vista Way

30. **House**   1914; W. C. Hays
2733 Buena Vista Way
A small-scale Florentine palazzo gracefully executed in the Berkeley shingle style.

31. Boynton House 1914; A. Randolph Monroe
2798-2800 Buena Vista Way

This romantic structure has more the quality of a garden ruin than a building. A local landmark both architecturally and culturally, the "Temple of the Wings" functions today as a shrine to the Berkeley that aspired to be the "Athens of the West." Although Maybeck was involved with the original concept, he had no contact with the present building which replaces one by A. R. Monroe destroyed in the 1923 fire.

32. Hume House 1928; John Hudson Thomas
2900 Buena Vista Way

The Spanish castle of popular myth whose convincing design was partly dictated by the wishes of the clients.

33. McCue House 1968; Gerald McCue
2902 Buena Vista Way

A rare house design by a prominent local architect whose major work has been in the industrial field.

34. Lawson House 1907; Bernard Maybeck
1515 La Loma St.

Built for the geologist who discovered the San Andreas Fault, this concrete house was designed to be earthquake-proof. The arched openings of the projecting, second-story porches, the bands of colored stone, and decorative sgraffito patterns give this house a distinctly "Roman villa" quality, grafted, with Maybeck's usual deftness, onto the most modern of building methods.

35. Jensen House 1936; William W. Wurster
1650 La Vereda at Hilgard

One of Wurster's early, "basic-box" designs which achieves perfection of scale.

36. Lezinsky House 1894
1730 La Vereda
Stylistically unusual for the area, this gambrel-roofed colonial house is a landmark from the streets below.

37. House 1905; A. E. Hargreaves
1705 La Loma
Everybody's idea of a Swiss Chalet designed by a man who worked in Maybeck's office.

38. Keeler Cottage 1895; Bernard Maybeck
1770-1790 Highland Pl.
Esther McCoy, in *Five California Architects*, has this to say of the Keeler house: "The various roofs, one a pagoda, had the feeling of a village street whose attached houses had been built by the same carpenter over a period of years."

39. Moody House "Weltevreden" 1899;
A. C. Schweinfurth
1755 Highland Pl.
A barely surviving design by an architect who died young leaving a small body of work of considerable significance. Its sensitive siting and some remnants of its original design can be seen from the streamside. The photo shows it in its original state.

photo: Bancroft Library

40. Oscar Maurer Photographic Studio 1907; Bernard Maybeck
1772 Le Roy Ave.
This building needs no sign saying "studio". Its side elevation is a controlled ramble along the stream.

41. Freeman House 1904-06; Coxhead & Coxhead
1765-69 Le Roy at Ridge
This manorial house derives much of its visual strength from the bold statement of the gambrel dormers. The lath garden houses along the east edge of the property are worth noticing, and the wall on Ridge St. is fine street furniture.

42. **Cloyne Court**   1904; John Galen Howard
2600 Ridge Rd.

    An unadorned shingled block with a pleasant three-sided central court and a strong utilitarian character.

43. **Graduate School of Public Policy (formerly Beta Theta Pi House)** 1899; Coxhead & Coxhead with Bakewell and Brown
Hearst at Le Roy Ave.

    More English in character than other Coxhead designs, this building has fine paneled interiors open to the public. The wing toward Hearst Ave. has been resurfaced.

44. The intersection of LeConte and Ridge Rd. marks a focal point of the **Graduate Theological Union,** an association of seminaries of several religious denominations. The top of "holy hill," as it is called, is occupied by the Pacific School of Religion whose plan and subsequent buildings were designed by Walter H. Ratcliff in 1923-24. Ratcliff also designed the original building of the Church Divinity School of the Pacific and its Chapel in 1926. The two most recent buildings at LeConte and Euclid were designed by Skidmore, Owings & Merrill: Shires Hall in 1957 and Parsons' Hall in 1965. The new library designed by Louis Kahn will be built in 1973.

44. Anthony House 1939; John B. Anthony
LeConte at Hearst Ave.

The best thing that has happened to a "V"-shaped lot since the flat-iron design—in Streamline Moderne.

●45. Normandy Village 1928; W. R. Yelland
1781-83, 1817-39 Spruce

Originally called Thornberg Village, this is really the Mother Goose Village par excellence—must be seen to be believed.

46. House c.1915; 1730 Spruce St.

A good example of the Prairie Style in local translation.

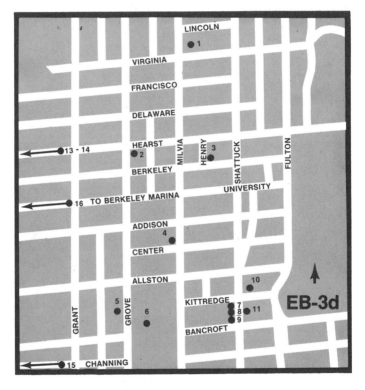

Downtown Berkeley has none of the character of the typical university town. It is rather a grab-bag of commercial buildings with no strong sense of time or place. Around the intersection of Shattuck and Center an attempt has been made to graft a modern curtain-wall image onto the central business district, but within a few blocks, the modest town of low density commercial-residential development resumes. Even the width of Shattuck Ave. with its center strip prevents the two sides of the street from pulling together to create a real "downtown" atmosphere.

1. **Whittier School** 1937; Dragon, Schmidts & Hardman
   Milvia between Virginia and Lincoln Sts.
   A veneer of Moderne decorative motifs applied to a standard educational plant.

2. **House** c.1905; 1905 Grove St.
   A vintage Colonial Revival style house fighting a probably hopeless battle with commercial development.

3. **Fire House No. 2** 1966; McCue, Boone & Tomsick
   Henry and Berkeley Sts.
   A striking mannerist essay in Brut-Concrete.

4. **Milvia Center Bldg. and Berkeley Center Bldg.**
   1966; L. L. Freels & Assoc.
   Milvia at Center St.
   Two buildings which provide some architectural unity for downtown.

5. **City Hall** 1908; Bakewell & Brown
   2134 Grove St.
   A rather free Beaux-Arts rendition of a French provincial town hall.

Berkeley High School (detail)

6. **Berkeley High School** 1938, 1940; Gutterson & Corlett
   Grove St. Buildings and Auditorium
   The most notable buildings in this large high school complex, designed in Streamlined Moderne style, with typical W.P.A. relief sculpture by Jacques Schnier extolling the virtues of work, industry, and science.

7. **Berkeley Public Library**   1930; James W. Plachek
   Shattuck & Kittredge St.

8. **The Pantry**   c.1930; 2270 Shattuck Ave.

9. **United Artists**   c.1930; 2274 Shattuck Ave.

10. **California Theatre**   c.1930; Kittredge & Shattuck
    The above four buildings are also in the Moderne style.

11. **Tupper & Reed Music Store**   1926; W. R. Yelland
    2277 Shattuck Ave.
    A note of the Berkeley "village" of the 1920s in a convincing if imaginary style.

12. **Bank of America-South Berkeley Branch**   1969;
    Charles Stickney
    2001 Ashby Ave.
    A well-executed design in the contemporary Brut-Concrete idiom.

The following two churches are the finest remaining examples of Victorian Gothic church architecture in Berkeley.

13. **Westminster Presbyterian Church (originally)** 1879
    8th & Hearst Ave.

    Church of the Good Shepherd   1878
    9th & Hearst Ave.

● 14. **Niehaus House**   1889; Edward F. Niehaus
    7th & Channing Way
    A striking advertisement for his business, this Stick Style villa with Eastlake detail was built by the owner of the West Berkeley Planing Mills.

15. Harbormaster's Building Berkeley Marina 1966; McCue, Boone & Tomsick

The Berkeley Marina is the first step in the development of a regional shoreline recreational area. The firm of McCue, Boone & Tomsick prepared a master plan which, when completed, will occupy 200 acres of land and water providing berthing facilities for about 800 boats in the present harbor as well as 110 acre boating basin and a waterfront park. The Harbormaster's Building has a steel frame within which walls of wood and glass are hung to allow for shrinkage, movement, wind, and settlement deformations.

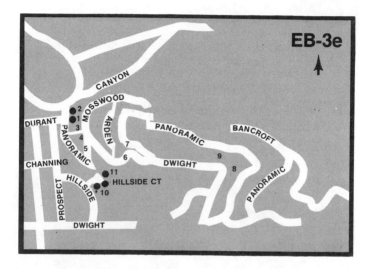

1. Torrey House c.1906; Coxhead & Coxhead
10 Canyon Rd.

This house is Coxhead's farewell to the shingle style. A major aspect of its design is the subtle entrance approach which leads the visitor up a zig-zag path to an entrance at the rear of the house. Only after entering through the livingroom windows could he see the magnificent view of the Bay.

2. Rieber House c.1905; Coxhead and Coxhead (?)
15 Canyon Rd.

Almost certainly the design of Ernest Coxhead, this large house follows the rim of the hill with unusual grace. The angled stair window is an interesting element of the design.

3. Steilberg House 1922; Walter Steilberg
1 Mosswood Lane

Designed by an architect-engineer who was the chief draftsman in Julia Morgan's office for many years.

4. **Boke House**   1903-04; Bernard Maybeck
    23 Panoramic Way
    This modest cottage has a plan, radical for its day, in which the living and dining areas become one through the use of sliding panels.

5. **House**   1929, Walter Steilberg; and 1954, Howard Moise
    69 & 71 Panoramic Way
    Originally a one-story house, the second-story addition complements the design and continues the fine tradition of the Berkeley shingle style.

6. **House**   1941; Harwell Hamilton Harris
    3 Arden Rd.

7. **House**   1941; Harwell Hamilton Harris
    255 Panoramic Way
    These two houses by an important architect in the field of residential design were among the most influential in the Bay Area. The upper house is made up of a stack of inverted prisms that seem poised for flight toward the sweeping view. Its extroversion is complemented by the introversion of the house below.

8. **House**   1952; Charles W. Callister
    3456 Dwight Way
    Concrete block piers raise this striking house off the hillside. Floor and roof beams project in a lively rhythm.

9. **House**   1968; R. W. Ratcliff
    3360 Dwight Way
    This "pavilion" house with its long veranda is a frequent design solution for the steep hillside site.

10. **Maxwell houses**   1907; John Hudson Thomas
    14 & 18 Hillside Ct.
    A pair of ingeniously designed Secessionist style houses which share the same entrance garden. The garage of 18 must have been for Cinderella's pumpkin.

11. **House**   c.1915; Julia Morgan
    10 Hillside Ct.
    A Shingle Style house with Classical features.

photo: Bancroft Library

The University of California graduated its first class in 1873. Ceremonies were held in front of the first two buildings, North and South Hall, designed in 1878 by David Farquharson in the Second Empire/Mansard Style. They were sited by the central axis of Frederick Law Olmsted's campus plan of 1866, which later became Campanile Way. For the next fifteen years, campus buildings were unaffected by any plan.

In 1894 Mrs. Phoebe Apperson Hearst became involved in University affairs through a desire to found a school of mining in memory of her husband. Upon the advice of Bernard Maybeck she sponsored an international competition for a new campus plan, which offered a $10,000 prize to the winner. This competition was elaborately presented by Maybeck and Regent J. B. Reinstem throughout the United States and Europe. By the time it was juried in 1899 it had attracted world attention. The winning design, a Beaux-Arts scheme of symmetrically placed plazas connected by major axes could scarcely have been a surprise. The winner, Emile Henri Bénard, declined the post of supervising architect; and the task of developing his scheme fell to John Galen Howard, a member of the fourth place team who then practiced in New York. During Howard's tenure as University Architect, he not only became the author of a revised campus plan and designed a number of the University's buildings, but also founded the Department of Architecture.

Later modifications of Bénard's and Howard's plans have largely ignored the system of axes; even the strongest one which followed Olmsted's University Ave. has been suppressed. For the most part the buildings have been "shoe-horned" into available sites so that it is only occasionally possible to sense an overall organization.

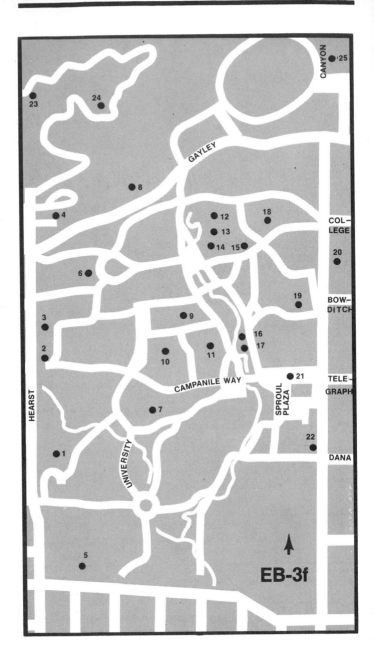

1. **University House** 1900; Albert Pissis

2. **Northgate Hall, "The Ark" (former Architecture Building)** 1906; John Galen Howard

3. **Naval Architectural Building** 1906; John Galen Howard

4. **Stern Hall** 1942 & 1959; Wurster, Bernardi & Emmons

5. **Warren Hall** 1955; Masten & Hurd

Hearst Mining Bldg.

6. **Hearst Mining Building** 1907;
John Galen Howard
Howard came to the University originally to design this building which later became one of the chief anchors of his master plan. The design combines a graceful Mediterranean Renaissance exterior with a fascinating steel arch and tile dome interior. The multiple chimneys house fume hoods and furnace flues, built independently of the building structure so as to be easily replaced.

7. **Moffitt Library** 1971; John C. Warnecke & Assoc.

8. **Hearst Greek Theatre** 1903; John Galen Howard; 1957 addition, Ernest Born

9. **Sather Tower** 1914; John Galen Howard

10. **Doe Library** 1911-1918; John Galen Howard

11. **South Hall** 1878; David Farquharson

12. **Women's Faculty Club** 1923; John Galen Howard

13. **Senior Men's Hall** 1906; John Galen Howard

14. **Faculty Club** original portion by Bernard Maybeck 1902; additions in 1903-04 by John Galen Howard, 1914 & 1925 by Warren Perry, and 1959 by Downs & Lagorio

Hearst Gym

15. **Hertz Hall** 1958; Gardner Dailey
16. **Pelican Building** 1957; Joseph Esherick
17. **Art Gallery (former power house)** 1904; John Galen Howard

18. **Wurster Hall** 1965; DeMars, Esherick and Olsen

19. **Phoebe Apperson Hearst Memorial Gymnasium for Women** 1925; Bernard Maybeck and Julia Morgan

20. **University Art Center** 1970; Mario Ciampi

21. **Sproul Plaza Student Union Complex:** Dining Commons, Student Union, Zellerbach Auditorium, and Eshleman Hall 1965; DeMars & Reay

●22. **Unitarian Church** 1898; A. C. Schweinfurth
Dana & Bancroft Ave.

Not designed for University use, this church is a landmark in the history of Bay Area architecture. The most distinctive elements of this low, shingled structure with broad gabled roof are the large circular window on the west end and the porches on the north and south ends supported by unpeeled redwood logs.

23. **Lawrence Hall of Science** 1965; Anshen & Allen
Canyon Rd. North & Grizzly Peak Blvd.

24. **Lawrence Radiation Laboratory 88 Inch Cyclotron**
1960; McCue, Boone, Tomsick
University of California

A visual landmark from the streets below but not open to the public.

25. **Strawberry Canyon Recreation Center (University of California)** 1959; Wurster, Bernardi & Emmons
Canyon Rd.

A gracefully sited example of the work of this firm strongly marked by the early California rancho tradition. It houses club and recreation rooms, kitchen, locker rooms, and snack bar for faculty, staff, and students.

photo: Glen Christiansen, *Sunset Magazine*

photo: Glen Christiansen, *Sunset Magazine*   Hearst Mining Bldg.

The heart of the original village of Berkeley still beats most strongly in the south-of-campus area bounded by Bancroft, Fulton, Woolsey, and Piedmont. The first tracts were platted in this area, and the first town hall was located in a house near Dwight Way and College Ave. Socially the area is still strongly tied to the University with much of the student-professor population living in the generous shingled houses set close together in the grid patterned blocks. A walk or drive along the streets of Piedmont, Benvenue, and Hillegass reveals the strong vernacular character of most of the buildings, only now succumbing to L.A. ticky-tacky apartment blocks.

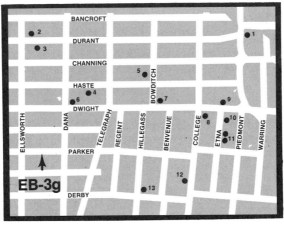

1. Thorsen House (now Sigma Phi Fraternity house)
1908; Greene & Greene
2307 Piedmont Ave.

One of the few houses outside the Pasadena area by this famous firm, it is characteristic in its rhythmic use of long projecting beam-ends, carefully rounded and smoothed. The broad, overhanging eaves cast lively shadows on the shingled walls, and large, uninterrupted glass windows replace the usual casements. The beautiful wood-paneled interiors are remarkable for the flush lighting fixtures integrated into the wood detailing of the ceiling. Notable also are the wrought iron gates and stained glass on the front door and side panels.

2. **Berkeley City Club**   1925; Julia Morgan
2315 Durant Ave.

An imposing variation on the Italian Gothic theme with a strong institutional character.

3. **McCreary House**   1904; 2318 Durant Ave.
A fine example of the Colonial Revival Style.

4. **Rochedale Village**   1971; Ratcliff, Slama, Cadwalader
Haste between Telegraph and Dana St.

A tasteful, well-planned student cooperative housing project clothed in a shingle skin.

5. **Anna Head School (originally)**   1895, Ernest Coxhead (?); 1930, Walter J. Ratcliff
Haste & Bowditch Sts.

As yet undocumented, this Eastern Shingle Style building has been popularly attributed to Ernest Coxhead. The later gymnasium building with its Maybeckian stenciled interior is the work of Walter Ratcliff.

6. **Town & Gown Club**   1899; Bernard Maybeck
2401 Dwight Way

This simply articulated shingle building with delicate outrigger roof bracketing looks about 50 years younger than it is.

7. **First Church of Christ Scientist**   1910, Bernard Maybeck; 1927, Sunday School Addition by Henry Gutterson
Dwight Way & Bowditch St.

One of the Bay Area's greatest architectural monuments, this church is Maybeck's masterpiece, showing his ability to combine such unrelated styles as Gothic and Oriental with an admixture of Romanesque and Craftsman. The interior illustrates his genius for fusing structure and ornament. All this with an imaginative use of such new materials as concrete, cement asbestos board, and industrial sash. Those interested in seeing the interior should call the church office for the hours of public tours.

8. **Newman Center and Rectory**   1966; Mario Ciampi
   College at Dwight Way

   A ponderous, poured-in-place concrete building in the Brutalist style of the 60s.

9. **Paget-Gorill House**   1891-92, Willis Polk; altered in 1910
   2727 Dwight Way

   Originally a half-timber structure with shingled gables, this much altered house has become more typical of the popular image of the Berkeley shingled cottage than of the work of Willis Polk.

10. **Cedric Wright House**   1921; Bernard Maybeck
    2515 Etna St.

    A small, simple but special cottage in a very private place. The studio room called "the barn" was the scene of many gatherings of Berkeley's cultural elite of the day.

11. **Two houses**   c.1910; Julia Morgan
    2531 & 2535 Etna St.

    The same site plan as 2814 & 2816 Derby St. with simpler houses.

12. **St. John's Presbyterian Church**   1910; Julia Morgan
    2640 College Ave.

    A straight-forward yet sophisticated meeting hall church from the architect's Craftsman period. Admirers of the building should address themselves to the congregation which is about to destroy it.

13. **Gifford-McGrew house**   1900; Bernard Maybeck and Charles Keeler
    2601 Derby St.

    This house with its restrained detail has a deceptively simple appearance. To gain an appreciation of its complex massing, the back should be studied from Hillegass.

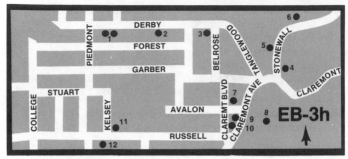

1. **Two houses** 1906 & 1910; Julia Morgan
   2814 & 2816 Derby St.
   A good site plan for congenial neighbors, these two houses face each other at right angles to the street giving each a private entrance.

2. **William C. Hays House** 1908; W. C. Hayes
   2924 Derby St.
   Another pleasantly understated shingled house.

3. **Randolph School (originally)** 1911; Bernard Maybeck
   2700 Belrose Ave.
   Designed as a school and now a private residence. The village-like collection of steep-roofed classroom pavilions opening on terraces presented a planning concept in advance of the times.

4. **Strauss House** 1939; William Wilson Wurster
   8 Stonewall Rd.
   A fine example of Wurster's frankly unpretentious, small house design. The flat roof with wide eave and expressed beam ends, and the crisply detailed balcony are identifying elements.

5. **Farley House** 1940; William Wilson Wurster
   91 Stonewall Rd.
   Another clearly signed Wurster design in his more delicate Regency style.

6. **Robbins House** 1959; Jacob Robbins
   139 Stonewall Rd.

7. **Seldon Williams House** 1928; Julia Morgan
   2821 Claremont Ave.
   A restrained mansion with Venetian Gothic tracery windows.

8. **Claremont Hotel** 1905; C. W. Dickey
   Ashby & Domingo Ave.
   This landmark resort hotel was part of the grand scheme real estate enterpreneur Frank C. Havens had in mind for the development of the East Bay Hills.

9. **House** c.1925; Henry Gutterson
   3016 Avalon Ave.
   Typical of Gutterson's personal eclecticism but more compactly designed for the small corner lot.

10. **St. Clement's Episcopal Church**   1907-08; Burnham & Co. (Willis Polk)
2 2 Tanglewood St.
This humble village church in shingle style is an odd job for this famous Chicago firm. The mystery is explained by the fact that Polk designed it when he headed their west coast office.

11. **Marquis House**   c.1910; 2827 Russell
An enormous house in Mission Revival Style.

12. **Smith House**   1927; William Wilson Wurster
1812 Russell St.
Who else would have thought of doing a miniature Regency Style manor house in rough-sawn redwood painted white? The low entranceway is a highly successful scale-giving element.

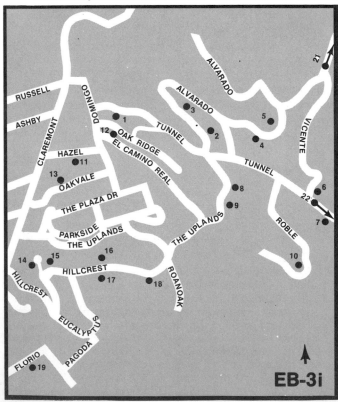

1. **Hoyt House**   c.1917; John Hudson Thomas
   26 Tunnel Rd.
   One of Thomas' infrequent timber houses.

2. **Sclater House**   1910; Louis Christian Mullgardt
   26 Alvarado Rd.
   A stucco bungalow made imposing by a battered-wall base.

3. **Lamberson House**   1942; Wurster & Bernardi
   62 Alvarado Rd.
   A good example of Wurster's simplified Monterey Colonial mode.

4. **House**   c.1925; Clarence Tantau
   190 Alvarado Rd.
   This large residence closely patterned after the courtyard houses of the Spanish Colonial Style has a stable that is hardly credible in the Berkeley hills.

5. **Atkins House**   1915; 215 Alvarado Rd.
   Said to have been designed by the owner, Henry Atkins, with the help of Harry Stearns of Willis Polk's office.

6. **Wintermute House**   1915; John Hudson Thomas
   20 Vicente Rd.
   The romantic curtain of vines on this great house obscures a collection of forms assembled with an abandon that few architects would dare to attempt.

7. **Tantau House**   1927; Clarence Tantau
   228 Tunnel Rd.
   The courtyard plan of this Spanish Colonial Revival Style house is apparent from the road. It should be compared with 190 Alvarado.

8. **House**   1970; Donald Olsen
256 The Uplands
Sited in wooded seclusion, this is a handsome house in the Harvard "box" tradition.

9. **DeMars House**   1951; Vernon DeMars
240 The Uplands
A rare residential design in the Bay Region Style of the 1950s by an architect famous for his work in public housing and the design of the Student Union complex on the University campus.

10. **Chick House**   1913; Bernard Maybeck
7133 Chabot at Roble Rd.
A fine example of Maybeck's mastery of design in wood. The broad gable roof ends in trellising at the gable eaves. Esther McCoy has this to say of it," The Chick house was developed under a gable roof, with particular emphasis on the upper half of the gable ends; it extended two feet beyond the first floor, forming a bonnet around the bank of second floor windows." The material of the gable projections is vertical redwood siding with alternating round and flat battens; the rest of the house is shingled.

11. **House**   1956; Roger Lee
56 Hazel St.
A most attractively sited house in the idiom of the 1950s.

12. **House**   1968; Dimitri Vedensky
20 El Camino Real
One of the few houses on the street that takes advantage of its hillside site.

●13. **Dangan House**   1915; John Hudson Thomas
41 Oakvale Ave.
A composition in roof gables pleasantly sited over a stream.

14. **Meyer House**   1916; John Hudson Thomas
10 Hillcrest Ave.
Stylistically this house falls between Thomas' strong Secessionist work and a comfortable adaptation of the California Bungalow.

15. House   1959; Joseph Esherick
125 Hillcrest Ave.

A stylish stucco house with a sonotube columned entrance and a plan generally typical of Esherick's work of this period.

16. House   c. 1910; 159 Hillcrest Ave.

A fine example of the Craftsman Style designed by a lumberman for himself.

17. House   c.1910; Charles W. McCall
158 Hillcrest Ave.

A well-designed house with a Prairie School tone.

18. Claremont Club   1912; Julia Morgan
214 Hillcrest Ave.

A pleasant and typical clubhouse in Craftsman Style.

19. Smith House   1926; Ernest Coxhead
6451 Florio St.

A Spanish Colonial Revival Style design heavily informed by Coxhead's tour of Southern France during World War I. The carefully designed fenestration makes a highly sophisticated facade.

●20. Talbert House   1965; Moore, Lyndon, Turnbull, Whittaker
141 Strathmore Dr.

One of the first "vertical box" designs by this firm. Because of the steep slope the house has a minimal joint with the ground, after which it "platforms" out to give the living spaces access to the view. It is attached to the road by a "gangplank" entrance.

21. Hiller Highlands   1967-1972; Callister & Payne; Landscape Arch't., Royston, Hanamoto & Beck
Hiller Dr.

A 67 acre planned unit development, ultimately 500 units of townhouses and apartments. Density: eight and one third units to the acre.

The city of Piedmont in the northeastern hill section of Oakland grew first around a horse car line which ran up Piedmont Ave. to the Oakland Cemetery in the 1870s and 80s. As the car lines multiplied wealthy families such as the Crockers and the Requas built residences higher in the hills than before, and Piedmont became the East Bay equivalent of the Peninsula's sections of stately homes. In fact, by 1907 when it was incorporated it boasted 32 millionaires giving it the largest per capita wealth of any community its size in the country. Around 1910 the very large estates began to be carved up into smaller parcels, although the homes built upon them were rarely small. Most of these houses, well exposed to public view because of the small lot size, express a variety of styles and offer a rich hunting ground to the student of eclectic architecture.

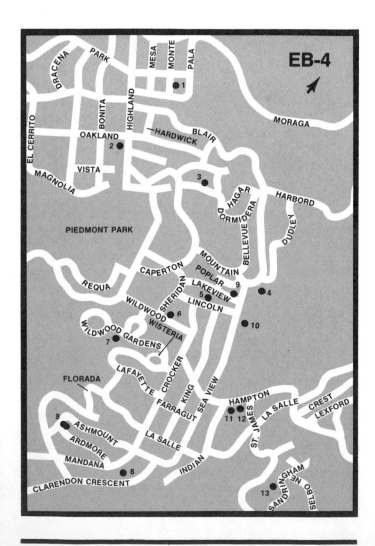

1. **House** c.1915; 1726 Oakland Ave.
   A handsome shingled house with multiple dormers and a roof design strongly reminiscent of the work of the English architect, Charles Voysey.

2. **House** c.1910; 104 Monte St.
   California Craftsman style.

3. **Fore House** 1909; Louis Christian Mullgardt
   444 Mountain Ave.

   One of Mullgardt's finest residential designs, this well-sited house displays such hallmarks of his work as the battered basement wall, banded windows on the stuccoed second story, and shallow gabled roof with wide, overhanging eaves. Compare with the Evans house in Mill Valley.

4. House

4. **Jorgensen House** 1907; Louis Christian Mullgardt
   43 Dormidera St.

   Stylistically related to the California Bungalow, this house makes good use of its site.

5. House

5. **House** c.1925; 37 Lincoln Ave.
   This improbable design is a concoction of Egyptian Revival and French Chateau with Neo-Bulgarian motifs.

6. **Kelly House** 1910; John Hudson Thomas
455 Wildwood Ave.
One of Thomas' largest houses, it commands the hillside impressively.

7. **Wildwood** 1906; Bernard Maybeck, Tiffany & Co., etc.
101 Wildwood Gardens
Designed for Oakland's major developer, Frank C. Havens, the conventional exterior of this house masks an interior of spatial adventure and surface opulence. Though originally designed by Maybeck, nearly all traces of his redwood building have disappeared beneath the successive encrustations of Tiffany & Co., various local decorators, and a host of highly skilled, anonymous Chinese craftsmen. What the house chiefly expresses is Mrs. Havens' fascination with all things Far Eastern.

8. **Three houses**; John Hudson Thomas
1016 Ardmore, 1020 Ashmont, 1121 Mandana Blvd.
These three houses are representative of Thomas' work prior to the '20s which was characterized by the over-scaling of such elements as engaged columns and monumental chimneys.

9. **House** c.1925; Julia Morgan
65 Sea View Dr.
A baronial manor to be compared with 2509 Claremont Blvd. in Berkeley.

10. **Crocker House** 1912; Willis Polk
86 Sea View Dr.
The bold use of classical detail particularly in the broken pediment with oversized scrolls over the entrance mark this as a Polk design.

11. **House** 1941-42; Serge Chermayeff & Clarence Mayhew
330 Hampton Rd.
This period piece design of the 1940s shows how the east coast Harvard "box" was tempered by the more rambling Bay Area style.

12. House c.1920; 320 Hampton Rd.
A fine example of Spanish Colonial Revival with a superb entrance portal.

13. House 1958; Campbell & Wong
111 Sandringham Rd.

EMERYVILLE

Balaam Bros. (orig. Cook Stove Oil Co.) 1940
1350 Powell, Emeryville
A 1930s wooden radio set stuccoed and blown up to building size.

TWELFTH ST—NORTH SIDE

More than any other Bay area city Oakland is the product of the interdependence of land and transportation development. Its first townsite, incorporated in 1854, was platted under the direction of an unscrupulous trio of easterners who gained squatters rights to a tract of land belonging to the rancho of Vicente Peralta. Surveyer Julius Kellersberger laid out a gridiron street pattern for the area bounded by 1st, 14th, West, and Oak Sts. This city grew modestly behind a busy waterfront in the area of the present Jack London Square. Of its three squatter-founders Horace Carpentier became the most infamous by acquiring control of the entire waterfront for a period of 37 years, a contract which not only prevented municipal development of a harbor, but also allowed him to negotiate a land deal with the "Big Four" of the Western Pacific Railroad for the location of the western terminus. The coming of the transcontinental railroad in 1869 inaugurated a period of intense real estate speculation during which most of the great oak groves were sacrificed to residential development and city resources were generally over-extended. By the mid-1870s Oakland had gained a reputation on both coasts as a city of gracious homes and spacious gardens. Its designation as the most popular suburb of San Francisco was a constant frustration to the civic-minded whose city perpetually hovered on the brink of surpassing "The City" across the Bay. While San Francisco had a port, it had no railroad, and in the closing decades of the 19th century the dominance of railroad interests made Oakland's accession seem inevitable. By the mid 1880s Oakland rose to second place in manufacture on the Pacific coast; by 1890 downtown traffic was so congested that the speed of horse-drawn vehicles had to be restricted to 5 miles per hour.

The first period of real civic concern began in 1905 when the city council ordered a plan presented to Mayor Frank Mott by New York planner-landscape architect Charles Mulford Robinson which recommended acquisition of park lands in the city and the hills connected by a system of scenic roadways. The plan was, as usual, too ambitious for the times but its major achievements, the development of park lands around Lake Merritt, has given Oakland its principal distinguishing feature. The recommendation for parks in the hills culminated in the 1933 East Bay Regional Park District Act enabling acquisition of land on utility district property. The present park system stretches from Charles Lee Tilden Park to Cull Canyon park east of San Lorenzo. After the 1906 earthquake Oakland, little damaged in comparison to San Francisco, received a bounty of refugees many of whom moved their businesses as well. Although the city fathers were con-

vinced that the opportunity to surpass San Francisco had at last come, city management lagged behind so that the expansion of facilities necessary to accommodate the influx never happened and most of the businesses moved back to the city within two years. Still Oakland's metropolitan aspirations had received a strong impetus manifested by street improvements, new schools, and a major hotel, the Hotel Oakland, built in 1910. In 1915, after two years of study, a report by the famous German planner, Werner Hegemann, was published which put major emphasis on developing the waterfront, legally acquired in 1911, as a harbor that would bind together railroad and water transport and create an independent zone which would become part of a unified harbor management for the Bay. Little came of the recommendation at first but some of its impact is evident in the fact that today Oakland has the second largest container port in the world. The greatest physical changes to the waterfront area came during World War II: the Alameda Naval Air Station and the Naval Supply Station established in 1941 extended the general land mass by 1500 acres. Since then the Metropolitan Oakland Airport has claimed 1500 acres from the Bay so far, and there are future expansion proposals.

Transportation needs, notably the common use of the automobile, made a further impact on Oakland with the construction of the **San Francisco-Oakland Bay Bridge** in 1936 (EB-5a-**1**). Four and one third miles long, this immense structure includes the only twin suspension bridge span and the largest bore tunnel in the world. The cantilever truss running from Yerba Buena Island toward Oakland was used because subsurface conditions made a suspension span unfeasible. The series of smaller truss spans which complete the bridge cross a shallow portion of the Bay where larger spans would have been extravagant, especially since the entire system was designed for maximum economy. The major figures in the bridge's design were: Charles Henry Purcell, Chief Engineer; Charles E. Andrew, Bridge Engineer; Glen B. Woodruff, Design Engineer; and Arthur Brown, Jr., Timothy Pflueger, and John Donovan, Consulting Architects.

A system of freeways tied to the Bay Bridge and somewhat ruthlessly carved through the northeastern residential areas has given transbay as well as East Bay traffic the means of circumnavigating Oakland without being conscious of any but the most superficial aspects of it. This is unfortunate as the essential character of Oakland was already hard to define. Gertrude Stein's famous remark, "There's no there there," is too easy a summing-up, even though the casual visitor fresh from the exhilarating atmosphere of San Francisco may agree with it. Since nearly a third of Oakland's present housing was built between 1910 and 1920, its architectural character is generally that of stucco or clapboard detached homes, of varying size depending on the district, in the stylistic categories of California Bungalow and Chicago Prairie School with some Classic Revival and English Tudor thrown in. The more contemporary, high density apartment area lies around Lake Merritt while the older housing of the Victorian era, largely razed by redevelopment, is scattered throughout East and West Oakland. Downtown is easily marked by the cluster of high-rise buildings south of the Bay Bridge where the major arteries of San Pablo, Telegraph, and Broadway cut through the grid pattern from the northeast to converge at 14th St. From here north to Grand Ave., west to Lake Merritt, south to the Nimitz Freeway, and east to Market St. lies the core area, which has experienced the pattern of growth, decay, and renewal typical of most American cities.

photo: Calif. Dept. Public Works

West Oakland, an area generally bounded by Market and West Grand Ave. was the "garden city" area which first brought fame to Oakland. At present it is a low-income ghetto with its remaining old 19th century houses hemmed in by industry, railroads, and freeways. Visually it presents the same mixture of the distressing and the interesting which has sparked hope here and elsewhere that renovation, if a magic way could be found to do it, would reclaim the area as a vital part of the city. In fact West Oakland has been in the throes of urban renewal for about ten years with two current projects, Acorn, designed by Burger & Coplans in 1971, and Oak Center, representing the two approaches: razing and rebuilding in the first case and rehabilitation in the second.

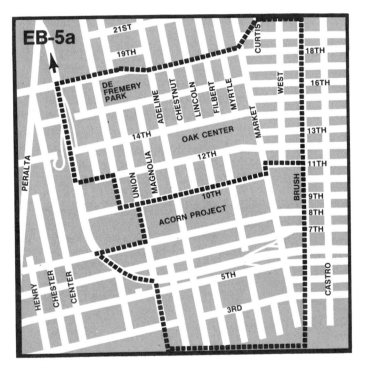

●1. Pardee House   1868; 672 11th St.

The finest remaining example of the Bracketed Italianate Villa Style complete with carriage house and water tower.

2. Commercial Buildings   c.1870-80

400 Block of 9th St. between Washington & Broadway

Oakland's first commercial district, built in response to the coming of the railroad in 1869, sprang up in the blocks stretching north from the station at 7th and Broadway. The 400 block of 9th, a product of preservation through stagnation, is the only one left intact. On the north side of the street starting at Broadway is the Delger Block, 1868-82. Next is the Portland Hotel, formerly Henry House, built in 1877 by Ashmun C. Henry, a prominent banker. The building on the corner of Washington is the former Nicholl House, later the Arlington Hotel Building, 1875-76. On the south side of the street are two brick buildings designed by the architect of the Portland Hotel, William Stokes, in 1865-79. Next at 461-471 is a building which was the Oakland Post Office from 1875-77; it got its stucco facade and ironwork in the 20th century. At the corner of 9th and Broadway is the Wilcox Block, pre-1869, reputed to be Oakland's first brick building, now stripped of its roof ornamentation. From 10th to 9th St. on Broadway and at 721-735 Washington are other buildings of the same vintage. Despite the general skid-row atmosphere, this part of the city is a lively one and contains a variety of food markets and thrift-junk shops among the cheap hotels and money-lending operations.

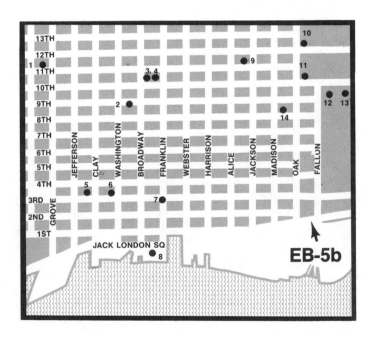

3. **Commercial Building** c.1890; 11th & Broadway
   Simplified Richardsonian Romanesque as is the building around the corner on 10th St. Across the street is an office building in Renaissance style a la McKim, Meade & White.

4. **T & D Theater** c.1905; Matthew V. Politeo
   425 11th St.
   A choice piece of theatrical fancy with elements of Art Nouveau.

3. Commercial Bldg.

5. **Brete Hart Boardwalk**   c.1896; 567-577 5th St.
   Brete Hart lived with an uncle in one of these houses. The group was restored in 1952 as restaurants and small shops.

6. **Western Pacific Station**   1915;
   NW corner 3rd & Washington Sts.
   A small scale version of the Beaux Arts railroad station in concrete.

7. South of the freeway around 3rd and Franklin Sts. is the **old produce area.** The brick warehouses with their corrugated iron and wood sidewalk canopies recall produce areas of the 19th century all across the country. Although it still functions, maintenance is minimal, and redevelopment could deal with it as mercilessly as it did in San Francisco.

8. **Jack London Square**
   Foot of Broadway at the waterfront
   So named because the Last Chance Saloon, a diminutive building now enshrined there, was a favorite haunt of this famous writer and native son. The cabin he occupied while prospecting in the Klondike has been moved here and looks equally like a movie prop. Because the foot of Broadway was the city's first waterfront, the plaza nearby became a social center, a place of famous restaurants and bars. The area declined and the glamorous scene departed, but beginning in 1958 a commercial redevelopment began which has succeeded in making the square the rival of Fisherman's Wharf in San Francisco. A boardwalk running along the water's edge gives the visitor a continuous view of the working port, an opportunity available nowhere else on the Bay, plus the chance to see a vintage fireboat which still steams across to San Francisco to put out waterfront fires.

Architecturally speaking there is little to note; the important thing is that Oakland is reclaiming its waterfront. Further south at the foot of Alice St. a residential and business development called Porto Bello will begin construction this year. The architects are James Babcock & Donald Sandy; landscape architect is Anthony Guzzardo. When completed, this development will link with Oakland Village, now under construction on a site adjacent to Jack London Square, to form a continuous strip with pedestrian walkways. A long range project to link Jack London Square with Lake Merritt by walk and bike ways will be a significant breakthrough of the large scale transportation barriers that separate the city from the Bay.

9. **California State Office Building**   1959
   Warnecke & Warnecke
   1111 Jackson at 12th St.

10. **Court House and Hall of Records**   1935
    W. G. Corlett & J. W. Plachek
    13th and Fallon Sts.
    A perfect piece of P. W. A. Moderne.

Oakland Museum

11. **The Oakland Museum**   1969; Kevin Rocke, John Dinkeloo & Assoc.; Landscape Arch't., Dan Kiley
    Oak between 10th & 12th Sts.

    One of the justly famous buildings of the Bay Area, this museum is also a monument to the civic pride and foresight of Oakland's citizens who approved a bond issue to house three separate museums, Natural History, History, and Art, in one building. The poured concrete structure occupies a four block site sloping down to Lake Merritt; the concept, successfully realized, is that of a park with much of the building underground.

12. **Laney College**   1971; Skidmore, Owings & Merrill
    900 Fallon St.
    A densely built, hard-edged campus for an inner city, vocationally oriented college.

photo: Ezra Stoller

13. **Building**   c.1940; 314 E. 10th St.

Streamlined Moderne, but almost International style in its vocabulary of horizontal banded windows and vertical corner stair tower.

14. **B.A.R.T. Headquarters Building**   1969
Yuill-Thornton, Warner & Levikov
800 Madison St.

A concrete slab building set in a plaza, it houses the main offices of the Bay Area Rapid Transit System.

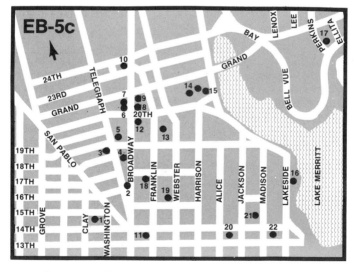

1. **Oakland City Hall**   1914; Palmer, Hornbostle & Jones
SE corner Clay and 12th St.

This highly ornamented building is composed of three tiers crowned with an elaborate top-knot. It recalls McKim, Meade & White's New York City Hall transformed and adapted to the west coast.

2. **The Federal Building** 1913; Benjamin G. Mc-
   Dougall
   Telegraph Ave. and Broadway
   A flat-iron building with a spikey top like a
   French chateau.

Around 20th St. at Broadway and Telegraph is the retail shopping district, remarkable for the fact that many
of the major stores, designed in the Moderne Style of
the 1930s, have not updated their facades. In addition
a program sponsored by the Downtown Property Owner's Association in 1932 fostered the modernization of
stores and business buildings by removing bays and
other irregular features while replacing Victorian
Gothic ornament with Zigzag or Art Deco detail. All
this has made the area a rich field for the fancier of
the Moderne.

3. **Fox Oakland Theater and Office Building** c.1923;
   M. I. Diggs
   1815 Telegraph Ave.
   One of a fast vanishing type of movie palace
   which evoked the mysterious and far-away; it
   has become even more exotic as its surrounding
   architecture has become more simplified.

4. **Singer Shop** c.1930; 1721 Broadway
   Zigzag Moderne with a horizontal band of windows with angled mullions and elegant terra cotta
   ornament above.

5. **Oakland Floral Depot** c.1930;
   1800 Telegraph Ave.
   A single story, black and silver terra cotta building in Zigzag Moderne style with a superb corner
   tower.

6. **I. Magnin & Co.** 1931; 20th & Broadway
   A restrained, dignified green terra cotta building
   of the early Moderne.

10. John Breuner Co.

● **7. Paramount Theater**   1930; Miller & Pfleuger
2025 Broadway

A tile mural billboard building. Its Buck Rogers interiors are being refurbished by Skidmore, Owings & Merrill to house the Oakland Symphony.

8. The Gray Shop   1931; Albert A Froberg
2000 Broadway

The early Zigzag Moderne rendered with almost classic restraint.

9. Barnes Wright Haberdashery   c.1925
2034 Broadway

A perfect period piece of the 20s with a "Ye Olde World" front.

10. John Breuner Co.   1931; Albert F. Roller
22nd & Broadway

Another example of an early Moderne building dressed in terra cotta. See also the office building at 333-339 14th St.

11. Oakland Tribune Building   1923; Edward T. Foulkes
13th and Franklin Sts.

A landmark and for years a symbol of the heart of Oakland.

12. Golden West Savings & Loan   1970; Skidmore, Owings & Merrill
20th & Broadway

A luxurious corporate image on a bargain basement budget. The cast plastic sculpture in the lobby is by James Grant; the wood sculpture in the court is by J. B. Blunk.

13. Blue Cross Building   1972; Skidmore, Owings & Merrill
1950 Franklin St.

14. **Kaiser Center Building** 1959; Welton Beckett & Assoc. **Kaiser Ordway Building** 1970; Skidmore, Owings & Merrill
Lake Merritt

    As the largest property owner in the area Kaiser was able to inaugurate the latest phase in Oakland's commercial development by building this complex. The Kaiser Center Building is a multiple use building containing offices, shops, and a garage. The bright-aluminum, curtain wall building by S. O. M. is the latest increment in the master plan.

photo: Bob Hollingsworth

15. **Buick Showroom (former Anthony Packard Showroom)** 1928; Bernard Maybeck
Lake Merritt

    Also located on the Kaiser property, this late Maybeck design was once in scale with the Lake front buildings. It now sits awkwardly on Kaiser's doorstep and may soon disappear.

16. **Cameron House** 1899; 1426 Lakeside Dr.

    The last relic of the period when stately mansions lined the lake front; the one story additions in the rear of this Italianate house were added when the building housed a museum.

17. **Park Bellevue Towers** 1967; Fisher-Friedman Perkins & Bellevue

    One of the better designed apartment buildings on the lake front.

18. **First Church of Christ Scientist** 1902; Henry A. Schultze
17th & Franklin Sts.

    A small, stone building in Romanesque Revival Style.

19. **Y.W.C.A.** 1915; Julia Morgan
1515 Webster St.

In 1915 Julia Morgan was the official architect for the National Y.W.C.A. in the West. This building, the one in San Jose, and others scattered throughout the West are her designs.

20. **Oakland Hotel** 1910;
Henry Janeway Hardenbugh and Bliss & Faville
270 13th St.

Building this hotel after the earthquake of 1906 was regarded as one of Oakland's first major steps on the path from village to metropolis. Its derelict state is a sad commentary on society's failure to make a creative use of its housing stock.

Scottish Rite Temple 1908; O'Brien & Werner
1433 Madison St.

One of the usual gutsy statements of the Mission Revival Style.

The following buildings are part of the Civic Center located in the area southwest of Lake Merritt:

21. **Oakland Public Library** 1949; Miller & Warnecke
125 14th St.

Streamlined P. W. A. Moderne carried on after World War II.

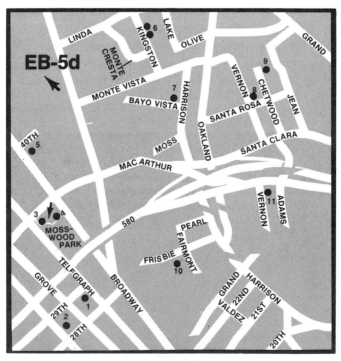

1. **Trinity Episcopal Church** 1892; W. H. Hamilton
29th & Telegraph Ave.

One of the finest remaining examples with unaltered interior of wooden Victorian Gothic Revival church architecture in the Bay Area.

2. **Durant School** 1912; Louis Christian Mullgardt
2820 West St.

   Horizontal hinged windows grouped in projecting picture frame units add unity and scale to this building whose monumental entrance stairway is the principal feature.

● 3. **Moss Cottage** 1864; S. H. Williams
Mosswood Park

   The finest, most elaborately detailed Gothic Revival cottage still standing in California.

4. **Mosswood Park Building** 1971; Stone, Marraccini & Patterson
MacArthur Blvd. & Broadway

   Proof that vernacular commercial architecture can happily swallow Paul Rudolph too.

5. **King's Daughters Nursing Home** 1912
Julia Morgan
3900 Broadway

6. **Two houses** c.1900; 778 & 780 Kingston Ave.

   Two very distinctive shingle houses which appear to have been joined together at one time.

7. **Lock House** c.1911; John Hudson Thomas
3911 Harrison St.

   A bold over-statement of both the favorite forms and decorative detail that Thomas used in his other Secessionist houses.

8. **Newsom House** c.1897; Samuel Newsom
202 Santa Rosa

   A gambrel roofed, shingle cottage by a firm which ran through the entire gamut of late 19th and early 20th century styles.

9. **House** c.1900; end of Chetwood, so. side.

   A small but impressive shingle house whose gabled end contains a central recessed panel within which are paned windows and a segment of the brick chimney.

10. **First Christian Church** 1928; 29th & Fairmont

    A picture-book example of the Spanish-Colonial Revival style in its "pretty" phase.

11. **House** 1909; 205 MacArthur Blvd.

    This large Craftsman style house should be compared with the Thorsen house in Berkeley to see how strongly it is marked by the work of Greene & Greene.

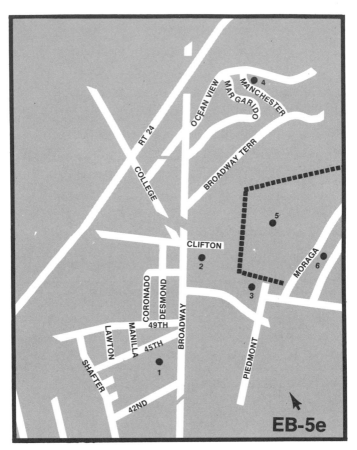

1. **Oakland Technical High School** 1914
   John J. Donovan
   4351 Broadway

   A stripped Classical design with Viennese Secessionist overtones, this building with its long colonnade and ample grounds makes an important place in an otherwise nondescript area.

2. **California College of Arts and Crafts** founded 1907
   5212 Broadway

   One of the oldest colleges of arts and crafts in the country. College Ave. was laid out as the connecting route with the University. The oldest campus building is Treadwell Hall built around 1880; the newest is a Library and Studio Building designed by DeMars & Reay and completed in 1967.

3. **Chapel of the Chimes** 1928; Julia Morgan
   1965; addit.; Aaron Green
   4499 Piedmont Ave.

4. **Ronada Court** c.1915; 157 Ronada Ave.
   Illustrated in the Werner Hegeman Planning Report of 1915 this group of one-story apartments strung together around an open court on a steeply sloping site looks as if it might have been stolen from the drawing board of Irving Gill.

5. **Wells House**   1915; Julia Morgan
   6076 Manchester Rd.
   A manorial house in Julia Morgan's personalized
   version of the Prairie School Style now painted
   gray and adorned with Regency wrought iron detail.

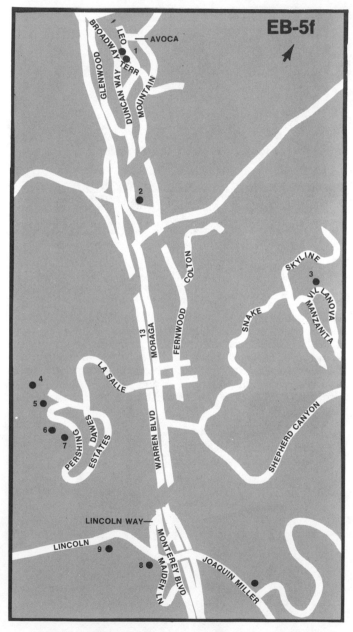

1. **Two houses**   1910 & 1912; Louis Christian Mullgardt
   6000 and 5960 Broadway Terr.
   The combination of a long veranda with gangplank entrance stairs, smoke stack chimneys,

and a pilot house on top gives this house a Mississippi steam boat quality that recalls the fact that Mullgardt practiced for some years in St. Louis, Mo. Its more restrained neighbor could, except for its fine detailing, be a skillful builder's version of the California stucco bungalow.

Fire Station

The community of Montclair above Moraga Ave., whose center stretches between La Salle and Thornhill, was first developed in the early 1920s and '30s. Districts such as those around Leimert Blvd. and Arcadia Ave. were laid out just before World War II; they contain a good cross section of typical builders' houses of the late '30s and early '40s. A major landmark is is the firehouse at 6226 Moraga Ave. in restrained "Mother Goose" style. The branch library at 1687 Mountain Blvd. in the Old-English-Half-Timber mode, was designed in 1930 by Mrs. Lucie Fisher, the wife of the donor.

2. **House** c.1935; Carr Jones
   1600 Fernwood Dr.
   Similar to those in Piedmont.

3. House

3. **House** 1971; MLTW/ William Turnbull
   200 Villanova Dr.
   The siting of this house was dictated by a legal setback; its "vertical box" design was directed by the 180 degree view.

4. **House** c.1930; Carr Jones
    6 Lexford Rd.

5. **House** c.1930; Carr Jones
    5 Pershing Dr.

These two Jones houses are the work of a remarkable "carpitect" who built some 50 houses in the Bay Area in the 1920s and 1930s. They are distinguished by the craftsmanlike concern for the materials used: old brick, irregular slate, well-weathered wood often reclaimed from older structures, hand forged iron work, and hand-made ceramic tile. Jones took apart the medieval, half-timber house, disposing its rooms in one and two-story irregularly placed blocks punctuated by round towers and curving walls. Like Maybeck, whose student he was, he personally built many of his houses and lovingly hand-finished their interiors.

6. **House** 1959; Donald Olsen
    115 Pershing Dr.

7. **House** 1955; Henry Hill
    339 Pershing Dr.

8. **Greek Orthodox Church** 1959; Reid, Rockwell, Banwell & Tarics
    1965; addit. Aaron Green

    A modern restatement of traditional Greek Orthodox church design with a steel-framed dome.

9. **Mormon Temple** 1964; Harold Burton
    4770 Lincoln Ave.

    One of the visual landmarks of the East Bay hills, the style of this building might be described as late Wizard-of-Oz.

East Oakland is the other area of the city which has retained a representative number of 19th century buildings. Within it is Oakland's first completed urban renewal project, Clinton Park, which with neighboring San Antonio Park formed the old town of Brooklyn. Funded for renewal before the legal apparatus for condemnation existed, the area was provided with new light poles, street trees, underground utilities, and street diverters to discourage through traffic. Consequently its strong neighborhood character survived. The area as a whole is a good hunting ground for Victorian architecture, particularly for those interested in the work of the Newsoms, prolific architects whose ideas, widely accepted and copied, contributed to the general character of the local architecture of the day.

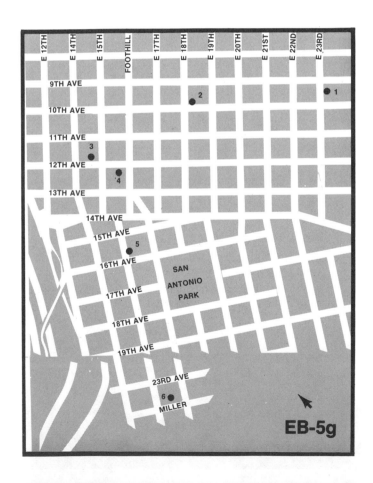

1. **Cottage**   1887; Newsom & Newsom
   2304 9th Ave. at E. 23rd St.
   A typical design from this firm with a horse-shoe arch porch entrance.

2. **Queen Anne Revival house**   1888; Newsom & Newsom
   1806 10th Ave.

3. **Brooklyn Presbyterian Church** 1887; Samuel Newsom
   E. 15th at 12th Ave.

4. **St. James Episcopal Church and Parish Hall**   1858
   1540 12th St. at Foothill Blvd.
   A very good example of the Victorian Gothic.

5. **St. Anthony's Church**   1966; Reed & Tarics Assoc.
   1535 16th Ave.
   A well-detailed wood and concrete structure with a three-lobed, hexagonal plan.

6. **Ina Coolbrith Library**   1917; C. W. Dickey & J. J. Donovan
   1449 Miller Ave.
   A very "prairie" Spanish Colonial Revival building more sensitive in design than either architect did by himself.

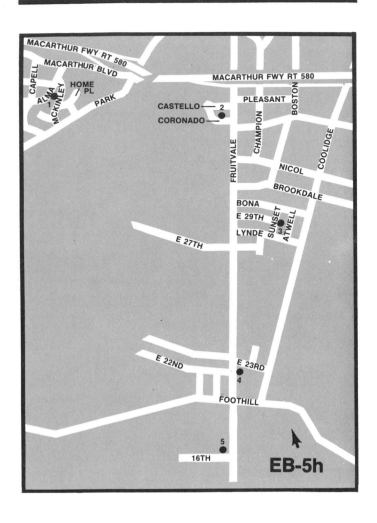

1. **Cielito Lindo Apartments**   c.1920; Casebolt Dakin
   1021 McKinley St.

   Variation and seclusion are provided in this Spanish Colonial Revivial apartment house with Moorish detail. It was designed by the architect for himself.

2. **Bungalow**   c.1910; 2708 Sunset Ave.
   A fine example of the bungalow of "oriental" persuasion with strongly articulated gables and carved beam ends.

3. **Fruitvale Congregational Church**   1908;
   Hugo Storch
   1601 Fruitvale Ave.

   A personal version of the Mission Revival style
   whose interior semi-circular space is ambiguously
   clothed in a rectangular envelope. It is about to
   be destroyed so see it while it lasts!

4. **Castello and Coronado—loop street**
   A well-maintained one-street-subdivision in builder's Spanish Colonial Revival style of the 1920s.

Medical Office Building   c.1940
22nd Ave. and Fruitvale Ave.

Small scale Streamlined Moderne. For another example of the Moderne period see Vert's Camera
Shop, 5795 Foothill Blvd., a letter-perfect Vitrolite
catalog store front design.

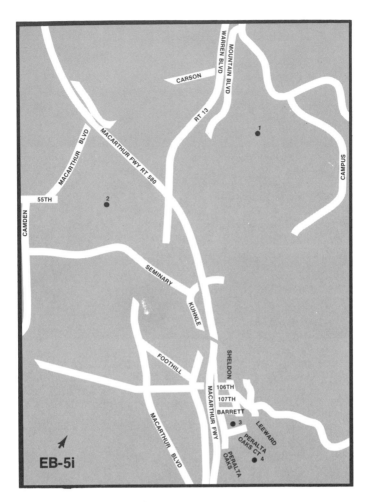

1. **Merritt College** 1972; Wurster, Bernardi & Emmons/Reynolds & Chamberlin; Lawrence Halprin Assoc., Landscape arch'ts.
Campus Dr.

The latest of the three contemporary junior colleges in the Peralta District, this group of brutconcrete buildings is coldly composed on its hilltop site.

2. **Mills College**   Trenor St. and Seminary Ave.

The oldest women's college in the West grew from a Young Ladies' Seminary established in Benicia in 1852 which moved to its Oakland site in 1871. The 127 acre campus, originally open fields, has been carefully planted with specimen trees much needed to screen the noise of the freeways which hem it in. There have been two major building periods, the first in the 1920s, the second in the 1960s. These have tended to split the architectural character between the Spanish Colonial Style and the contemporary concrete idioms. A map locating all the buildings and giving their architects is available at the reception desk in Mills Hall.

Physical Sciences & Mathematics Building   1970; Gerald McCue & Assoc.

● **The Campanile**   1904; Julia Morgan

Library   1906; Julia Morgan; 1954, addition by Milton T. Pfleuger

Mills Hall   1871; S. C. Bugbee & Son

Life Sciences Building   1969; Gerald McCue & Assoc.

Life Sciences Bldg.

Mills Hall

Rothwell College Center   1969; Chan/Rader & Assoc.

Ege Hall, Reinhardt Hall, White Hall, and Founders Commons   1970 Skidmore, Owings & Merrill

Art Gallery   1925; Walter H. Ratcliff

Warren Olney Hall   1917; Walter H. Ratcliff

Orchard Meadow Hall   1919 & 1921; Walter H. Ratcliff

Lucie Stearn Hall   1965; Ernest J. Kump

Isabella Cowell Health Center   1966; Ernest J. Kump

Music Building   1928; Walter H. Ratcliff

Walter A. Haas Pavilion   1971; Ernest J. Kump

Chapel   1967; Callister & Payne

Mary Morse Hall   1935; Walter H. Ratcliff

Ethel Moore Hall   1926; Walter H. Ratcliff

3. **Moore Business Forms, Inc.**   1966; John Bolles & Assoc.
2950 Peralta Oaks Ct.
Several stories of contemporary offices waterfall down a slope with well-landscaped parking terraces.

4. **Dunsmuir House**   1899; Eugene Freeman
2960 Peralta Oaks Ct.
A Colonial Revival mansion evocative of the "old South" with an appropriately tragic-romantic history. The house and property, whose original landscaping was by John McLaren, are now a city park open to the public Sundays, noon to four, with admission fee of $.50 for the garden and $1.00 for the house tour.

photo: Ezra Stoller

Oakland-Alameda Co. Coliseum Sports Arena and Stadium   Skidmore, Owings & Merrill
66th Ave. and Coliseum Way
The arena which seats 14,000 people is one of the largest structures with a cable-supported roof yet built; the Stadium seats 53,000. There is also an exhibit hall between the Stadium and the Arena. The complex is the result of a 1964 bond issue.

Metropolitan Oakland International Airport Administration Building and Terminal   1962-71
J. C. Warnecke & Assoc.
Hegenberger Overpass

The first tracts in Alameda were laid out at its eastern
end in the early 1850s. Developers used some colorful
sales techniques, including offering free weekend ferry
service which served free lunches and watermelons
in an attempt to lure prospective buyers from San Francisco. A lively commercial district grew up at the western end of the island complementing that of the original town. Most of the development occurred during the
boom decade of 1870-80 as the railroad and ferry network grew up around the Bay. From the beginning
Alameda was highly touted in real estate brochures
as the ideal bedroom community providing "Healthful
climate, perfect sewage, finely macademized streets,
park-like drives, charming homes, pure artesian well
water, and pleasant, convenient rail and ferry service."
Development was steady but orderly until World War
II, when seven shipyards operated full time in the city.
Some 6500 units of housing were constructed, using up
all the available land, but the greater part of the labor
force came from elsewhere through the two-lane Posey
Tube and over the crowded bridges. Although few

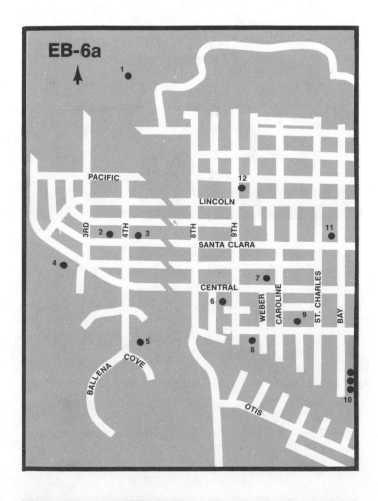

traces of this stressful period remain, Alameda suffered another, more durable encrustation of unwanted housing during the 1960s when the Utah Construction Co. succeeded in pulling off a bay fill operation stretching nearly the length of the southeastern shore. The once gracious shoreline, the only Bay front residential development of the 19th century, is now sadly landlocked exchanging a view of ordinary tract housing for that of the Bay sweeping across to San Francisco. Concerned Alameda citizens are still fighting unwanted Bay fill development which threatens to overburden city facilities and destroy a way of life that makes the community a truly successful backwater on the cluttered and wasted East Bay shore.

1. **College of Alameda** 1970
   Perkins & Will/Stone, Marraccini & Patterson/ Leaf, Ruana, Mowry/Reynolds & Chamberlin
   555 Atlantic Ave.

   One of the three new campi for the Peralta College District designed in the contemporary concrete idiom. The others are Laney and Merritt Colleges in Oakland.

2. **House** c.1885; 325 Santa Clara Ave.
   A very thin, spindly Queen Anne house.

3. **Cottage** c.1889; 529 Santa Clara Ave.
   A Queen Anne cottage with a few tinges of Islamic decoration.

4. **Encinal High School** 1950; Ernest J. Kump
   210 Encinal Ave.
   A typical plan from this firm whose schools are legion in the Bay Area.

5. **Ballena Bay Complex** 1969-70; Fisher-Friedman
   Ballena Blvd. at Tideway Dr.
   One of the large, stylish developments by this prolific firm; it should be compared with the Bay Farm Island developments, Islandia I and II, near the end of this section.

6. **Bungalow block** c.1915; 1300 block of Burbank St. The California Bungalow in its small, single-story version is a building type found in abundance in Alameda. This block with its tall, skinny palms is a complete period piece.

During Alameda's most prosperous decades from 1870-1900, the pre-Bay-fill area of the south shore from Weber to about Chestnut St. was known as the "Gold Coast". Declining fortunes have naturally affected the general scene, but it is still in this area that one has the strongest sense of the "ideal bedroom community" that Alameda was and is. Standing at the foot of any of these quiet cul-de-sac streets, one can only mourn the unfortunate Bay fill development across the estuary which has seriously curtailed their outlook. Still the streets are worth walking down for the trees, the gardens, and the houses—interesting variations of traditional styles of the late 19th and early 20th centuries.

7. **House** c.1895; 1001 Weber St. Shingle style.

8. **Cottage** c.1890; 1279 Weber St. Eastlake style.

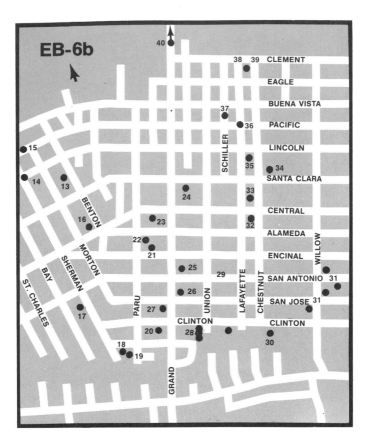

EB-6b

40

38 39 CLEMENT

EAGLE

BUENA VISTA

37
36 PACIFIC

LINCOLN

15

SCHILLER
35 34 SANTA CLARA

14 13

24 33

BENTON

16 23 CENTRAL

MORTON

22 32 ALAMEDA

21 ENCINAL

WILLOW

SHERMAN

25 29 SAN ANTONIO 31

BAY

26 31

ST. CHARLES

PARU 27 SAN JOSE

17 UNION LAFAYETTE CHESTNUT

20 CLINTON CLINTON

18 28 30

19 GRAND

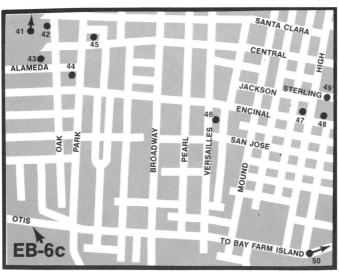

41 42 SANTA CLARA

45 CENTRAL

HIGH

43 ALAMEDA 44 JACKSON STERLING 49

ENCINAL 47 48

46

OAK PARK BROADWAY PEARL VERSAILLES SAN JOSE MOUND

OTIS

EB-6c TO BAY FARM ISLAND 50

9. **House**   c.1905; 1031 San Antonio Ave.
   Colonial Revival style.

10. **Cottages**   c.1910
    End of Bay St., E side
    Three harmoniously sited redwood cottages in early Bay Region vernacular.

11. **Mastick School**   1938; Kent & Haas
    Santa Clara Ave. & Bay St.
    A pleasantly scaled school building in the Moderne style.

12. **1630 Pacific St.**

13. **1500 Block of Benton St.**

14. **1600 Block of Sherman St.**

15. **1200 &1300 Blocks of Pacific St.**

16. **Cottage**   1884; Joseph C. Newsom
    1423 Central Ave.
    An exuberant Queen Anne cottage by one of the Newsom brothers. Some ornament has been removed and new windows have been added to the second floor.

17. **House**   c.1905; 1221 Sherman St.
    The off-center porch is an example of some of the liberties taken with the Classic Revival style in the West.

18. **House**   c.1890; 1098 Sherman St.
    As sophisticated a Queen Anne Shingle style house as any in the East.

19. House   1893; Fuller Claflin
723 Paru St.
An Islamic Revival style house now stripped of its third floor which was bedecked with Arabian Nights ornament and crowned with two onion-domed turrets.

20. House   1892; Willis Polk
1620 Clinton Ave.
A rare, early Polk design showing a personal approach to the small, Shingle style house. The dormer windows and front porch have been altered.

21. House   c.1915; 1617 Encinal Ave.
A whimsical bungalow.

22. House   c.1900; 1222 Paru St.
This house deserves more than a passing glance for its fanciful porch columns and subtle use of stock detail in the windows.

23. House   1876; 1630 Central Ave.
Built by railroad official John Anthony, this house is the finest example remaining in Alameda of the Bracketed Italianate style so prevalent in the 1870s.

24. Stephens Center (former Greenley house)   1892-94
1724 Santa Clara Ave.
Although as yet undocumented, this house is very probably the work of Ernest Coxhead. The interior has been altered, but the entrance sequence and first floor hall are intact. It is open to the public.

25. House   c.1880; 1717 San Antonio Ave.
Bracketed Italianate.
Grand St. is worthy of its name. Although the houses are not mansions, many of them are large and set in enough land to give them a stately quality. Most are

mixtures of the highly decorated Eastlake-Queen Anne style.

The difference in mass and treatment of the Eastlake-Queen Anne style can be seen by comparing the houses at 1001, 1007 & 1011 Grand St. (c.1815). The corner house represents the most sophisticated approach.

26. House   c.1870; 900 Grand St.
Bracketed Italianate style.

27. House   c.1895; 815 Grand St.
Stock decorative detail such as the ceramic inset of stylized rosettes in the chimney of this Eastlake-Queen Anne house can be seen elsewhere in Alameda.

28. Three houses   c.1890; 891, 893, 899 Union St.
There are few streets anywhere in the Bay area that can boast of houses as impressive as these. Built within a few years of each other, allegedly for sea captains, they are particularly rewarding for students of the stylistic variations of the 1890s. 899 has lost the diamond-paned windows of the towers and much of its ornamental detail.

29. Double house   c.1890
1832-34 Clinton Ave.
Queen Anne style.

30. House   c.1910; 2000 Clinton Ave.
A small house showing a sophisticated handling of the common elements of the Shingle style.

31. Four houses   c.1890
2070 & 2103 San Jose Ave.; 2105 & 2258 San Antonio Ave.
These houses present most of the vocabulary of the Eastlake-Queen Anne Style. Although hard to imagine in this undecorated era, old street photographs indicate that it was the vernacular architecture of its time on both small and large scale. In fact, it was in a way a democratic style since it depended on the wide use of stock ornamental designs which could be applied to the workingman's cottage as well as to the large house of his employer. Almost all of the cottages, like the houses of today, were designed by the builder-speculator, not by architects.

32. First Congregational Church   1904
Daniel F. Oliver
Central Ave. at Chestnut St.
A good example of Romanesque Revival church design.

33. Immanuel Lutheran Church   1891; F. Kraft
1420 Lafayette St.
Typical of late Victorian Gothic style wooden church design.

34. **First Presbyterian Church**   1904; Henry H. Meyers
2001 Santa Clara Ave.
A Roman-Renaissance Revival design with elegant fenestration.

35. **1538 Lafayette St.**

36. **1900 Block of Pacific St**

37. **1700 Block of Schiller St.**

38. **1917, 1919 Chestnut St.**

39. **1920-28 Lafayette St.**

40. **Government Island—U.S. Coast Guard: Recruit Dormitories**   1970; Marquis & Stoller; **Mess Hall** 1970; Skidmore, Owings & Merrill
A well-designed concrete and steel complex easily seen from the freeway.

41. **City Hall**   1896; Santa Clara Ave. and Oak St.
This Richardson-Romanesque style building lost its tower in the 1906 earthquake.

   Public Library   1936; 2264 Santa Clara Ave.
   Roman-Renaissance style.

Because the South Pacific Coast Railroad ran along the northern edge of the island, the more modest neighborhoods are located on this side. Whole streets of small cottages in the Eastlake-Queen Anne style of the 1890s still exist. All were built by speculator-builders, not by architects, and are examples of early tract architecture. The best examples are:

43. **Alameda Theatre**   1931; Miller & Pflueger
2315 Central Ave.
Designed by the famous San Francisco firm that produced most of the notable Moderne buildings in the Bay area. Other buildings in the Moderne style may be found along Park St.

44. **Business block**   c.1890
SE cor. Park St. & Alameda Ave.
Romanesque Revival style.

45. **U.S. Post Office**   1912; John Knox Taylor
Park Ct. & Central Ave.
A good example of the quality of design of most large and small federal buildings of this era.

46. **House**   c.1852; 1238 Versailles Ave.
Reputed to be the oldest house in Alameda, the split columns and "icicles" on the verge boards indicate its early date and close affinity to the Gothic Revival style.

47. **Commercial Building**   c.1890; Encinal & High Sts.
Eastlake-Queen Anne style.

   Cottage   c.1890; 3241 Encinal Ave.
   Eastlake-Queen Anne style.

49. Bungalow block   c.1915
3200 block of Sterling Ave.

These bungalows have such small lots that the block assumes the character of a bungalow court. Note the nicely scaled street lights.

Since the 1890s the heart of Alameda's business district has been around Park St. and Central Ave. The following buildings are the principal monuments of the area:

50. Islandia I & II   1966-69; Fisher-Friedman
Bay Farm Island—Island Dr., Catalina Ave., Fontana Dr., & McCartney Rd.

A large, award-winning residential development with a recreation center. This somewhat monotonous development represents a step forward in design and a step backward in planning for location. It brings to the town of Alameda an unwelcome population increase which threatens to overextend municipal resources while thoughtlessly multiplying itself.

San Leandro began about 1850 as a stage coach station on the East Bay shoreline from Oakland to San
Jose. It takes its name from the Rancho San Leandro,
bounded by the coastal hills on the east, the Bay on
the west, and Mission San Jose on the South. The only
relic from these early days is the Ignacio Peralta house
(1), 561 Lafayette Ave., built in 1860 by W. P. Toler and
reputed to be the first brick house in the county. It is
now the Alta Mira Club, and though altered by a front
porch addition and a rear wing, its interiors are worth
seeing. Also notable is the warping of the street pattern
to save the house with its two great magnolia trees in
front. As with most Bay communities, San Leandro became a city from 1940-44, increasing its population 57%

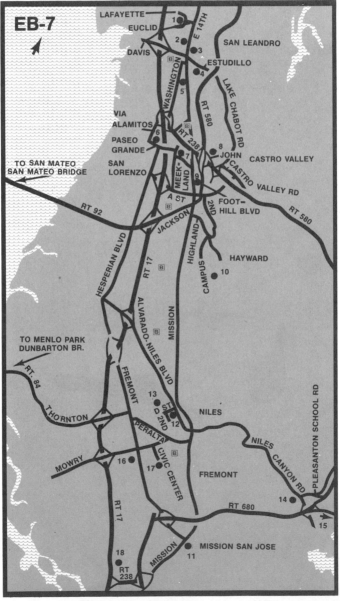

because of wartime industrial expansion on the Bay. The Civic Center **(2)**, 835 E. 14th St., was begun about 1938; its latest component is the Public Safety Building by Wong & Brocchini, 1967. Collectors of Corbusian concrete slab office buildings can add to their list the Pacific Telephone Directory Assistance Building **(3)**, 550 E. 14th St., Howard Johnson, 1971; while fanciers of the Moderne Style can seek out the Medical Building **(4)** at 333 Estudillo and Frieden Calculating Machine Co. **(5)** at 2350 Washington, by Fred H. Reimer, 1940.

To the south is San Lorenzo, an example of a postwar "new town" of low-cost housing with its own shopping centers, schools, and recreation centers, planned by the David D. Bohannon Organization in 1944. The major architectural monument is the San Lorenzo Community Church **(6)** at 954 Paseo Grande, designed by Bruce Goff in 1946 for the Seabees at nearby Camp

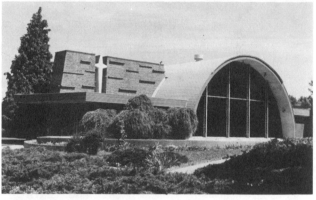

Parks. As a member of the unit, Goff was given the job of designing several buildings for the base within the government regulations for materials and construction. The camp closed a year later and the buildings were demolished except for the Chapel which was mustered out to the Community Church for $1. They dismantled the structure and reassembled it on the present site. There it stands, the most successful of many attempts to make architecture out of quonset huts. The cast concrete sea creatures in the pool were designed by M. H. Coe.

Nearby is the Meek Estate **(7)** on Hampton Rd., a handsome Bracketed-Italianate villa, c. 1860, home of William Meek who pioneered the fruit industry in the west. Originally the grounds covered 10 acres and were landscaped with imported trees, shrubs, and fountains. Now considerably smaller, the estate is a park and open to the public.

East of San Lorenzo is the modern town of Castro Valley. The Cathedral at the Crossroads, by Welton Beckett, 1969 **(8)**, is prominently sited on a hill by the freeway intersection of 580 and Rt. 238 at 20600 John Dr. It looks more like a performing arts center than a group of religious buildings. It may best be described as a mission from Southern California dedi-

cated to the spiritual enrichment of the Northland.
Further south is the town of Hayward, first a stagecoach stop hotel built by William Hayward in 1852.
The town holds little of architectural note except for
the former City Hall, c. 1940, now the Police Department **(9)** in a style best described as Otto Wagner

Revival. In the hills above is the windswept campus
of Cal State University Hayward **(10)**. The multi-story
Administration Building, designed by the State Division
of Architects in 1963, is an unfortunate landmark
from the hills below. Other buildings are: Cafeteria
Building, 1968, Wong & Brocchini; Speech and Drama
Building, Smith, Barker & Hanssen; Alexander Meikel-
john Memorial Building, 1968, Skidmore, Ownigs &
Merrill. To the southeast is Mission San Jose, founded
in 1797, one of the most prosperous of the California
missions. Sold and secularized in 1846 it has since returned to the church. Much of the building was restored
in 1916; only part of the original living quarters was
preserved. Next door is the church of St. Joseph **(11)**,
built soon after the 1906 earthquake. Fragments of the
19th century town are scattered along the main street.

About 5 miles north on Mission Blvd. is Niles. Here
the transcontinental railroad pierced the last barrier
of hills to reach the Pacific Coast in 1869. Niles became
an important rail center for the Southern Pacific and
Western Pacific lines; it had another brush with fame
when it was the location of the Essenay Studios of
the silent movie era. The railroad declined in importance; the film industry departed, but if you stand in
front of the Courthouse and Jail **(12)** on Second St. at
I St., you can easily conjure up a scene with Charlie
Chaplin or Ben Turpin. The principal monument is
the adobe of Don Jose de Jesus Vallejo, brother of
General Mariano Vallejo and first administrator of
Mission San Jose, built in 1853 **(13)**. It is on the grounds
of the California Nursery at Nursery Ave. and though
somewhat restored preserves a piece of the past in its
setting of eucalyptus trees.

To follow the historic path of the railroad, take the
Niles Canyon Rd. This leads through the hills to the
town of Sunol. Nearby is the Water Temple, designed
by Willis Polk in 1910 **(14)**, marking the place where

the San Francisco water supply is filtered on its way to Crystal Springs Lake from the Sierra. Reputedly Polk's favorite design, the Classical rotunda presents a romantic aspect unrivalled by any other structure in this landscape of rolling usually brown hills. A side excursion out of Sunol is a trip up Kilkare Canyon (12), whose name tells you what it is all about. Built up over the period from the 20s to the present, the canyon is almost continuously lined with hideaways in various styles and sizes.

The Kaiser Research Center, J. C. Warnecke & Assoc., 1969, on Sunol Blvd. off 680 So. **(15)**, is a complex of buildings in contemporary concrete slab idiom, very eye-catching at freeway speed. A closer look reveals a pleasant, sunken courtyard where members of the Kaiser "think tank" find an oasis sheltered from the view if not the noise of the freeway.

The route of the railroad continues into the Livermore Valley through the towns of Pleasanton and Livermore. Both of these cities were originally platted in 1869, the spawn of railroad fever, but grew slowly until the post-war building boom began in the 1950s. The laying of the interstate highways of 580 and 680 assured such a steady urbanization of the valley that the town of Pleasanton was moved in 1972 to vote against further development. There is little of architectural importance in the area, most of which is an object lesson in slurban sprawl. Livermore has a new Library, end of Carmen off Livermore Blvd., by Ratcliff, Slama & Cadwalader who also did the master plan for the Civic Center.

The city of Fremont, created in 1956, stretches over most of southwest Alameda County, incorporating as districts the former towns of Niles, Centerville, Mission San Jose, Irvington, and Warm Springs. The planning department, responding to citizens' requests, created a strongly unified plan for the city whose projected population by 1985 is 300,000. By 1970 the town contained 100,000 people and much of its planned urban pattern had become clear. Originally the plan called for a continuous system of Radburn-type greenways. During the early 1960s some of these were realized, most notably in the one crossing Fremont Blvd. at Brookvale Shopping Center, extending southwest to Patterson School, and northwest to Brookvale Park. Other main components include the planned central business district, now a loose chain of shopping centers along Mowry from the Fremont hub on the southwest side of Fremont Blvd. to the Fashion Center northeast of Paseo Padre near the BART station. On Fremont Blvd. near the intersection of Mowry is the Chadbourne Carriage House, 1886 **(16)** a Victorian moment in a sea of contemporaneity. Looking east on Mowry one has a perfectly planned vista of Mission Peak which serves as a splendid backdrop for the Civic Center Building, 1969, designed by Competition winner Robert Mittelstadt**(17)**. There is something improbable about this European-International, brut-con-

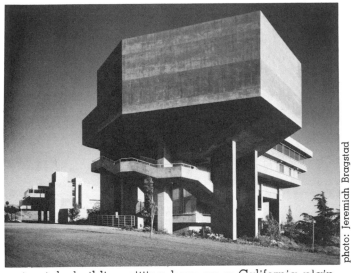

photo: Jeremiah Bragstad

crete style building sitting here on a California plain, but the design successfully conveys a spirit of civic monumentality. The fact that it is still missing a wing is directly expressed by having the construction sliced off at the appropriate juncture. The view from the balconies of Central Park with its lake and boating facilities is particularly pleasant.

18.   General Motors Assembly Plant   1963
General Motors Corp., Argonaut Realty Div.
45500 Fremont Blvd.

Rising out of the plain in splendid isolation, this industrial complex is the Bay Area's most successful piece of architecture at the freeway scale.

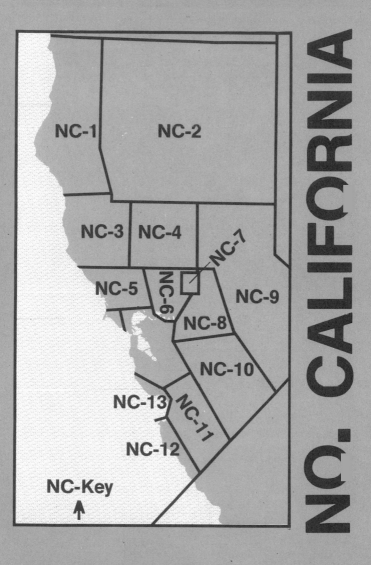

NC-1
NC-2
NC-3
NC-4
NC-7
NC-5
NC-6
NC-9
NC-8
NC-10
NC-13
NC-11
NC-12
NC-Key

NO. CALIFORNIA

NC

ARCATA

Arcata was founded in 1850 and was originally named Uniontown. In 1860 the town was renamed Arcata. During the decade of the 50s it was an active transportation center for pack trains which supplied the mines in the northern mountains. Arcata's pre-eminence gave way to its southern neighbor Eureka because the silting mud banks of northern Humboldt Bay prevented the development of an extensive deep water harbor. By the early 90s Arcata was described as ". . . a residential town, being more free from fog than its larger neighbor."

The street pattern of the town is the usual checkerboard with the main business district facing a pleasant open square. There are a few historically significant commercial buildings to be found in the downtown area, such as the Jacoby Bldg. (started in 1857, cor. 8th St. & H St.), but these are on the whole of only marginal architectural interest. As has occurred in a number of California communities, the 101 Freeway has forcibly split the town, with a small residential area and Humboldt State College to the east, and the remainder of the town to the west.

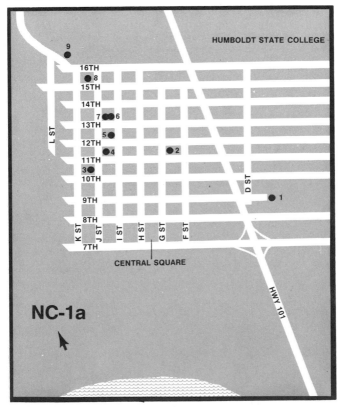

1. **House** mid 1880s; 380 9th St.

    A Queen Anne house with some Eastlake detailing. Boasts an impressive octagonal high peaked roof tower and coupled spindle and sawed work on entrance porch and in gable ends.

2. **First Presbyterian Church** 1916;
   Franklin B. Georgeson
   NE cor. G & 11th Sts.
   A modernized Gothic as seen through the Crafts-man movement.

3. **Cottage** c.1860; 1022 10th St.
   A Victorian Gothic Revival cottage set in spacious grounds.

4. **Cottage** c.1880; 986 12th St.
   A story and a half Eastlake/Queen Anne cottage.

5. **Bair House** mid 1880s; attrib. Samuel and Joseph C. Newsom
   916 13th St.
   Queen Anne. This house is a must for those fascinated by Victorian architecture. Its entrance porch with its 2/3 arched opening, its rich spindle work and original balustraded steps is rare. Its octagonal tower, with inset decorative panels on the third floor is similar to the tower on the house at 380 9th St.

6. **Jackson House** late 1880s; 902 14th St.
   A two story Queen Anne house—one of a pair on 14th St., each located at the oposite end of the block. The second house at 980 is identical but reversed. Both have a spacious entrance porch, corner round towers with high conical roofs, and are set back in ample well-maintained grounds.

7. **House** late 1880s; 980 14th St.
   Two story Queen Anne house, reverse plan of house at 902 14th St.

8. **St. Mary's Roman Catholic Church** c.1860s
   N side 14th bet. L & J Sts.
   A Victorian Gothic Revival wood church.

9. **Arcata High School** 1947 & 49; Masten & Hurd. 1953-56; Ernest Winkler. 1960-62; Falk & Booth
   905 6th St.
   The classroom building is a good example of the International style with slight post World War II touches of the Streamline Moderne.

NC-1bc   Eureka

Significantly, this city was founded one year after the adoption of the California State seal with its motto "Eureka." The source of the place name is obvious. Its appropriateness was, however, not immediately obvious, since for many years Eureka was remote from the best mines in the area and was dwarfed by such nearby settlements as Uniontown (now Arcata) and Humboldt City. But with its excellent harbor and the lumbering boom of the 50s, Eureka fulfilled the promise of her name and developed a lucrative business, still evidenced by a constant parade of redwood logs and the fetid smell of pulp mills.

The city was laid out in the usual gridiron pattern in 1850. The original street layout was slightly askew of the cardinal points of the compass. As the city developed to the south away from the bay, this "error" was corrected; and the streets from Wabash Ave. on run north-south, east-west. In 1856 the town was incorporated, and it was in this year that Eureka finally became the seat of Humboldt County. In 1883 (completed in 1887) a magnificent courthouse in the Italianate/Mansard style was designed by the San Francisco architects Curtis and Bennett. Regrettably this dominating landmark has been destroyed.

Like many of northern California's coastal cities, Eureka is fogbound for much of the year, and the natural longing of its inhabitants is for sunshine. The streets and the lawns and gardens around the houses have on the whole been kept free of trees so as to encourage as much natural light for the houses as possible. The town does not have many public parks, but in a way this is made up for by Sequoia Park which contains a wonderful redwood grove and an extensive playground for children.

If any community in California has the potential of being developed as the West Coast Williamsburg, it is Eureka. A majority of its business buildings and its houses built during the decades of the 70s, 80s and early 90s are still standing. As a writer noted in 1889, Eureka has ". . . a host of magnificent residences, in which are housed her lumber millionaries, which are many." The most famous Victorian house of the western U. S., the William Carson house, is located here. The brothers Samuel and Joseph C. Newsom designed not only the rich and flamboyant Carson house, but numerous other large residences and many smaller speculative cottages. In all, there are well over 75 well preserved Victorian houses in Eureka, ranging from the Italianate to the later Queen Anne Colonial Revival. But it is the Eastlake and Queen Anne styles which predominate, and these help to give the community a strong historic unity.

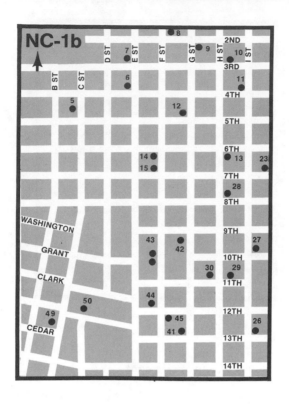

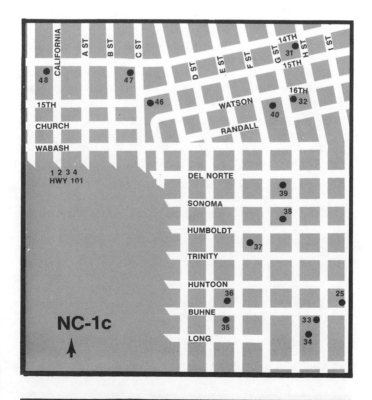

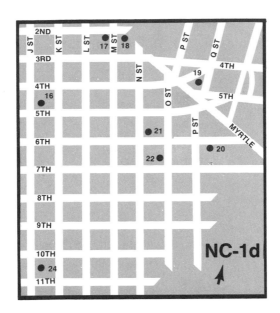

1. **College of the Redwoods** 1970; Falk & Booth; Matson & Nielson
   2 mi. S of Eureka on Rt. 101, Tompkins Hill Rd. turnoff
   A series of low redwood pavilions follow the contours of the hillside.

2. **Berta Ranch Covered Bridge** 1936
   S Eureka on Rt. 101; Elk River Rd. S 2 mi. to Berta Rd. then to Elk River
   Except upon close examination, one would find it difficult to believe that this wooden bridge had been built in the mid 1930s.

3. **Zane Ranch Covered Bridge** 1937
   S Eureka on Rt. 101; Elk River Rd. S 3 mi. to Zanes Rd. then to Elk River
   Another 1930s covered bridge still in use.

4. **Fort Humboldt** 1853-1866
   S edge Eureka, off Rt. 101 at Highland Rd.
   The restored Commissary Bldg., a simple white clapboard structure, is all that remains of this famous fort. The main entrance to the Commissary with its side lights and transom light is Federal style in feeling.

5. **International Order of Moose Building** 1902
   109 5th St.
   Except for the store sign on the ground floor, this wooden building has been little altered. The low relief engaged columns and the fan windows of the second floor place it loosely within the Colonial Revival.

6. **Clarke Memorial Museum (formerly the Bank of Eureka)** 1912
NW cor. 3rd & N Sts .

A sophisticated version of the turn-of-the-century Roman-Renaissance Revival. Its interior space functions very well in its new role as a museum of natural history and history.

7. **Commercial Office Building** c.1910; 350 E St.
Roman-Renaissance Revival office building in the spirit of McKim, Meade and White. This and the Clarke Memorial Museum building are the only two examples of the City Beautiful image brought to Eureka.

8. **Store and Office Building** late 1870s
NE cor. 2nd & N St.

An impressive French Empire Mansard building; its long facade on 2nd St. is centered on an imposing two-story entrance pavilion.

9. **Humboldt National Bank** c.1870s; 600 2nd St.
A three story brick building, somewhat Italianate in style. The windows are round arched above, and arched openings are used as well on the street level.

10. **Store and Office Building** c.1880s; 717-719 E St.
A mixture of Eastlake and Queen Anne details.

11. **Eureka Title Company Building** 1971
Trump & Sauble
735 4th St.

A low one story building of shingles and redwood, well oriented both to its own parking area and to the public streets. Fits in very well with the older buildings nearby.

12. **State Theatre** 1920; Richard Sweasey
W side G St. bet. 4th & 5th Sts.

A strange mixture of Sullivanesque ornament overlaying classical details.

● **13. St. Bernard's Roman Catholic Church**   1886
James Simpson
SE cor. 6th & H Sts.

The high steeple of this wooden church forms a dominant landmark in the community. It is an excellent and sophisticated example of Victorian Gothic Revival. Note the Parsonage next door, which is Queen Anne in style.

14. Eureka Theatre   c.1937
W side F St. bet. 6th & 7th Sts.

Streamline Moderne; note the building up of "cubist" volumes to form the theatre sign, and also the projecting canopy with its banded and curved end.

15. Carnegie Public Library   1902
NW cor. 7th & F Sts.

The frontispiece of this building is a very delicate almost Colonial Revival temple front, with four widely spaced Corinthian columns. A recessed arched entrance leads into the building.

16. House   c.1880s; 937 5th St.
A two-story version of the Eastlake style.

17. Carson (the Younger) House   1887
Samuel and Joseph C. Newsom
SE cor. 2nd & M Sts.

Queen Anne in style, though overshadowed by the William Carson house across the street, this house contains the full vocabulary of the Newsom brothers when they were working in the Queen Anne style. In excellent condition, both inside and out.

● **18. William Carson House** (now a private club)   1884-86; Samuel and Joseph C. Newsom
SW cor. M & 2nd Sts.

"The" example of "Victorian" architecture. This, the largest residence designed by the Newsoms stands on a low hill overlooking the harbor and the east end of town. It is impossible to label the style of this building. Overall it is Queen Anne, but there is also a little of everything else ranging from the Italianate to the Eastlake styles. The original contract for the house (1884) reads, "day labor, $25,000. The following year a second contract notice was for $50,000.

19. **Boyd House** 1885; Samuel and Joseph C. Newsom
NE cor. 4th & Myrtle Sts.
An Eastlake house by the Newsoms; some changes have been made on the lower floor and on the entrance porch.

20. **Cottage** 1887
attrib. Samuel and Joseph C. Newsom
1528 6th St.
A Queen Anne cottage exhibiting fine carved and spindle work on its entrance porch and a large, arched window with delicate curved wood mullions.

21. **Cottage** late 1870s; 1305 6th St.
A remarkable blending of Italianate and Eastlake with bold fat columns, brackets and ornament. Also note the house at 1226 6th St. which seems to be Italianate, Eastlake and Queen Anne, all in one.

22. **House** late 1870s; 1331 7th St.
Italianate.

23. **Wilson House** 1912; 630 J St.
A West Coast version of a Prairie School house.

24. **House** late 1870s; 1035 J St.
Italianate; also note one-story store building to rear.

25. **House** c.1905; 2424 J St.
A two-story bungalow sheathed in shingles.

26. **House** c.1880s; 1237 I St.
An Eastlake style house.

27. **House** c.1870s; 933 I St.
A small story and a half Mansard roofed house.

28. **House** c.1900; 703 8th St.
A very handsome Queen Anne Colonial Revival house. The arch is the major motif on the front of the house, being used for the large dormer, as the opening in the second floor porch, and again as an arched window on the first floor.

29. **First Church of Christ Science** 1914; Frank T. Georgeson. **Sunday School Building** 1968; Gerald Matsen
SW cor. 11th & H Sts.
A Craftsman/Prairie School Church building, similar to churches from the East Bay area.

30. **Veterans Memorial Building** 1935
    W side H St. bet. 10th & 11th Sts.
    W.P.A. Moderne.

31. **Christ Episcopal Church** 1939; Lewis F. Hobart
    NW cor. 15th & H Sts.

    This church building well illustrates how a sensitive architect can carry on the tradition of an older style. This board and batten Gothic Revival Church replaced an earlier (1869) building which was situated further downtown. In the new building the architects used a number of pieces from the older structure including the altar, altar rail, pulpit, pews, etc. The older fragments blend perfectly with the new structure.

32. **Cottage** c.1880s; 1604 H St.

    An Eastlake cottage.

33. **Attached houses** c.1937; 2400 H St.

    A perfect example of the Streamline Moderne, right out of a Hollywood film set of the late 1930s. The tour de force of the front elevation is the large centrally placed circular window with its pod-like planting box below.

34. **House** 1936; 2505 G St.
Streamline Moderne with glass bricks, circular windows and curved metal railings.

35. **Puter House** c.1915; Arthur S. Heineman
2434 E St.
A loose flowing single floor bungalow, highly reminiscent of the Pasadena houses of Charles and Henry Greene.

36. **House** c.1900; NW cor. Buhne & E Sts.
A shingled Mission Revival house.

37. **House** c.1880s
SE cor. Humboldt & E Sts.
Eastlake style, profusion of sawed ornament.

38. **House** c.1880s; 2031 F St.
A two-story Eastlake house.

39. **First Methodist Church** 1931
SW cor. Del Norte & F Sts.
Colonial Revival (of the 30s); a New England Church set down on the Pacific Coast.

40. **House** c.1890s; 1604 G St.
Queen Anne/Colonial Revival; an unusual grouping of architectural fragments ranging from the large circular tower wrapped with garlands, to the Baroque splayed steps leading to the classical entrance porch, to the delicate sawed ornament found in the gable ends.

42. **Simpson House** 1884
Samuel and Joseph C. Newsom
904 G St.
Queen Anne in style. The Newsom brothers in a more restrained mood; the highly ornamented porch, windows and doors pose as picture frames placed out in front of the simple undecorated clapboard walls of the house. Classical touches can be seen in the broken curved gable over the entrance porch and in the curved lintels over the groups of windows. The octagonal tower is pure Queen Anne, while the arches of the entrance porch are pointed Gothic.

43. **Two Cottages** mid 1880s; 944 & 1000 F St.
2 Queen Anne cottages, almost identical. There are a number of paired cottages in Eureka; other examples can be seen at 911 & 931 3rd St., 905 & 911 F St., and 944 & 1000 F St.

44. **Eureka Municipal Auditorium** 1936
NW cor. 12th & F Sts.
W. P. A. Moderne.

45. **House** early 1880s; 1207 F St.
Eastlake/Queen Anne. A commodious dwelling entailing a potpourri of Eastlake and Queen Anne details.

46. House mid 1880s; 1461 C St.

Eastlake/Queen Anne. A rather straightforward house with a small elegant entrance porch with fat lath-turned columns.

47. Cottage c.1884
attrib. Samuel and Joseph C. Newsom
SW cor. 14th & C Sts.

Eastlake in style, with Queen Anne touches. Certainly one of the impressive "Victorian" houses of Eureka, with its sumptuous entrance steps and balustrades, and a rich array of sawed and turned ornament, especially on the gable ends.

48. The Wooden Garden 1972 and earlier
Romano Gabriel
1415 Pine St.

One of the delights of Eureka. A folk fantasy of wooden images colorfully painted which creates a forest in front of the small residence. Romano Gabriel has sawed the figures out of ordinary wood boxes, assembled them in attached groups and has then painted them with brilliant colors. The images represent animals, human figures and flowers.

49. House c.1880s; 1228 C St.

Eastlake with a few slight Queen Anne details. The street elevation is a delightful frontispiece— starting at the top with a cantilevered covered balcony down to the entrance porch with its cusped "Islamic" arches.

50. Houses on Hillside St. early 1880s through the 1890s

Hillsdale St. is only two blocks long, but in this short length it exhibits houses which trace the changes in architectural fashion from the early 80s through the 90s. 216 and 220 are a mixture of Eastlake and Queen Anne and are attributed to Samuel and Joseph C. Newsom.

The site of Ferndale was first settled in 1852, though the town itself was not established until 1860. In contrast to its larger neighbors to the north, Ferndale was from the beginning an agricultural town, a center of the extensive dairy activities of the Salt River Valley. By the late 1880s it had basically assumed its present form and it was described as "thrifty and improving." Some newer housing has been built to the northwest, and a few buildings have been added since 1900 to the central area of the town, but basically Ferndale remains as a beautifully preserved Victorian community, entirely oriented around Main Street. The three blocks of Main Street between Eugene Street and Washington Street are a show place of Eastlake and early Queen Anne commercial architecture.

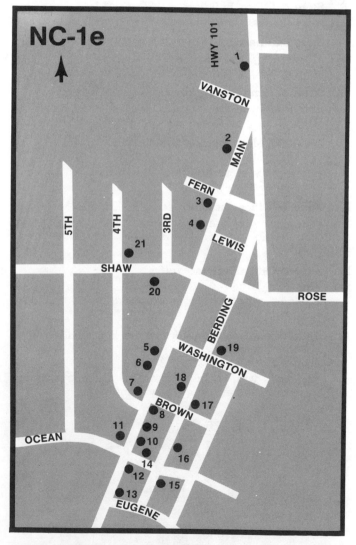

1. **House** c.1880s; 923 Main St.
   A combination of Eastlake and Queen Anne.

2. **House** c.1880s; 831 Main St.
   A little Italianate mixed with Queen Anne.

3. **Carnegie Public Library** 1908
   SW cor. Main & Fern Sts.
   Roman/Renaissance a la 1893 Chicago World's Fair.

4. **Cottage** c.1860s; 703 Main St.
   A perfect Victorian Gothic Revival cottage beautifully set back from the street behind its white fence and surrounded by a heavily wooded garden.

5. **Store & Office Building** c.1880s; 507 Main St.
   A wooden Eastlake commercial building.

6. **Store & Office Building** c.1880; 475 Main St.
   A well preserved Eastlake store building.

7. **Store Building** c.1880s
   W side Main St. opp. Brown St.
   Eastlake in style.

8. **Bank of America Building** 1911; 394 Main St.
   Roman/Renaissance a la McKim, Meade and White.

9. **Ferndale Meat Market Building** early 1880s
   370 Main St.
   A one-story store building with a high false front in the Eastlake style.

10. **Store & Office Building** early 1880s; 366 Main St.
    Eastlake, with impressive ornament, especially around the entrance which leads to the second floor.

11. **Store & Office Building** c.1880
    NW cor. Main St. & Ocean Ave.
    Eastlake, with elaborate brackets supporting the roof.

12. **Victorian Village Inn** (formerly a Bank and Office Bldg.) c.1880s
    SE cor. Main St. & Ocean Ave.
    Eastlake, with some Italianate touches; richly decorated second story bay windows.

13. **Masonic Hall** late 1870s
NW cor. Main & Eugene Sts.

Italianate, with engaged columns on second floor. Unusual grouping of round headed windows with gabled pediments above to suggest the Gothic style.

14. **Berding Cottage** c.1860s; 455 Ocean Ave.

A Victorian Gothic Cottage, still surrounded by an Eastlake fence and gates; wonderful grounds around house with cypress trees clipped into the form of giant gum drops. Note the stable facing on Berding which is Eastlake in style.

15. **Church** c.1870s
SE cor. Oregon Ave. & Berding St.

Victorian Gothic Revival church, now closed.

16. **House** c.1880s; 363 Berding St.

A Queen Anne house.

17. **House** 1894; NE cor. Berding & Brown Sts.

Said to have been built in 1894, though its use of the Eastlake style would seem to be earlier. This is one of the lagest houses in Ferndale, and one which is very well preserved. It is rich in turned and sawed wood ornament.

18. **House** c.1880; 439 Berding St.

Queen Anne with some Eastlake details.

19. **Church of the Assumption** (Roman Catholic) c.1880s
NE cor. Berding & Washington Sts.

An impressive Victorian Gothic Revival church, similar to the Catholic church in Eureka.

20. **House** c.1880s; 464 Shaw Ave.
Queen Anne.

21. **Our Savior Lutheran Church** c.1870s
N side Shaw Ave. bet. 3rd & 4th Sts.
Victorian Gothic Revival.

This town, initially founded in the 1860s, was first named Springville, then Slide, and then to encourage real estate speculation it was renamed Fortuna. Its layout is the conventional gridiron scheme, with streets labeled in the usual fashion of numbers and letters. The downtown commercial area has been remodeled so that little of its 19th century character can be experienced; but there are a number of houses, especially in the area north of Main Street, which are excellent and characteristic examples of late 19th century Victorian architecture.

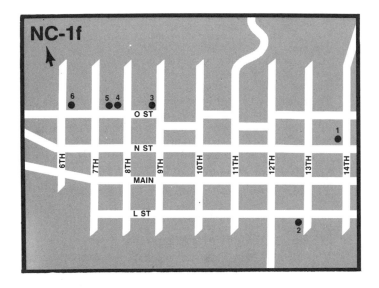

1. **St. Joseph's Roman Catholic Church**   c.late 1860s
   NW cor. 14th & N Sts.
   A Victorian Gothic Revival clapboard church.

2. **House (now Fortuna Missionary Baptist Church)** c.1880s
   SW cor. 13th & L Sts.
   Queen Anne in style.

3. **House**   c.1880; NW cor. 4th & N Sts.
   Italianate with Eastlake details.

4. **House** c.1880s; 812 O St.
   Eastlake, with a pair of two-story bay windows and a delicate entrance porch placed between.

5. **House** c.1880s; 822 O St.
   Eastlake in style.

6. **House** c.1900; 624 O St.
   Colonial Revival; with center projection dominated by two large scaled Corinthian columns.

LOLETA

A small railroad community which is a shipping point for dairy products produced by the neighboring farms in the rich Eel River Valley and Delta area. (No map)

Bank of Loleta   1921; F. T. Georgeson
W side Main St., bet. Church & Loleta Sts.

A modest, well designed small bank in the turn of the century Roman/Renaissance style.

Loleta Community Evangelical Free Church   1898
SE cor. Railroad Ave. & Church St.

An Eastlake version of a wood Gothic church, romantically situated alone on the low rising hill.

SCOTIA

Scotia is one of the few wholly company owned towns still operating in California. The Pacific Lumber Company established its first large mill at this site in 1886. The mill buildings themselves are impressive examples of industrial architecture and are well worth a visit. (No map)

Winema Theatre   1920; Alfred Henry Jacobs
W side Main St., bet. Church & Bridge Sts.

A small log cabin raised to gigantic scale; wonderful porch across the front with 10 redwood trunks as classical columns.

Visitors Center   1920; F. T. Georgeson
E side Main St., across from Bridge St.

A classical Roman/Renaissance bank building rendered in redwood with redwood tree trunks as primitive Doric columns.

Winema Theatre

SISKIYOU, MODOC, LASSEN, PLUMAS

These counties contain some of the most magnificent scenery in the world. Here it is very apparent that God's architecture is superior to man's. **Crescent City** used to have some fine old places, but they were mostly swept away by a flood a number of years ago. On Battery Point, a lighthouse dating from 1856 and including many of the old furnishings has been turned into a museum.

On the other side of the mountains, **Yreka** has some quaint houses and the usual brick Odd Fellows Hall (1859). South of Yreka on State Route 3 is **Callahan** where the ample Callahan Ranch Hotel (1854) in late Georgian mode with Greek Revival details asserts an early importance for the area that has now vanished. Still farther east, **Susanville** is a pretty place where on Weatherlow Street you can see Roop's Fort (1854), a large log cabin which was a stopping place for immigrant trains, though it got its name from being a defense post during the Sagebrush War of 1863. On Route 89 just south of Crescent Mills you may turn off on County Route A22 seven miles to **Taylorsville,** a town of substantial houses and barns, the Taylor Hotel (1860) and, of course, an Odd Fellows Hall (1874). At **Quincy** is a frame Masonic Hall (1855) with projecting second-story supported by simple columns—also a Wells Fargo Bank (1969), by Henrik Bull, where there is a very pleasant wedding of the pioneer plainstyle to contemporary design.

On the Little Fork of the Salmon River south and east of the town of Somesbar on the road to Sawyer's Bar is an 82 ft. wooden covered bridge built as late as 1924. There may be many fine things that we have missed in the Northern Counties—and we hope to be told about them—but at this point it would seem foolish for anyone looking principally for architecture to go out of his way to investigate this area. On the other hand, in such natural beauty who needs architecture?

FRENCH GULCH
Three miles north of Route 299, this village was one of the richest diggings in the 1850s. Today it has a picturesque main street with a few stone buildings of the mining days. The most striking sight in town is, however, the tiny Gothic Revival church which you see on the east side of the road as you enter the town.

WHISKEYTOWN DAM
What was left of the rip-roaring settlement at Whiskeytown was submerged a few years ago in the reservoir backed up by the new Whiskeytown Dam. Overlooking the reservoir, eight miles from Redding on Route 299 is the Visitors Reception Center—four canopies each supported by a center post and an office facility in rough stone designed by the firm of Smith, Hunter, Hartman and Cox and built by the Division of Architecture of the U.S. Park Service in 1965-66.

SHASTA

As one passes through the ruins of Shasta's old business district today, it is difficult to realize that this was once the center of a thriving town of 2,500 gold-seekers. The long row of surprisingly uniform store-fronts, built in brick with iron shutters to avoid the hazard of fire that twice swept the town in the early 50s, is a very picturesque ruin on both sides of Route 299 six miles west of Redding. The Masonic Hall (1853) has been restored as have the jail and courthouse which may be visited 10 a.m. to 5 p.m. daily. Unfortunately the famous Classical Revival Shurtleff House (1851) burned to the ground several years ago.

SHASTA DAM

North of the City of Redding (on Hwy. 5; Hwy. 151) are two important monuments of the W. P. A. and of the Streamline Moderne of the late 1930s. These are Shasta Dam and its various outbuildings (Gordon B. Kaufmann & Earl C. Morris, consulting architects) which display many of the characteristic forms and ornament of the Moderne; and south and west of the Dam site is Project City which contains government-built housing and other buildings of the period. Construction on the Dam started in 1938 and was finished in the 1940s. Project City as its name suggests, was built to house those who worked on the construction of the Dam.

WEAVERVILLE

This small village is a well-preserved and unusually credible mining town. In spite of several devastating fires, sixteen of the brick buildings of the 1850s remain including the Courthouse (originally a saloon, 1856) at the corner of Main (Route 29) and Court Streets, and the Oddfellows Hall and the Clifford Building directly across from each other on Main Street just east of the Courthouse. Both of the latter have outside, iron spiral staircases from upper galleries to sidewalk beneath, a method of saving first-floor space almost unique in the United States. Most of the other architecturally notable buildings also stand near the Courthouse. Next door is a beautifully maintained and very chaste example of a Classical Revival house of the mid-nineteenth century and just north of the intersection of Court with Center on the east side of Court is a one and a half story house in the Queen Anne/Colonial Revival idiom of the last years of the century. Across the street from the Courthouse is a charming late Eastlake bandstand (1902). The most colorful building in town is off Main Street at the eastern edge of the business district—the Chinese Joss House (1869-1875) now set in a park and maintained by California Division of Beaches and Parks as a state monument. It was restored in 1957 and has recently been refurbished. In the same park is a museum of local history particularly emphasizing the contribution of the Chinese immigrants to the culture of the California frontier.

Weaverville Courthouse

REDDING

Redding is the county seat of Shasta county and has been a commercial center and cross-roads town since the gold-rush days. It is obvious from the paucity of Victorian architecture that in the nineteenth century it remained economically backward compared to the much smaller Red Bluff to the south, but in the twentieth century business flourished, and today it is a recreation center for the upper Central Valley. In process of construction (summer, 1972) on Market Street is an enclosed, air-conditioned mall, two blocks at present and one and a half blocks to be added later. It has been designed by Phil Patterson of Patterson, Langford and Steward of Medford, Oregon, and is the only such project besides a similar mall in San Bernardino. Several blocks of parking facilities have been planned on the west side. Hidden behind trees at 2100 West St. is the woodsy Saelzer House designed by Bernard Maybeck.

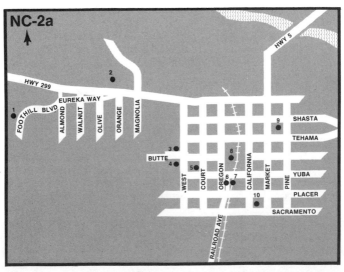

Redding NC-2

1. **Pilgrim Congregational Church** (United Church of Christ) 1959; Frank Lloyd Wright
   2850 Foothill Blvd. (S on Almond from Eureka Way (Route 299), then W on Foothill.)
   Latterday Wright.

2. **Shasta High School** 1926-27; Dorn and Dorn
   Eureka Way near Magnolia Ave.
   High Spanish Colonial Revival with a Byzantine flavor.

3. **House** c.1885; 1440 West St. at Butte St.
   Eastlake—a rarity in this town where Victorian architecture never sems to have flourished.

4. **Richard B. Eaton House** c.1865; 1520 West St.
   A clapboard Classical Revival cottage, somewhat remodeled.

5. **Shasta County Courthouse** c.1950
   W side Court St. bet. Yuba & Butte Sts.
   A huge International Style pile with recent additions.

6. **U.S. Post Office** c.1935
   SE cor. Yuba & Oregon Sts.
   Typical W. P. A. Moderne.

7. **Veterans Memorial Building** 1939
   SW cor. Yuba St. and Railroad Ave.
   Late W. P. A. Moderne.

8. **Southern Pacific Railroad Station** c.1910
   Off Oregon St. at Butte St.
   Turn of the century classical with delicate Tuscan columns—all this set in a beautiful row of palms.

9. **Fire Station** 1939; Masden & Hurd
   S side Shasta St. bet. Market & Pine Sts.
   One of the most striking examples of Streamline Moderne in the state.

NC-2b Red Bluff

10. Cascade Theater c.1938

E side Market St. bet. Sacramento & Placer Sts.

This Streamline Moderne movie palace is enriched by a fine sculptural frieze depicting the various industries of northern California in the robust realism generally connected with W. P. A. art.

RED BLUFF

(Reached from north or south by Interstate 5, and from Chico to the southeast by State Route 99)

Red Bluff is the commercial center of Tehama County, as well as being its county seat. Situated at the head of navigation of the Sacramento River, the town was an early stopping-off-point for Easterners who followed the Lassen Trail across the Cascade Range to northern California. The town was laid out in 1850 in the usual grid plan. Its site on the river is picturesque. As in many other California cities, Red Bluff is divided into two distinct parts by the Southern Pacific Railroad. In the early days produce from the rich farms to the south, lumber from the mountains to the east and west, and wool from the grazing lands that stretch off to the north as far as Oregon made Red Bluff the chief commercial center of the upper Sacramento Valley. In 1883 a fire destroyed most of the business district and recent developers have not spared such spectacular monuments of Victoriana as the Tremont Hotel, demolished in 1965 to make way for Peter Lassen Square. Nevertheless, the general appearance remains that of a prosperous country town of the late nineteenth century, all the more interesting because its houses and public buildings are modest in size, though sometimes flamboyant in detail.

In domestic architecture the crisp Italianate style, so popular in northern California towns in the 80s, is much in evidence. The extremely fine wood-carving (such as on the Kelly-Griggs House Museum) and the compact composition of the dwellings suggests that at least one master craftsman was at work in the period. Really unusual houses are rare, but almost all the streets, particularly Washington and Jefferson, can be traversed with little evidence of interference with what is essentially a period piece. Red Bluff is especially attractive on a hot, clear, summer day when palms and cottonwoods which line the streets cast cool shadows across well-kept lawns.

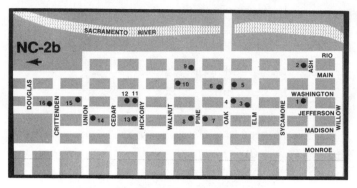

1. **Kelly-Griggs House Museum** c.1880
   NW cor. Ash and Washington Sts.
   A two-story, rigidly symmetrical Italianate bracketed house.

2. **House** c.1865
   Ash St. bet. Main & Rio Sts.
   An Italianate house with much Classical Revival detail.

3. **St. Paul's Episcopal Church** c.1890
   Ernest Coxhead
   NE cor. Jefferson & Elms Sts.
   A delightful, characteristic Coxhead Church, dollhouse in scale, sheathed in shingles and topped by a witchhat shingle tower. Minimal remodeling inside and out has not interfered with the original conception.

4. **Red Bluff City Center** 1967-68; Richard Smart and William Clabaugh
555 Washington St.
A low, one-story building with immaculate brick-work.

5. **State Theater** c.1935
S side 300 block on Oak St.
A colorful Moderne building, typical of the times.

● 6. **I.O.O.F. Hall** c.1870
NE cor. Washington & Oak Sts.
A well-preserved Italianate building, lodge rooms above and retail stores below. It still retains its original ground floor loggia.

● 7. **First Baptist Church** c.1885
SW cor. Pine & Jefferson Sts.
This basically Gothic Revival structure's light stone fabric is enhanced by red sandstone trim.

8. **House** c.1880
NW cor. Pine & Jefferson Sts.
A late Italianate bracketed house.

9. **Daily News Building** (formerly Bank of America) 1920; NE cor. Main & Pine Sts.
A beautifully proportioned classical building sheathed in white terra-cotta.

● 10. **Cone-Kimball Building** 1886
SW cor. Walnut & Main Sts.
The round, three-story tower, surrounded by clock faces and topped with an open cupola, dominates this building.

11. **House** c.1880; 905 Washington St.
One and a half story Queen Anne Cottage.

12. **House** c.1880
W side Washington St. bet. Hickory & Cedar Sts.
A small, story and a half Mansard roofed house with original patterned shingle roof.

13. **Herbert Kraft Free Library** c.1910
NW cor. Hickory & Jefferson Sts.
This simple classical building is on the model of many libraries built in this period.

14. **House** c.1885; 1055 Jefferson St.
A Queen Anne-Eastlake house with handsome towered entrance porch.

15. **House** c.1895; 1111 Washington St.
A Queen Anne house strongly touched by the late nineteenth century Colonial Revival.

16. **House** c.1898; 446 Crittenden St.
This defies stylistic categorization, though a Moorish effect seems to have been attempted. Even though small, this house boasts numerous dormers and a pair of low, bulbous towers.

● **17. William B. Ide Adobe** c.1850
1½ mi. NE of Red Bluff (N on Main St., then E on Adobe Rd.)

This house, the home of the first and only President of the California Republic, was restored in 1958. Perched under an oak on a bluff above the Sacramento River, it is a nostalgic stage set of California in the 1850s.

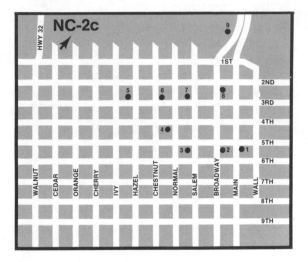

CHICO

Here is an example of nineteenth century civic responsibility. In the late 1840s John Bidwell, a leader of the first overland party of Americans seeking a home in California, bought the land where Chico now stands and called it Rancho Chico. He founded the town in 1860 just south of the place where he was to build his fine home. After the Civil War, in which he was a general in the state militia, Bidwell donated land for schools, churches, and for a Normal School, now Chico State University. His interest in agriculture and horticulture led him to develop a huge experimental farm which included not only a wide variety of exotic trees but also a vineyard which he soon dug up when he joined the temperance crusade (he was candidate of the Prohibition Party for the Vice Presidency in 1892). The family continued his benevolence after his death, donating vast acreages for parks.

Bidwell Park itself contains an impressive 2400 acres which have now regrettably been sliced in two by the Hwy 99 Freeway. On the extensive shaded campus of Chico State University are several buildings which reflect the 1920s version of brick Lombardian Romanesque, which was a popular style for educational buildings throughout California in the late teens and through the 20s.

Today Chico still shows signs of Bidwell's interests. It is the commercial center of a rich agricultural region, which among other things produces one-fifth of the world's almonds.

1. **Senator Theater** c.1936
   SW cor. W 5th and Main Sts.
   Extravagant adjectives come easily to mind in describing this monumental mixture of Moderne and Mayan motives.

● 2. **Post Office** 1914; Oscar Wenderoth, sup. architect
   SW cor. Broadway & W 5th Sts.
   This is a particularly graceful expression of the Italian Renaissance Revival.

3. **House** c.1875; 307 W 5th St.
   An imposing Italianate villa with not quite the quality of the Bidwell Mansion nearby, but very fine.

4. **House** c.1865; 410 Normal Ave.
   A wooden, late Classical Revival house with Italianate detail.

5. **House** c.1880; 238 Hazel St.
   A Queen Anne—Eastlake extravaganza.

6. **House (now Building D)** c.1915
   W 3rd St. at NE cor. Chestnut St.
   A pleasing composition in the West Coast Prairie Style.

7. **Episcopal Church** c.1885; NW cor. 3rd & Salem Sts.
   Almost invariably the most distinguished nineteenth-century church in northern California town is the Episcopal. This brick and shingle Gothic Revival structure with Eastlake details follows the rule. Notice the graceful apse.

8. **United California Bank** c.1928
   SE cor. W 2nd & Broadway Sts.
   Monumental Moderne.

● 9. **General John Bidwell House** 1865-67
   Henry W. Cleaveland
   On the grounds of Chico State University
   Bidwell, who owned the land on which Chico stands, desired a house to reflect his status and hired a famous eastern architect to do the job. Both the exterior and interior of this elegant villa have been recently restored. It is a State Historic Monument and is open to the public daily from 10 to 5.

10. **Matador Motel** c.1935
    SW cor. W 10th Ave. on Esplanade, about 1½ mi. from the City Plaza
    The red tiles, white walls and graceful arches of the Spanish Colonial Revival are set in beautiful grounds.

11. **Roman Catholic Church of Our Divine Savior**
1970; Quinn and Oda

566 Lassen Ave. (From north take Eaton Ave. exit from Interstate 99. Proceed E along Eaton about $\frac{1}{4}$ mile to Godman. Turn right on Godman about $\frac{1}{2}$ mile to Lassen. Church will be to your right. From south go N on Esplanade about $2\frac{1}{2}$ miles to Lassen. Turn E about $\frac{1}{2}$ mile.)

This church won a 1971 National Honor Award from the American Institute of Architects. It is a low white plaster box with steep shingle roof nicely faceted.

PARADISE
Several miles west of the town of Paradise on the Honey Run/Humbug Road is the Honey Run Covered Bridge (1894). This 230 ft. long covered bridge over Butte Creek is situated in a pastoral wooded area. Among the covered bridges in California it is one of the best preserved.

CLOVERDALE
At the juncture of Route 128 (to Mendocino and Fort Bragg) with Route 101, Cloverdale is the center of an agricultural area producing wool, hops, stock, citrus and grapes. In fact, her preeminence in orange groves and vineyards once led an early admirer to say that "Cloverdale appears as a winter bride in her orange blossoms and again as a russet-robed matron when the vineyard workers are calling blithely on the warm slopes." Amidst this boozy bliss is some good architecture.

As you enter the business district on Cloverdale Boulevard, you see at Second Street the First National Bank (c. 1890), a rare example of Richardsonian Romanesque with a well-related modern addition at the rear. To the east of it at the northeast corner of Main and Broad Streets is the quaint Episcopal Church of the Good Shepherd (1888), a wooden Gothic Revival building with Eastlake ornament and charming interior woodwork. Probably the most distinguished building in town is the shingled Gothic Revival Congregational Church (1889) on Cloverdale Boulevard near the intersection with University Avenue, just north of the business district. Some details, such as the bowed window at the south side, suggest that the architect was Ernest Coxhead, but it was actually N. A. Comstock.

Some worthwhile houses occur in various parts of town. At 210 Third Street is a Gothic Revival house with Eastlake decoration and lovely garden surrounded with picket fence. A pretty Queen Anne is at 221 Jefferson between Second and Third Streets. At 305 Washington Street is a late Shingle-Style (moving into Craftsman) house that is worth some study.

Congregational Church

ASTI

About five miles south of Cloverdale on Route 101, Asti is the home of the Italian Swiss Colony Winery. The principal sight is the Gothic Revival (with Baroque touches) Church of Our Lady of Carmel (c. 1890) which is in the shape of half a wine barrel.

FORT BRAGG

Founded as a military post in 1857, this town soon turned to other tasks—poultry-raising, fishing and particularly lumbering. The Union Lumber Company, on the site of the old fort (of which only an unimpressive building remains), is clearly the center of the economy.

The downtown has a number of old wood and stone commercial buildings, of which the Eastlake style Hardell General Merchandise Store at 145 Laurel Street is the most interesting. By far the most impressive building in the central district is the huge Shingle Style F. L. Johnson House (1892) on the west side of Redwood Avenue between Laurel and Main Streets. It is now a guest-house for the lumber company.

The residential district northeast of the town center has a few good houses such as the Shingle style house at 619 Fir Street, but the highlight of Fort Bragg is the little colony of Craftsman bungalows on Brandon Way, Winifred Street, Bush Street and Perkins Way. Almost all are worthy of comparison with similar houses and bungalows in Berkeley and Pasadena. The two story shingle house (c.1910) at 501 Bush Street with its oriental hanging lamp and quaint garden looks as if it had come out of the *Craftsman* magazine.

MENDOCINO

Mendocino City, as yet unspoiled, seems a bit of Cape Cod shipped around the Horn. It was a prosperous seaport and milltown in the days before the hills were stripped of Virgin timber. Now not a trace of the lumber industry or the wharf remains—only a beautiful cove, a town of picturesque houses, and an extreme oddity in the Masonic Hall with wavy-line verge-board and a cupola vaguely modeled on the Choragic Monument of Lysicrates surmounted by a wooden sculptural group—Father Time hovering over a strange little girl.

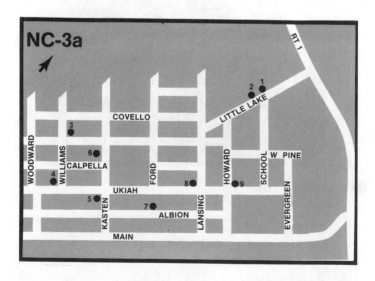

1. **Spenser Hill House** 1855
   On Little Lake Rd. at end of School St.
   Gothic Revival.

2. **Joshua Grindle House** 1879
   On Little Lake Rd. nr. end of School St.
   An Italianate one-story cottage.

3. **House (now jewelry store)** c.1880
   450 Little Lake Rd. at NE cor. Williams St.
   A Queen Anne house stripped of most of the details of that style.

4. **House** c.1855
   NW cor. Williams and Ukiah Sts.
   Board and batten Gothic Revival.

5. **House (now arts and crafts shop)** 1878
   SW cor. Kasten & Ukiah Sts.
   A very late Classical Revival house with quoined corners.

6. **House** c.1855
   600 Kasten St.
   A good board-and-batten house now painted yellow.

7. **House** c.1855; 740 Albion St.
   This imposing Gothic Revival house is most romantically viewed across a pond directly below it on Main Street.

8. **Masonic Hall** 1865
   NW cor. Lansing & Ukiah Sts.
   One of the strangest buildings in the state. The sculpture "Time and the Virgin" on the cupola is based on one of the familiar symbols of Freemasonry.

9. **House** c.1885
   NE cor. Howard & Ukiah Sts.
   Shingled Eastlake.

10. **Presbyterian Church** 1867
    On Main St. nr. end of Howard St.
    A late example of the Gothic Revival spectacularly placed on the bluff overlooking Big River Beach and the Pacific Ocean.

UKIAH

The name Ukiah is a phonetic spelling of the Indian word "yokaya," meaning deep valley between high hills, and was originally applied to a large rancho of which the present town comprises only a small part. The Yankees established a town there in 1850, and in 1859 the tiny village was made the seat of Mendocino County. It is now the commercial center of the valley which produces pears, prunes and grapes.

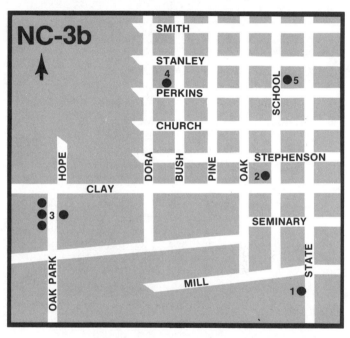

1. **Ukiah Theater** c.1935
   Nr. SW cor. S State & W Mill Sts.
   This grand ensemble of Streamlined Moderne includes a lobby and office structure connected at a right angle with the main auditorium. A tower of glass brick topped with something that looks like a bottle cap, and a neon sign in tune with the style complete the picture of one of the few elements of grandeur in the thirties.

2. **House** c.1885; 308 S School St.
   A house in the Eastlake style of a quality rare in a town where the nineteenth century was not very grand.

3. **Group of houses** 1910
   Oak Park Ave. nr. W Clay St.
   Several Craftsman bungalows, notable because one sees so little of this woodsy style north of Berkeley.

4. **Church of St. Mary of the Angels** 1923
   NW cor. N Bush & W Perkins Sts.
   A very late example of the Mission Revival.

5. **Mendocino County Courthouse** c.1910
   SE cor. W Standley & N School Sts.
   A fine classical facade in dressed, red sandstone—almost French in its elegance.

WILLITS
Willits is the eastern terminus for the romantic California Western Railroad which winds through the mountains to the coast at Fort Bragg. The town was first settled in 1865 and was incorporated in 1888. In addition to its chief architectural glory, its railroad station, Willits contains some well preserved Eastlake and Queen Anne houses and cottages. Several of the Eastlake cottages can be seen on School Street between Mendocino St. and Wood St. (note especially 118 School St. and the small cottage at the cor. of School St. and Wood St.)

1. **Northwest Pacific and the California Western Railroad Station** 1914-15; D. J. Patterson
   Commercial St. (3 blocks east of Main St.)

2. **Cottage** c.1880s; 84 State St.
   A Queen Anne cottage with a small tower.

LAKEPORT
Lakeport, which was at first named Forbestown, was established in 1859. On Clearlake Avenue and on Forbes Street are a number of older 19th century buildings including the 1871 County Court House, but the most important architectural monument in town is St. John's Episcopal Church of c.1889 designed by the turn of the century Bay area architect Willis Polk (with recent additions by Jack Payne). West and north of Lakeport is Bachelor's Valley which is filled with

wonderful wood barns (Bachelor's Valley can be reached by driving north of Lakeport on Hwy. 29 to Upper Lake, then west on Hwy. 20 to the Witter Springs Rd.)

COLUSA
Colusa lies about 28 miles west of Marysville on Rt. 20. Its architecture and place on the river give Colusa affinities with Mississippi River towns. The architectural gem is the Courthouse (1861) whose Classical Revival portico and cupola are almost completely hidden in trees. As in other California county seats, the next striking building is the I.O.O.F. Hall (1892). The residential district is very pleasant. In fact, Colusa seems a must for the nostalgia cult.

MARYSVILLE
(At the intersection of State Routes 70 and 20)
Originally called New Mecklenberg, Marysville was founded in 1842 and was named for Mary Murphy, one of the survivors of the historic Donner party. It is the only successful settlement of the eight cities which were laid out in this area during the height of the gold rush. After the nearby gold deposits gave out, Marysville became an important commercial center for the rich surrounding agricultural region. In 1850, when Yuba County was formed, Marysville became the county seat.

The town is situated at the confluence of the Yuba and Feather Rivers. The Yuba River very early filled with silt from the gold mines, thus raising the river bed and causing a series of disastrous floods. Since 1875, high levees have been constructed, and the town now lies well below the nearby river bed. Time has not been kind to the old district situated between First and Second streets. What was once a colorful assemblage of Victorian architecture is now in poor repair. As one proceeds north along E Street, the modern (undistinguished) business district presents itself. To the east and west of this was an area of fine houses and other buildings of the pre-Civil War period. Urban renewal has slashed through this district demolishing among other things, the marvelous Gothic Revival Court House (1854), which at the time of its demise was the second oldest public building in the state. But Marysville still has several fine Gothic Revival buildings, one of which, the Aaron House, is now a museum of local history. The town also has one of the state's oldest Chinese "Joss" Houses (Bok Kai Temple). This building, a reminder that Chinese labor was used in the building of the Southern Pacific and Western Pacific railroads is situated in the shadow of the river levee.

NC-4a Marysville

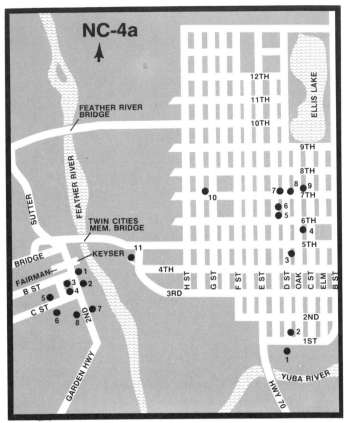

1. **Chinese Joss House (Bok Kai Temple)** c.1875
   S end D St.
   Chinese detail applied to a simple structure.

2. **Tower Theater** c.1935
   E side 100 block on D St.
   Moderne.

3. **Ramirez House ("The Castle")** c.1856; 220 5th St.
   A two-story Gothic Revival house with a projecting central bay and with very delicately detailed
   verge-boards, porch columns, and cast iron fence.

4. **City Hall**   1939; Starks and Flanders (W. P. A.)
   SW cor. C & 6th Sts.
   Art Moderne in its classical phase.

5. **House** c.1860; 618 D St.
   A well-proportioned Classical Revival house with
   Federal, fan-lighted door and Italianate detail.

6. **Stephen J. Field House** c.1860; 630 D St.
   A brick house, undistinguished architecturally,
   but the home of a Williams College graduate
   who went from being alcalde of Marysville to the
   United States Supreme Court, and as associate
   justice influenced the court in a number of extremely important decisions.

7. **Mary Aaron House (now a Museum)**   1855
   704 D St.
   A tiny California version (in brick and wood trim)
   of Strawberry Hill; certainly the most fanciful
   surviving example of the Gothic Revival in California.

8. **House** c.1870
   329 - 7th St. at D St.
   A large Italianate villa in a style not much used
   in Marysville.

9. **St. Joseph's Catholic Church** 1855
   NW cor. 7th & C Sts.
   This academic Gothic Revival structure has been
   stuccoed over on the exterior and remodeled
   (after a fire) on the interior, but it is still imposing.

10. **House**   c.1855; NW cor. G & 7th Sts.
    A story and a half Gothic Revival house with
    two handsome bays and very elegant detail.

11. **Western Pacific Railroad Station**   c.1910
    On a spur off J St. nr. its intersection with 4th St.
    This Mission Revival structure built on a levee
    has been abandoned as of 1972.

The town of Yuba City was plotted in 1849, and like Marysville it is now protected by high levees along the Feather River. In contrast to its sister city across the river, Yuba City presents a rather irregular pattern of streets. Originally quite rich in 19th century buildings, only a few have survived down to the present day.

1. **Masonic Hall** c.1905
   NE cor. B & 2nd Sts.

   A classic Mission Revival composition with a pair of square towers topped by low-pitched hipped roofs, and between the towers a scalloped gable and the usual star window (except in this case the window is a vent for the attic).

2. **Sutter County Office Building**   1953
   Harry J. Devine
   Across St. E from old Courthouse bet. B & C Sts.

   A good example of the type of modern architecture which was being used for public buildings in the 1950s. Tile mosaic decorates the entrance and the upper hall.

3. **Hall of Records**   1891; SW cor. B & 2nd Sts.
   A strange, squat Romanesque Revival building.

4. Sutter County Courthouse

4. Sutter County Courthouse c.1860
NW cor. C & 2nd Sts.
An Italianate bracketed cornice embellishes this otherwise Classical Revival building with its two story temple front and cupola on roof.

5. House c.1880; 241 C St.
A typical one-story Eastlake cottage with a high basement and two bays projecting from the front corners of the structure.

6. House c.1875; 224 C St.
A large Italianate house with modern Italianate porch and office addition connected by an International style corridor. It comes off very well.

7. House c.1860; 423 2nd St.
A two-story Classical Revival house with Italianate touches. The doorway is especially fine. The one-story porch across the front may be later.

8. House c.1870; 422 2nd St.
A two-story Italianate house.

9. Farm Securities Administration Projects 1936-39; Vernon DeMars
S of Courthouse about 2 mi.; second street to Garden Hwy. Turn E at Miles Ave. Housing project is behind row of houses on Garden Hwy.
A good example of low-cost housing as it was realized in the New Deal era.

OROVILLE

Even though Oroville is probably located on a rich gold deposit, not all of her history is lodged in her name. The first settlers came for gold in 1849 and gold was a major factor in the economy well into the 1880s. But Orville also developed as the commercial center of a rich agricultural region, and since the construction of the Oroville Dam in 1968 has become the hub of a large recreation area as well.

That in the nineteenth century Oroville was able to adapt to changing economic situations is well illustrated in her architecture, particularly on Bird Street where Victorian taste is strongly concentrated.
Incidentally, one is again impressed by the fact that so much of California is still rural-small town.

1. Judge Charles Fayette Lott House 1856
1067 Montgomery St.
Beautifully maintained by the city as a museum, this house and grounds exhibit the fact that the Eastern amenities were easily transferred to the West—the exact opposite of the stereotype of the frontier. The house is a mixture of Gothic Revival and Classical Revival details.

2. **Chinese Joss House** 1863; 1500 Broderick St.
Not as colorful as some of the other Joss Houses in the State, this one is perhaps more authentic than most and is open as a museum. It is estimated that Oroville once had as many as 10,000 Chinese in her population.

3. **First Congregational Church** 1912
SE cor. Oak & Bird Sts.
A late contribution to the shingled Gothic Revival.

4. **Post Office** 1932; Frederick H. Meyer
SE cor. Oak & Robinson Sts.
Cleaned-up Renaissance.

OROVILLE DAM AREA

At Kelly Ridge (off Hwy. B-2) is a 19th century Suspension Bridge and Tollhouse which originally stood at Bidwell Bar but was moved with the construction of the Oroville Dam. The bridge was fabricated in Troy, New York, and was then shipped around the Horn in 1853. The stone tollhouse is a rarity in California.

Also close to the Dam site off Hwy. B-2 is the Thermalio Hydroelectric Complex of 1971, designed by Frank V. Lee. One should contrast the styling of this hydroelectric complex with the Moderne version at Shasta Dam.

WOODLEAF

About 18 miles west of Oroville on Hwy. B-1 is the Woodville House Hotel, a large two story Greek Revival structure of 1858.

STRAWBERRY VALLEY

About 5 miles beyond Woodleaf where Hwy. B-1 becomes A-14, one comes into an area that is well known for its picturesque weatherbeaten wood barns.

LA PORTE

14 miles beyond Strawberry Valley on Hwy. A-14 is the Union Hotel, a really fine example of the Greek Revival in California. This two story building with a two story porch was built in the 1850s.

FORT ROSS

Fort Ross, situated at the mouth of the Russian River, was settled by the Russians as a trading post in 1812. The site of the Fort and its few remaining buildings was acquired by the State in 1906, and it is now a State Historic Monument. The only two major buildings still remaining at the time it was acquired were the Commander's House and the picturesque redwood Russian Orthodox Chapel with its hexagonal tower topped by a round cupola. During the 30s and later much of the Fort was restored including the surrounding stockade. In 1971 the Chapel burned to the ground. Plans are now underway for its reconstruction.

CALISTOGA

The name Calistoga was coined by the town's founder and promoter Samuel Brannan from "California" and from "Saratoga." It was Brannan's vision that the town would become the fashionable Saratoga of the West Coast. In 1866 he built a hotel and a group of 25 cottages near the hot springs, and he also managed to bring a branch railroad to his new community. The only signs left of the original resort are one of the cottages, Brannan's own store on Wapoo Ave. and a line of Palm trees. Several of the Brannan cottages have been moved; one may be seen at 1311 Cedar St., another at 109 Wapoo St. Along Lincoln Ave., the town's major street, are several late 19th century commercial buildings.

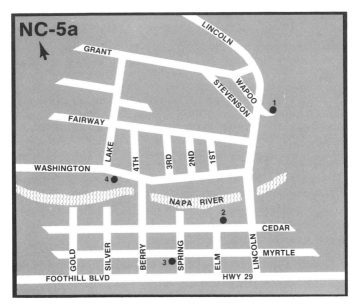

1. **Sam Brannan Cottage** 1866
    S of junction of Lincoln & Wapoo Aves. (Not original site)

    The cottage is small and consists of a simple rectangular volume covered by a hipped roof. Its only pretense is to be found in the porch which with its scalloped arches is somewhat Islamic in feeling.

2. **House** late 1870s; 1300 Cedar St.
    An Italianate house with a Second Empire Mansard roof.

3. **House** late 1870s
    NW cor. Martle & Spring Sts.

    An impressive and quite substantial stone house. In style it represents the Second Empire Mansard mode.

4. **Russian Orthodox Church** after 1900
    W side Washington St. bet. Lake & 4th Sts.

    A 20th century version of the Old Russian Orthodox Church at Fort Ross set in a thickly wooded garden.

HEALDSBURG

Healdsburg was incorporated as early as 1850. Its economic orientation then and now was toward agriculture. Its street pattern is basically that of two gridiron systems laid out in an oblique angle to one another. The commercial downtown area centers on a pleasant square, and several of the buildings facing the square such as the Trisch Building on the north side are almost Greek in their classical flavor. North St., between Fitch St. and East St. exhibits a number of modest late 19th century houses. The largest residences are located on Johnson St. north of the town square and on Matheson St. to the East. The eastern side of town forms a gradual pre-freeway transition between the open country and the residences of the town.

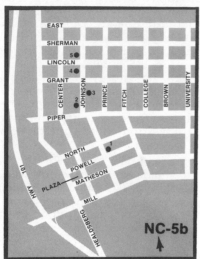

1. **Church of Christ** c.1880s; 301 Powell St.
   A modest Eastlake church building, with delicate spindle work in the open tower.

2. **Cottage** c.late 1880s; 152 Johnson St.
   A Queen Anne cottage.

3. **House** c.late 1880s; 343 Johnson St.
   A two-story Queen Anne house.

4. **House** c.late 1880s; 607 Johnson St.
   A Queen Anne house.

5. **House** c.late 1870s; 619 Johnson St.
   A two-story Italianate house with a later Colonial Revival porch.

6. **Cottage** c.1890s; 423 Matheson St.
   An unusual Queen Anne/Mission Revival cottage, with small tower to the east, and several handsome quatrefoil windows.

7. **Cottage** late 1880s; 403 Matheson St.
   A small Queen Anne cottage.

The first gridiron pattern of streets was laid out in Napa in 1848; other gridiron sections were laid out later, none of which line up with the original grid— with the result that Napa's street pattern presents the most picturesque assemblage which can be obtained through the use of the grid pattern. The site of the city is flat, but it has forcibly avoided the usual dullness of a level site through the lushness of its vegetation and the smaller scale of its public, commercial and residential architecture. Its largest park, Fuller Park, is an impressive tree shaded public glen. As is characteristic of most California cities, none of the city parks or open spaces take advantage of adjoining waterways, in this case the Napa River and the smaller Napa Creek.

Both the commercial and public downtown as well as the surrounding residential area are still essentially Victorian in feeling. The 1878 Courthouse hidden behind its trees still dominates the center of town, and the First Presbyterian Church forms a public transition from central downtown to the residential area. While the ground floors of almost all of the retail store buildings have been remodeled from time to time over the years, their upper floors and many of their projecting roof cornices remain as originally built. A number of newer buildings have recently been built in the central area, and on the whole they fit well and comfortably with their much older neighbors.

For those interested in late 19th century domestic architecture, Napa is a must! Numerous examples of houses built from the mid-1870s on exist, and even more important, here one can find whole blocks of residential streets which have fully retained their 19th century flavor. The city is especially rich in examples of the Italianate style, though regrettably a number of these have been destroyed in the past few years.

1. **Napa County Court House**   1878
   Samuel and Joseph C. Newsom; Ira Gilchrist
   Brown St., bet. 2nd & 3rd Sts.

   A version of governmental Italianate; regrettably the building has lost its octagonal tower which was topped with a fanciful onion dome.

2. **The Napa Opera House**   1879
   Samuel and Joseph C. Newsom; Ira Gilchrist
   E side Main St., bet. 1st & Pearl Sts.

   Commercial Italianate; except for present fire escape, the upper part of the building is well preserved; the ground floor retail store fronts have been extensively altered.

3. **Bank of America** (originally the Bank of Napa)
   1923; NW cor. Main & 2nd Sts.

   A tasteful small Roman-Renaissance bank building.

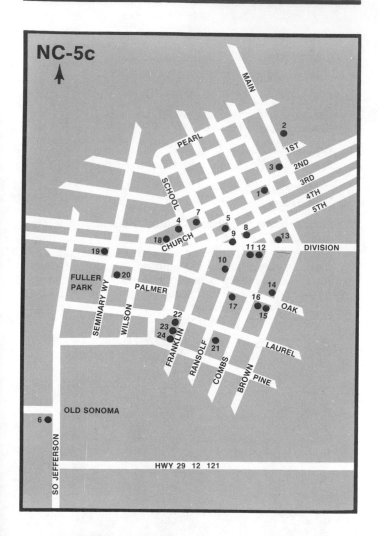

4. Redwood National Bank 1965
Neil Smith & Assoc.
SW cor. 2nd & School Sts.

A sensitively scaled and detailed small bank building.

5. First Presbyterian Church 1874; Daley & Eisen.
Replaced older 1857 structure
SW cor. 3rd & Randolph Sts.

Still one of the dominant landmarks in the city. An impressive well maintained example of late Victorian Gothic; all in wood; sculpture on third level of tower unusual.

6. Drive-in-Shopping Center c.1940
SW cor. S. Jefferson St. & Old Sonoma Rd.

An example of the Streamlined Moderne; the tower with glass is especially interesting.

7. House c.1870s; 833 Franklin St.

Small Italianate house with central three-story tower.

8. **House** c.1880s; 608 Randolph St.
   Queen Anne with Eastlake touches.

9. **House** c.1870s; 569 Randolph St.
   An example of the Italianate Style.

10. **House** c.early 1880s; 555 Randolph St.
    Eastlake Style house.

11. **House** c.1880s; 1225 Division St.
    Mixture of Eastlake and Queen Anne styles.

12. **House** c.early 1880s; 1211 Division St.
    Eastlake style.

13. **House (now the Napa County Historical Society)**
    c.1880; 508 Combs St.
    This house is basically Queen Anne in style; it exhibits many fanciful elements of this style ranging from its tall three-story corner tower, to its oval opening in the porch above the front entrance, to the classical inspired railings and columns of the main porch.

14. **Goodman House** c.late 1870s
    NW cor. Oak & Brown Sts.; (originally faced on Brown St.)
    A large and impressive Italianate house which boasts a third floor mansard roof and dormers; the entrance porch, doorway and entrance hall are elaborate and well preserved.

15. **Churchill House** c.late 1870s; later addition in the 90s
    485 Brown St.
    A substantial Italianate house to which was added in the 90s (?) a two-story Colonial Revival porch; said to be one of the largest existing private residences in Napa.

16. **Churchill House (no. 2) (later "Cedar Gables Inn")**
late 1890s; Ernest Coxhead
486 Combs St.
A classic Coxhead production combining in an impossible fashion elements of Classical architecture with the vernacular Shingle style. The central round tower with its conical roof supported by four short columns is similar to several other houses designed by this architect.

17. **House** late 1880s; 492 Randolph St.
Displays almost all of the essential trademarks of the Queen Anne—corner tower, elaborate entrance porch with curved openings, sawed and spindle work; a wide array of textured surfaces, including stucco work on the south side of the house.

18. **House** late 1870s; 1567 3rd St.
Italianate.

19.   **House**   c.1885-1890; 741 Seminary Wy.

Queen Anne Revival house with a wonderful display of spindle work and different textured surfaces; note second floor bay windows each facing onto triangular spindle and column enclosed openings.

20.   **Cottage**   c.1900

NE cor. Seminary Way & Palmer St.

Colonial Revival; a turn-of-the-century bungalow with the curved porch now transformed into an outdoor living room.

21.   **Cottage**   c.1880s; 330 Randolph St.

Eastlake.

22.   **Double house**   late 1870s; 397 Franklin St.

Italianate.

23.   **House**   early 1880s; 333 Franklin St.

An Eastlake house with a finely detailed entrance porch.

24.   **House**   late 1870s; 313 Franklin St.

Large Italianate house very rich in sawed and carved ornament; unusual "V" pediments above doors and windows.

25.   **Salvador Vallejo Adobe**   1850s (?)

1006 Monticello Rd.

Single story adobe house.

PETALUMA

Petaluma was founded on the need of San Franciscans for food, principally potatoes. By the early 1850s Petaluma had developed truck farming to the point that it was the wealthiest and commercially liveliest community in Sonoma County. The association with "the big city" shows today in an array of Victorian architecture that resembles on a small scale the variety of Eastlake, Queen Anne and Italianate styles that still give quality to the Bay Area. Nowhere else in California can you see so many Italianate, iron storefronts, many of them with a plate giving the name of the foundry in San Francisco where they were produced.

As in the larger city, the town fathers adopted a grid plan, but since Petaluma was laid out on a curve of the Petaluma River, the grid was bent, so that the town is divided into two parts, neither of which is oriented on the points of the compass. It is very confusing. But the variety and excellence of the architecture are worth the difficult problems of navigation.

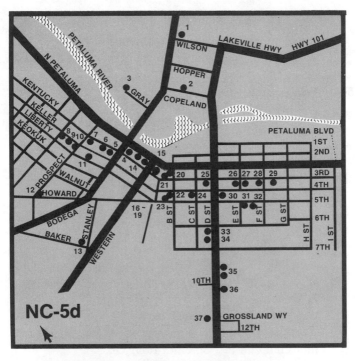

2. Northwestern Pacific Railroad Station

NC-5d　Petaluma

1. **House** c.1885
   NE cor. Washington & Wilson Sts.
   A combination of Eastlake and Queen Anne modes very characteristic of California and almost unique to this state.

2. **Northwestern Pacific Railroad Station** c.1905
   Nr. NE cor. Washington & Copland Sts.
   Mission Revival.

3. **Grain Elevator** c.1920
   At N end Gray St.
   A monumental reminder of Petaluma's place in agriculture.

4. **Sonoma County National Bank (now Westgate Realty)** c.1910
   SW cor. Washington St. & Petaluma Blvd. N
   A classical pile that you could have confidence in.

5&6. **Two houses** c.1885
   219 Kentucky St., 233 Kentucky St.
   Both are variations on the Eastlake-Queen Anne combination.

7. **House** 1880; 253 Kentucky St.
   Queen Anne in a purer form.

8. **House** 1885
   SE cor. Keller & Oak Sts.
   A good example of the Eastlake style.

9. **House** 1885; 311 Keller St.
   Another Eastlake house.

10. **House** c.1880; 200 Prospect St.
    A Queen Anne house with a lovely fence.

11. **House** c.1895; 226 Liberty St.
    A plain Queen Anne house which shows signs of merging with the Colonial Revival.

12. **House** c.1885; 516 Prospect St.
    An Eastlake cottage.

13. **Elim Lutheran Church** c.1880
    NW cor. Baker & Stanley Sts.
    A Gothic Revival structure with especially imaginative tower. Unfortunately the original wood has been stuccoed.

14. **I.O.O.F. Building** c.1880
    111 Petaluma Blvd. N
    As usual, the Odd Fellows have a striking building. In this town they have a three-story, iron front with a curved Mansard roof. Like most of Petaluma's iron fronts, this building has been "modernized" on the first floor.

15.　Wells Fargo Bank c.1915
NW cor. Western St. & Petaluma Blvd. N

Another classical bank in competition with the one at the Washington end of the block on Petaluma.

16.-19.　A row of iron fronts c.1885
S side Western St. from Petaluma Blvd. to Kentucky St.

This row of Italianate iron fronts is really unmatched in California architecture. The Masonic Building (16) at the east end of Western is a three-story structure with odd Mansard cupola at the corner. The next two smaller buildings (17, 18) are also variations on the Italianate mode with Second Empire decoration, so common in the late phase of the style. The Mutual Relief Association Building (19) at Western and Kentucky appears to be the finest of the lot partly because the crisp, cast iron decoration has been further delineated by being painted green and set against a tan background. It has a plaque at its base announcing that it was made at the Pendergast Foundry, San Francisco, 1885. Certainly this row must be the pride of Petaluma!

20.　Commercial Building 1886
23 Petaluma Blvd. N

Another cast iron of great quality above, remodeled below.

● 21.　McNear Building 1886
On Kentucky St. at a bend in the street and just around the corner two buildings from the Mutual Relief Association Building.

Another Italianate iron front with extremely delicate ornamentation. This one was made by O'Connell and Lewis, Architectural Iron Work, 230 to 236 Stewart Street, San Francisco.

22. Evangelical Free Church c.1880
SW cor. 5th & B Sts.
Gothic Revival.

23. Petaluma Women's Club 1913
B St. across from 515.

A Craftsman structure with Prairie Style windows.
The Craftsman style is closely associated throughout the State with the architecture of women's
clubs which were burgeoning in the period just before World War I.

● **24. St. John's Episcopal Church** c.1890
Ernest Coxhead
NW cor. 5th & C Sts.

Coxhead, who might be called the official Episcopalian architect in the late 80s and early 90s,
worked his usual magic here. The feeling is a
fairy-tale church out of an imaginary English
countryside. The entrance porch should be particularly noted since it is a playful interpretation of
English Queen Anne decoration. One wishes that
the shingles had not been painted.

25. Post Office c.1930
120 4th St. at D St.

Stripped Spanish Colonial Revival with green
marble trim.

26. House c.1875; 222-4th St.

An Italianate structure with beautiful fence and
yard.

27. Heritage House of Petaluma 1894
300-4th St. at E St.

A small Queen Anne cottage.

28. House 320-4th St. at F St.

A two-story Italianate house with a great deal of
gingerbread.

29. House c.1880; 404-4th St.

A very simple cottage with a Queen Anne door, a
little Eastlake decoration and some very unusual
stepped, curved sawed work on the gable end
facing the street.

30. House c.1885; 501-D St.

An Eastlake-Queen Anne house with a Moorish flavor.

31. House c.1875; 300-6th St. at E St.

A chaste Italianate villa with a magnificent magnolia tree in the front yard.

32. House c.1885; S side 6th St. bet. E & F Sts.

It is possible that this Eastlake-Queen Anne House with its handsome entrance porch was designed by Samuel and Joseph Newsom.

33. House 112-7th St. at D St.

A Queen Anne-Eastlake cottage.

34. House c.1890; 758-D St.

A huge Queen Anne-Shingle building.

35. Two houses c.1930; 849-D St., 853-D St.

Both are Georgian Revival, the first of wood and the second of brick, and are sophisticated designs in a style that has until recently been dismissed by the avant-garde.

36. House c.1910; 901-D St.

A two-story building with two gigantic classical columns supporting the entrance porch.

37. House c.1930
1000 D St.

The twentieth century Colonial Revival at its best. A design showing that an architect with imagination can express himself and his client's wishes within the confines of a historic style.

Vallejo Adobe ("Casa Grande")
About 4 mi. E of Petaluma off Sonoma Rd. (Rt. 116)
This was the country residence of General Mariano Guadalupe Vallejo and is the largest adobe structure in Northern California. It was begun in 1836 and expanded through the years by this hero of the Mexican War and loyal American after the peace treaty. Restoration was begun by the State in 1951, and it is now a very complete museum of the mid-nineteenth century Mexican-American heritage. Open to the public.

Union District School

About five mi. SW of Petaluma on Point Reyes Rd. is this charming example of the Classical Revival of the 1860s.

ST. HELENA

The town of St. Helena was founded in 1855, and almost from the first its life and economic base have been organized around the wineries and vineyards which surround it on all sides. Main Street, which is a short segment of State Hwy. 29, is both the spine and the commercial center of the town. To the east lies the railroad and other commercial activities; to the west on a gradually rising hill is the residential district. All of the buildings of the town, from the one and two story commercial buildings on Main Street, to the churches, schools and houses on the hill are small and modest in scale. The wineries and the occasional large scale houses of their owners lie outside of or just at the edge of the town. Many of these buildings represent some of the most impressive 19th century examples of architecture in stone to be found in California. North of St. Helena along Hwy. 29 are several large 19th century houses placed on the hillside overlooking the valley. One can obtain a glimpse of an Italianate/Eastlake house about a mile north (on the west side of the Hwy.), of Christian Brothers Winery, and a little further up the Hwy. on the same side of the road is "Rockland," a Queen Anne style house. Across the road just before Deer Park Rd. are the Charles Krug stone winery buildings which were started in 1868 and completed in 1884. South of St. Helena on several of the smaller roads are located Gothic Revival cottages dating from the 1860s.

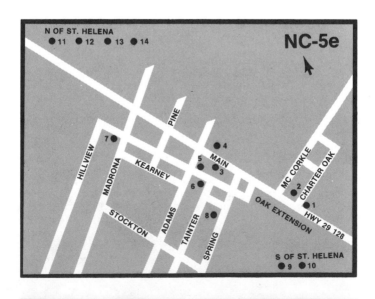

1. **House** c.1860s; 738 Main St.
   Victorian Gothic Revival house.

2. **Old St. Helena Winery** 1880
   NE cor. Main St. & Charter Oak Ave.
   A well proportioned stone building with arched windows and projecting corner quoining.

3. **Richie Block** 1892; 1331 Main St.
   A fanciful example of a Queen Anne store and office building. The second floor balconies with their curved lattice work ingeniously connect the three projecting bays.

4. **I.O.O.F. Building** 1885
   E side Main St. bet. Adams St. & Hunt Ave.
   A rather severe Queen Anne Revival commercial building. The street facade exhibits an interesting rosette design in pressed brick.

5. **Carnegie Public Library Building** 1906
   NE cor. Oak & Adams Sts.
   Turn-of-the-century Mission Revival.

6. **Catholic Church of St. Helena** 1889
   attrib. to Fr. R. Becker
   SW cor. Tainter & Oak Sts.
   A Victorian Gothic Revival church completely rebuilt in 1946 after the fire of the previous year.

7. **Cottage** late 1880s; 1551 Oak St.
   A Queen Anne Revival cottage.

8. **First Presbyterian Church** 1874
   1428 Spring St.
   A wood Victorian Gothic Revival Church.

9. **Robert Mondavi Winery** 1966; Cliff May
   Just N of Oakville on Hwy. 29
   A 1960s version of the Mission Revival, though the large arch opening with the tower to one side is a compositional device much more reminiscent of the 19th century Richardsonian Romanesque Revival.

10. **Inglenook Winery** 1879; William Mooser
    At S edge of Rutherford on Hwy. 29

    A large three-story building of stone which defies any stylistic pigeon hole. The old tasting room to the right of the main entrance is Eastlake in flavor.

11. **Beringer House (now the wine tasting and selling center for the Beringer Winery)** 1883
    William Mooser
    At York Creek, N edge St. Helena, off Hwy. 29

    A San Francisco architect's version of a Rhine Villa; the well preserved interior is a mixture of Eastlake and Queen Anne Revival.

12. **The Christian Brothers Winery** (formerly the Greystone Winery) 1889; Percy & Hamilton
    N of St. Helena on Hwy. 29

    Another stone winery by a San Francisco architectural firm. The arched entrance and other details place this building loosely within the fold of the Richardsonian Romanesque Revival.

13. Gristmill

13. **Gristmill (Old Bale Mill)** 1846
    3 mi. N of St. Helena on Hwy. 29

    An often photographed highly picturesque build-
    ing dominated by its very large overshot wheel.

14. **Sterling Vineyards** 1971-72; Martin J. Waterfield,
    designer; Keeth Assoc. Engineers
    4300 St. Helena Hwy.

    A contemporary Italian monastery set romanti-
    cally on a high hill which overlooks the valley.
    The interior tiles for walls and floors were de-
    signed and produced by Nancy Genn.

SANTA ROSA

Santa Rosa became a post office in 1852, a township
the following year, the county seat in 1854 and was incorporated in 1868. In 1870 the Southern Pacific Railroad reached the city, and in 1887 the Santa Rosa &
Carquinez Railroad was finished. As a railroad center
the city became the major shipping point for the produce of the area. Santa Rosa is one of the largest
cities north of the Bay area, and as such it has many
of the assets and problems which are being faced by
larger communities. For one interested in architecture
and planning it presents a rather complete picture of
what has been going on in California over the past 100
years or more.

One can enter Santa Rosa via two major routes, each
of which characterizes in a way different periods in the
history of California. The approach which most people
experience is via the Freeway—Rt. 101, which like
many urban Freeways manages to beautifully cut the
community into two distinct parts. The second way of
entering the city is from the east via Hwy. 12, which
gently follows the curves of Santa Rosa Creek to the
south. The visual and factual impact of the Freeway,
plus the usual problems faced by the older commercial centers of a city led to the deterioration of the business district. The area south of Fourth Street is now
undergoing renewal, and in this instance the results
are most laudable. A number of the older commercial

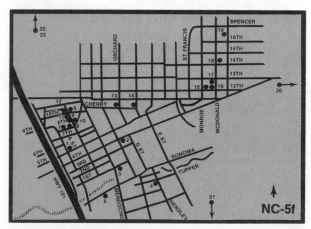

buildings have been well integrated into the new plan, along with a new group of public as well as private buildings. The public buildings are low in scale, and are set in open park-like settings. The only contrast to this horizontal scale is the new 14 story Bethlehem Tower.

Several fragments of the 19th century residential area are still in existence north of Fourth Street. The best preserved of these is the area centered around McDonald Street and the old McDonald House.

1. **U. S. Post Office Building** (no longer in use)
   1905-06; James Knox Taylor
   A dignified Roman-Renaissance revival building.

2. **Rosenberg's Department Store Building** 1937
   Hertzka & Knowles
   SE cor. A & 4th Sts.
   The commercial Streamlined Moderne style of the 30s on a large scale.

3. **Santa Rosa City Hall** 1970
   DeBrer, Bell, Heglund & Assoc.
   SE cor. Santa Rosa & 1st Sts.
   An exposed concrete structure set in its own large park; a covered walkway leads into a two story inner court which is dominated by a double exterior staircase which leads to the council chambers. The building expresses a strong play between the formal and the informal in its composition.

4. **Bethlehem Tower** 1971
   Duncombe, Roland and Miller
   Cor. Tupper & Hendley Sts.
   This tall 14-story tower dominates the skyline of Santa Rosa. It contains 160 units of housing for the elderly.

5. **Baptist Church** 1902
   Sonoma Ave., bet. A St. & Santa Rosa Ave.
   The fame of this church rests on the fact that it was built from one redwood log. As a design it is a good example of the turn-of-the-century late Victorian Gothic Revival. Buttresses and dormer windows dominate the sides of the building, while the tower and its tall spire form the frontispiece.

6. **Medical Building (now an employment agency)** c.1935-40; NE cor. B & 10th Sts.
   A small single story Streamlined Moderne office building.

7. **Cottage** c.1880s; 421 8th St.
   An unusual, highly ornamented Eastlake cottage. Of special interest are the hooded windows and the small classical columns which form part of the brackets supporting the overhang of the roof.

8. **House** c.late 1870s; 535 B St.
   A two-story Italianate house.

9. **House** c.late 1870s; 537 B St.
   A two-story Italianate house.

10. **House** c.late 1880s; 558 B St.
    A late blending of the Eastlake and Queen Anne Revival styles.

11. **St. Rose Catholic Church** 1900; Shea and Shea. Recent addition and remodeling 1964; J. Clarence Felciano
    SW cor. B & 10th Sts.
    One of the few examples of the Richardsonian Romanesque still standing in northern California.

12. **House** c.1880s; 625 B St.
    An example of the Eastlake style.

13. **House** c.1870s
    NW cor. Cherry & Orchard Sts.
    Stick style plus Eastlake.

14. **House** c.1870s; 825 Cherry St.
    Another mixture of the Stick style and the East-
    lake. The original fence is still in place so that
    one has a better idea of how the house was re-
    lated to its garden and to the public street.

16. **Cottage** c.1880s or later
    702 Monroe St.
    The corner angled bay window has been carried
    above the porch roof to form a low tower with a
    high pitched roof.

17. **Cottage** c.1880s; 805 McDonald St.
    A small Eastlake cottage.

18. **Wright House** c.1880s; 815 McDonald St.
    A mixture of Eastlake and Queen Anne Revival
    styles with impressive spindle work displayed on
    the porches, balconies and beneath overhangs.

19. **House** c.late 1870s; 900 McDonald St.
    Italianate.

20. **McDonald House** 1877-78
    W side McDonald St. bet. 16th & Spencer Sts.
    One of the major classics of late 19th century
    domestic architecture in California. This story and
    a half cottage still occupies a city block, and both
    the gardens and the house are well preserved.

21. **Bethlehem Lutheran Church** 1972
    Duncombe, Roland, Miller
    1300 St. Francis Rd. (2 blocks N of Sonoma Hwy.
    12)
    A shingle-covered pyramid provides a simple
    and at the same time impressive interior space.

22. **Sonoma State College (at Cotati)** 1961-present
    SW cor. Petaluma Rd. & Rohnert Expwy.
    Campus Plan and first buildings 1961
    John Carl Warnecke & Assoc.
    Cafeteria 1968; Marquis & Stoller
    Student housing and Cafeteria 1972
    Hardison & Komatsu

23. **Fountain Grove Colony** 1875-80
    Fountain Grove Winery Rd. (private); off Mendo-
    cino Ave. bet. Don Martin Rd. & the Old Redwood
    Hwy.

    The large round red barn of the Colony may be
    seen from the Freeway or from Mendocino Ave.
    The main house, which is Italianate in style, and
    the other buildings may not be seen from the
    public roads.

24. **Windsor Winery** 1970; Duncombe, Roland, Miller
    Old Redwood Hwy., one mi. N of Windsor

    The building consists of four ramp-like forms
    which build up to the central square volume.
    Narrow open ramps lead the visitor into the main
    building.

SEA RANCH

The Sea Ranch and especially Condominium I of 1965
designed by Moore, Lyndon, Turnbull and Whitaker is
the California architectural monument of the 1960s. As
a development, the Sea Ranch represents the more
sophisticated and complex approach which some
large scale developers have been taking toward the
land and architecture during the 60s and early 70s.
The site upon which this 5,000 acre development has
been placed was originally a forested coastline resplendent with thick groves of redwood, fir and pine.
During the 1880s and 90s this section of the coast was
logged off. Afterwards the coastal plain itself became
a grassy meadow on which sheep grazed. The only
specific man-made intrusions were occasional windbreaks of cypress trees and a scattering of barns and
other farm buildings. Like most of the coast of northern
California, the climate tends to be cool, foggy and at
times very windy.

In 1964 Oceanic Properties engaged Lawrence Halprin and Assoc. to make a study and prepare a master
plan for the area. Detailed studies were made of the
site, its soil, climate, the winds it experienced, the
days of sunlight it could expect, and finally how a low
density urban residential community could be imposed

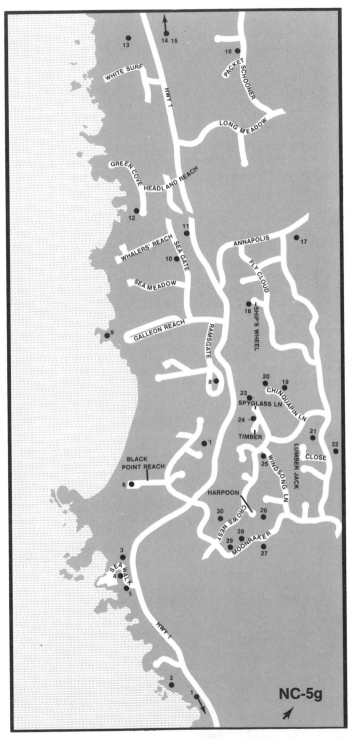

on the site without ending up (as is usually the case) by destroying it. The original concept was to leave as much open land as possible especially in the gently sloping coastal plain which was almost treeless. This was to be accomplished by keeping the living units in groups close together, either in condominium groups, or free standing single family houses treated as units. In the wooded hills above, a looser residential pattern was established, less dense, but at the same time laid out so that the pattern of roads and the buildings themselves would not compromise the character of the place. Strict architectural controls were drawn up, again assuring that the man-made object would be part of, not opposed to, the site.

In addition to the housing, a small community commercial center was created to house a general store, restaurant, hotel, etc., and several recreational centers were projected for swimming, tennis, golf, etc. Some changes and modifications have been made by the developer since the project opened in 1965, but the Sea Ranch remains as an impressive scheme, both in regard to rational land use and in the remarkable quality of the architecture and the graphics of its individual buildings.

(A note as to addresses and directions: The houses at the Sea Ranch are not given street addresses, therefore we have sought to indicate the street the building is on, which side of the street in many cases, and the nearest junction. The user of the Guide will find that he must rely very heavily on the map itself.)

1. **House** 1969; Moore & Turnbull (MLTW)
   W end Yardarm Dr.

   A large redwood sheathed house; internally oriented around vertical space and semi-open court yards.

2. **House** 1967; Moore & Turnbull (MLTW)
   Hwy 1, SW of junction with Yardarm Dr.

   A small but highly complex series of shed roofed volumes.

3. **General Store, Restaurant, Land Office, Lodge, etc**
   Original building 1965; Joseph Esherick & Assoc. Additions 1970; Alfred Boeke and Louis McLane, & AGORA. Supergraphics by Barbara Stauffacher

   A group of one to three story shed-roof units designed to form a single composition.

4. **Condominium I** 1965; Moore, Lyndon Turnbull, Whitaker
   End of Seawalk Dr.

   Still the most impressive and the most famous of the buildings at the Sea Ranch. The ten units of the Condominium submerge themselves into history—i.e. the rural traditional architecture of northern California and the landscape itself—and yet in the end their strong geometry dominates the place. The interior spaces of the condominiums are as dramatic as their complex exteriors.

5. **Condominium** 1971-72; Mackinlay & Winnacher
Seawalk Dr., E side
A regrettable siting for this condominium in relationship to the original Condominium I by MLTW.

6. **Hedge Row Housing** 1965
Joseph Esherick & Assoc.
W & S sides of Black Point Reach
These are the first free standing residential units built at the Sea Ranch. These six houses stand as a group and are closely related to the Cypress windbreak. Several of these shed roof houses have sod roofs.

7. **Swim and Tennis Club ≠1** 1966; Moore & Turnbull (MLTW). Supergraphics by Barbara Stauffacher
N side Moonraker Rd.
An impressive example of design, site planning and supergraphics realized in one building of very modest cost.

8. **House** 1968; Moore & Turnbull (MLTW)
Ramsgate Rd.
One of Moore and Turnbull's early spine houses; note the Gaudi-esque wood chimney.

9. **House** 1968; McCue, Boone & Tomsick
S end Galleon Reach Rd.
Oriented around a partially enclosed courtyard.

10. **House** 1968; Esherick, Homsey, Dodge & Davis
Sea Gate Road, S side, bet. Whalers' Reach & Sea Meadow Dr.

11. **House** 1967; Esherick, Homsey, Dodge & Davis
Sea Gate Rd., N side, opp. junction with Whaler's Reach Rd.
"Mini-Mod I," a prototype house for the Sea Ranch.

12. **House** 1969; Moore & Turnbull (MLTW)
    SE end Green Cove Dr.

13. **Swim and Tenis Club #2** 1970
    Moore & Turnbull (MLTW)
    W of junction of Hwy. 1 and Whitesurf Rd.

    A functional and at the same time highly abstract response to the needs of the program and of the site; placed behind a high cypress windbreak, sunk into the ground and partially surrounded by man-made earth mounds.

14. **Cluster Housing** 1970-72; Moore & Turnbull (MLTW)
    Off Hwy. 1, S side, beyond Sea Ranch Stables

    Five demonstration units have been built and others are planned to follow. Mini lot ownership clustered together to provide the type of open space associated with a condominium unit together with the more traditional desire for single family attached housing.

15. **House** 1970; Moore & Turnbull (MLTW)
    Off Hwy. 1, S side, beyond Sea Ranch Stables
    Building as land form.

16. **House** 1971; Moore & Turnbull
    Schooner Dr., W of Packet Close Dr.

17. **Sea Ranch Corp. Yards;** & next door the **Slyvia Corp. Yards** 1965 & 1967; Moore & Turnbull
    NE side Annapolis Rd., NE of Timber Ridge Rd.

18. **House** 1971; Duncombe, Roland, Miller
    S end of Ship's Wheel Close

    A vertical composition sheathed in shingles.

19. **House** 1968; AGORA
    Chinquapin Ln., N side just above turn around.
    A small L-shaped redwood house with a separate bunkhouse.

20. **House** 1969; Moore & Turnbull (MLTW)
    End of Chinquapin Ln.

    A vertical spine ties the garage and interior spaces of this house together.

21. **House** 1967-69; Moore & Turnbull (MLTW)
    S side Timber Ridge Rd., W of junction with Lumber Jack Close.

    One of a series of prototype houses designed for the Sea Ranch. Others can be seen on the south side of Fly Cloud Rd. west of junction with Constellation; one at the end of Constellation, another at the east side of Constellation and Fly Cloud Rd. In the meadows below, one of the prototype houses can be seen on the southwest side of Black Point Reach, just south of its junction with Moonraker Rd.

22. **House** 1967; Esherick, Homsey, Dodge & Davis
Timber Ridge Rd., junction with Lumber Jack Close
Another Mini-Mod I, prototype house.

23. **House** 1969; Moore & Turnbull (MLTW)
W end Spyglass Ln.

24. **House** 1967; Marquis & Stoller
SW cor. Spyglass Ln. & Timber Close
Two vertical shafts, one the house proper, the other the stair tower.

25. **House** 1970; Esherick, Homsey, Dodge & Davis
SE cor. Crow's Nest Dr. & Windsong Ln.

26. **House** 1967; Esherick, Homsey, Dodge, & Davis
End of Harpoon Close, off Crow's Nest Dr.

27. **House** 1967; Esherick, Homsey, Dodge, & Davis
NE side Moonraker Rd., bet. Windsong Ln. & Crow's Nest Dr.

28. **House** 1965; Moore & Turnbull (MLTW)
SW side Moonraker Rd. S of junction with Wind Song Ln.
A small square house, which internally is a house within a house.

29. **House** 1966; Moore & Turnbull (MLTW)
SW side of Moonraker Dr., E of junction with Crow's Nest Dr.

30. **House** 1966; Moore & Turnbull (MLTW)
S side Crow's Nest Dr., W of junction with Moonraker Rd.

SEBASTOPOL

Like many other towns in Sonoma County, Sebastopol was first settled in the mid 19th century (1846). Its street plan is that of the usual gridiron scheme loosely overlaying the more irregular routes of the highways which go through and converge on the community. Architecturally the main interest of the town is not its 19th century buildings, but rather examples of the Moderne of the 1930s. (No map)

Emmanji Temple after 1900
Hwy. 116 (Gravenstein Rd.), at S end of town nr. the junction of Gravenstein and Cooper Rds.
A well maintained replica of an Oriental temple.

Analy Theatre c.1940
S side 300 block of N Main St.
A Streamlined Moderne motion picture theatre; its tall sign with its curved base and curved glass front dominates this end of Main St.

Medical Building c.1935; 7207 Bodega Ave.
A sophisticated example of the Streamlined Moderne of the 30s with tower of glass and stucco, corner windows and glass brick.

Analy High School 1935
Louis S. Stone & Henry O. Smith
Cor. Analy & Bonnardel Aves.

The projecting entrance pavilion with its insert lettering creates a classic Streamlined Moderne building.

Sebastopol Union Elementary School 1936
Bodega Ave. bet. Dutton & Washington Aves.

A little International Style mixed with the Streamlined Moderne.

Craftsman Bungalow c.1910; 482 Vine St.

A shingle bungalow set in a Craftsman garden.

SONOMA

The Pueblo de Sonoma was laid out around a central open plaza in 1835 by Gen. Mariano Guadalupe Vallejo. The streets were arranged in gridiron scheme running north-south and east-west. Broadway which enters the Plaza from the south provides an impressive entrance into the town being axially oriented to the stone Mission Revival City Hall. The Plaza of Sonoma forms part of the National Historic Landmark, and a number of the buildings facing the Plaza are of adobe and date from as early as the 1840s. In addition to the restored Mission San Francisco Solano there are a number of two story buildings still remaining in Sonoma which beautifully characterize the unification of the Mexican adobe structure with the mid 19th century Anglo Greek Revival. Just east of the town are a number of impressive Italianate farm houses, but these are set so far back from the public roads that it is impossible to catch anything more than a brief glimpse of them. In addition to these buildings, Sonoma possesses several good examples of the wood clapboard Greek Revival, the Victorian Gothic and the Italianate. Several of the wineries in and around Sonoma contain stone buildings built in the 1850s and 1860s. North and east of Sonoma were located a number of fashionable warm springs spas, but almost all of the buildings constructed for these resorts have been destroyed or converted to other uses.

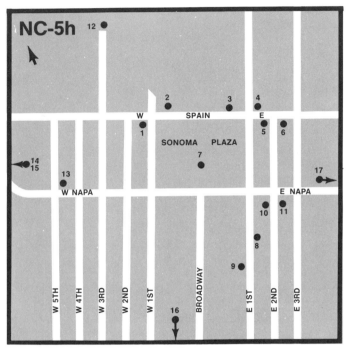

1. **Salvador Vallejo Adobe** 1840s
   415 1st St.
   An early adobe which faces directly onto the Plaza; the second floor of wood construction was added later.

2. **"Swiss Hotel,"** (originally the Salvadore Vallejo house) c.1840
   18 Spain St.
   One of the earliest of the adobes still standing.

3. **"Mexican Barracks"** 1836
   NE cor. Spain St. W & 1st St. E
   A two-story structure with a two-storied balconied porch; a direct precursor of the Monterey Colonial Revival style of the 1920s and 30s.

4. **Mission San Francisco Solano** 1840
   NE cor. Spain St. W & 1st St. E
   An unornamented very direct building covered with a gabled tile roof, much restored after 1903. A Mission revival version of what a California Mission should be.

5. **Blue Wing Inn** 1840; 133 Spain St. E
   Its two-storied balconied porch covers the public sidewalk; to the rear is a secluded garden.

6. **Ray House** 1847; 205 Spain St. E
   An adobe with very strong Greek Revival details in the windows and doors.

● 7. **Sonoma City Hall** 1906; H. C. Lutgens
   S side of Plaza facing Broadway St.
   A very fine example of the Mission Revival, only in this case in stone.

8. **Cottage** c.1860s; 564 1st St. E
   A small story and a half Victorian Gothic revival cottage of wood.

9. **Nash House** c.1847; 579 1st St. E
   A single floor adobe.

10. **House** c.1870s; 531 2nd St. E
    A two-story Italianate house situated in a large spacious garden.

11. **House** c.1860s; 530 2nd St. E
    A handsome two-story clapboard Greek Revival house, made even more "correct" by later re-modeling.

12. **Gen. M. G. Vallejo House "Lachryma Montis"** 1851-52; 3rd St. W
    The main house is a story and a half prefabricated Victorian Gothic cottage; the nearby "Swiss Chalet" of 1850 is of half timber with brick infill.

13. **Wells Fargo Bank Building (Napa Branch)** 1965
    John Carl Warnecke & Assoc.
    NE cor. 5th St. W & Napa St. W
    This contemporary bank building has sought to fit itself gently into the historic fabric of the community. Its scale detailing and landscaping are quite successful.

14. **St. Leo the Great Roman Catholic Church** 1968
    McSweeney, Schuppel, Michael Kelley Assoc.
    Agua Caliente Rd. W of Hwy. 12 (N of Sonoma)
    The central hipped roof of the sanctuary seems to grow out of the thick masonry walls below.

15. **"Wolf House," of Jack London** 1911; Albert Farr
    Glen Ellen. N of Sonoma, E to Jack London State
    Park.
    The U.S. has all too few romantic ruins. "Wolf
    House" burned before it was completed. Stylis-
    tically the house was a loose mixture of the
    Shingle style and the post 1900 Arts and Crafts
    movement.

16. **Temelec Hall (Swift House) (now a private coun-
    try club)** 1858
    3.8 mi SW of Sonoma, off old Petaluma Rd.
    A really grand mid-19th century country house.
    The main house with its two-story balconied
    porch is pure Greek Revival, although much of
    the exterior and interior detail is Italianate. Two
    small Victorian Gothic Revival summer houses
    pose at each side of the garden front of the house.
    On the other side of the road may be seen the
    two-story stone barn topped with a high dove
    cote.

17. **Buena Vista Winery** 1857
    2½ mi E of central Plaza of Sonoma; E on Napa St.
    to Old Winery Rd.
    Built by Agostin Haraszthy, the founder of the
    modern California wine industry. The winery con-
    sists of a group of large stone buildings set ro-
    mantically in a narrow heavily wooded valley.
    The buildings back up against the north hillside
    which contains man-made caves for aging the
    wine.

AETNA SPRINGS RESORT

Angwin-Pope Valley turn-off from Rt. 29, $\frac{1}{2}$ mi N of St. Helena.

East of the Napa Valley lies the Pope Valley ringed with hills which once formed a volcanic crater edge. The valley floor is beautiful grassland studded with oaks and devoted principally to ranching. It presents a picture of the traditional, 19th century rural pattern preserved in part by the barrier of the hills around. Appropriately, one of the vanishing institutions of the 19th century, the mineral springs resort, survives here in good health.

Aetna Springs is one of California's oldest resorts. The springs, which still bubble from the ground at a temperature of about 98°, were first discovered by miners in the 1850s. About 1860 the first building, a simple, square, wood frame structure with cupola, was built along with a bottling works, now destroyed. The popularity of "taking the waters" was such that the resort expanded its building program to include a dining hall in 1902, a social hall in 1904, and a club house in 1906. These buildings are in the best tradition of rustic, resort architecture with great, exposed wooden truss roofs, and strong, simple interiors featuring fireplaces of mighty masonry. Although undocumented they are attributed to Bernard Maybeck. A number of shingle cottages are grouped around the site. Those named Francis Marion, Munro, Locust, and Caroline were designed by Albert Farr from 1923-29. The whole complex is not only a treasure from the past, but continues to serve the public well from May 29 to Sept. 14. Further information about accommodations may be acquired from the resort.

BENICIA

Benicia was founded in 1847 on a site overlooking the important Carquinez Straits. The Straits at this point are deep enough so that ships could dock directly onto the shore. In the same year that the town was founded, the U.S. Army established the Benicia Barracks on a site to the east which commanded the eastern end of the Straits and Suisun Bay. The town enjoyed the spotlight of history and of famous historic personages during the 19th century. Its high points were the years 1853-54 when Benicia was briefly the state capital of California. Frequent attempts were made throughout the 19th century and even in the 20th century to transform Benicia into an important city, but none of these attempts succeeded.

The plan of the city is that of a gridiron scheme of streets, with the major streets running on a NE SE axis. From an architectural point of view Benicia is highly important for an understanding of the development of California architecture. It still has several wooden buildings which were prefabricated in the East and shipped to California, while its public buildings represent several of the earliest examples of the Greek Revival and of the Victorian Gothic Revival. The scale of the town and of its buildings is such that many of the older structures are still the dominant landmarks in the community. Of equal importance architecturally, is nearby Benicia Barracks which contains some of the finest and most impressive stone architecture to be found in California.

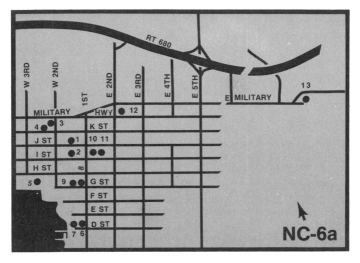

1. **Protestant Church** c.1870s; 132 W. J St.
   A wooden Victorian Gothic Revival Church.

2. **Masonic Hall** 1850; 110 W. J St.
   A crisp, clean Greek Revival building; the first Masonic Temple building in California.

3. **Bungalow** c.1910; 1121 W 2nd St.
   A shingle Craftsman bungalow.

4. **House** c.1880s; 231 W. K St.
   A large Queen Anne house, set in an ample garden.

5. **House** c.1880s
   SE cor. W. H & W 3rd Sts.

   A good sized Eastlake house, almost devoid of ornament; romantically situated on extensive tree covered grounds which extend directly down to the river.

6. **Store (now the What Not Shop)** 1848
   123 W. D St.

   A wooden clapboard building prefabricated on the East Coast and sent by ship to California.

7. **"Salt Box" House** c.1850; 145 W. D St.

   Another clapboard building, prefabricated in the East.

● 8. **State Capitol Building** (originally built as the City Hall) 1852; NW cor. 1st & G Sts. W

   Greek Revival; a two-story brick temple form, with a central recessed porch containing two Doric columns. Both the interior and exterior have been restored to original condition. Now a state monument and open to the public.

9. **Fischer House** 137 W. G St.

   Originally built as a hotel in the late 1840s. In 1856, after a fire, it was purchased, moved to its present site and extensively remodeled. In style this house is much more reminiscent of the East Coast Federal style c.1800 than the later Greek Revival. This house is now part of the State Capitol Building Monument and will eventually be open to the public.

10. **St. Paul's Episcopal Church** 1860
    SE cor. 1st & E. J Sts.

    A stern straightforward version of mid-century Victorian Gothic architecture.

11. **McAllister House (now the Rectory of St. Paul's Episcopal Church** 1864; 120 E. J St.

This house was originally built in 1790 and stood in Torrington, Conn. It was purchased by Julian McAllister, taken apart, and shipped around the Horn to Benicia. The house is a characteristic New England Salt Box to which has been added (1865) a master bed room and kitchen.

12. **Walch Cottage** 1849; 235 E. L St.

A Victorian Gothic cottage, one of three houses built in Boston and shipped to California. One of these houses was erected in San Francisco and is no longer in existence, the other was purchased by Gen. Vallejo and was erected on the outskirts of Sonoma for his own use.

13. **Benicia Arsenal and Barracks (now the Benicia Industrial Park)** 1849-later; E end E. M St.

It is to be hoped that the older part of the Benicia Arsenal and Barracks will eventually be created as a major California historic monument. Architecturally it possesses a number of excellent examples of stone architecture, several of which are unequaled in the state. The most significant of these buildings are:

> **Camel Barns** (originally built as Warehouses and later modified) 1853-54
> Contains one of the earliest Otis Elevators, still intact.
>
> **Post Hospital** 1856
> **Powder Magazine** 1857
> **Clock Tower Building** 1859
> The most imposing building at the site. Originally it was a three-story structure with two towers placed diagonally at opposite corners. The building was damaged by a fire in 1912 and was then rebuilt, removing the third floor and the rear tower. The scale of the stone

work and such details as the lower gun ports convey some of the same feeling and scale of the fantastic architecture of Ledoux and Boulee in late 18th century France.

Commandant's House 1860

A restrained Italianate house of brick which has been stuccoed over. The scale of its entrance porch and of the public rooms on the main floor is most imposing.

Double Officer's Houses 1860

Italianate, similar to but having less ornament than the Commandant's house.

WOODLAND

Woodland was officially established as a post office in 1861. In the following year the town was selected as the seat for Yolo County. By the mid 1860s it had become an important and prosperous center for the rich surrounding agricultural area—as it still is today. The town site is basically flat and upon this has been imposed the typical gridiron scheme. This gridiron plan has been somewhat modified to the south where several configurations of gently curved streets have been laid out for the newer suburban areas. The downtown section is unusual in that there are two principal paral-

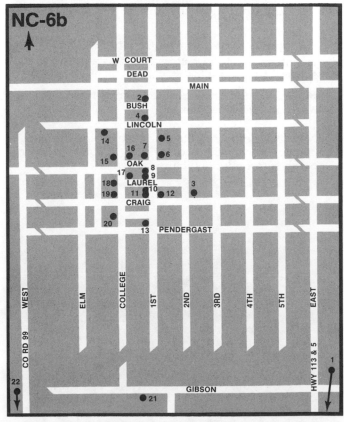

lel arteries: Main Street, which is essentially commercial, and to the north, Court Street, where the city and county public buildings are located.

The downtown area contains a number of older buildings, the Woodland Opera House of 1891 (the West side of 2nd St., north of Main Street), and the Julian Hotel of 1893 (across the street from the Opera House) are simple straightforward brick buildings. On Main Street itself are situated several older business blocks, including the former Bank of Woodland Bldg. (1916) at 435 Main Street, the Porter Bldg. (1914) at 511 Main Street, and the much older Armstrong & Alge Bldg. (1890) at 606 Main Street. At the corner of 3rd and Main one will find the arcaded three story Mission Revival Odd Fellows Bldg. of 1905. On Court Street are located the City and County Library Bldg. (1904 & 1914, bet. College & First Streets), a building which while essentially classic has a Mission Revival flavor; and the rather dry but entirely correct Roman-Renaissance Revival County Court House (1918, bet. Second and Third Streets). It is in the area south of Main Street between West Street and East Street that one will discover numerous examples of Italianate, Eastlake and Queen Anne Revival clapboard houses. These residential streets lined with tall trees and the houses set back in their own gardens and lawns conjure up a vision of what the small California city was like just before and after the turn of the century.

1. **House** c.1880
   SW cor. of Hwy. 113 and County Rd. 24a
   A characteristic two-story Italianate farm house set well back from the road.

2. **McGrew Building (Jackson Apartments)** 1890
   NW cor. 1st & Bush Sts.
   Unquestionably one of the exotic wonders of Northern California. Its shingle-clad bullet-shaped corner tower dominates the simple two-story porch-surrounded structure below.

3. **Rhodes-McGrath Cottage** 1879
   704 2nd Ave.

   A simple rather straightforward Gothic Revival cottage. The projecting bracketed roof is quite unusual for a Gothic Revival house. Another Gothic cottage is located at 5th and Court Sts. c.1865.

4. **Lowe House** 1890; 458 1st St.

   A large substantial Queen Anne house with octagonal tower and finely detailed porch with intricate lath work.

5. **Cottage** c.1890s; 527 1st St.

   A small single floor Queen Anne cottage.

6. **Muegge Cottage** 1874
   NE cor. 1st & Oak Sts.

   (Now occupied by the Daughters of the Golden West.) A single story Italianate house with bold brackets supporting the roof overhang; the porch contains a handsome classical balustrade.

7. **Hunt-Powell House** 1875
   NW cor. 1st & Oak Sts.

   A variation of the typical two-story Italianate house of the 1880s.

8. **Cranston Nicholson House** 1890
   610 1st St.

   A late story and a half Queen Anne house with impressive porches on both the east and south sides of the house.

9. **House** c.1915; 618 1st St.

   This is one of several impressive Colonial Revival houses to be found in Woodland. Others are the earlier (c.1900) house at 804 College St., the remodeled house at 803 College St. (remodeled in 1911), and the later house (c.1920s) at 41 Palm Ave.

10. **Merritt-Campbell Cottage** 1886
    632 1st St.

    The rich exterior detailing of this Queen Anne (with a touch of Eastlake) cottage are worth careful study; note especially the classical detailing used in the north and east gable ends and on the two small porches below.

11. **Cottage** early 1880s; 638 1st St.

    A lively detailed Eastlake cottage exhibiting a number of moon-shaped openings around its exterior front and side porch.

12. **Gable House** 1885; 659 1st St.

    This large two-story house displays a strange, rather mysterious mixture of the Stick style and the Italianate.

13. **Stevens House** 1916; John Hudson Thomas
756 1st St.

An impressive house with a Maybeckian flavor designed by the Berkeley architect John Hudson Thomas. At 742 1st St., to the north of the Stevens house, is a later house (of the 1920s) by the same architect—designed in his personal version of the English Tudor style. Another house, at 515 1st St., is attributed to Thomas.

14. **Brown House** 1880; 422 Lincoln Ave.
A beautifully restored two-story Italianate town house.

15. **Bickford Cottage** 1885; 546 College St.
A small single floor Italianate cottage.

16. **House** c.1915; 555 College St.
A flat roofed stucco covered Mission Revival house, with unusual corner windows and a wide pergola porch at the front.

17. **Adams House** 1899; 619 College St.
An expansive two-story Queen Anne house (with a touch of Eastlake) which exhibits a three-story circular tower, open at the top, fine turned and sawed detailing, and interesting terracotta inlaid panels in the south chimney.

18. Pendegast-Terhene House

18. **Pendegast-Terhene House** 1876; 640 College St.

A classic two-story Italianate house. A similar house built in 1890 is located next door at 648 College St.

19. **Pendegast-Harling House** 1882; 656 College St.

Another Italianate house, similar in plan to those located at 640 and 648 College St.

20. **Gaddis-Harkness Cottage** 1890; 734 College St.

A small Queen Anne cottage with a low Islamic dome, and impressive detailing especially on the projecting southeast bay.

21. **Gibson House** 1849; 1857-72; 1890-1910
512 Gibson Rd.

A two-story gabled temple front with four Ionic columns faces north toward the road. The original house (before it was later remodeled) had a two-story porch around both the north and west sides. The present two-story portico was added around 1900.

22. **Bullard House** 1863; 1900-1912
$\frac{1}{4}$ mi W of junction of County Rds. 27 & 99 (S of Woodland)

The original house was built in 1863; it was brought up to date in the Colonial Revival style c.1900, and the classical portico was added in 1912.

FAIRFIELD

Fairfield's contribution to architectural fame is the beautifully situated turn of the century Renaissance Revival Solano County Court House, designed in 1911 by E. C. Hemmings and W. A. Jones. Its classical two-story portico and long flight of steps are axially oriented to look down Union Avenue.

Fairfield also has the latest in competition designed Civic Centers, also located on Webster Ave. It is the work of Hawley Stowers & Assoc., with Ribera & Sue, landscape architects, and was completed in 1972.

ROCKVILLE

(North of Hwy. 80; 4 miles west of Fairfield)
In and around this small community are a number of interesting buildings of finely cut stone which were constructed during the 1850s and 60s. In the Rockville Public Cemetery is situated the Rockville Stone Chapel. This chaste Greek Revival church was built in 1856. North of the Chapel on the Suisun Valley Rd. is the Baldwin Stone Barn of 1865. South of Rockville on the Suisun Valley Rd. is the 1861 Martin house. A mile SE of town on the east side of Suisun Creek is the Barbour house of 1859.

About 28 miles southwest of Sacramento on Hwy. 80 is the town of Vacaville. The town, platted in 1851, was named after Don Manuel Vaca. The present freeway skirts the town to the south so that its downtown and older residential area have remained intact. In an all too familiar tale of northern California communities, Vacaville has suffered both from fires and also from the 1892 earthquake. As a result her business district is quite late in time. However, there are several buildings of architectural interest, the most exotic being the former City Hall-Fire Station and Jail which, with its open domed corner tower and strange bulky columns, defies any stylistic pigeon-holing. The former City Hall building is located on the S side of East Main St. a short distance east of its junction with Davis St. At the SW corner of East Main St. and Davis St. is a small cast iron fronted store.

The delight and charm of Vacaville is to be found in its older residential area situated on Buck Ave. (the western extension of West Main St.). Buck Ave. is and was *the* residential street of the town, and here one will discover residences dating from the late 1870s through the 20s and even later. At the SE corner of East Main/Buck Ave. and West St. is a small Mission Revival Church, c.1900 (now the Christian Science Society Church). At 201 Buck Ave. is a Queen Anne house (c.1887) with an octagonal tower; across the street at 212 is a small raised-basement Eastlake/Queen Anne cottage (c.1885). At 225 is a large two-story brick sheathed Eastlake/Queen Anne house (early 1880s). Further west at 301 is a large Queen Anne residence, and on the other side of the street at 308 Buck Ave. is a perfect example of the Colonial Revival phase of the late Queen Anne (c.1900). Just west of 308, on the same side of the street, is an impressive essay in the Mission Revival (c.1915).

City Hall—Fire Station and Jail

WINTERS

The town of Winters lies just off Hwy. 505, 11 miles north of Vacaville. Like many northern California towns it was named after one of the original land owners, in this case Theodore W. Winters. Today the town still possesses much of its turn of the century atmosphere and there are a half a dozen or more modest residences which present an appealing picture of domestic architecture in the late 1890s and early 1900s. Worth mentioning are a group of houses on Russell St., nos. 129, 202, 206 and 413; and also the house at 25 Baker St. All of these are late Queen Anne in style with a touch of the Colonial Revival. On Main St. will be found a small Mission Revival monument, the Pioneer Church, built c. 1905.

DAVIS

Davis, a small town some 14 miles west of Sacramento on Hwy. 80 was originally named Davisville after its first settler and landholder. With the coming of the railroad it became a shipping point for agricultural products grown on the rich surrounding farm lands. In 1905 the University of California Farm was established and the name was changed to Davis. For some years the study of agriculture mainly took place in the fields, requiring only a few residence halls and a number of barns. The transformation of agriculture into an industrial-scientific field forced major physical changes on the campus. During the post-World War II decades of the 50s and 60s, after Davis had become an independent campus of the University, the building program accelerated and more than doubled the size of the campus.

Entering the campus from Hwy. 80 on 1st Street, one comes directly to the heart of the old campus, the East-West Quad. On the east side are North Hall, 1908; East Hall, 1909; and South Hall, 1912, the original buildings. Other buildings on the Quad are the Library by Stark & Flanders, 1940, and the Memorial Union by Confer & Willis, 1955. The area is ringed with venerable cork oak trees. To the west are the newer parts of the campus which finally feathers out into the vast open fields of the agricultural station. Fine old barns and some new ones in the same vernacular dot the campus and fields. A pleasant linear park along Putah Creek designed by Ted Osmundson forms a barrier between the southeast edge of the campus and the freeway and railroad right-of-way. Across the creek a former livestock judging pavilion has been transformed into an arena theater as part of a complex that includes a waterside snack bar and faculty club (Dean Ungers, 1969).

Two other imaginative designs for old farm structures are the Architecture and Engineering Building, a former dairy barn of c.1914, and the Silo, c.1920, which is now a student center. The buildings were originally designed by the San Francisco firm of Cunningham & Politeo, and have been successfully remodeled by

Clifford C. Jay, campus architect, and his staff. Of the other buildings on campus the following deserve mention: Student Health by John Funk, 1952; the residence complex of Ryerson, Malcolm, & Gilmore; and Bixby Halls with Segundo Dining Hall by Kitchen & Hunt John Funk, 1960; the Chemistry Library by John Funk, 1971; Biology Laboratory, Smith, Barker, Hanssen, 1971; and the Swimming Pool complex by Marquis & Stoller, 1971.

The town itself has remained small and primarily residential. Even as late as the 20s and 30s there were a number of interesting 19th and early 20th century buildings to be found along Davis's streets. Today the only remaining building of historic interest is the small Mission Revival Southern Pacific Railroad Station, 1914, designed by the Architectural Bureau, So. Pacific R.R., located at the east end of 2nd St.

SACRAMENTO

The first town on this site was laid out in 1849 by John A. Sutter, Jr. His father's fort which was established earlier in 1839 lay to the west. With the great importance of water transportation in the mid-19th century, the selection of this site was a logical one, being situated on the Sacramento River a short distance from its confluence with the American River. In 1855 Sacramento became the capital of California. Work on the capitol building was started in 1860 and was completed in 1874. The commercial area of the city was at first oriented to the Sacramento River front, and it was here that the stores and other business buildings were built. With the coming of the railroads and the increased importance of Sacramento as the state capital, the business district spread east and just south of the City Plaza (on J St. bet. 9th & 10th Sts.) Major fire and floods occurred throughout most of the 19th century, with the result that the city's architectural inheritance from the earliest years is minimal.

Many of the first houses in Sacramento were prefabricated in the East and shipped around the Horn. In 1849 one traveler to Sacramento noted that "Our brig had no less than 13 (prefabricated houses) on board finished even to the glazing." Ten to 15 years after its founding, the city conveyed the general architectural feeling that it was a midwestern Greek Revival town. Its fire house, its porticoed Court House, and such business structures as the D. O. Mills Co. Bank, and a number of houses suggest through details here and there that their allegiance was to the Greeks. In the 60s and 70s the Italianate style became the latest mode both for commercial buildings and for large and small dwellings. The Governor's Mansion, the Crocker House and the Stanford-Lathrop house attest to the zeal and passion of the citizens for this style. In the decades which followed, Sacramento, like other California cities and towns, went through the usual array of late 19th century styles, including several examples

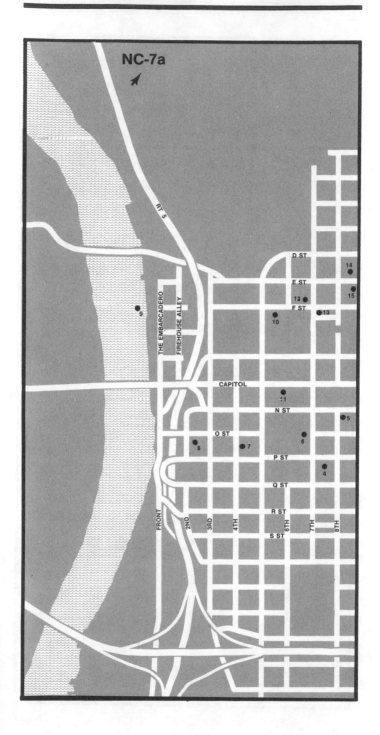

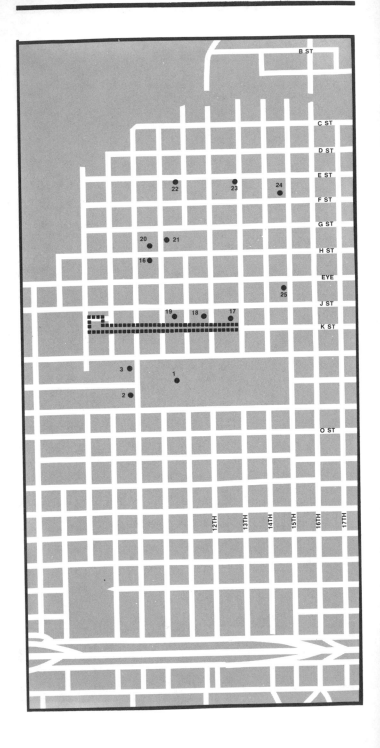

of the Richardsonian Romanesque Revival. But the visual character of the city was firmly established by its adherence to the classical tradition, expressed initially by the State Capitol building itself, later by the turn of the century City Beautiful movement. The new State Library building and the new State Office building were in the Renaissance Revival style, and so also were the major city buildings: the City Hall, the Library and the U. S. Post Office building.

In 1948 the city embarked on an extensive urban redevelopment project which in the end would affect the whole of the west part of the city. In 1949 they engaged the Los Angeles firm of Neutra and Alexander to prepare a general proposal. This was followed by further studies by Catherine Bauer and Davis McEntire. Later the San Francisco office of Skidmore, Owings and Merrill (in 1963 and in 1968) made a detailed study of the commercial area of the redevelopment project. Extensive sections were leveled (with the usual loss of a number of significant buildings), and it is currently being developed into four separate city functions: a ceremonial mall, the Capitol Mall, running from the bridge over the river to the State Capitol Park (and symbolically lined by opulent highrise buildings occupied by offices of major corporations); to the north a pedestrian mall which has replaced several blocks on N street; a new major shopping center with extensive underground parking in and around 5th and J Streets; and finally a posh low and highrise residential district centered around 5th and O Streets.

Even more than urban renewal has been the impact of the freeway system on the city. Since Sacramento is the capital of the state which has been most devoted to the automobile and the freeway systems, it is quite logical that it should be transformed into the full image of the freeway city. Rt. 5, the freeway running parallel to the Sacramento River, is the one which has impinged itself the most on the city. It has cut right through the old business district and has in effect completely severed the city from the river front. What has been left of the old commercial district between the freeway and the river has been planned as a Historic District (planning by DeMars, Reay and others in 1963). The concept was to develop an "old town" atmosphere combining historic buildings and the continued commercial use of the area in the form of small shops and restaurants. Little of this has so far been realized, and the area conveys the feeling that it is just waiting for the bulldozer. If and when it is developed, the area should be a great asset to the city, though its proximity to the freeway and the highrise buildings on the Capitol Mall raise doubts as to whether it can ever recapture any of its original scale and historic atmosphere.

With a few very important exceptions Sacramento has lost most of its impressive Victorian houses of the 19th century. But it should be noted that the area north of the city Plaza (D through H Streets, as far east as 29th

St.) contains many modest single floor raised basement cottages and two-story houses. In style most of these are Italianate and Eastlake with a few Queen Anne scattered here and there. Further to the east on J St. between 40th and 50th Streets one will find wooded residential streets lined with Period Revival houses of the late teens and 20s.

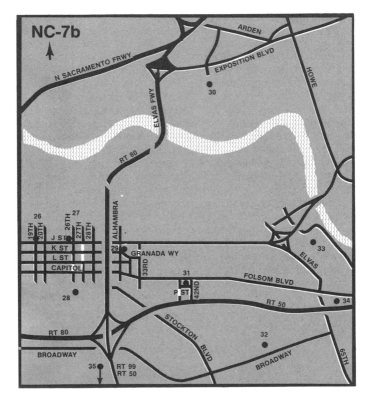

● 1. **The Capitol Building, State of California** 1860-74; Miner F. Butler. Completed by Reubin Clark, G. P. Cummings and A. A. Bennett. Remodeled with the addition of 70 rooms 1906-08; Sutton & Weeks Capitol Park, bet. 10th & 12th Sts., L & N Sts.

Described as a "classical structure in the florid Roman-Corinthian style." Within the rotunda are a series of mural paintings by Arthur F. Mathews (1913), which from the point of view of style are a mixture of the late 19th century neo-classicism of Puvis de Chavannes, with a strong Pre-Raphaelite tone.

2. **The State Library Building** 1913-28; Weeks & Day NE cor. N & 9th Sts.

Renaissance Revival. The sculpture in the pediments is by Edward Field Stanford, Jr.; the neo-classical murals in the vestibule are by Frank van Sloun; the large, mildly modern murals in the James L. Gilles Hall are by Maynard Dixon.

3. **The State Office Building** 1913-28; Weeks & Day
SE cor. L St. at 9th St.

Renaissance Revival, matches the State Library Bldg. across the mall, and the two buildings very effectively frame the State Capitol Bldg.

4. **State Office Building Nos. 8 & 9** 1969
Fred Hummel (state arch.)
714 P St.

Large cast plastic sculpture by Bruce Beasley in the plaza.

5. **Stanford-Lathrop House** 1860; Seth Babson
800 N St.

Italianate, with a mansard roof. A good example of how un-provincial California could be in the 19th century, for this house in style, in size, and in detailing could have been placed in New York or Boston and would have fit perfectly with the then-current fashions.

6. **Capitol Tower Apartments** 1958, 1965; Wurster, Bernardi, Emmons; Edward L. Barnes; DeMars & Reay
1500 7th St.

Part of the Sacramento urban renewal project. The low rise units were built first, then the high rise in 1965. The tower is mildly International style.

7. **Governor's Square Apartments** 1970; Donald Sandy, Jr., James A. Babcock
1500 4th St.

The latest Bay Tradition style brought to Sacramento. Some of the units are clothed in shingles, others in stucco. Extensive use has been made of sloped shed roofs. Another unit is presently being built in the block bound by P and N Sts., and 5th and 6th Sts. All of these units are part of the urban renewal project.

8. **Crocker Art Gallery: Crocker House** 1852; Seth Babson. **Crocker Art Gallery** 1883-84; Seth Babson. **R. A. Herold Memorial Wing** 1969; Dodd, McCabe, Cox, Liske
W side 3rd St. bet. O & P Sts.

Like the nearby Stanford-Lathrop house, the original Crocker house (actually built for B. F. Hastings) can loosely be called Italianate, though it is a much more knowing example of the style than is generally found in California. The later Art Gallery is more early 19th century Renaissance than Italianate, while the Herold Wing at the rear of the building is fashionably contemporary in design.

9. **Historic Old Sacramento (Waterfront Redevelopment Area)**
The Embarcadero, Firehouse Alley, bet. Eye & L Sts.

Small scaled commercial buildings dating mostly from the 60s and 70s. Redevelopment scheme by DeMars & Reay, in assoc. with Candeub, Flessig & Assoc., 1963.
A few of the brick buildings are of architectural interest, but the main visual asset which will be conveyed when the project is finished will be the general atmosphere of the business district of a 19th century town. (Though, as always seems to happen in such transformations the visual sense of the place will appear more as a stage set than a 19th century town.)

10. **Downtown Plaza** 1971-72; John S. Bowles, Assoc.
In, around and over the junction of 5th & J Sts.
Part of the Sacramento urban renewal project. The multilevel city of the future realized.

11. **I.B.M. Building** 1964; Dreyfuss & Blackford
520 Capitol Mall
An 8-story office block with all but the ground floor defined by precast window units.

12. **Security Pacific National Bank** 1912; Willis Polk
NW cor. J & 7th Sts.
A well thought out Renaissance Revival building.

13. **Crocker National Bank** 1915-16; R. A. Herold
SE cor. J & 7th Sts.
Renaissance Revival.

14. **U.S. Post Office Building** 1932; James A. Wetmore, acting superv. arch.
S side Eye St. bet. 8th & 9th Sts.
Late Renaissance Revival.

15. **Sacramento Public Library** 1918; L. P. Rexford
SW cor. Eye & 9th Sts.
Described when built as "Florentine Renaissance style."

16. **Sacramento City Hall** 1907-11; R. A. Herold
N side Eye St. bet. 9th & 10th Sts.
A Baroque version of the Renaissance Revival style. The building is set back beautifully in its landscape grounds which face out onto the City Plaza.

17. **Downtown Shopping Plaza (K Street Mall)** 1965
K St. bet. 5th & 13th Sts.
K Street has been closed off for a 7 block section. The street and the cross street have been replaced by a mall with plantings, fountains, and street furniture.

18. **Esquire Theatre** 1940; William B. David
1217 K St. (in the Downtown Shopping Plaza)
A late Streamlined Moderne theatre building.

19. **Cathedral of the Blessed Sacrament** 1886-89
1017 11th St. (in the Downtown Shopping Plaza)
Described as "Late Italian in style."

20. **University Club** (formerly a private residence) late 1870s; 917 H St.
Italianate, with Eastlake details, especially in the attic story and around the porch. One of the few large Italianate houses still standing in Sacramento.

21. **Governor's Mansion** (formerly the Albert Gallatin House) 1877-78; N. D. Goodel
SE cor. H & 11th Sts.
Italianate in style with a wonderful Charles Adams tower. No longer used as a residence for the governor, now open to the public.

22. **House** c.1880; 1100 E St.
An Eastlake house.

23. **House** c.1880; 1312 E St.
An Eastlake house.

24. House c.1880; 1511 F St.
An Eastlake house.

25. Sacramento Memorial Auditorium 1925-27
15th St. bet. Eye & J Sts.
Described as of "Italian Romanesque design."
The brick work and the arcaded entrance portico
are impressively handled.

26. Western Pacific Railroad Station 1910; Willis Polk
N side K St. bet. 19th & 20th Sts.
A single floor Mission Revival railroad station;
the proportions of the arcaded porch and the
deeply recessed quatrefoil windows in the gable
ends reveal the hands of a sensitive designer.

27. House c.1880; 2620 J St.
A two-story Eastlake house.

28. Sutter's Fort 1839-44
L St. bet. 26th & 28th Sts.
The central two-story building is all that remains
of the original fort; the walls and other sections
of the fort were restored during the years 1890-
91—one of the earliest of the restorations which
eventually led to the Mission Revival and finally
the Spanish Colonial Revival.

29. Alhambra Theatre 1927; Starks & Flanders
E cor. Alhambra & K Sts.
A Spanish Colonial Revival movie palace of the
20s, set far back from the street and approached
through a long theatrical walkway.

30. California Exposition (State Fair Grounds)
Exposition Blvd. off Elvas Freeway (A-80), N side
of American River
The State Fair Grounds were moved to this site
and, during the late 60s, a number of new buildings were added. These include a new fountain and landscaping by Lawrence Halprin; a
new Floricultural Bldg. by Callister & Payne, and
the Florin Shopping Center by Fisher-Friedman.

31. **4100 Folsom Blvd. Apartments** 1966
Dreyfuss & Blackford
4100 Folsom Blvd.

A 10-story apartment building housing 40 apartment units and other facilities. The exterior walls are of precast concrete.

32. **Low Cost Housing Project** 1972
Broadway bet. Stockton Blvd. & 57th St.

A HUD Operation Breakthrough Project built on the eastern section of the old State Fair Grounds. A few of the older brick buildings are still to be found in the Fair Grounds.

33. **Sacramento State University** (formerly Sacramento State College)

A number of new academic buildings have been added to the campus over the past few years, the most interesting of which is the Psychology Bldg., designed by Naht and Lewis in 1971. This building is a concrete structure with its two functions —classrooms and offices, and windowless research space—fully separated. The architectural high point of the campus is the married student housing provided in Collegetown, 1970, (located on Collegetown Dr. at the south edge of the campus). These were designed by Neil Smith & Assoc. and the landscaping was by Lawrence Halprin. The housing units are redwood sheathed two story units each with its own enclosed courtyard. The site plan and the landscaping are as impressive as the buildings themselves.

34. **Sacramento Municipal Utility District Office Building** 1965; Dreyfuss & Blackford
6201 S St. off Hwy. 50

A low well-proportioned Miesian box raised above its site on stilts.

35. **Cosumnes River Jr. College** 1971; Nacht & Lewis; Cox, Liske, Lionakis, Beaumont
Duluth Rd., off South Sacramento Freeway (Hwys. 50 & 99), W on Duluth Rd.

A precise rectilinear scheme—almost the ideal city. The buildings are placed on a raised podium, walkways are axially oriented to the roadways and to the buildings. The new planting on the site has just been started so that the geometry of the scheme is openly apparent.

STOCKTON

The city of Stockton was founded by Captain Charles M. Weber in 1847. Weber originally called it Tuleburg in reference to the tule swamps which lay about the area, but his growing earnestness in urban development led him to resurvey the town in 1849 and rename it for his friend Commodore Robert F. Stockton of San Francisco. It was now ready to receive the 49'ers who got their supplies in Stockton before they moved on to the southern mines. Then, as today, its most unusual natural feature was the deep water channel which jutted into the old center of the city allowing ocean-going vessels to enter the Embarcadero from San Francisco Bay, eighty-eight miles away.

The original grid plan was aligned on this long arm of water stretching roughly from east to west. A shifting of the grid, still not on the points of the compass, occurred with the building of Smith's Canal above which a fine residential area developed in the twenties. The grid here was punctuated by a series of elongated loops and an "Oxford Circle" just above the end of the canal, a pattern which can lead to some hilarious confusions of direction for those unacquainted with the vagaries of city planners.

Urban renewal has all but destroyed the old business section of the town and replaced it with parking lots, the inevitable mall (with no discernible center of interest) and motels, one of which has been given the prime land at the end of the deep water channel. In fact, nowhere in all of California is there a greater confusion of priorities than in the few blocks at the end of the old channel.

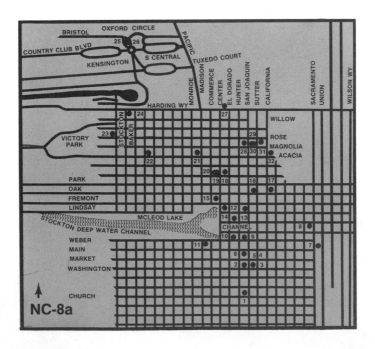

This observation should not detract, however, from the fact that Stockton has some real architectural treasures. The Civic Center, in spite of some recent building, still gives an idea of the classical "city beautiful" movement of the turn of the century. The Civic Auditorium (1924) was designed by Glenn Allen, a local architect who did many unusual buildings in California and other parts of the West. Indeed, if you see any buildings in Stockton that pleasantly mystify you, they are bound to be by Allen whose aggressive hand also designed the Christian Science Church (classical), the Henery Apartments (French Baroque, with the Renaissance Revival Clark Garage, also by Allen, next door), and the outlandish Dawson Storage Warehouse (Egyptian Revival) to name only his most salient works. But the business district also includes a fine Episcopal Guild Hall by Ernest Coxhead and the interesting Trethaway Block, Masonic Building, and Hotel Stockton.

But to know Stockton you must visit the residential area where there is much fascinating material from the Victorian period (the Newsoms were here) up to the 1940s and 50s (William Wurster was here). Not incidentally, the beauty of the residential districts is augmented by a liberal sprinkling of parks which, we never tire of pointing out, is a rare phenomenon in California.

One of the newest residential extensions of Stockton, almost in the nature of a new town is the development to be found north of Mile Slough off Benjamin Hoyt Drive.

1. **House** c.1895
   Just below E Sonora on W side of S San Joaquin
   Now painted white, this is a relatively rare example of the Shingle style given increased interest through balancing Mission style quatrefoil windows in the gable.

2. **St. Mary's Catholic Church: Nave and Bell Tower** 1861; **Facade** 1893
   201 E Washington St.
   A late and very striking example of the Gothic Revival in red brick.

3. **Clark Garage** 1916; Glenn Allen
   125 Sutter St.
   The fact that the Henery Apartments next door are by the same architect gives special zest to this Renaissance Revival building by Stockton's greatest architect.

4. **Henery Apartments** c.1916; Glenn Allen
   121 Sutter St.
   The architect seems to have used similar buildings in New York as his model for this French Neo-Baroque edifice, now crying out for restoration.

5. **Masonic Building** 1921
SW cor. Market & Sutter Sts.
A distinguished example of the Spanish Colonial Revival especially notable for its ornate entrance screen.

6. **Fox Theater** c.1925
S side Main St. bet. San Joaquin & Hunter Sts.
This time the Spanish Colonial Revival is accented with a tower.

7. **Western Pacific Railroad Station** c.1910
Nr. NW cor. Main & Union Sts.
A Mission Revival building now abandoned and waiting for some new use—certainly this station is worthy of preservation.

8. **Southern Pacific Railroad Station** c.1910
Just S of Miner Ave. at Sacramento
Another Mission Revival station but without the quality of the Western Pacific station nearby.

9. **Trethaway Block** 1892; 229 E Weber Ave.
A three story commercial building difficult to place stylistically. Some elements, such as the heavy cornice, remind us of the work of the Philadelphia architect, Frank Furness. A bit of Queen Anne decoration appears in the two bays.

10. **Hotel Stockton** 1910; E. B. Brown
NE cor. Weber Ave. & El Dorado St.
This vast monument of the Mission Revival is now being converted to the county administrative offices. It was the first steel-reinforced concrete building in Stockton.

11. **Sperry Flour Mill Office**   1888
148 W Weber Ave.

A fine and rare example of Victorian commercial architecture, this building with its hipped roof and pointed windows is now occupied by lawyers.

12. **St. John's Episcopal Church: The Guildhall**   1889-90; Ernest Coxhead. **The Church**   1892; Walter King
NE cor. El Dorado St. & Miner Ave.

The Guildhall is a mixture of English Queen Shingle style with a little Richardsonian Romanesque added. Though not designed by Coxhead, the church closely follows his early sketches for the building.

13. **Post Office**   1932; Bliss & Fairweather; Howard G. Bissell; James A. Wetmore
400 block of San Joaquin

The date clearly proves the W.P.A. Moderne was not an invention of the New Deal. The stripped classicism of this building is enhanced by a restrained use of flat "cubist" decoration.

14. **City Hall**   1923-26; Davis-Holler-Pearce; Peter E. Sala; Losekinn and Clowdsley; John L. Clowdsley
S side Civic Ct. bet. El Dorado & Center Sts.

A better than average essay in the Renaissance Revival idiom made famous by McKim, Mead & White.

15. **Memorial Civic Auditorium**   1924; Glenn Allen, W. J. Wright, Ivan C. Satterlee. Joseph Wicks, sculptor
N Center bet. Fremont & Oak Sts.

Allen's feeling for classical mass is nowhere more conspicuous than in this focal point of the Civic Center. The note of uplift is continued in Wicks' sculpture over the doors. The interior hall, once premonitory of Nervi's domes, has now been remodeled (1965) in order to provide adequate acoustics. The building is nevertheless a masterpiece of overstatement.

15. Civic Auditorium

16. **Fanning House**   c.1880s
NW cor. Oak & Sutter Sts.
Queen Anne with marvelous ornament.

17. **Dawson Storage Warehouse**   1918; Glenn Allen
700 block N California St. with wing on Oak St.
The nineteenth century took Egyptian architecture
seriously. The twentieth did not. The California
Street facade of this building has been stripped
of its ornament; but the Oak Street portion, though
lacking its original polychrome, still exhibits a
broad misconception of Karnak and a frieze, possibly by Joseph Wicks, of a medley of dancing
girls and an odd couple (Antony and Cleopatra?)
on a chaise lounge. Allen outdid himself here. Will
Stockton meet his challenge?

18. **House**   c.1880; 11 Flora St.
Eastlake-Queen Anne.

19. **First Church of Christ, Scientist**   1927; Glenn Allen
NW cor. Central & Flora Sts.
A squarish, domed variation on the Mother
Church in Boston. The Sunday School wing on
Flora Street is more tightly organized than most
of Allen's work.

20. **Weber Primary School** 1873
55 Flora St.

The belfry is gone, but this Italianate structure in red brick is a fine building. Moreover, it is one of the last remaining structures to remind us that Stockton was once called "The Brick City."

21. **Swett House** 1883; Samuel & Joseph C. Newsom
143 West Acacia St.

One of the Newsoms' more modest designs in the Queen Anne style.

22. **Kenning House** c.1880
745 W Acacia at Baker St.

A very successful essay in Queen Anne composition, this house with its corner tower and enclosing porch has Moorish as well as Eastlake details.

23. **Pioneer Museum and Haggin Galleries** 1931
Pershing at Rose St.

There is a hint of the Baroque on the exterior of this Depression era building, but it is rather washed out. The interior, however, contains important exhibits of western history and has several rooms furnished with pieces from the Stockton area.

24. **House** c.1935; 1505 N Stockton

A small, one-story Streamlined Moderne structure.

25. **Field House** 1941; William W. Wurster
1030 Bristol Ave.

This house and the one next door are Wurster in his American Colonial Revival phase.

26. **Sanderson House** 1934; William W. Wurster
920 Bristol Ave.

27. **Hurrle-Weston House** 1906
5 Harding Wy. at Center

An American Colonial Revival house, possibly by Glenn Allen.

28. **Bennett Apartments** 1925
135 E Magnolia at Hunter St.

Again, the strange rendering of this statement of the Spanish Colonial Revival suggests that its author was Glenn Allen.

29. **House** c.1900
205 E Magnolia at Hunter St.

A fine example of the Shingle Style.

30. **Newell House** 1880
1107 N San Joaquin at Magnolia St.

The quality and many of the specific details of this two-story, beautifully preserved Queen Anne house tend to associate it with the Newsoms.

31. **House**   c.1880
    1120 N San Joaquin St.
    Another fine Queen Anne house.

32. **Superintendent's House, Stockton State Hospital**
    1900; 521 E Acacia at California St.
    A flamboyant example of McKim, Mead and White Classicism probably designed by Glenn Allen.

33. **San Joaquin Delta College**   1971-73
    Ernest Kump & Assoc.
    Entrance on Pacific Ave. at Yokut

34. **Holt House**   1957; Joseph Escherick & Assoc.
    4000 Wagner Heights Rd.
    (Just below the city limits Pacific Avenue branches into Sacramento and Thornton roads. Take the left branch (Thornton) across Bear Creek and beyond city limits to Wagner Heights Road.)

LOCKEFORD

The pattern of Lockeford's streets was established in 1859, and the founders of the new city dreamed that it would become the major port at the headwaters of the Mokelumne River. Today it presents a nostalgic picture of a small 19th century Central Valley community. On Main Street at the southwest corner of Tully Road is just the sort of building one should find in a small 19th century town: a two-story Queen Anne red brick store building with a white painted round tower and dome projecting out over the corner of the building. On Elliot Rd., one block from Main Street, is the former Congregational Church (now Grace Church) which was built in 1869. Further up Elliot Rd. is the brick two-story Locke house of 1865, and behind it an impressive brick barn. Southwest of Lockeford on Locke Rd. is the deserted brick Community Church, built in a simple Gothic style during the late 1850s.

WOODBRIDGE

Woodbridge was laid out in 1859 on the south side of the Mokelumne River. On the main street (Sacramento Rd.) is a two story I.O.O.F. Bldg., the lower floor of which was built in the 60s, the upper floor in 1874. Certainly one of the most unusual 19th century buildings still existing in northern California is the narrow, very tall Masonic Hall of 1882. This brick structure employs a hard very stiff rectangular version of the late Gothic Revival style. The windows of its upper floor are capped by crisp gabled pediments, its central gable has a stepped pattern as a cornice, and thin cast iron columns were used in the ground floor store front.

At nearby **Lodi** is one of the only remaining Mission Revival ceremonial arches still in existence in California. It is located at the corner of East Pine and Sacramento Streets. This three arched structure was built at the high point of the Mission Revival in 1907, and recently (1956) it was rebuilt.

FOLSOM

The town of Folsom, up the American River from Sacramento (off Hwy. 50) was laid out in 1855, and enjoyed its greatest period of prosperity during the 1860s. Today, scattered here and there in the business district one will discover stone and brick commercial buildings dating from the 60s and 70s, and on the tree lined streets of the residential districts are a number of well preserved 19th century houses. Just outside of Folsom on the south bank of the American River is Folsom State Prison which was built in 1880. Next to the buildings at Stanford University, the prison is the largest still standing example of Richardsonian Romanesque in California. Its thick fortress-like walls serve as a cold monumental backdrop to the impressive Richardsonian arch which leads into the prison.

COURTLAND

Anyone with an afternoon free for exploration should drive along Hwy. 160 which follows the Sacramento River between Walnut Grove and Sacramento. Levee-topped roads run along both sides of the Channel and link together fragments which seem at one moment to be part Mississippi River, part the Frontier West, and part from faded pages of various 19th century architectural pattern books. Among the highlights: Walnut Grove where the latest elegant high fashion bank design from the 1970s confronts its counterpart from the early teens of this century (The Bank of America Bldg. and the First Federal Savings Bldg.); the town of Locke a mile north of Walnut Grove, a false-fronted, wooden sidewalked, galleried Chinese community dating from 1916 (don't miss the view down Main Street which parallels the highway at the bottom of the Levee); George H. Greene House built in 1876 just south of Courtland's city limits—a very fine essay in the Italianate with an obliquely joined tower.

NC-9a Lake Tahoe

Long famed as one of the largest and most beautiful of America's mountain lakes, Tahoe in recent years has become a symbol of the intense battle between conservationists and land developers. Bit by bit the waters of this crystalline clear lake have become polluted, and the magnificent timbered shores have sprouted townhouses, clustered houses and commercial developments of all types. It has become increasingly apparent, even to those involved in the development of land, that in the case of Tahoe one can easily destroy that which makes it worthwhile. Joint planning has recently been coordinated between the states of California and Nevada (the lake lies on the boundary between the two states) and now one can but wait and see whether planning can rescue what remains.

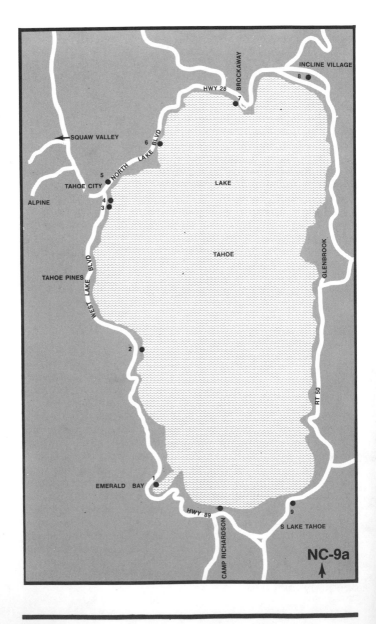

Lake Tahoe NC-9a

The lake was discovered in 1844, and in 1862 the first hunting and fishing resort was built. In the following year Tahoe City was laid out, but during the first years of its existence it was more of a primitive lumbering town than a resort community. With the coming of the railroad and later good roads and the automobile, Lake Tahoe became a resort primarily for people living in the Bay area. A number of lodges were built on its shores, one of which remains in operation, a reminder of the traditional, genteel, lakeshore summer resort built in the first decade of the 20th century. It is called Glenwood and is located on the Nevada shore. Slowly individual cabins and in a few instances large estates came into being. During the decades from the 20s through the mid-50s, the lake shore communities were essentially upper middle class retreats. Because of the life style and small number of residences, the resources and the character of the lake were not over-extended or compromised. But by the late 50s and on into the 60s all of this changed. Second home communities were becoming the thing, and large corporations started to enter the speculative land and housing market. Lake Tahoe was a golden apple ready to be picked.

Around Lake Tahoe are a few remnants of its 19th century past, but these are of only marginal architectural interest. There are a few turn-of-the-century buildings of note: at Emerald Bay just north of Eagle Creek stands the romantic stone pile of Vikingsholm (a lakeshore house designed for Mrs. Iona Moore Knight in 1928-29 by Lennart Palme. This house is a perfect 1920s version of how the Vikings should have lived). Further up the west shore of the lake adjacent to Sugar Point State Park is the Hellman house of 1901-03 designed by Walter Danforth Bliss. The Hellman house is a large three-story shingle house topped by large stone chimneys. In style it fits comfortably into the late turn of the century West Coast Shingle tradition.

In and around Tahoe City and along the shores of the lake are individual houses designed by many of the major practitioners of the Bay area—Maybeck, John Hudson Thomas, William Wurster and others. But as is true in Carmel and other resort communities, these houses are generally not visible from the public roads and have therefore not been listed.

Of the most recent work to be found at Lake Tahoe, the various types of cluster housing have made the most notable architectural contribution. At Tahoe Taverns is a development designed by Henrik Bull with later units by James Morton. In Tahoe City itself is a handsome ski-lodge & Wells Fargo Bank building by James D. Morton (1968). Overlooking Carnelian Bay just above Tahoe City is the "Chinquapin" clustered housing designed by James D. Morton (1970-72). Over the California-Nevada line, in Incline one will find what is probably the most successful of the clustered housing, Forest Pines, designed in 1971 by James Flood. Returning to the lower part of the lake at South Lake Tahoe is another group of cluster housing, Lakeland Village, designed in 1971-72 by MacKinlay and Winnaker.

NC-9b Squaw Valley

Northwest of Lake Tahoe off Highway 89 is Squaw Valley where the 8th Winter Olympic games were held in 1960. Many of the facilities designed for the games were of a permanent nature and have remained intact. Olympic Village itself was designed by the firms of Corlett, Spackman, Kitchen and Hunt between 1957 and 1960. The major building of this group was the Olympic Tent constructed of steel decking suspended by cables from a framework above. The other buildings are good 50s versions of the late Bay tradition, and on the whole they fit non-assertively into the site. The most recent addition to the facility is a large monolithic concrete and glass structure which houses the machinery for the cable car system. The machinery, and in fact all of the mechanical innards are on public display through the glass sections of the building. This structure was designed in 1969 by Shepley, Bulfinch, Richardson and Abbott. Close by is a condo-

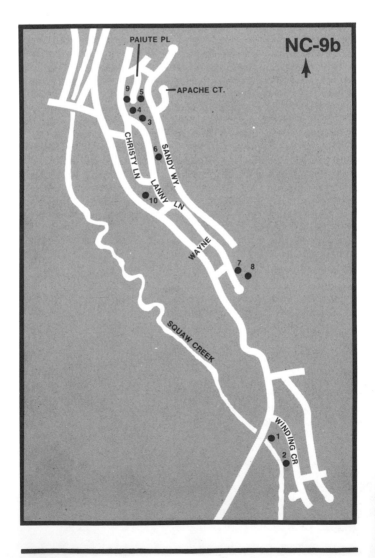

minium group (Squaw Valley North) designed by Alfred Wastlhuber (1968 +). These units are well sited and fit handsomely into the hillside. Both Squaw Valley and Alpine Meadows are dotted with woodsy single family second homes.

1. **House**   1956; George Rockrise
   N side Squaw Valley Rd. nr. junction with Winding Creek Rd.

2. **House**   1959; Henrik Bull
   S side Winding Creek Rd.
   Has been described as a "shoebox with chevron designed siding."

photo: Stone & Steccati

3. **House**   1958
   Anshen & Allen (James Morton, designer)
   N side Lanny Lane nr. junction with Christy Lane
   A successful A-frame house.

4. **House**   1965; George Rockrise
   N side Lanny Lane
   Another A-frame house.

5. **House**   1965; Bull, Field, Volkmann, Stockwell
   End of Paiute Place

6. **House**   1955; Henrik Bull
   S side Lanny Lane
   An early house by this important Bay area designer.

7. **House** 1956; Henrik Bull
   N side Lanny Lane

8. **House** 1968; Jerry Weisbach
   S side Lanny Lane

9. **House** 1972; David Tucker
   S end Paiute Pl.
   A sharp angular form with a bridge entry.

10. **House** 1971; David Tucker
    N side Squaw Valley Rd. opp. the Meadow
    A large round window penetrates the sculptural
    forms of this house.

11. **House** 1965; James Morton
    Squaw Valley Rd. & Hwy. 89, on Truckee River
    A modern version of a Greene & Greene bunga-
    low.

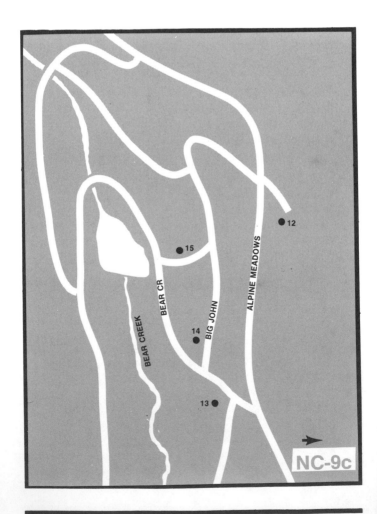

12. **House**   1966; James Morton
N side Alpine Rd., Alpine Meadows

13. **House**   1963; Henrik Bull
S side Bear Creek Dr., Alpine Meadows

14. **House**   1965; Bull, Field, Volkmann, Stockwell
NW cor. Bear Creek Rd. & Big John Rd., Alpine Meadows

15. **House**   1964; Bull, Field, Volkmann, Stockwell
N side Bear Creek Dr., Alpine Meadows

Lake Tahoe: Tahoe Taverns

YOSEMITE

Yosemite's spectacular scenery—just as the West should be—has been a major tourist attraction for well over 100 years. It was in 1855, only four years after its discovery, that the valley experienced its first tourist expedition; and two years later in 1857 regular tourist travel began. In 1859 the first hotel was built and in 1864 the valley itself became one of California's first State Parks. In 1890 the surrounding area became a federal National Park, and in 1906 the state ceded its park to the federal government. Over the years a conscious effort has been made to preserve a number of older buildings of the area. At the Old Village is a simple but charming board and batten Chapel of 1879, and at Wawona is situated the Pioneer Yosemite History Center. The major attraction of the Center is the Wawona Covered Bridge, built in 1858, covered in 1875, and restored in 1956. Nearby is the old Wawona Hotel, part of which dates back to 1885; also a Wells Fargo Office, a jail, a wagon shop, and several cabins. In other areas of the Park one will find odds and ends typical of Smokey Bear park architecture of the 20s and 30s, i.e. comfort stations of heavy timber and stone, rest areas, bridges, etc. Architecturally the gem of the Park is the Ahwanee Hotel designed in 1926 by the Los Angeles architect Gilbert Stanley Underwood. Here one can, with no effort whatsoever, go back into the atmosphere of a "rustic" park hotel of the Flapper Age.

Like other federal and state parks Yosemite seems slowly to be settling under the dust of automobiles, campers, rock music, and vast hordes of people. A number of studies are now being made to see how people might be accommodated and transported in and out of the valley so as not to destroy the natural beauty of the place.

BRIDGEPORT (& BODIE)

Though well off the beaten path of travel, Bridgeport and nearby Bodie are well worth a visit for those interested in 19th century architecture in California. At Bridgeport is one of the rare remaining examples of a California Italianate Courthouse (for Mono County of which Bridgeport is the County seat). This beautifully kept 1880 wood building has all of the ingredients of the Italianate style: bracketed and pedimented canopies over windows, engaged columns and quoining at the corners, and a delightful miniature cupola with round headed windows and a curved mansard roof broken by small circular windows.

At Bodie, which lies south and east of Bridgeport, one will find America's equivalent to Europe's Gothic and Classical ruins—a perfect decayed ghost town of the mining days. Fortunately the town is now a State Historical Park so, like its European counterparts, it will continue to exist and be visited in the years ahead. Within the town there are 168 buildings still standing, most of which were built between the years 1876 and 1880. These include a Methodist Church, a Miner's Union Hall and Odd Felows Hall, and other buildings, all of which are just what one would expect in a real ghost town or in a Hollywood stage set for a Western film.

This highway, circling through the foothills of the High Sierra, is rich in the lore of the gold mining era. Who can fail to be dazzled by place-names of towns along it—Goodyear's Bar, Humbug, Grass Valley, Cool, Fiddletown, Drytown, Mokelumne Hill, Chili Gulch, Angel's Camp, Jackass Hill, Roaring Camp, Squabbletown, Moccasin Creek, Mt. Bullion, Mariposa? But, whatever the romantic associations these names evoke, the reality is often disappointing unless you are prepared to erase neon signs, log trucks, campers, not to mention tourist traps, from your idea of things past. Most of the towns, each with its own variation on the theme of violence and riches, have been modernized, their main streets fronted with buildings remodeled with the intention of making them commercially arresting. Consequently they are best viewed from the rear. The side streets, if any, are often the only places you can get an idea of the nineteenth century. Even there the evidence of awareness of the elaborate contemporary styles of architecture is rare—and, being rare, the more interesting. What remains of the 1850s (almost all the towns had disastrous fires in the 1850s) and 1860s is usually nondescript, utilitarian architecture with the well known "false front," meaning a false attic, and the iron shutters, intended for fire protection, being the only really picturesque accents. A few towns, commented upon below, preserve a glimpse of their heritage, the common architecture of the pioneer. But, if you have the conventional approach to architecture as a matter of styles, you will be disappointed in most of the towns. The styles are better seen in nearby commercial centers such as Marysville, Sacramento, and, of course, San Francisco. As is true in Mississippi and Alabama, the fine houses and public buildings are usually not in the areas which produced the riches but in the places where the middle-man resided.

Nevertheless, there is a charm about the villages along and near Route 49, a contrast of pioneer civilization with lovely to spectacular scenery. And, some towns, particularly Nevada City, make claims to the interest of the architectural historian. Significantly, it is an area where little modern architecture of any distinction exists, though somewhat farther east around Lake Tahoe there is a great deal of recent work, mainly by San Francisco and Sacramento architects. On Route 49 we see the shards of an exploitative culture. The major monuments are the tailings of abandoned mines and brick ruins. Everywhere there are signs that time, not always beneficiently, passed this area by.

The route is traced with side trips, from North to South. Many towns are by-passed by new road construction.

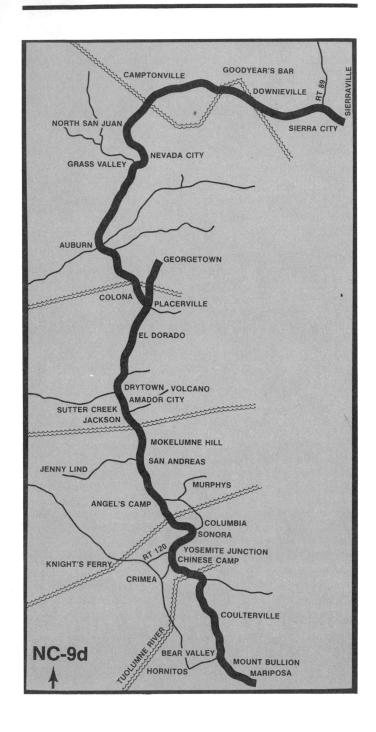

SIERRAVILLE

Essentially Route 49 begins here in this pleasant crossroads town. If you approach from Route 89, you can take a side trip by turning southwest near Blairsden to visit Johnsville, one of the best preserved of the old wooden towns of the 1870s.

SIERRA CITY

A pretty and very old place, largely because fire which destroyed almost all the towns along Route 49 was usually put out here due to the plentiful water supply. One building which did not escape was the Busch Building (1871) on Main Street. A fire in 1948 destroyed the wooden third floor but left the brick lower floors. Notice the "E.C.V." over the door. The letters stand for E Clampus Vitus, a local society which erected the building.

DOWNIEVILLE

This town preserves elements of the Greek and Gothic revivals, and with its beautiful trees has the look of rural New England about it. In spite of its tranquil appearance, it has been flooded several times and even more often swept by fire. Nevertheless, much remains that is old. The Museum and the Costa Store were both built in 1852, the latter with walls four feet thick at the foundation. The Catholic Church (c. 1855) on the hill is whitely chaste.

NORTH SAN JUAN

A few pre-1900 brick and wood buildings of a simple commercial vernacular are still to be found along the main street of North San Juan. The major monument of architectural interest, though, is the Covered Bridge of c.1862 located at Freeman's Crossing. This 105 foot long bridge is located 3 miles north of San Juan on Highway 49, then east on Ridge Road to where it crosses Oregon Creek.

FRENCH CORRAL

Just south of this small mining town is the largest span Covered Bridge still standing in the West. This bridge, the Bridgeport Bridge, is located on the Pleasant Valley Rd. where it crosses over the South Yuba River. This 233 foot long bridge was built in 1862 and was in use as late as 1971. The roof as well as the sides of the bridge are covered with shingles, and the two long segmented wooden arches are emphasized by a curved row of shingles.

NEVADA CITY

Only a few years ago, this town was one of the prettiest in the state. Then came the freeway, a vast white scar where once Route 20 wandered through lovely scenery! Nevertheless, if anger at highway engineers is calmed, the visitor to Nevada City will still find much that is charming. Besides scattered relics of the Gothic Revival, the domestic architecture shows a great debt to the Italianate classicism of the 1860s and 70s. The well preserved commercial area has the usual simple pioneer buildings, but many have Eastlake details added. This city is worth the attention of the admirer of architecture as well as the gold-country buff.

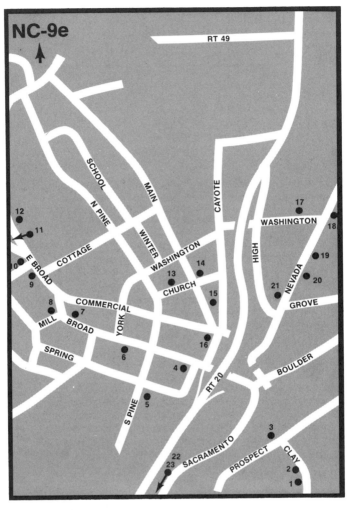

1. **House**   c.1865; 208 Clay St.
   An Italianate house whose classical composition is emphasized by a Greek Revival door and a cupola on the roof.

2. **House**   c.1885; 212 Clay St.
   A large, two-story Queen Anne Revival house.

3. **The Red Castle**   1860
   Prospect St. at end of Clay St.
   A Gothic Revival house in a Gothic setting on a wooded hill high above Deer Creek. Best seen from below on Sacramento Street. It is now a hotel.

4. **The National Hotel**   1854, rebuilt in 1856 and 1857
    At the foot of Broad St.

    Essentially nondescript with Eastlake details add-
    ed much later, this is nevertheless the oldest hotel
    in the state and has been restored to its supposed
    appearance in the mid-nineteenth century with
    modern conveniences placed where necessary.

5. **House**   c.1880; 203 S Pine St.
    A Queen Anne cottage framed in trees.

6. **City Hall**   1937; George C. Sellon
    317 Broad St.

    A small, two-story Moderne building with stream-
    lined details. The lettering and design above the
    second-story windows are notable.

7. **Firehouse No. 2**   1861; 420 Broad St.
    A simple, belfried structure, interesting to compare
    with Firehouse No. 1 on Main Street (No. 15 in our
    listing) which though basically of the same char-
    acter was remodeled in the 80s and now, with its
    Mansard roof and gingerbread, presents a more
    striking appearance.

8. **First Methodist Church** 1864
NW cor. Broad & Mill Sts.
An Italianate structure with Eastlake detail.

9. **House** c.1865; 449 Broad St.
Italianate with a long, low veranda giving unusual horizontality to this basically vertical style.

10. **House** c.1865; 517 Broad St.
Italianate.

11. **House** c.1865
522 Broad St. (in V separating E & W Broad Sts.
A Queen Anne turret tops this Italianate house.

12. **House** c.1865; 524 E Broad St.
Again Italianate—this time a classical composition with an almost Georgian portico given Victorian movement through projecting bays at either side. A single architect or builder's guide must have been responsible for this Italian colony. We have mentioned only a few of such houses.

●13. **Placer County Courthouse** 1936-37
George C. Sellon
N side Church St.
This WPA Moderne structure and the Streamlined Moderne City Hall offer strong visual contrast to this otherwise Victorian town.

14. **First Baptist Church (originally Congregational)**
1864; NE cor. Main & Church Sts.
Brick Gothic arches on the sides dignify this otherwise nondescript building.

●15. **Firehouse No. 1** 1861; 214 Main St.
A utilitarian structure with Mansard roof, with belfry and gingerbread added. This building is now a museum.

16. **Bank of America** 1971; Francis Lloyd, assoc. with Owen L. Jones and John Beltz.
201 Commercial St.
An example of adapting Victorian detail to International Style composition which is being followed by this banking system and the Wells Fargo Banks along Route 49.

17. House c.1890; 441 Washington St.
Queen Anne moving off into the Colonial Revival.

18. House c.1870; 316 Nevada St.
Another contribution to the Italianate collection.

19. House c.1855; 236 Nevada St.
The Greek Revival at its purest.

20. House 226 Nevada St.
A Greek Revival cottage with Eastlake details!

21. Trinity Episcopal Church 1854
Nevada St. at end of Grove St.
A board and batten, Gothic Revival church typical of the strong influence of Richard Upjohn on Episcopalians.

22. House (off map) c.1885
515 Sacramento St. just S of intersection with Zion St.
Queen Anne cottage.

● **23. William Morris Steward House** (off map) 1850-60
Zion St. just W of Calvary St.
Certainly for age, grounds, and the purity of its classicism, this Greek Revival house with two-story (Monterey Style) portico is the most impressive in town.

GRASS VALLEY

The North Star Mine, the oldest and deepest gold mine in California, is still an inspiration to the town's economy. Although a fire destroyed some 300 buildings in 1855, Grass Valley has many old buildings and on Mill Street near West Main Street is a row of old store buildings with wooden awnings which are almost unique. Considerable local color is added to the town when you consider the fact that both Lola Montez, the dancer, and Josiah Royce, the philosopher, once called it home. In fact, both lived on Mill Street (Lola at 248 and Josiah at site of present library).

Grass Valley is easily toured for most of the notable buildings are on Mill Street or nearby.

The Union Building c.1905; 151 Mill St.
A wooden Classical building with curved glass windows.

Bank of America 1917
NE cor. Mill & Bank Sts.
A small pantheon in the Renaissance Revival style popularized by McKim, Mead, and White.

Del Oro Theater c.1935; Mill St. at Neal St.
Another Streamlined Moderne structure of the Buck Rogers era.

Wells Fargo Bank   1969; Dean F. Unger
214 Mill St. nr. Neal St.
A blending of old and new which seems appropriate in this frontier town.

Emmanuel Episcopal Church   1858
S Church St. on E side bet. Walsh & Neal Sts.
This Carpenter's Gothic (board and batten) structure demonstrates Richard Upjohn's influence.

Two Queen Anne Houses   c.1880s
518 Walsh St. & 403 Neal St.

Lyman Gilmore School   1968; George G. Higgins & Assoc.
W Main St. at City Limit
A low group of concrete buildings, some monumental in proportion.

"Empire Cottage"   c.1895; Willis Polk
E Empire St. N side Grass Valley off Hwy 20/49
A stone cottage and other buildings by one of the proponents of the early Bay tradition.

AUBURN

Named after Auburn, New York, this mining town presents a mostly turn-of-the-century appearance except for a few buildings on Commercial street and on the Old Plaza. Lawyer's Row (Commercial Street) is a series of false-fronted buildings (of the 1850s and 60s) which step down the ravine to the old town whose most impressive bit of architecture is the mansard-roofed Fire Station (1852; roof 1891), an ironic sight since fire so often devasted Auburn. The Neo Classic Courthouse (in places almost Italianate in feeling), designed in 1894 by the architect John M. Curtis, is situated on the hill. Its size and elegance indicate Auburn's high aspirations.

The older part (which lies in the valley) of town has been preserved and to a considerable extent restored. On the hill above the older part of town is the lightly Gothic styled Methodist Church of 1858. Higher up on a gentle hillside are the new Placer County Administrative Offices designed in 1967 by Robert Lilles. These offices consist of 5 interlock hexagonal based domes covered with diamond shaped aluminium panels. This variation on Buckminster Fuller's Geodesic dome theme creates the feeling of a space colony on the moon.

COOL

Between Cool and Pilot Hill on the west side of the road is the Alcandor A. Bayley House (1862), a three-story structure with simplified classical portico. Bayley, a native of Vermont, believed that the railroad would be built near the building and contemplated a grand hotel. Unfortunately the railroad engineers by-passed Bayley's dream.

COLOMA

The Gold Rush started here. Little remains of it except ruins and simple houses. Probably the most interesting sight is the Gothic Revival Emmanuel Episcopal Church (1856). East of Coloma on a side road is Georgetown which, though unspoiled save by fire, has nothing of real architectural significance except the Shannon Knox House (1852), a Monterey Style structure built of lumber supposedly shipped around the Horn.

PLACERVILLE

Since the entire Main Street has been modernized, this is one of the best places to view the old town from the rear. The Wilcox Warehouse (1852) is a fine building of rough native rock. It and the Episcopal Church of Our Savior (1866) in the Gothic Revival are about all that are interesting from the architectural point of view. A lot was here, but now it is mostly "site of."

About ten miles south-west of Placerville on Route 50 at Ponderosa Road in Shingle Springs is the new Ponderosa High School by Nacht and Lewis.

COPPEROPOLIS

This town's great period of prosperity was in the 1860s when its copper mines were at the height of production. At the south end of town are situated several brick buildings of the 1860s: the Federal Armory, and the Office and Warehouse Bldg. for the Consolidated Mining Company. At the other end of town is the brick former Congregational Church c.1860 (later an I.O.O.F. Hall and now a Museum) which is Gothic Revival in style.

SUTTER CREEK

Along the streets of this gold rush town one will find a good number of buildings dating from the end of the 1850s through the early 80s. Among these are the Masonic and I.O.O.F Halls of 1865, the Brignole Bldg. (1859) and the Belletti Inn (1860). Among the houses one should see are the Voorhies house (now Sutter Creek Inn) and the Downs house. Like other houses in Sutter Creek they are lightly New England in feeling.

IONE

Ione, named for the heroine of Bulwer Lytton's *The Last Days of Pompeii*, was settled in 1848. There are still a few 19th century commercial buildings on the town's streets, but the main structure of architectural interest is the brick Gothic Revival Methodist Church which was completed in 1862. Its brick tower is surmounted by a witch's hat roof.

AMADOR CITY

This tiny village boasts two hotels. The Amador, dating from gold rush days (c.1856), is Monterey Style; and the Imperial (c.1870) is in the pioneer plain-style with a false castellated attic, in which Gothic Revival arches are inscribed in brick, strongly, if coincidentally, resembling the effect of Latrobe's St. Paul's Church (1817) in Alexandria, Virginia. Thus travels civilization!

JACKSON

This town is notable for its stone architecture on Main and Court Streets. The Odd Fellows Hall (c.1870) is an extremely tall, brick, three-story building. But the principal sight is the A. C. Brown House (c.1862), now the County Museum. The National Hotel (1862) at Water and Main Streets was modernized in the 1930s but later restored. At the end of town is St. Sava's Serbian Orthodox Church (1893), suggesting the cosmopolitan nature of the search for gold.

VOLCANO

About fifteen miles east of Jackson on a side road is Volcano, now mainly ruins but once supposed to have had a population of 5000 and seventeen hotels. Only one of these remains, but in beautiful condition and still functioning—the Monterey Style Hotel St. George (1854).

Volcano Bar

MOKELUMNE HILL

Now by-passed by Route 49 and badly in need of restoration, this town was once one of the richest gold
diggings in the state. The three-story, stone Adams and
Company building (1854, with third story added by the
Odd Fellows in 1861) reflects the past status of the
town, as does the two-story, Monterey Style Leger Hotel (1852). The Congregational Church (1856) is a fine
Classical Revival building with board and batten siding.

ALTAVILLE

Altaville's most interesting piece of architecture is the
Prince and Garibardi Store (1852) a nondescript stone
structure with beautiful wrought iron balcony.

MURPHYS

At Angel's Camp, which, despite its connection with
Mark Twain, has little of architectural importance, you
may take a side road, Route 4, northeast about eight
miles to this beautiful village. The buildings are old,
famous, and quaint, but the best is the much-photo-
graphed Classical Revival elementary school house
(1860) at the southwest edge of town.

(By retracing your route a few miles and then turning
south on a well-marked spur you can take a lovely,
winding road to Columbia without having to go all the
way back to Hwy. 49.)

COLUMBIA

For a short time the capital of California, Columbia is
now a museum administered as a State Park. It is, unlike Murphys, alive with tourists at almost all seasons
of the year. Nevertheless, it is unquestionably the place
to see the pioneer, plain-style at its best. Columbia had
a fire in 1854 and thus everything dates from the late
1850s, but frontier institutions—black-smithing, saloons,
candy stores, even dance-hall girls—have been re-
created to give you the feel of gold-rush days. Many
of the buildings (e.g. the Express Office, 1857) have
lovely wrought iron balconies. The best architecture is
reserved for the churches—the Presbyterian, an exact
replica (1954) of the original 1854 structure, and St.

Anne's Catholic Church (1856), also Gothic Revival with its strange altar painted in 1880 by James Fallon, the son of a local hotel-keeper.

SONORA

If you think that the traffic is bad as you enter the central section of Sonora, imagine how it was in the 1850s when Washington Street, the main street, was crowded day and night with thousands of gold-seekers and fellow-travelers! Although many of the buildings downtown are old, almost none show many signs of it. The trees have been cut down and the street widened so that you must poke into alleys to get any idea of the building of the old town. Actually, the best building is the Bank of America, built in the mid-1960s.

The residential areas are more rewarding. At the head of Washington Street stands St. James' Episcopal Church, (1859), one of the loveliest board and batten Gothic tributes to the influence of Richard Upjohn on Episcopalian architecture. The Frank A. Morgan House (1886-1888) across the street (West Snell) from it is certainly one of the most manneristic houses in the state, worthy of Samuel and Joseph Newsom who may, indeed, have been the architects.

Morgan House

KNIGHT'S FERRY

A diversion of 12 miles at Yosemite Junction south on Route 120 will take you through Jamestown (see the Eastlake style Emporium, 1897) to this very picturesque town. On the main street is a Classical Revival bank (c.1860) of dressed stone with bracketed cornice and columned porch. On the hill above the town is the Dent House (c.1852) where the young army officer Ulysses S. Grant visited his wife's brother in 1854. It was during this visit that Grant is supposed to have designed a covered bridge which spanned the Stanislaus River. The original bridge was swept away by the flood of 1862, but a new one, an exact copy, was rebuilt on the raised foundations of the original in 1864. Incidentally a similar covered bridge at O'Byrne's Ferry nearby was demolished in 1957.

HORNITOS

Built around a square, this sleepy town, reached from Bear Valley or Mt. Bullion, is very close to being a ghost town. Mostly in ruins, it evokes a violent past. The ruins of the store where D. Ghirardelli began his climb to riches are marked. No significant architecture remains.

MARIPOSA

Founded on John C. Fremont's Rancho Las Mariposas, this town exhibits some architecture of real interest largely because it was a commercial center as well as a mining town. In 1854 the residents ordered that a courthouse "sturdy and classical" be built and it still stands sturdy and classical. In 1866 the Monterey Style Schlageter Hotel was built. The lovely Carpenter's Gothic St. Joseph's Catholic church dates from 1862.

MERCED

Now an agricultural center, Merced was founded in what once was cattle country. Its existence is due to the coming of the Southern Pacific Railroad in 1872. Now bypassed by Route 99, it is one of the most pleasant towns in the state. The planning, architecture, tree-lined streets, and even the summer heat remind one of some of the county-seats in the lower Midwest. Originally surrounded by cattle-ranches, Merced now manufactures food and wood products. But it has, so far, escaped urban renewal and other horrors of the Age of Progress.

It thus exhibits some fine examples of the popular styles since the 1870s. The best is undoubtedly the Italianate Merced County Courthouse—sculpture still in place—designed by A. A. Bennett, one of the early architects of the Capitol at Sacramento. When in 1875 the members of the Inspection Committee recommended the acceptance of the building by the County, they congratulated themselves "and the people generally of the County of Merced that we have in our judgment full value received for the money [$30,000] expended." After almost a century, the judgment still seems valid. A number of good buildings are near the Courthouse. At the northeast corner of 21st and L Streets is a curious house (c.1910) in a sort of stripped and squared-off Mission Style with pergola connecting it to a garage in the same style—a nice ensemble. Another Mission Style structure is the Central Presbyterian Church (c.1905) at the northwest corner of 20th and L Streets. St. Luke's Episcopal Church (c.1880) at 2030 M Street has been modernized, but its board and batten Gothic still is picturesque.

PLANADA

This was, as the name implies, a planned Mission Revival community laid out in 1911. It barely got off the ground. Now very little even of the plan exists except Broadway with trees in the divider and a few closed shops along it. A real disappointment!

Until the 1870s Modesto was simply a tiny ferry-cross-ing on the Tuolumne River servicing traffic to and from southern mines. The Southern Pacific changed the pic-ture, making the town the commercial center of a rich agricultural region of Stanislaus County of which Mo-desto is the seat. Significantly the City Hall, Court-house and Mission Revival Railroad Station (disap-pointing) are within a radius of three blocks. The rela-tion shows again in the grid which aligns itself on the railroad running from the southeast to the northwest corners of the original square plat. In more recent ad-ditions the grid has been changed to conform to the points of the compass, so that in looking at a street map, it is quite clear how the city grew.

It is also clear from the map that Modesto has, in the twentieth century, been conscious of the need for parks. About thirty dot the city, many of them on Dry Creek (it is wet) and the Tuolumne River. Like Merced to the south and Stockton to the north, Modesto seems to be a very pleasant place to live.

Unfortunately, progress-oriented politicians tore down the magnificent Italianate Courthouse (1872) a number of years ago and replaced it with a building that is merely functional. A new library has also been built, but the old McHenry Library building has been trans-formed into a really excellent museum of the city. A few good Victorian commercial buildings, all "modern-ized" on their first floors, and some houses of the nine-

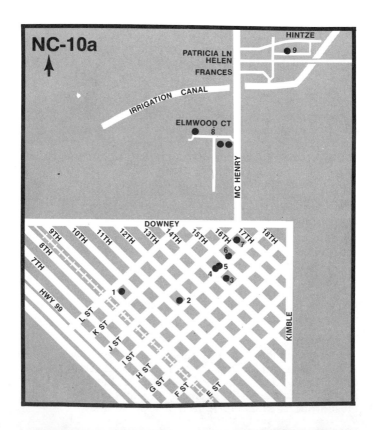

teenth century remain. But the pleasantest areas of Modesto, besides the parks, are the residential sections east and west of McHenry Avenue and east of Kimble. Here the twenties, thirties, and forties are reflected in eclectic forms and in a relaxed style of life.

In 1911 an illuminated arch was constructed across I Street at Ninth and on it was inscribed the slogan "Water, Wealth, Contentment, Health." That just about says it for Modesto.

1. **Ford Garage** c.1935
   SE cor. L & 9th Sts.
   Streamlined Moderne, wonderful round tower.

2. **Post Office** 1932; James A. Wetmore, act. & superv. archt.
   NW cor. 12th & I Sts.
   Renaissance Revival with a touch of the Zigzag Moderne.

3. **McHenry Museum (formerly Library)** 1911; addition, 1928
   SE cor. 14th & I Sts.
   A strange classical building with the columned portico entrance on the corner. Inside, the circulation desk was under a domed rotunda. Very impressive!

4. **First United Presbyterian Church** 1910
   NE cor. 14th & I Sts.
   A Mission Revival structure very similar to the Presbyterian Church in Merced.

5. **Modesto-Stanislaus Library** 1971; Austin, Field & Fry
   I St. bet. 14th & 15th Sts.
   A white pavilion very much in the Edward Stone manner.

6. **Oramil McHenry House** c.1875
   906 15th St.
   Probably this was always the finest Victorian house in town. Most of the others have been demolished. But this Mansard-roofed mansion, the home of Modesto's most distinguished citizen, has withstood progress admirably.

7. **Chuck Wagon** c.1928; SE cor. 16th & J Sts.
   The Spanish Colonial Revival at its most ebullient.
   Actually this includes a small shopping center as
   well as a restaurant.

8. **Three houses** c.1930
   211 Elmwood Court, 118 Elmwood Court, 422 Elmwood Ave.

   These houses, the last two almost connected, can
   best be described as Hansel and Gretel architecture. Their confectionary effect is enhanced by the
   use of pastel washes under the eaves. The
   Berkeley architect W. R. Yelland comes to mind.

●9. **Heckendorf House**   1941; John Funk
   215 E Patricia Ln.

   This house, illustrated on the cover of Elizabeth
   Mock's *Built in U. S. A., 1932-1944* (Museum of Modern Art, 1944), has weathered the stylistic storms
   of the decades since it was built and remains a
   classic of modern architecture.

Note: There is a very late Frank Lloyd Wright house in
Modesto, but it is utterly impossible to see it from the
public streets.

Northeast of Modesto on Route 120 is **Escalon** with its
John Wheeler Jones House of 1867, a square house
made of local bricks. Directly east of Modesto on Route
132 about thirty-two miles is **La Grange** where there
are a number of nineteenth century buildings among
them St. Louis Catholic Church and the ever-present
I.O.O.F. Hall.

● **INTERSTATE HIGHWAY #5**   completed 1972
Bet. Tracy and 12 mi. S of Bakersfield
This new 240 mile section of the Valley Freeway
visually, and factually, represents the ideal of the
open freeway. It avoids all of the major towns of
the Valley, and since it goes through a sparsely
settled section, it forms the dominant man-made
element (along with the California Aqueduct
which runs occasionally very close to the freeway). The two ribbons of concrete have been
beautifully fitted into the terrain, and the infrequent interchanges with their bridges create patterns in the landscape which are impressive,
whether driving on the freeway or seeing it from
the air.

● **CALIFORNIA AQUEDUCT**   1959 to present
Driving on Interstate #5 one can catch occasional
glimpses of this great canal as it winds its way
down Southern California. Like the new Interstate
#5, the serpentine course of this waterway makes
a deep impact on the landscape. At present the
project starts at Oroville Dam north and west of
Redding and ends up in Los Angeles County.
With the current critical concern for conservation
and ecology, it is doubtful that the project will be
completed as it was originally planned in the late
1950s.

HOLLISTER

Hollister is another of those California towns which lies
just far enough off the usual path that it is seldom visited by tourists, let alone those who might be interested
in architecture. It lies in a rich agricultural valley of
its own and the town conveys a feeling of quietness
and prosperity. The history of its founding is rather
unusual. In 1868 a group of fifty farmers formed the
San Justo Homestead Association and purchased
21,000 acres from the old Rancho San Justo. The land
was then divided equally into fifty parcels, and near
the center one hundred acres was set aside for the
town site of Hollister. A simple grid pattern was imposed on the town site, but irregularities occurred from
the beginning. There are a number of short streets,
many of which are called Alleys. Forming the north
boundary of the town is Hollister Hill, which is a large
public park, while in the southern part of the town
several small parks have been provided. Architecturally there are no "great" buildings in Hollister, but
there are a number of good houses which run from the
Italianate of the early 70s through the Spanish Colonial Revival of the 20s.

    House   c.1887; 582 5th St.
A Queen Anne house, with an excellent stained
glass window on the porch.

    House   c.1870; 528 5th St.
Italianate.

Catholic Church c.1880s
SW cor. 5th & College Sts.
A late Gothic Revival church.

House c.1872; 801 South St.
A narrow Italianate house with very sophisticated details—the curved brackets and the bold dentals under the overhang, a low mansard-roofed tower which grows out of the front two-story bay, and a fine entrance porch and doorway.

Cottage c.1870s; 477 South St.
A single floor spindled Eastlake cottage. The house itself is simple undecorated board and batten, but around this has been placed a light very delicate porch of spindles and thin wood arches.

House c.1915; 472 South St.
A simple version of the West Coast Prairie style.

House c.1870; 464 South St.
Another excellent Italianate house. A new porch has been added, but to the side of this is the original gable front of the house with a round window in the attic, a pair of round-headed windows on the second floor, and a projecting bay with its own round-headed windows on the ground floor.

House   c.1870s; 864 Powell St.
An Italianate house.

House (a double house)   c.1912
380 Hayden St.
This is an unusual version of the West Coast Prairie style; note the handling of the windows on the second floor at the rear as a continuous band.

House   c.1880s; 800 Montgomery St.
A two story Queen Anne house.

San Benito Nursing Home   c.1912
910 Montgomery St.
In the Mission Revival style.

House   c.1925; 1564 San Benito St.
Spanish Colonial Revival.

SAN JUAN BAUTISTA

The Mission of San Juan Bautista was founded in 1797; work on the church and its related buildings was started in 1803 and completed in 1812. The Mission buildings at San Juan were among the first to be restored (in 1884) when the newcomers to California became increasingly self-conscious of "their" Hispanic past. Though other Mission buildings were larger and certainly more sophisticated architecturally, the simple forms of the San Juan Mission became one of the major sources for the new Mission Revival of the 90s and early 1900s.

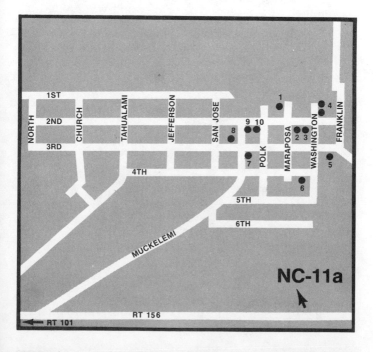

Even before the Mission was secularized in 1835, several private adobe houses had been built around the open Plaza which lies to the southeast of the church. These were later joined by other one and two-story adobes, and by the 1850s a few Anglo wood buildings had been constructed. During the 19th century, the town was a major stopping off place for travelers between San Francisco and Monterey. Fortunately, in the 20th century, when the highway (#101) and later the freeway (which keeps getting wider and wider) were built, they were located several miles to the west of the town, so that the 19th century feeling of the place still remains. The Plaza area has been turned into a State Historic Park, and other historic structures have been restored over the years. Because of the importance of the Mission and of the Spanish-Mexican period in San Juan, little mention is made of several excellent wood clapboard buildings dating from the 1850s and 1860s. Yet these buildings, ranging in style from the Greek Revival to the Italianate, occupy an important place in the history of architecture in California.

● 1. **Mission San Juan Bautista** 1803-1812; restored 1884 & 1907
NW side of Plaza off 2nd St.

The long low arcade of 20 arches covered by a low tiled shed roof conjures up the romantic image of California in pre-Anglo days. The church building itself is rectagular, covered by a low pitched gable roof. A series of arches provides the major divisions of space.

2. **Plaza Hotel** 1813-14; 1858
SE cor. 2nd & Mariposa Sts., facing the Plaza
Two single floor adobe buildings were joined together and a second floor of wood was added in 1858.

● 3. **Castro Adobe** 1840-41
SW cor. 2nd & Washington Sts., facing the Plaza
This two-story adobe with its projecting second floor balcony, and the Larkin House in Monterey, are rightly considered to be *the* most handsome

buildings in the mid 19th century Monterey Style. This house and the Plaza Hotel next door have been restored and are open to the public.

4. **Zanetta House**   1868
   SE side of Plaza, off 2nd St.

   Adobe bricks from the former Mission Nunnery were used for the first floor of this building, while the upper floor was constructed of wood. The whole was then sheathed in clapboard. The bracketed projecting roof, the detailing around the windows, doors, and porch, set this house within the Italianate mode.

5. **Casa Juan de Anza**   c.1850
   Cor. Franklin & 3rd Sts.

   An early adobe, now restored.

6. **Adobe House**   c.1850
   Cor. Washington & 4th Sts.

   A two-story adobe house.

7. **Glad Tidings Church (originally the Baptist Church)**   1863; SE cor. 3rd & Muckelemi Sts.

   An austere dignified Greek Revival Church. The small lattice work tower originally had a spire which came down in the 1906 earthquake. The proportions of its gabled front with its central single door and the tympanum above are as pure as one will find the Greek Revival in California.

8. **Kemp House**   1860
   502 3rd St.

   A single floor Greek Revival cottage set back in its own garden.

9. **Texas Lodge No. 46**   1868
   SE cor. 2nd & Muckelemi Sts.

   A two-story wood lodge building with a small cupola.

10. **Crane House**   1857; 401 2nd St.

    Monterey Style, though relying heavily upon the Greek Revival.

For those who travel back and forth between San Francisco and Los Angeles, the remembrance of Salinas is most likely that of stopping off at a restaurant or a motel near one of the freeway exits. But if you leave the freeway and travel west into the main section of town, a pleasant surprise awaits, for there are many well preserved 19th century residences to be found along the streets, and there is the Monterey County Courthouse, a gem of the WPA Moderne style of the 1930s. Nearby in the Post Office building and the Salinas Californian building one will find other good examples of the pre and post-World War II Streamlined Moderne style.

The city was founded in 1856 and rapidly grew as a major center for the cattle industry of the Salinas valley. At the end of the 19th and the beginning of the

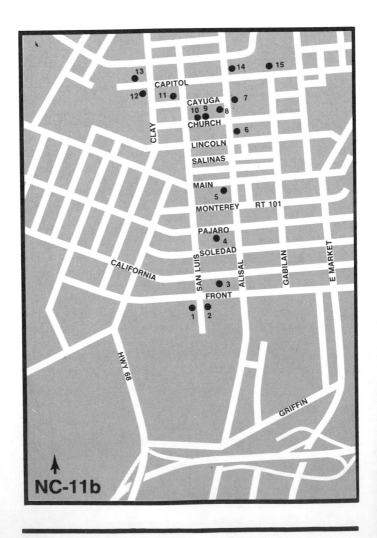

20th centuries, the rich soil and excellent climate of the valley came to be increasingly utilized, and today Salinas' economy and that of the lower valley is oriented to such crops as lettuce and sugar beets. As in other California cities, its town plan presents a hodgepodge of separate grid iron patterns which go off in one direction or another. Today the freeway and the railroad separate the community into two parts, of which the northern and eastern section is basically a product of the 50s and 60s.

1. **House**   c.1890; 403 Front St.
   A Queen Anne house with a tower.

2. **Cottage**   c.1885; 347 Front St.
   A large scale pattern of a rose in shingles jumps out of the front gable of this Queen Anne cottage.

3. **Three cottages**   c.1885
   329, 331, 333 California St.
   A group of small Queen Anne cottages, probably built by a single builder.

4. **Valley Baptist Church**   c.1880s; 327 Pajaro St.
   A little Gothic revival together with Eastlake and Queen Anne touches.

5. **Crocker Bank Building**   c.1930
   SE cor. Main & E Alisal Sts.
   A six-story Moderne bank and office building.

6. **U. S. Post Office & Federal Building**   1936; Louis A. Simon. 1959, two wings added
   NW cor. W Alisal & Church Sts.
   A stark but very dignified example of WPA Moderne.

● 7. **Monterey County Courthouse**   1937
   Robert Stanton
   NW cor. W Alisal & Church Sts.
   WPA Moderne. One walks through a high two-story porch composed of square fluted piers into an interior courtyard garden. The two-story wings of the building are surmounted by a glass walled third floor which has strongly rounded corners. Sculpture abounds: heads of individuals in the spandrels, over the major entrance, and cast in metal relief on doors leading into the courtyard. This building is really a perfect example, inside and out, of the WPA Moderne style of the 30s, and also an excellent example of a concrete building whose surface is articulated by the pattern of the form boards.

8. **Salinas Californian Building**   1948
   Berham & Richards; Charles Butner
   SW cor. W Alisal & Church Sts.
   A post-World War II continuation of the Streamlined Moderne style of the 30s. Note the composition of the exterior clock and its ornament placed in the parapet above the main entrance.

9. **Double Cottage**   c.1875; 334-336 Church St.
   A raised basement Eastlake double house.

10. **Cottage**   c.1880; 336 Church St.
    An Eastlake cottage, broken into 4 bays, each of which is covered with its own high pitched roof and delicate sawed wood ornament.

11. **House**   c.1885; 402 Cayaga St.
    A story and a half Queen Anne house, overflowing with ornament—a number of horseshoe windows and decorative areas, and elaborate sawed and turned work around the porch and on the eaves.

12. **House**   c.1925; 165 Clay St.
    A Period Revival house of the 20s, in this case using the English rural cottage tradition.

13. **House**   c.1937; 510 Capitol St.
    A single floor, compact Streamlined Moderne house.

14. **House**   c.1888; 246 Capitol St.
    A Queen Anne house with unusual groups of turned columns on the entrance porch and the second floor porch above.

15. **House**   c.1870s; 119 Capitol St.
    A small mansard roofed house.

16. **House**   c.1900; 154 Central Ave.
    A Shingle Style house which looks back to the Queen Anne.

17. **Cottage (now the John Steinbeck Memorial)**
    c.1887; 132 Central Ave.
    A carefully restored raised basement Queen Anne Cottage.

Mission San Antonio

Twenty miles south and west of King City near the town of Jolon are two important architectural monuments. The first of these is the Mission San Antonio de Padua. This mission was founded in 1771, but the existing church was not started until 1810 and was completed in 1813. Like other missions, the church and its outbuildings fell into ruins in the late 19th century. In 1903 the ruins were stabilized, and in 1948-49 an extensive restoration took place. The building presents just what the image of a California Mission should be: a simple two-story church covered by a low pitched tile-covered gable roof; in front of the church is a screen of arches and low bell towers, and to the side is a long one-story arcade. Behind the arcade and the rooms beyond is the classic enclosed patio. Before one reaches the mission, and in fact it is often mistaken for the mission, is Las Milpitas, the former headquarters of one of William Randolph Hearst's extensive ranches (now a part of the Headquarters Building of the Hunter-Liggett Military Reservation). Las Milpitas, which was described as a "hunting lodge" for Hearst, is a splendid Mission Revival building designed in the early 1900s by Julia Morgan. While pure Mission Revival in style, the building exhibits many very personal almost idiosyncratic views of the style.

While traveling to and from the Mission and Las Milpitas, note the delightful late 19th century wooden Gothic St. Luke's Episcopal Church in Jolon (on Hwy. G 14 to King City). Further along the highway to King City one will discover a number of characteristic California wood barns, with their central two-story naves and their low shed roofed aisles to each side.

Gilroy's fame rests on its Town Hall of 1905 designed by Samuel Newsom (with Wolfe and McKenzie), one of the two brothers who designed the well-known Carson house in Eureka. For those who have some difficulties in separating styles, it should be noted that the Town Hall at its dedication was described as "in the Mission style" though it must be admitted that no church father of the early 19th century would have recognized it as such. The Town Hall is located on the main street (Monterey St.) at the northeast corner of 16th Street; further uptown to the north on the same side of the street is a two-story Mission Revival commercial building which could well have been designed by Newsom. South of the Town Hall at Monterey and Depot Streets is a sort-of Mission Revival Railroad Station. Across the tracks, east of Montgomery Street (at NE cor. Forest & Martin Sts.) is an excellent carpenter's version of a Gothic Revival church—the Church of the Nazarene.

City Hall

GONZALES & SOLEDAD

In Gonzales at the southeast corner of 9th and Day Streets is the late 19th century Community Church of Gonzales with its shingle and clapboard tower and crenelated silhouette. West of the town of Soledad is the Mission Nuestra Señora de la Soledad which was founded in 1791. The church and other buildings were started in the 1790s. From the 1830s on, the church was in a ruinous condition. In 1954 the small chapel of the complex was restored.

Until the year 1849 Monterey was the chief city of California. The Spanish Presidio at the site was established in 1770, and in 1775 Monterey was declared the capital of California. In 1822 California, with Monterey still as its capital, became a part of the Republic of Mexico. In 1846 the city, along with the rest of the state, was taken over by military forces of the United States. Four years later in Colton Hall in Monterey the constitution of the State of California was adopted and California became a state in the Union. With the discovery of gold and the rapid rise in importance of San Francisco, the town of Monterey became first a small and quiet fishing village, and later, with the completion of the railroad to the Peninsula and the building of the Hotel Del Monte in 1879-80, it assumed its present role as a resort community.

Even as late as 1900 Monterey was described by visitors as a perfect Mexican village with white adobe walls and tile roofs; but one by one the adobes were demolished and were replaced by brick, wood and later concrete stores, hotels, and office buildings. Fortunately, just after the turn of the century Monterey, as well as the rest of California, began to experience the Mission Revival in architecture. A large number of the remaining adobes were saved, restored or in some cases simply moved to new sites. Some continued in private ownership while others were slowly acquired by civic groups, by the State, and most recently by the National Trust for Historic Preservation. In the early 1960s the Custom House Redevelopment Project was organized and forty-five acres of land in and around the custom house were acquired and leveled in a classic urban renewal fashion, leaving only a few remaining historic adobe and stone buildings. Lighthouse Avenue, which went diagonally across the area, was

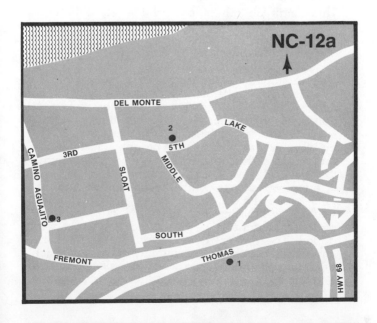

carried through a tunnel, and a new Custom House Plaza was established. It was hoped that much of the remaining land would be utilized for a major shopping center, hotels, restaurants, and housing. Unfortunately this has not so far been realized, and with the building in 1967 of the extensive Del Monte Shopping Center on the outskirts of the city, it is unlikely that Monterey can support a second major shopping center.

Like Santa Fe, New Mexico, Monterey is a tourist-oriented town, pleasant to walk through and to browse in. Except for the present bleak Urban Renewal area, the scale of its buildings, its irregular streetscape, and its beautiful location overlooking Monterey Bay make it one of the most pleasant cities to visit in California. Architecturally it is a gold mine of early California adobe architecture, from small single floor adobes to a number of classic examples of two-story Monterey style buildings with their 19th century classical detailing of projecting second floor porches. Though the community is not rich in late 19th century architecture, there are individual 19th century houses to be seen on the hill to the west of downtown. Back of Monterey to the south one will find streets lined with many small cottages built in a variety of Period styles of the 20s. Still higher up on the hill are located newer houses including several important examples of the work of Charles Moore, William Turnbull and others. (Those buildings with an asterisk are open at certain times to the public.)

*1. **St. John's Episcopal Church**   1891; Ernest Coxhead
SW cor. Thomas & Josselyn Canyon Rds. (originally located in Del Monte)

This small church is one of the great Shingle Style buildings in California, and it is unquestionably one of the most enticing of Coxhead's churches. The surface pattern of the shingles changes and varies, sometimes curving up and over to emphasize a window or a door, or on occasion to draw attention to dormers and window hoods. The scale of the church is that of the perfect doll house (even though it was cut in two and extended). This is best seen on the south side of the building where the roof is brought close to the ground, and the door and window protrude into the low roof. The child-like quality of the exterior is equally realized within, where space and details are reduced to an Alice in Wonderland world. The building was moved to its present site and at that time a new entrance vestibule was added. The present composition shingle roof unfortunately destroys the continuity of surface which originally existed, for the wood shingles were carried around the curved eave line tying the walls and roof surfaces together.

1. St. John's Church

2. **U.S. Naval Post Graduate School (formerly Del Monte Hotel)** 1925-on
S side Del Monte Ave., W of Camino Aguajito
Before World War II this was the site of the famous Del Monte Hotel, one of the really great social spas of the late 19th and 20th centuries. The first hotel building in the Stick style was constructed in 1879 and burned in 1887. It was replaced during 1887-88 by a Swiss Chalet style building. The central section of this building burned in 1924, and a new central section in the Spanish Colonial Revival style designed by Lewis P. Hobart and Clarence A. Tantau was built in 1925.

Carefully placed in a magnificent stand of oaks on the grounds of the old hotel are the five reinforced concrete buildings by Skidmore, Owings & Merrill, housing the teaching and technical facilities of the school. The five-story Laboratory Sciences Building and the one-story Auditorium are visible from Rt. 1; the remaining three are north of these and only visible from within the grounds. They represent one of the high points of the earlier work of this firm.

3. **666 Office Building** 1968; Hall & Goodhue
666 Camino Aguajito
An International Style building, very European in feeling; even its site overlooking the lake and park is highly reminiscent of similar buildings in Switzerland and elsewhere.

4. **G. T. Marsh & Co. Oriental Goods Building** c.1915
699 Fremont St.
Outrageously oriental, but still fittingly Mission Revival in style.

5. **Girl Scout Headquarters (formerly First French Consulate)** c.1830
Camino del Estero, bet. Franklin & Anthony Sts. located in the park.
A single floor adobe which was moved to its present site in 1932. It was formerly located at the corner of Fremont and Abrego Streets. The end gable walls have been projected out to enclose two sides of the long front porch.

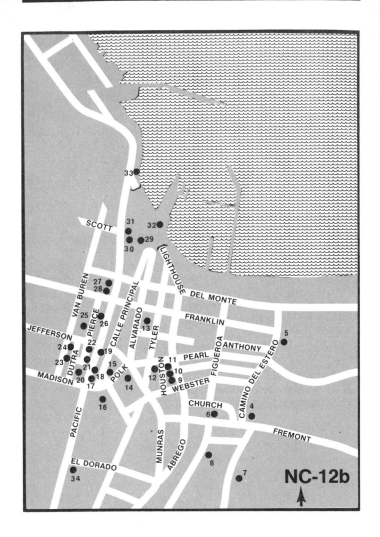

*6. Royal Presidio Chapel of San Carlos de Borromeo
1794; Sculptor: Antonio Valesquez
S side Church St. opp. Figueroa St.

A severe Neo-Classical screen surmounted by a scalloped gable sits as a frontispiece before the simple gabled roof volume behind. The first church on the site had been built in 1770, but was severely damaged by an earthquake in 1789.

7. Casa Bonifacio 1835
E side Mesa Rd., beyond Perry Ln.

An adobe house which was moved in 1922 from the central area of town to its present site.

8. Casa Boronda 1817
Boronda Ln., off E side Major Sherman Ln.

The oldest house still standing in Monterey; a single story adobe covered by a gabled shingle roof.

9. **Casa Abregio**   c.1840
NW cor. Abregio & Webster Sts.
A single floor adobe house with a long porch running parallel to the street.

10. **Casa Madariaga**   early 1840s; 615 Abregio St.
A single floor adobe house.

11. **Casa Pacheco**   1840; 602 Abregio St.
A large two-story adobe much remodeled on exterior and interior.

*12. **Stevenson (Gonzales) House**   c.1830s
530 Houston St.
A two-story adobe. The entrance with its side lights, transom light, and bracketed projecting eaves is Italianate in feeling.

13. **Estrada Adobe**   1823; 456 Tyler St.
The building which we now see is a restored version of the original two-story balconied house of 1823. In 1880 a third floor (of wood) was added and it became the St. Charles Hotel. In 1902 further remodelings and additions were made and it was called the Mission Inn. In 1964 the adobe was restored by the Monterey Savings and Loan Association.

14. **Cooper-Molera Adobe**   1826; 506 Munras Ave.
Just what one thinks a Monterey adobe should be: a two-story adobe with balconies carried on both sides.

15. **Casa Amesti**   1825; 516 Polk St.
A perfect example of the two-story Monterey style house. Beautifully restored and in perfect condition.

16. **Stokes House**   late 1830s; 500 Hartnell St.
A two-story adobe with a two-story porch; situated in a characteristic California garden.

17. **Casa Gutierrez**   1841?; 580 & 590 Calle Principal
A pair of two-story adjoining adobe town houses, both with classical (Italianate) detailing and recessed entrances.

18. **The House of the Four Winds**   c.1830
546 Calle Principal
A story and a half adobe which during its long history has served as a residence, a store, and a hall of records. The hipped roof is topped by a famous weather vane.

●*19. **Larkin House**   1835; 464 Calle Principal
The acknowledged masterpiece of the Monterey Style. The perfect marriage of the Anglo Greek Revival with the earlier adobe style of the Spanish and Mexican periods.

*20. Colton Hall   1847-49
Friendly Plaza; W side Pacific St., bet. Madison &
Jefferson Sts.

A large two-story rectangular stone building with
a two columned classical pedimented portico and
a pair of outside stairways leading to the second
floor balcony. As originally built, the lower floor
was devoted to school rooms while the entire upper floor was a single large meeting hall. Colton
himself wrote of the building shortly after completion that, "It is not an edifice that would attract
much attention among public buildings in the
United States, but in California it is without rival."

21. Gordon House   1849-50; 526 Pierce St.
A single story clapboard frame house, pure Yankee in appearance.

22. Casa Tores   1852; 502 Pierce St.
A small three room adobe to which later lean-tos
have been added.

23. Casa Alvarado   1836; 510 Dutta St.
The 24 inch thick adobe walls of this house are
covered on the exterior with clapboard; this white
siding, shuttered windows and long wooden
balustraded porch make the house seem more
Greek Revival than adobe.

24. Casa Vasquez   c.1840; 546 Pierce St.
A second floor of wood construction was added
at a later date to this single floor adobe.

25. Casa Soto   1842; 460 Pierce St.
A small single floor adobe with deep set windows,
restored in 1931.

26. Casa Serrano   1843; 412 Pacific St.
A story and a half adobe. Projecting end gable
walls enclose the sides of the long corridor-like
front porch; an outside wood stairway leads to
the second floor loft.

27. Casa Soberanes   c.1830; 336 Pacific St.
Another of the impressive two-story Monterey style
adobes, set well back from the street in a large
garden.

28. Merritt House   c.1860s; 386 Pacific St.

A two-story adobe; its front narrow end carried forward to form a Greek Revival two-story porch. An unusual use of 3 square columns for the temple-front porch.

*29. Pacific House   1835-47; 200-222 Calle Principal

This large adobe was built as a hotel and saloon; later in its history it became a residence; presently its lower floor is a museum. The second floor balcony which serves as the corridor to the rooms was carried around all sides of the building.

*30. The First Theatre   1844 & later
SW cor. Pacific & Scott Sts.

A single floor building constructed of both wood and adobe. Originally built as a saloon and boarding house, later (1847) converted into a theatre.

*31. Casa del Oro   pre 1846; 200 Oliver St.

A two-story gabled roof building of native chalk stone and adobe. (Now a museum.)

*32. Old Custom House   1814 & later
NE cor. Custom House Plaza

The oldest public structure in California. The one and two-story sections of the building are constructed of stone and adobe. (Now a museum.)

33. Whaling Station (Wright Adobe)   1855
391 Decatur St.

This two-story adobe was built as a residence and later became a boarding house for fishermen. The projecting second floor balcony was added when the house was restored in 1903. Behind the stone walls to the sides and rear is an extensive garden. Nearby at 351 Decatur St. is a plain two-story brick house (built in 1848). This is said to be the first brick house constructed in California.

34. Sota Adobe   c.1820?
End of Via Joaquin, off El Dorado St.

A single floor adobe which was restored and added to in 1942.

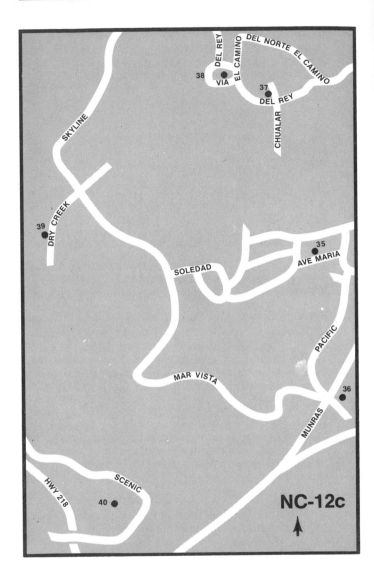

35. **Howard House & Studio**   1929; Charles Greene
86 Ave Marie Rd., E of junction with San Bernabe Dr.

A romantic exercise in the shingle cottage tradition by the famous exponents of the California bungalow. Like many houses of the 20s in and around Monterey and Carmel, the scale of this house is doll house-like, and its references are more historic (i.e. English rural cottage) than the earlier work of the Greenes.

36. **Del Monte Shopping Center**   1967
J. C. Warnecke & Assoc.
SE cor. Munras Rd. & Soledad Dr.

The new major retail center for the Monterey area, set far back from the major roads. The landscaping and the buildings themselves are modest, non-assertive in form and size.

37. House 1959; Charles W. Moore
10 Chualar Place
An early house by this architect which from the point of view of style falls easily within the late wood Bay tradition of the 40s and 50s.

38. House 1957; Charles W. Moore
325 Via Del Rey Dr.
A single floor wood house, somewhat Japanesque in character.

39. House 1966; Moore & Turnbull (MLTW)
780 Dry Creek Rd.
A vertical box on end, set on a steep hillside in the pines. The window openings are organized to take in both close and distant views from this high hillside location.

40. General Community Hospital of the Monterey Peninsula 1963; Edward D. Stone
Carmel Hwy. (68), bet. Skyline Forest Dr. & Hwy. 1
Though low and informal in grouping, the total effect of the building is characteristic of Stone: formal, almost classic, the detailing highly polished and refined.

41. House c.1910, 301 Lighthouse Ave.
Perhaps Mission in style, with an unusual tower.

42. House c.1890s; 361 Lighthouse Ave.
A two-story wood extravaganza; all the features of late 19th century architecture rolled into one building.

PACIFIC GROVE

This community was established in 1875 as a Methodist summer encampment. In 1883 the land was acquired by the Pacific Improvement Company who laid out the small-scale gridiron scheme on the slope of the hill facing towards Monterey Bay. The town itself was incorporated in 1889. The image which the town has sought to cultivate is that of the Chatauqua of the West, and in one form or another this image of the community has been carried down to the present day in the Asilomar Conference Center. The downtown area of Pacific Grove still contains a few late 19th and early twentieth century commercial buildings. The Crocker National Bank building at the northwest corner of Lighthouse and Forest Avenues is a successful version of the Spanish Colonial Revival commercial building of the mid-1920s. Off Asilomar and Lighthouse Avenues, at Point Pinos, is one of the earliest stone lighthouses (1855) on the West Coast.

NC-12d

Pacific
Grove

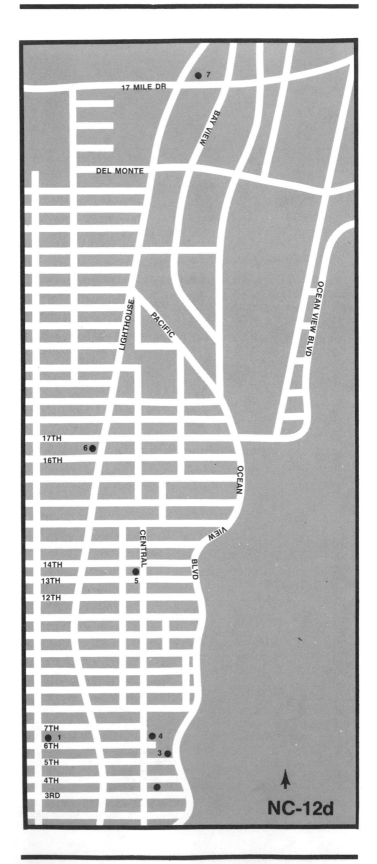

1. **Trummer House**   c.1889; 230 6th St.
A very good example of the Queen Anne style,
with sawed and spindle work on the porch, and
a tower on the north side.

2. **Cottage**   c.1880; 312 Central Ave.
A small Queen Anne cottage.

3. **Green Gables Inn (originally the Pudar House)**
1878; 104 5th St.
A half-timber, step-gabled Queen Anne house,
closer to the English version of Queen Anne than
to the American.

4. **Cottage**   c.1875; 288 Central Ave.
Somewhat Queen Anne, though much of its detailing is typical of the earlier Stick style.

5. **St. Mary's by the Sea Episcopal Church; Parish
House**   1893; Coxhead & Coxhead. **Church** 1887;
W. H. Hamilton, enlarged in 1910 by Louis Hobart
Cor. 13th St. & Central Ave.
Though somewhat altered, this is still an interest-
ing set of buildings; in the church itself one will
discover a set of windows by Tiffany, and a
group of windows by Bruce Porter (1896-).

6. **"Maison Bergerac"**   c.1890
1649 Lighthouse Ave.
A cleaned-up Queen Anne house with a witch's
tower.

7. **House**   c.1888
NW cor. Lighthouse Ave. & 17 Mile Dr.
The perfect picture of a late 19th century country
house set well back from the street in its own extensive grounds. In style, late Queen Anne, almost into the Shingle style.

8. **Asilomar Conference Center**   1913-1973
Asilomar Blvd. bet. Sunset Dr. & Pico Ave.
Here one can obtain a clear picture of Julia Morgan's informal wood Craftsman architecture,
ranging from the early stone gates at the entrance

to the Administration building. The later additions by Warnecke, and by Smith, Barker, Hanssen show how well the Bay Tradition of the 1950s and 60s merges with the much earlier buildings.

Buildings by Julia Morgan: Entrance Gates, 1912-13; Administration Bldg., 1913; Chapel, 1915; Crocker Hall, 1927; Scripps Hall, 1927; Merrill Hall, 1927-28.

Buildings by John C. Warnecke & Assoc.: Surf & Sand Complex, 1959; Seascape, Woodland, & Kitchen & other additions to Crocker Hall, 1961; Sea Galaxy Complex, 1964; View Crescent Complex, 1968.

Buildings by Smith, Barker, Hanssen: Northwood Complex, 1972; Eastwood Complex, 1972-73.

PEBBLE BEACH & 17 MILE DRIVE

Del Monte and its world famous 17 Mile Drive is one of those beautiful but at the same time frustrating places for those of us interested in experiencing architecture. There are a dozen or more major landmarks of California domestic architecture to be found at Pebble Beach and in other parts of Del Monte, but with the fewest of exceptions these houses cannot be seen from the public roads. All that one can really do is to gain a general feel of the area and here and there to catch a fragmentary glimpse of these houses along the public roads or in a few instances from the beach itself. To sense why Pebble Beach has been described as the Riviera of California, one should go down to the beach where public access is permitted and experience the way these great seaside villas pose among the rocks with the dark forests as background.

Part of the land which is now contained in Del Monte was purchased in 1878 by the first developers of the area, the Pacific Improvement Company. Other properties were added and in 1919 the present Del Monte Properties was incorporated. 17 Mile Drive itself was basically laid out in 1878-80 as a winding dirt road which went from the Del Monte Hotel through Monterey and ended at Carmel. The present 17 Mile Drive now starts at Pacific Grove and ends just north of Carmel. The strong desire to transform the coastal section of Del Monte (especially the Pebble Beach area) into a New World Riviera dates from 1915, and most, although not all, of the great seaside villas were built during the late teens and the 20s. Here one will find houses designed by almost all of the major California domestic architects of the 20s: Bakewell and Brown, Lewis P. Hobart, Johnson, Kaufmann & Coate, Bernard Maybeck, Miller and Warnecke, Addison Mizner, Julia Morgan, Willis Polk & Co., George Washington Smith, and Clarence Tantau. Of the houses produced by these designers, the most important are the stone Byzantine house of 1927-28 designed for Mrs. Paul Fagan, the courtyard-oriented Spanish Colonial Revival Vincent house of 1924, and the Hatley house of 1926 (also Spanish Colonial Revival) all designed by George Washington Smith. Addison Mizner (who did only two houses in California) is represented by the stone, somewhat Romanesque, Chase house of 1924; and Bernard Maybeck created a highly personal version of the Spanish Colonial Revival in his Ford house (1924) with its many

Fagan House

separate gabled roof volumes. All of these houses can be seen to one degree or another along the coastal strip between the Del Monte Lodge and Cypress Point Golf Course. Of the more or less "public" buildings found in Del Monte, mention should be made of Del Monte Lodge itself, designed in 1915 by Louis P. Hobart; Clarence A. Tantau's Club House of 1925 for the Monterey Peninsula Country Club, and finally George Washington Smith's Cypress Point Golf Club House of 1928-29. All of these buildings are in the general Spanish Colonial Revival style.

Carmel, the Village by the Sea, has battled growth for growth's sake from its founding in the 1890s. Its desire has been, contrary to the usual California syndrome, to remain small, rural and non-commercial. For many years it realized its ideal as a place where painters, sculptors, and writers could congregate and at the same time find a place as far removed as possible from the usual American or California city. Even after it was incorporated in 1916 it fought against the introduction of paved streets and electricity. To this day street addresses are unknown. The theme of the Artists' Colony was played on in the 20s (not of course by the artists themselves) and by the end of the 20s, Carmel had become a major tourist attraction. Quaint little fairy-land shops and restaurants and low Spanish Colonial Revival buildings were built in and around Ocean Avenue and Dolores Street, and more and more

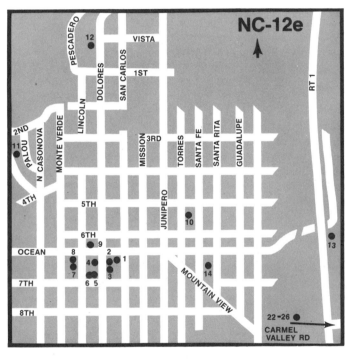

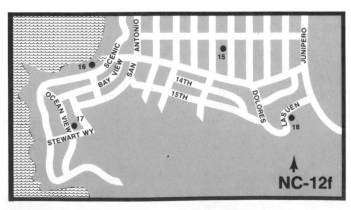

cottages were built in the residential areas. Today one can sense the two worlds of Carmel: the visitor oriented downtown area generally bustling with tourists, especially on the weekends, and the quiet residential streets, lined by small cottages, which are almost empty of people or automobiles. Though few changes are occurring in the town itself, Carmel Valley to the south is rapidly being urbanized, so that in not too many years Carmel will probably find itself as the western seaside end of a narrow urban corridor which will stretch as far west as Carmel Valley Village. Scattered throughout the Carmel area are a good number of really important houses by Richard Neutra, Henry Hill, Mark Mills and others. Almost all of these houses are close to impossible to see from the public roads. They have therefore not been included in the list of buildings in and around Carmel.

1. **Las Tiendas Shop (Patio Shops)** c.1925
   S side Ocean Ave., bet. San Carlos & Dolores Sts.
   A group of small shops in the Spanish Colonial Revival mode.

2. **Pernie's of Carmel Shop** c.1925
   E side Dolores St., bet. Ocean & 7th Aves.
   A shop in the Spanish Colonial Revival style.

3. **The Tuck Box Shop** c.1925; Hugh Comstock
   E side Dolores St., bet. Ocean & 7th Aves.
   The best and most delightful of the Hansel and Gretel doll houses; a perfect Hollywood stage set.

4. **China Art Center** c.1925
   W side Dolores St., bet. Ocean & 7th Aves.
   A two-story Spanish Colonial Revival commercial building which is Mission in feeling.

5. **Commercial Building** c.1927
   NW cor. Dolores St. & 7th Ave.
   Certainly the strongest Spanish Colonial Revival commercial building in Carmel. Note the successful handling of the outside staircase and the upper porch.

6. **Cyprus West Inn** c.1920
   NE cor. 7th Ave. & Lincoln St.
   Contains an elaborate "Churrigueresque" entrance.

7. **La Rambla** c.1927
   W side Lincoln St. bet. 7th & Ocean Aves.
   A group of small courtyard-oriented shops in the Spanish Colonial Revival style.

8. **El Matador Shops** c.1925
   S side Ocean Ave., bet. Lincoln & Monte Verde Sts.
   Another group of shops in the fairy tale mode, probably designed by Hugh Comstock.

9. **Harrison Memorial Library**   1927
    Bernard Maybeck, consulting architect
    NE cor. Ocean Ave. & Lincoln St.

    Though the building has been added to in recent years the strong Maybeck touch is apparent in the proportions of the building, its low pitched tile roof, its arched windows with tile inserts below, and in the interior with its exposed wood gable ceiling.

10. **Cottage**   c.1925; Hugh W. Comstock
    E side Torres St., bet. 6th & 5th Aves.

    A cute cottage with bent roof and rustic fence. Also note another cottage in the same style at the SE corner of Torres St. and 6th Ave. This was also designed by Comstock.

11. **House**   1966; Moore & Turnbull (MLTW)
    W side Palou St., W of junction of Palou & Casonova Sts.

    A shingle house divided into two distinct parts by a central walk-through porch.

● 12. **Carmel Woods School**   1941; Kump & Falk
    W side Dolores St., at junction with Vista Ave.

    A pre-World War II school composed of a single long gable unit; individual class rooms open to the rear into their own walled outdoor class room space.

13. **Carmel High School**   1939 & 1949
    Franklin, Kump & Assoc.
    SE cor. Hwy. 1 & Dolores Watson Place

    Separate units of wood and stone follow along the contours of the site, connected together by open corridors, some of the detailing of which is almost Wrightian.

14. **Converse House**   1933; William W. Wurster
    W side Santa Rosa St., bet. Ocean & Mountain View Aves.

    An early but at the same time highly abstract version of the Colonial Revival with a pinch of the Monterey Colonial Revival. This and other houses of the early 1930s in and around Carmel illustrate Wurster's ability to take the period house and transform it into something highly personal—something modern and at the same time highly practical.

15. **Charles Greene Studio**   c.1918; Charles Greene
    W side Lincoln St., bet. 13th & 14th Aves.

    All in stone with carved wood detailing; very medieval and romantic in feeling; a small scale version of his large 1918 James House at Carmel Highlands (see ≠20).

15. Greene Studio

16. Walker House 1952; Frank Lloyd Wright
W side Scenic Dr., bet. Martin Way & Ocean View Ave.
An often illustrated Wright classic of thin layered stone with porcelain enamel roof and outward stepped windows, set on a small rocky promontory jutting out into the sea.

17. Robinson Jeffers' "Tor House" 1926-27
Robinson Jeffers
Scenic Dr. bet. Ocean View Ave. & Stewart Way
A 1920s Craftsman stone house poses behind and to the side of the small medieval tower which looks out over the Pacific.

●**18. Mission San Carlos Borromeo Del Rio Carmelo**
1793-97
SW cor. Rio Rd. & Lasuen Dr.
This Mission church and that of Santa Barbara are the most famous of the early Spanish churches in California. The stone detailing around the main entrance are late 18th century Neo-Classic, but the general grouping of the towers, the curved gable end and the quatrefoil window are late Provincial Baroque from Mexico. The Carmel Mission was one of the first of the Mission churches to be restored; the first restoration, which was none too accurate was carried out in 1884. A more archaeologically correct restoration was carried out between 1936 and 1940. The Mission at Carmel served as a frequent source for details and even massing of buildings which were built during the Mission Revival of the late 90s and early 1900s.

19. Carmelite Monastery c.1920
E side Hwy. 1, S of Carmel, by San Jose Creek
Just what a Spanish Colonial Revival building should look like; beautifully set on a darkly wooded hillside overlooking the southern part of Carmel Bay.

20. James House   1918; Charles Greene
S of Carmel on Hwy 1, W side of highway in Carmel Highlands (can be seen at the view turn-off opposite the Highlands Inn)

A large stone house set high on a cliff overlooking the ocean. In style it is loosely "Mediterranean," though it has a Craftsman feeling about it.

21. House   1928; Charles Greene
S of Carmel in Carmel Highlands; Spindrift Rd. at bottom of hill

The second of the large houses in the Carmel area by Charles Greene; somewhat similar to the James house, but like Charles Greene's own studio house in Carmel this house is more specifically Medieval than the James house. Except for the impressive gates and the fine stone wall the house cannot be seen from the public road.

22. Office Building   1972; Sebastian J. Bonaro
S of Carmel, Carmel Valley Rd., approx. 4 mi. W of junction with Hwy. 1, N side road

A small office building composed of connected but visually independent boxes and enclosed patios.

23. Carmel Valley Junior High School   1962
Ernest Kump & Assoc.; Alston & Cranston
S of Carmel, Carmel Valley Rd., approx. 2½ mi. E of junction with Hwy 1; S side of Rd.

A characteristic Kump school composed of separate hipped roofed buildings.

● **24. Carmel Valley Manor**   1962
Skidmore, Owings and Merrill
S of Carmel, Carmel Valley Rd., approx. 4 mi. W of junction with Hwy. 1, N side of road

A retirement community inspired by Mediterranean and Monterey Colonial stucco architecture. The angled forms of white stucco walls and shingle roofs are placed so as to interact strongly with each other and the surrounding landscape.

25. White Oaks Theatre   1963
Duncombe, Roland, Miller; Don, James, Clark Assoc.
S of Carmel, Carmel Valley Village, Carmel Valley Rd., just beyond junction with Fort Rd.

A square structure covered with a high pitched hipped roof; impressive woodsy interior.

26. Studio of Dance   1969; D'Amico
S of Carmel, Carmel Valley Village, Carmel Valley Rd. to Pilot Rd. just beyond junction with Del Fino Pl.

A small redwood building with a well planned interior dance space.

SEASIDE & SAND CITY

On the sandy slopes below Fort Ord, between that giant military base and Monterey lie the bedroom communities of Seaside and Sand City. Originally these were little more than squatters' villages for World War II and after camp followers. Since then the towns have made a real effort to transform themselves into modest but amenable permanent settlements for workers. Much of the reconstruction took place using federally aided rehabilitation and development programs. The flavor of the accomplished work can be seen by driving east off Hwy. 1 at the Hwy. 218 interchange, following Canyon del Rey Road (Hwy. 218) to Carlton Drive, then right on Plumas to Mescal Street. Follow Mescal Street along top of hill to Broadway, then return to the center of town below. On the whole most of these projects are perfectly adequate examples of urban renewal, but they look a little pallid beside the really successful low cost housing project, Villa del Monte, designed by Moore and Turnbull (MLTW) (1966-68). The Villa del Monte illustrates that even with stringent financial and other limitations, a distinguished piece of architecture can be produced within the confines of a low cost housing program.

Two other buildings in Seaside should be seen. One is the Streamlined Moderne Del Rey Theatre at the southwest corner of Broadway Avenue and Fremont Blvd. This theatre of the late 30s exhibits a cylindrical tower with the theatre's name lighted on four sides. Just southwest of the junction of Hwy. 218 and Harcourt Ave. is the new, rather intimately scaled City Hall designed by Edward D. Stone (1968).

SANTA CRUZ

The Santa Cruz Mission was established in 1791 on an elevated mesa overlooking the Bay and the San Lorenzo River. A few years later, in 1897, the Villa de Branciforte—a second community—was established on the lower flatlands. In 1866 the State of California granted a charter to the city and in 1876 the city which now included both the original Mission community and the Villa de Branciforte was incorporated. Though lumbering and manufacturing were important in the early days of Santa Cruz, its fame in the late 19th century was that of a seaside resort. In 1890 the great wooden Sea Beach Hotel was completed and eventually the beach and the boardwalk boasted a roller coaster, a merry-go-round, and in the 20th century a new casino, natatorium and pleasure pier were built. The Hotel is gone, but the amusement park still dominates the harbor area.

The San Lorenzo River, the irregular coastline, and the many hills effectively divide the city into very distinct areas. The hill directly back of the beach and boardwalk was once a fashionable residential area, but in recent years the older houses have one by one been torn down and replaced by nondescript motels and

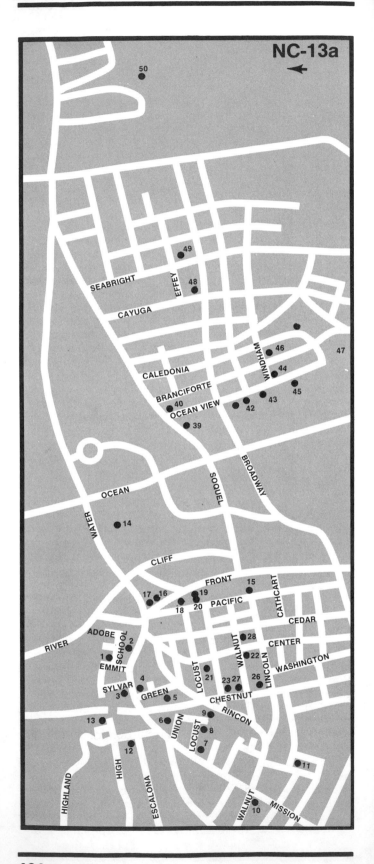

NC-13a

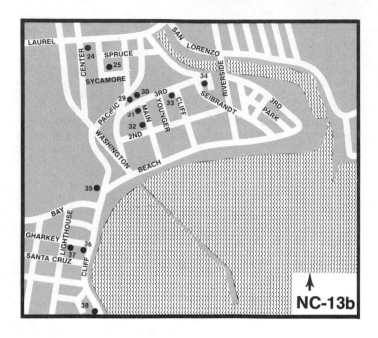

apartment buildings. The downtown commercial area and the older residential streets to the west are presently undergoing a renaissance, with a new drive-through mall on Pacific Street, many older buildings being tastefully restored, and a number of new commercial and public buildings being constructed. The County buildings formerly located in the heart of downtown have been moved to new quarters in a spacious park east of the San Lorenzo River. The mesa and hillside north and west of downtown is presently a very mixed area, part residential and, as one proceeds west, roadside commercial. There are though, some really outstanding Victorian houses scattered here and there. The hill and flat tableland east of the San Lorenzo River is also quite mixed, with strip commercial developments along its major streets, a few new shopping centers and many streets lined with small residences of the 20s and later. The hill on the east side of the river mouth is another place where one can still discover the 19th century flavor of Santa Cruz. This is particularly true of the houses which line Ocean View Avenue. In the opposite direction is the West Cliff area which exhibits a few architecturally significant houses dating from the late 19th century through the early 20th. In addition, the West Beach area contains an unusual street pattern composed of concentric circles (laid out before 1900), and also a lighthouse at Point Santa Cruz. As with most California cities, Santa Cruz has very few small neighborhood parks or extensive parkways. This is in part made up for by the large

Redwood Parks (such as De Laveaga Park) which are situated on the hillsides back of the city, and of course the Beach area forms a major place of recreation for those living in the community. The visual and factual independence of the city of Santa Cruz has appreciably diminished during the decades of the 50s and 60s. The new campus of the University of California has transformed the community to a remarkable degree, and to the east, Santa Cruz now really forms a continuous urban pattern with adjoining Soquel, Capitola, Aptos and Rio Del Mar.

1. **Mission Santa Cruz** 1793-94
   NE cor. Emmit & School Sts.

   The Santa Cruz Mission was built of stone and adobe during the years 1793-94. Its fabric was damaged by an earthquake in 1840 and it was completely destroyed by a second earthquake in 1857. In 1931 the present half size replica was built.

2. **Neary-Hopcroft Adobe** c.1810; 136 School St.

   This one-story adobe was most likely built as the Mission Guard's quarters. Its date is not fixed, but current evidence would seem to point to the year 1810. The north facade of the building is placed directly up against School Street, and on the south side the house opens to the garden.

3. **Willey House** 1893; 105 Sylvar St.

   The general character of this house is that of the Eastlake style, though it is a late date for this style in Santa Cruz.

4. **House** c.1870s; 207 Mission St.

   Without doubt one of the great Eastlake houses still remaining in Santa Cruz. The entrance porch and three-story tower are both fascinating variations on the usual Eastlake scheme.

5. Cottage   c.1860s; 127 Green St.
The basic form of this house, its pitched central gable, and its porch across the front are Victorian Gothic Revival; but the entrance, the windows and the general balanced symmetry points to the Greek Revival.
Note the two-story Italianate house nearby at 123 Green St., c.1870s.

6. House   c.1912; 332 Union St.
A two-story Craftsman Prairie style house, sheathed in redwood clapboard below, stucco above, and covered with a low pitched gable roof.

7. House   c.1880s; 603 Mission St.
An Eastlake/Queen Anne house.

8. House   c.1880; 419 Locust St.
Stick style, plus Swiss Chalet.

9. Two Apartment Buildings   c.1937
110 & 112 Pine Place
Two Streamlined Moderne apartment buildings; one of three units, the other of four; because of their site on the brink of the steep hill they are visible from the east side of the downtown area below.

10. Cottage   late 1890s; 914 Mission St.
Colonial Revival/Queen Anne; note the very low Palladian windows.

11. House   mid to late 1880s; 724 California St.
Eastlake with some Queen Anne overtones, especially in the tower. Another of the large and important Victorian houses of Santa Cruz.

12. McPhetres House   c.1870; 203 Highland Ave.
A charming French Mansard roof house complete with small rectangular tower and large palm tree in front lawn.

13. Calreta Court (originally named Piedmont Court)
1912; William Bray
NE cor. High St. & Highland Ave.

An impressive Mission Revival 50 room apartment house. When built it was described as of "Moorish Design," and it was famed for its ornamented interior court with fountain.

14. Santa Cruz Governmental Center 1967
Rockwell & Banwell
SW cor. Water & Ocean Sts.

Two buildings consisting of a 5-story office block and a one story court rooms building, situated in an open park on the east side of the San Lorenzo River, (part of Santa Cruz's urban renewal). The 5 story office block is self-consciously constructivist within the New Brutalist phase of the late 50s and 60s.

15. Pacific Street Mall 1969-70
Kermit Darrow, arch., Roy Rydall, landscape arch.
Pacific St., bet. Front & Cathcart Sts.

A serpentine drive-through mall. The scale and the pattern of the street, plus the very heavy planting creates a strong anti-urban feeling.

16. Commercial Buildings c.1870s-1890s
Front St., bet. E Water & Cooper Sts.

Here one can find a number of well preserved 19th century commercial buildings, some of wood, others of brick and cast iron.

17. U. S. Post Office Building 1911
Oscar Wenderoth; James Knox Taylor
SE cor. Front & E Water Sts.

Roman/Renaissance (more Italian Renaissance than Roman); a restrained dignified classical revival building.

18. County Bank of Santa Cruz c.1890
NE cor. Cooper & Pacific Sts.
Richardsonian Romanesque Revival.

19. Records Building, County of Santa Cruz 1882
A. W. Burril
SW cor. Front & Cooper Sts.

A 19th century gem; a small brick octagonal building which, according to local tradition, was modeled after the 1855-56 U.S. gold piece.

20. Cooper House (formerly the County Court House Bldg.) 1894; Comstock; Thomas Beck
SW cor. Cooper & Pacific Sts.
Richardsonian Romanesque Revival building, now being used as a retail store.

21. Santa Cruz City Hall 1937-38; C. J. Ryland (WPA).
New addition to the west 1967; Robert Stevens Assoc.
W side Center St., bet. Cooper & Locust Sts.
The original one-story building, with a porch

around the U-shaped court yard, is the ideal of what one expects of a small California City hall. In style the original building is Monterey Colonial Revival. In the new two-story addition to the rear, the architects have sought to harmonize their design with that of the older building.

22. **Calvary Episcopal Church** 1864
Edmund Jones & Samuel Sharp
532 Center St.
A wood Victorian Gothic Revival church building.

23. **Medical Building** c.1937; 343-345 Church St.
A Streamlined Moderne medical building.

24. **House** c.1880s; 319 Laurel St.
Eastlake; a plain two-story house in front of which is a wonderful jigsaw porch in the Islamic style.

25. **Cummings House** 1884-90
NE cor. Cedar St. & Sycamore Ave.
A very unusual hexagonal house with curved mansard roof, bold sawed out porch arches, and a front door cut through one of the corner angles of the hexagon.

26. **Five attached row houses** late 1880s
NE cor. Chestnut & Lincoln Sts.
Queen Anne; a tastefully restored group of small town houses.

27. **Pair of cottages** c.1880
240 & 244 Walnut St.
Two Eastlake cottages, each with its own small tower.

28. **Lindsey Cottage** c.1880s; 219 Walnut St.
A restored Queen Anne cottage with a handsome wide paneled front door with small paned beveled glass sidelights.

29. **House** c.1940; 1034 3rd St.
A two-story white stucco Streamlined Moderne house equipped with portholes, curved walls, metal railings and a garden folly of stone with a metal roof.

30. **McLaughlin House** 1891; T. J. Welch
924 3rd St.
Queen Anne in style, visually the most prominent Victorian house in Santa Cruz. When the house was under construction in 1891 it was noted that "The style of the exterior is the modern renaissance of the design of Queen Anne's time, adopted by the architect to the out-of-door life which is the great attraction to sojourners in Santa Cruz." A number of later changes have been made in the house, but externally the most apparent is the enclosure of the third floor of the tower. When built, this was entirely open with columns and arched openings.

31. **Cottage** c.1880s; 1005 3rd St.
A raised basement Eastlake cottage, similar to many which were built in the late 70s in San Francisco.

32. **House** c.1890s; 311 Main St.
A two-story Colonial Revival/Queen Anne house.

33. **House** c.1890s; 417 Cliff St.
Another Colonial Revival/Eastlake house.

34. **Barfield House** 1890; 611 3rd St.
A sharp angular Eastlake house; note the ornamental panel on the second floor bay window on the west side of the house.

35. **Sedgwick House** 1876; 170 W Cliff Dr.
An Italianate house which still commands the west harbor area from its hilltop site.

36. **House** c.1905; 314 W Cliff Dr.
A Mission Revival house overlooking the ocean.

37. **Cottage** c.1880s; 135 Gharkey St.
An Eastlake/Queen Anne cottage, complete with fenced garden.

38. **House** c.1890s; 544 W Cliff Dr.
Colonial Revival/Queen Anne.

39. **House** c.1890
Present entrance bet. 514 and 522 Soquel Ave.
Colonial Revival/Queen Anne; well ornamented with large round tower.

40. **Cottage** c.1880s; 540 Ocean View Ave.
Eastlake.

41. **House** c.1880; 512 Ocean View Ave.
Eastlake.

42. **Cottage** c.late 1880s; 407 Ocean View Ave.
Eastlake/Queen Anne cottage.

43. House c.late 1880s; 325 Ocean View Ave.
Eastlake/Queen Anne.

44. Smith House c.1890
SE cor. Ocean View Ave. & Windham St.
Queen Anne with Eastlake touches; one of the Victorian show places of Santa Cruz; handsome grounds surrounded by Queen Anne wooden fence.

45. House c.1880s; 245 Ocean View Ave.
Eastlake in style.

46. House c.1890; 220 Windham St.
Queen Anne with some Eastlake details.

47. Reed House c.1870s; 90 Caledonia St.
When built, this was an Italianate farm house far from the edge of town.

48. House c.1880; 1205 Broadway St.
Mansard/Eastlake styles.

49. Gault Elementary School c.1920s
SE cor. Seabright Ave. & Effy St.
A school building in the Spanish Colonial Revival style.

50. Hagermann Cottage c.1880
SW cor. Montel Ave. & Agnes St. (house cannot be seen from the street)
A rare fragment of California of the 80s. A long winding driveway through a thick eucalyptus grove brings one to the cottage. Although modest in size, the cottage is elaborately ornamented and has two low towers at each of the front corners.

51. Dominican Santa Cruz Hospital 1967
Rex Whitaker, Allen & Assoc.
SE cor. Paul Sweet Rd. & Heights Dr.
Each of the hospital rooms has a projecting angular exterior wall with an L-shaped window at the corner.
Note the handsome small redwood medical building across the street at the NW cor. of Paul Sweet Rd. & Heights Dr.

52. Oakwood Memorial Park c.1900
Paul Sweet Rd., N of junction with Heights Dr.
Wonderful gate posts—one surmounted by a large anchor, the other by a harp.

53. Covered Bridge 1892
Branciforte Dr., into picnic area of De Laveaga Park
An 83 ft. covered wood bridge which has been moved to its present site over Branciforte Creek. This is one of three covered bridges to be found near Santa Cruz. For the others see #s 57 & 58.

54. Pasatiempo Estates (A private Golf Club and development)
Thomas Church, Landscape Architect
Hwy. 1, N of Santa Cruz, off at Rancho Dr., W under fwy. to entrance

This golf course with its surrounding low density housing was laid out in the 1920s. A number of the early houses were designed by William W. Wurster; among these are:

(a) Field House 1934
17 Pasatiempo Dr.

(b) Berry House 1931
2 Hollins Dr.

(c) Hollins House 1931
33 Hollins Dr.

(d) Butler House 1931-32
41 Hollins Dr.

These houses are all typical of Wurster's early work; they loosely employ a variety of stylistic forms ranging from the Monterey Colonial Revival to the Regency Revival of the late 20s and 30s.

55. University of California, Santa Cruz
The site for the campus was selected in 1961 and stands on the old Cowell Ranch which enjoys a superb view over the city of Santa Cruz below and of the bay beyond. The concept of this new campus was that of a series of independent cluster colleges. These were to be grouped at the edge of the redwood grove overlooking the open grass-covered fields which slope down to the outskirts of the city. The site plan was prepared in 1962-63 by Carl Warnecke and Thomas D. Church. The first of the cluster colleges, Cowell College, opened in 1965. Since this date, five additional colleges have been built, and a number of general structures have been added to the site. With the exception of the new student apartments, all of these buildings have been grouped and, one might add, to a considerable extent hidden within the redwood grove. From the beginning, the Regents of the University of California and those involved with the administration of the Santa Cruz campus have sought to make it a showplace of architecture. The roster of those who have designed buildings at the Santa Cruz campus is impressive, not just on a state level, but nationally.

Cowell College 1965
Wurster, Bernardi & Emmons

Adlai Stevenson College 1967
Joseph Esherick & Assoc.

Crown College 1967; Ernest Kump & Assoc.

Merrill College 1968-69; Campbell & Wong

Kresge College 1966-73
Moore & Turnbull (MLTW)

Central Service Bldg. 1965
Ernest J. Kump, Assoc.

Field House 1965; Callister, Payne, & Rosse

Natural Science Bldgs. (2) 1965, 1969
Anshen & Allen

University Library 1968; John Carl Warnecke

Outdoor Theatre 1968
Royston, Hanamoto, Beck & Abey

Communications Bldg. 1968
Spencer, Lee & Busse

Cowell Student Health Center 1970
John Funk

Student Apartments 1971
Ratcliff, Slama, Cadwalader

Performing Arts Center 1971; Ralph Rapson

Applied Science 1971; Reid & Tarics

Class Room Unit #1 1972; Marquis & Stoller

College V 1969-70; Hugh Stubbins, Jr.

56. **House** 1967
William Turnbull, (MLTW) Moore & Turnbull
517 Meder St. (off map)
Located just below the U. C. Santa Cruz campus
is this two-story redwood sheathed house. A gentle
shed roof which flows out and covers most of the
house is abruptly terminated by a second shed
roof placed at a right angle to the main roof.
Within, the two levels of space are closely brought
together by the two-story hall.

57. **Covered Bridge (Paradise Park, a private community)** 1872
Off Hwy. 9 at Keystone Rd., then proceed to San
Lorenzo River crossing (off map)
180 ft. long; the sides of the bridge have a number of small windows.

58. **Covered Bridge (Felton Bridge)** 1892
N Covered Bridge Rd. off Mt. Hermon Rd., just E
of the small community of Felton (off map)
130 ft. long; no longer in use.

59. **"Scottish Castle" Howden House** 1926
Robert Howden
N edge of Ben Lomond; SW side Hwy. 9 just before
crossing San Lorenzo River (off map)
A delightful 20th century architectural folly; a
miniature castle perched on the edge of a low
cliff overlooking the San Lorenzo River.

60. Mobile home parks

In recent years, several large mobile home parks have been established in the Scotts Valley area. One of the most sumptuous of these and one well placed in the landscape is Montevalle Mobile Home Park located at 552 Bean Creek Rd., off Scotts Valley Rd., Much of it is presently under construction.

61. Gregory Farm house (not visible from public road)

1927; William W. Wurster

Canham Rd. off Glenwood Dr., Scotts Valley area

One of the classics of domestic architecture in California, and certainly one of the most impressive of Wurster's houses. The L-shaped farm house encloses a court yard, and to the front is the tall water tower which is set back from the gates. The Gregory Farm house illustrates this architect's ability to take the simple forms of the California ranch house, add a little bit of period architecture (loosely a Monterey Revival ingredient) and produce an architectural high art object. Nearby are two other Wurster houses, one dating from the 30s, the other from the 50s.

SOQUEL - APTOS - SEA CLIFF - RIO DEL MAR

With the coming of the railroad to this section of the coast in the 1860s, a number of communities (including Santa Cruz itself) developed as seaside resorts. In recent years these communities have tended to lose their individual identity and to merge into one continuous beach strip. The freeway (Hwy. 1), which runs a little inland and basically parallel to the beach, has strongly divided the area, with Soquel and Aptos remaining more open and rural, and the beach communities becoming more compressed, not only because they back up against the freeway, but also because of the several state beaches in the area.

SOQUEL

Willbanks House   c.1870
4500 Soquel Dr.
A really fine Italianate house with central projecting pavilion, pedimented windows, and deep corner quoining.

Congregational Church   1870
4931 Soquel Dr., E of junction of Soquel Dr. & Porter St.
Basically a very simple Greek Revival church building.

APTOS & SEA CLIFF

Cabrillo College   1962; Ernest J. Kump Assoc., Masten, Hurd & Gwathmey. Later buildings by Kump, Masten & Hurd
Soquel Dr. at College Dr.
A modern version of the Monterey Colonial Revival style, plus an echo of the rural California barn.

Bay View Hotel   1870, 1883; 8041 Soquel Dr.
Italianate with Mansard roof; the original building was constructed in 1870, the mansard roof third floor was added in 1883, and the building was moved to its present location in the same year.

Group of Streamlined Moderne beach houses
c.1940; 421, 423, 429 Beach Dr.
Most of these beach houses were built before World War II, though a number of them have been remodeled since then. Architecturally the most interesting of these are 421 with its large round window on the second floor and 423 which comes close to being International Style rather than Moderne.

CAPITOLA

House   c.1880; 921 Capitola Ave.
A mansard roof house with an extensive porch.

House   c.1915; 1564 Prospect Ave.
A Maybeckian Swiss Chalet which comes close to being a pure architectural folly.

Episcopal Church of St. John the Baptist   c.1890
SE cor. Oakland Ave. & Escalona Dr.
A small scaled Gothic Revival church in shingles.

WATSONVILLE

Watsonville lies just far enough off Highway 1 that it is often missed when one travels from or to Monterey and Carmel. Both in and around the city are a number of very good examples of 19th and 20th century architecture. The city was founded in 1852, though most of the present commercial buildings in the center of town date from the 90s and later. Even as late as the 1950s, Watsonville possessed a score or more of really fine Italianate houses of the mid to late 1870s; but one by one these have disappeared. One of the latest casualties to progress and a parking lot was the Gothic Revival Methodist Church of 1874.

1. **Store & Office Building**   c.1910; 307 Main St.
   A Mission Revival commercial building with an off-center composition of a quatrefoil window, and a small bay which projects above the roof as a round tower.

2. **Wells Fargo Bank Building**   c.1930
   NW cor. Main & Peck Sts.
   Basically a Renaissance Revival building with Moderne ornament.

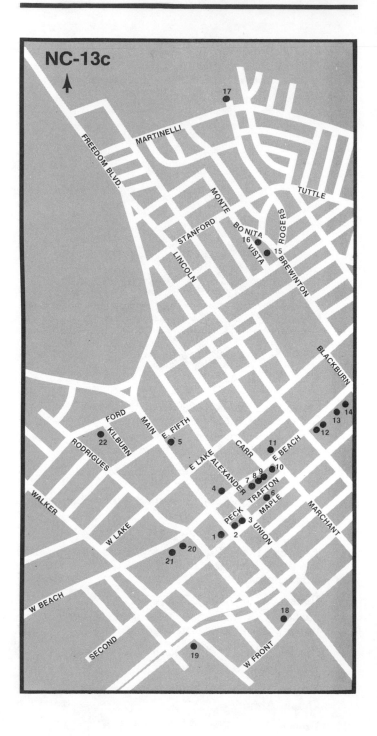

NC-13c

3. **I.O.O.F. Building** 1893; E Beach St., opp. Union St.
Richardsonian Romanesque. While the ground floor has been remodeled, the upper floor and the central tower are well preserved.

4. **Marinovich Block** 1899
SW cor. Union & Peck Sts.
A mildly classical (almost Colonial Revival) wooden office and store buildings.

5. **Gasoline Station (no longer in use)** c.1930
NE cor. Main & E 5th Sts.
Art Deco Moderne, an angled cubist composition.

6. **Houses**
E. Maple St., bet. Union & Marchant Sts.
A block of late 19th century houses, ranging from the early Eastlake style to the Queen Anne/Colonial Revival.

7. **House** c.1887; 104 E Beach St.
Eastlake/Queen Anne; note spindle work on the upper part of the entrance porch.

8. **House** c.1884; 124 E Beach St.
A small Eastlake house.

9. **House** c.1890; 128 E Beach St.
Queen Anne.

10. **House** late 1870s; 134 E Beach St.
Italianate.

11. **House** c.1887; 265 E Beach St.
Queen Anne with Eastlake touches in its ornament.

12. **Two Queen Anne/Colonial Revival houses** c.1900
302 & 308 E Beach St.

13. **House**   c.1890; 316 E. Beach St.
A shingle Queen Anne house.

14. **Bockius House**   late 1870s; 332 E Beach St.
A handsome Italianate house set far back from the street in a wooded garden surrounded by a white wooden fence.

15. **House**   c.1938; 505 Brewington Ave.
A classic Streamline Moderne house of the late 1930s, with corner windows, pipe railing, and other characteristic details of the "new" architecture of those years.

16. **Biskamp House**   1933; William W. Wurster
523 Brewington Ave.
A two-story Monterey Revival house. In houses such as this, one can readily see why Wurster was able to establish such a strong reputation by the early 1930s, a reputation among architects for the ease with which he could develop forms out of historic precedent which were modern and very liveable.

17. **All Saints Episcopal Church**   1962
Ernest J. Kump, Assoc.
437 Rogers Ave.
A really Baroque Moderne church; purposely emotive, visually demanding with a concave gable roof topped at its ridge with a skylight.

18. **House**   mid 1870s; 18 W. Front St.
A large two-story Italianate house.

19. **Warehouse**   c.1910
SE cor. Riverside Dr. & Walker St.
A wood Mission Revival warehouse. Watsonville once boasted a good number of Mission Revival commercial buildings, public buildings, and houses. Most of these are now gone or have been remodeled.

20. **Cottage**   late 1860s; 137 W Beach St.
A small Gothic Revival cottage.

21. **House**   c.1895; 143 W Beach St.
A late Queen Anne house with Colonial Revival detailing. Architecturally one of the most interesting buildings in Watsonville.

22. **House**   late 1870s; 108 Ford St.
Italianate.

23. **House**   c.1895
7 mi. E of Watsonville on Hwy. G-12, N side
A Queen Anne farm house.

24. House c.1875
4 mi. E of Watsonville on Hwy. G-12, junction with San Miguel Canyon Rd., S side

A perfect Italianate farm house with richly ornamented front porch.

25. House c.1870
2083 Beach Rd., SW of Watsonville

Greek Revival/Italianate. Another architectural gem—a symmetrical two-story house with Italianate detailing; wonderful topiary in the grounds between the house and the road.

26. Pajaro Dunes
SW end of W Beach St., SW of Watsonville

South of the road is Pajaro Dunes which is a private beach club not open to the general public. Within the club are several recently built beach houses of real architectural interest (among these are two houses designed by Mike Lee Assoc.), but these and the other houses cannot be seen from the public road. North of the road on the dunes overlooking the beach is a large condominium complex (Shorebird Homes) made up of 9 buildings (310 units) on a 40 acre site. These have been designed by Frank L. Hope Assoc. (1971-72).

27. Castro Adobe c.1840s?
184 Old Adobe Rd. (NW of Watsonville, off Larkin Valley Rd. & Buena Vista Dr.)

A two-story adobe with a large ballroom on the second floor and a two-story balconied porch with an outside staircase.

21. House

PHOTO HISTORY

SF-12 (7)   Mission San Francisco de Asis (Mission Dolores), San Francisco. 1782.

NC-12e (18)   Mission San Carlos Borromeo del Rio Carmelo (Carmel Mission), Carmel. 1793-97.

NC-11   Mission San Antonio de Padua, nr. Jolon.
      1810-13.

NC-11α (1) Mission San Juan Bautista, San Juan Bau-
      tista. 1803-12.

NC-2b (17)   Ide Adobe, Red Bluff.   c.1850.

NC-12b (19)   Larkin House, Monterey.   1835.

NC-11α (3)   Castro Adobe, San Juan Bautista.   1840-41.

NC-11   Barn, nr. Jolon.   c.1900.

NC-13b (58)   Felton Covered Bridge nr. Felton.   1892.

NC-2   I.O.O.F. Hall, Weaverville.   c.1857.

NC-9   Fire Station, Auburn.   1852 & 1891.

NC-9e (15)   Fire House No. 1, Nevada City.   1861.

NC-3α (8)   Masonic Hall, Mendocino.   1865.

NC-6α (8)   State Capitol Bldg., Benicia.   1852.

NC-7α (1)   State Capitol Bldg., Sacramento. 1860-74. Miner F. Butler; completed by Reubin Clark, G. P. Cummings & A. A. Bennett

NC-9   Elementary School House, Murphys. 1860.

Plates 17, 18

NC-9e (23)   Steward House, Nevada City.   1850-60.

SF-3 (8)   Octagonal House, San Francisco.   1857.

NC-8   Community Church, Lockeford.   c.1850s.

NC-4α (7)   Aaron House, Marysville.   1855.

EB-5d (2)   Moss Cottage, Oakland.   1864-65.
Heston & Williams

NC-8   Masonic Hall, Woodbridge.   1882.

NC-2c (9)   Bidwell House, Chico. 1865-67. Henry W. Cleaveland

NC-1b (13)   St. Bernard's Roman Catholic Church Eureka. 1886. James Simpson

EB-5α (1)   Pardee House, Oakland.   1868.

SF-2 (11)   Casebolt House, San Francisco.   1865-66.

NC-10   Merced County Courthouse, Merced. 1875.
A. A. Bennett

NC-6b (7)   Hunt-Powell House, Woodland.   1875.

NC-2b (6)   I.O.O.F. Hall, Red Bluff. c.1870.

NC-5d (21)   McNear Store Bldg., Petaluma. 1886.

NC-2b (10)   Cone-Kimball Bldg., Red Bluff. 1886.

NC-5e (3)   Richie Block, St. Helena. 1892.

SF-10 (36)   Nightingale House, San Francisco.   1882.

EB-3d (14)   Niehaus House, Berkeley.   1889.

NC-1b (18)   Carson House, Eureka.   1884-86.
Samuel & Joseph C. Newsom
NC-8α (30)   Newell House, Stockton.   1880.   Attrib.
Samuel & Joseph C. Newsom

P-10α (10)   Stanford University, Palo Alto.   1887-91.
Shepley, Rutan & Coolidge

SCV-1g (15)   Art Museum (formerly Post Office, Public Library), San Jose.   1892.

M-6 (9)   San Francisco Theological Seminary, San Anselmo. 1897. Wright & Sanders

NC-2b (3)   St. Paul's Episcopal Church, Red Bluff. c.1890. Ernest Coxhead

NC-5d (24)   St. John's Episcopal Church, Petaluma. c.1890. Ernest Coxhead

SF-4 (24)   Polk House, San Francisco. c.1892. Willis Polk

EB-3f (22)   First Unitarian Church, Berkeley. 1898.
A. C. Schweinfurth
P-4 (17)   Southern Pacific Railroad Station, Bur-
lingame. 1894. George H. Howard

SF-2 (24)   Church of the New Jerusalem (Sweden-borgian), San Francisco. 1894.
A. Page Brown

NC-5i (7)   City Hall, Sonoma. 1906. H. C. Lutgens

NC-8   Ceremonial Arch, Lodi. 1907.

EB-5i (2)   Bell Tower, Mills College, Oakland. 1904. Julia Morgan

SF-6 (14)   Ferry Bldg., San Francisco.   1894.
A. Page Brown
(Photo: Security First National Bank)

SF-3 (17)   Bourn House, San Francisco.   1894.
Willis Polk
(Photo: Morley Baer)

SF-2 (18) Waybur House, San Francisco. 1902. Ernest Coxhead

P-8 (3) Josselyn House, "Vinegrove," Woodside. 1906. Clarence Tantau
(Photo: Morley Baer from *Here Today*)

SF-1 (12) Roos House, San Francisco. 1909.
Bernard Maybeck

EB-3f (14) Faculty Club, University of California,
Berkeley. 1902. Bernard Maybeck

EB-3g (7)   First Christian Science Church, Berkeley. 1910. Bernard Maybeck

EB-3i (13)   Dangan House, Berkeley. 1915. John Hudson Thomas

EB-3c (24)   Mathewson House, Berkeley. 1916. Bernard Maybeck

SF-14 (4)   Gingg House, San Francisco. 1915. Glenn Allen

SF-8 (19) Hibernia Bank Bldg., San Francisco. 1892. Albert Pissis

EB-3f (10) The Library, University of California, Berkeley. 1911-18. John Galen Howard
(Photo: University of California)

SF-3 (23)   Spreckels House, San Francisco.   1913.
MacDonald & Applegarth

NC-2c (2)   Post Office Bldg., Chico.   1914.
Oscar Wenderoth

SF-2 (1)   Palace of Fine Arts, San Francisco. 1915.
Bernard Maybeck

SF-8 (17)   City Hall, San Francisco. 1913-15.
Bakewell & Brown

EB-3c (45)   Thornberg (Normandy) Village, Berkeley.
1928. W. R. Yelland

EB-3c (32)   Hume House, Berkeley.   1928.
John Hudson Thomas

P-9 (4)   Heller House, Atherton.   1926-27.
George Washington Smith

NC-13b (61)   Gregory Farm House, nr. Santa Cruz.
1927. William W. Wurster

SF-7 (12)   450 Sutter Street Bldg., San Francisco. 1929-30. Timothy Pflueger

SF-7 (25)   Sommer & Kaufmann Store Bldg., San Francisco. 1929. Kem Weber & A. F. Roller

EB-5c (7)   Paramount Theatre Bldg., Oakland.   1929-
             30. Miller & Pflueger
P-10α (32)   Hanna House, Palo Alto.   1937.
             Frank Lloyd Wright

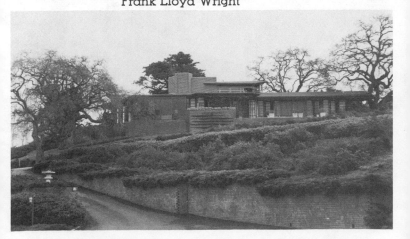

SF-5 (10)   Kahn House, San Francisco. 1939.
Richard J. Neutra

EB-3h (4)   Strauss House, Berkeley. 1939.
W. W. Wurster (Photo: Roger Sturtevant)

NC-10α (9)   Heckendorf House, Modesto.   1939.
John Funk

EB-1 (1)   Kaun Beach House, Richmond Shores.
1939. R. M. Schindler

M-2 (8)   Owens House, Sausalito. 1939.
Gardner Dailey (Photo: Roger Sturtevant)

EB-3e (7)   Havens House, Berkeley. 1941.
H. H. Harris

(Photo: Roger Sturtevant)

SCV-1c (6)   Administrative Offices, Schuckl Canning
Co., Sunnyvale.   1942.
Wurster, Bernardi & Emmons

SF-12 (5)   Valencia Gardens, San Francisco.   1943.
Wurster, Bernardi & Emmons/Thomsen

NC-12e (12) Carmel Woods School, Carmel. 1941. Kump & Falk

NC-9e (13) Placer County Courthouse, Nevada City. 1936-37. George C. Sellon

NC-11b (7)   Monterey County Courthouse, Salinas. 1937. Robert Stanton

SF-2 (22)   Howard House, San Francisco. 1939. H. T. Howard

NC-2α (9)   Fire House, Redding.   1939.
                    Masden & Hurd

SF-6 (45)   Union Oil Company Bldg., San Francisco
                    1940. Lewis P. Hobart

EB-3α (3)   House, Berkeley.   1954.
Joseph Esherick & Assoc.

EB-3c (16)   House, Berkeley.   1958.
Charles Warren Callister
(Photo: Les Flowers, Jr.)

P-3 (4) Mills High School, Millbrae. 1958. John Lyon Reid & Partners

SF-6 (21) John Hancock Bldg., San Francisco. Skidmore, Owings & Merrill

(Photo: Roger Sturtevant)

M-7 (3)   Eichler Housing Project, Terra Linda. 1955-60. Anshen & Allen

M-4 (24)   House, Mill Valley.   1961.
Marquis & Stoller
(Photo: Ezra Stoller Assoc.)

NC-12f (24)   Carmel Valley Manor, Carmel Valley.
1962. Skidmore, Owings & Merrill
(Photo: Morley Baer)

EB-3b (2)   House, Berkeley.   1963.
Richard C. Peters & Peter Dodge
(Photo: Morley Baer)

NC-5g (4)　　Condominium #1, Sea Ranch. 1965.
　　　　　　　　Moore, Lyndon, Turnbull, & Whitaker

EB-3i (20)　　Talbert House, Oakland. 1965.
　　　　　　　　Moore, Lyndon, Turnbull, & Whitaker

(Photo: Alexandre Georges)

M-4 (7)   Mill Valley Library, Mill Valley.   1969.
          Wurster, Bernardi & Emmons

SF-4 (5)   The Cannery, San Francisco.   1968.
          Esherick & Assoc.

(Photo: Kathleen Kershaw)

NC-1d (48)   The Wooden Garden, Eureka.   1969-73. Romano Gabriel

SF-6 (19)   Bank of America World Headquarters Bldg., San Francisco. 1970-71. Wurster, Bernardi & Emmons; Skidmore, Owings & Merrill with Pietro Belluschi

(Photo: Ezra Stoller)

NC-7b (33) Collegetown, Sacramento State University, Sacramento. 1970. Neil Smith & Assoc.

SCV-1i (3) Eastridge Shopping Center, San Jose. 1971. Avner Naggar

(Photo: Joshua Freiwald)

Plate 103

NC-10   California Aqueduct and Interstate 5, upper San Joaquin area.
(Photo: Dept. Public Works, State of Calif.)

Glossary   G

ARCHITECTURAL STYLES FOUND IN NORTHERN CALIFORNIA

One of the delightful pastimes which architecture can provide is the searching out and identification of styles (of fashions). Being a human product, the specific-ness of a style can never enjoy the precision of species and sub-species found, say, in botany or zoology. Architects and their clients seldom turn out to be complete purists in their products. More often than not an individual building will exhibit a potpourri of architectural styles, some old fashioned, some "right up and at'em," some "way-out" and futuristic. Still it is possible to identify and to pin down the major stylistic trends of a period and through this process to identify and loosely date a building. The following list outlines the most important styles of the past two hundred years which are to be found in Northern California. For those who would like to pursue the taxonomy of architectural styles further, no better handbook can be found than Marcus Whiffen's, *American Architecture Since 1780: A Guide to Styles* (M.I.T. Press, Cambridge, 1969).

THE LATE 18TH AND EARLY 19TH CENTURIES:
The Hispanic Phase (c.1770s-1850s)
The Spanish-Mexican phase can be divided into two sub-phases: the rural adobe, used both for secular and religious buildings; and the Mexican provincial Neo-Classic style which is present in only a few of the Mission buildings.

photo: Title Ins. and Trust, San Diego

THE MID TO LATE 19TH CENTURY:
Greek Revival (c.1850s-1860s)
More correctly, mid-century Classical Revival; the Monterey style was a mixture of the early adobe Hispanic and the Greek Revival.

Gothic Revival   (c.1850s-1900s)

Divided into three phases: The Early Gothic Revival, (1850s-1860), the High Victorian Gothic (late 1860s-early 1880s), the early Archaeological Gothic Revival (1890s, on into the 20th century.

Italianate Style   (c.1860s-1880s)

Divided into two phases: The Italian Villa (c.1850s-1880s); the Bracketed Italianate style (1860s-1890s).

Mansard Style   (c.1860s-1880)
The Second French Empire style.

Stick Style   (c.1870s-1890)
Often mixed with the somewhat later Eastlake style.

Eastlake Style   (c.1870s-1890)
Early examples mixed with elements of the Stick style; later examples combine with features of the Queen Anne.

Queen Anne Revival (c.1880s-1890s)

    Seldom pure in detail or form, often exhibits Eastlake, Romanesque, and even Colonial details.

Richardsonian Romanesque (late 1880s-1900)

THE PERIOD OF THE 1890s THROUGH 1920:

Colonial Revival (c.1890s-1920)

    Often mixed together with the Queen Anne and with the Shingle style.

Glossary   G

Shingle Style   (c.1890s-1920)
In the San Francisco region, the **First Bay Tradition** was in part an aspect of the Shingle style; most Shingle style buildings contain some decorative elements of the Colonial Revival.

Roman-Renaissance Revival   (c.mid 1890s on into the early 1930s)
The City Beautiful movement was an aspect of the Roman-Renaissance Revival.

Mission Revival   (c.1890s-1915)
After 1900, examples of the Mission Revival style absorbed many features of the Arts and Crafts movement.

Craftsman Style   (c.1900-1920)
Expressed itself through the following forms: the Bungalow, the Prairie style, the Mission Revival, the English Cottage mode, and the Secessionist style.

THE DECADES OF THE 20s AND 30s:

Spanish Colonial Revival   (c.1915-1930s)
Sometimes labeled the Mediterranean Revival; sub styles include Andalusian, the Churrigueresque Revival, and the Italian Revival.

Monterey Revival   (c.1925-1930s)
A strong mixture of the Colonial Revival of the 1920s and 30s, with the original Monterey style and the rural board and batten ranch house.

The Second Bay Tradition (c.1930 on through 1942)

A mingling of the rural California ranch house, the Monterey Revival (in some cases) and the International style.

photo: Roger Sturtevant

Zigzag Moderne (1925-early 1930s)

The American version of the European Art Deco.

Period Revivals (c.1920s and 1930s)

The open use of past historic forms; the preferred ones being the Hansel and Gretel cottage, the French Provincial, the English half-timber, and the Colonial Revival.

W.P.A. Moderne   (c.1930-1942)

The Roman-Renaissance mode cleaned up with added elements of both the Zigzag and the Streamlined Moderne.

Streamlined Moderne   (1933-1942)

The marriage of the aesthetics of the industrial designer and the International style.

THE YEARS FROM 1945 THROUGH 1973:

Late Second Bay Tradition   (1945-present)

Several variations came to the fore: the Post and Beam mode, the California Ranch house, and new variations on the Monterey Revival.

Glossary

G

Corporate International Style (1945-present)
The many variations on the Miesian glass box.

photo: Joshua Freiwald

The Pavilion Mode (1955-present)
Classical principles applied to the International Style.

photo: Jack Laxer

Brutalism (1960-present)
The building as sculpture, usually concrete sculpture.

photo: Rondal Partridge

Cut-out Vertical Box (1960-present)
The third Bay Tradition.

B Bibliographical Note

The following list of books and articles is intended to provide the interested reader with a general introduction to the architecture and the planning of Northern California. In order to keep the bibliography in bounds, much has been left out. For example, none of the excellent histories and bibliographies of counties and cities have been included, though they were consulted by the authors in preparing this guide. If one wishes to look into the history of a given place, these histories and bibliographies are essential. Fortunately a number of these (originally published by Thompson and West) have been reissued by the Berkeley publisher Howell North. In the matter of travel guides to San Francisco and Northern California, we have attempted to list those we found most useful. Since few of us travel solely to look at buildings or city plans, it is suggested that one also take along one or more of the general guides published by the Lane Magazine and Book Company of Menlo Park (such as *Northern California, Gold Rush Country, California Wine Country, The California Missions* or *San Francisco*). For the person who would really like to obtain a more detailed background on 19th century Northern California architecture, it is suggested that he read Harold Kirker's *California's Architectural Frontier*, and also the catalogue prepared by David Gebhard and Harriet Von Breton (*1868-1968 Architecture in California*) for the 1968 centennial of the University of California. Two other important sources for the 19th century—and a delight to go through—are the series of volumes produced by that remarkable Northern California architectural family of Samuel, Joseph C., J. J. and Thomas D. Newsom, and the various issues of *The California Architect and Building News* (1879-1899). During the present century the buildings and planning of communities in Northern California has been well published in all of the national architectural and planning journals, and in such regional California publications as *The Architect and Engineer, Arts and Architecture*, and in the popular *Sunset Magazine*. In recent years the problem of California and its environment has been published in *Cry California*, and in the many publications of SPUR and the Sierra Club. Critical analysis of buildings and planning have been written for the *San Francisco Chronicle* by Allen Temko, and for *Architectural Forum* and other publications by Roger Montgomery. Copies of the following articles and books (many of which are out of print and difficult to find) can, with much searching, be found at the following Northern California libraries: The California Historical Society, the Society of California Pioneers, the San Francisco Public Library, the Oakland Public Library, the California State Library at Sacramento and the University of California, Berkeley (the Library of the School of Environmental Design, and the Bancroft Library).

Anon.
  1891. *Memorial and Biographical History of Northern California.* Chicago.
  1893. *The Bay of San Francisco, the Metropolis of the Pacific Coast and its Suburban Cities, A History* . . . . Chicago.
  1912. "California's Contribution to a National Architecture." *The Craftsman*, Vol. 22, August, pp.532-560.
  1941. "Work of Some San Francisco Architects." *Pencil Points*, Vol. 22, May, pp.348-363.

Bibliography   B

1941. "Works of 17 Northern California Architectural Firms." *The Architect and Engineer*, Vol. 145, June, pp.16-53.

1949. "Is There a Bay Style?" (Brief comments by William W. Wurster, Albert Henry Hill, John Ekins Dinwiddie, Gardner Dailey, Frederick L. Langhorst, Francis Joseph McCarthy, Robert Royston, Francis Violich, Edward Williams). *Architectural Record*, Vol. 105, May, pp.92-97.

Adams, Kramer A. 1963. *Covered Bridges of the West*. Berkeley.

Abeloe, William N. (Hoover, Mildred B., Rensch, H. E., & Rensch, E. G.) 1966. *Historic Spots in California*. Stanford.

American Institute of Architects, Northern California Chapter. 1960. *Historic California: Sonoma, Benicia*. San Francisco.

Baer, Kurt. 1958. *Architecture of the California Missions*. Berkeley.

Baird, Joseph A. 1962. *Time's Wonderous Changes: San Francisco Architecture, 1776-1915*. San Francisco.

Bangs, Edward G. 1960. *Portals West: A Folio of Late 19th Century Architecture in California*. San Francisco.

Bartholomew, Harland. 1925. *The San Francisco Bay Region: A Statement Concerning the Nature and Importance of a Plan for Future Growth*. San Francisco.

Beebe, Lucius M. 1902. *San Francisco's Golden Era*. San Francisco. (Republished by Howell-North, Berkeley, 1960).

Bernhardi, Robert. 1971. *The Buildings of Berkeley*. Berkeley.

Bohn, Dave. 1971. *East of These Golden Shores*. Oakland.

Buchanan, Agnes F. 1906. "Some Early Business Buildings in San Francisco." *The Architectural Record*, Vol. 22, July, pp.15-32.

Burnham, Daniel H., & Bennett, Edward H. 1905. *Report on a Plan for San Francisco*. (Edited by Edward F. O'Day), San Francisco.

Clark, Arthur B. 1921. *Art Principles in House, Furniture and Village Buildings*. Stanford.

Clark, Robert J. 1966. *Louis Christian Mullgardt, 1866-1942*. Santa Barbara.

Coffman, Arthur. 1969. *An Illustrated History of Palo Alto*. Palo Alto: Lewis Osborne.

Crandall, Chuck. 1972. *They Chose to be Different: Unusual California Homes*. San Francisco.

Crofutt, George A. 1878-9. *Crofutt's New Overland Tourist and Pacific Coast Guide*. Chicago.

Croly, Herbert. 1906. "The California Country House. *Sunset Magazine*, Vol. 18, November, pp.50-65.

Crown Zellerbach Corp. 1960. *The Cities of Gold: The Story of City Planning in San Francisco*. San Francisco.

Cross, Ralph Herbert. 1954. *The Early Inns of California*.

Davoust, Martial 1903. *Illustrated Souvenir, Showing a Few Alameda Country Homes*. Oakland

——1910. "Art and Architecture in San Francisco." in *San Francisco, the Metropolis of the West*. San Francisco.

Department of Parks and Recreation, State of California 1971. *California Historical Landmarks*. Sacramento.

B   Bibliography

Delkin, James Ladd. 1941. *Monterey Peninsula*. Stanford.

Dobyns, Winifred S. 1931. *California Gardens*. New York.

Doxey, S. F. 1897. *Doxey's Guide to San Francisco: the Pleasure Resorts of California*.

Duell, Prentice 1923. "The New Era of California Architecture: II San Francisco." *The Western Architect*, Vol. 32, Nov., pp.126-128.

Elliott, W. W. 1885. *Oakland and Surroundings Illustrated and Described*. Oakland.

Flamm, Roy, & Ackerman, James. 1957. *A Collection of Photographs of a Group of California Buildings*. San Francisco.

Garnett, Porter. 1915. *The Stately Homes of California*. Boston.

Gebhard, David. 1964. *"The Bay Tradition in Architecture."* *Art In America*, Vol. 52, pp.60-63.

_____1964. *George Washington Smith*. Santa Barbara.

_____1965. "Charles Moore: Architecture and the New Vernacular. *Artforum*, Vol. 3, No. 8, May, pp.52-53.

Gebhard, David, & Von Breton, Harriet. 1968. *1868-1968 Architecture in California*. Santa Barbara.

Giffen, Guy, & Giffen, Helen. 1949. *The Story of Golden Gate Park*. San Francisco.

Gudde, Erwin G. 1969. *California Place Names: Origin and Etymology of Current Geographical Names*. Berkeley.

Guillermo, Prieto. 1938. *San Francisco in the Seventies*. San Francisco.

Gunn, Harry Lawrence. 1926. *History of Solano County and Napa County*. Chicago.

Hamlin, Talbot F. 1941. "California Whys and Wherefores." *Pencil Points*, Vol. 22, May, pp.339-344.

Hamilton, Frederick. 1911. "The Work of Willis Polk and Company," *Architect and Engineer*, Vol. 24, April, pp.35-73.

Hannaford, Donald R. 1931. *Spanish Colonial or Adobe Architecture of California, 1800-1850*. New York.

Hays, William C. 1917. "One Story and Open-Air Schoolhouses in California." *The Architectural Forum*, Vol. 27, Sept., pp.57-65.

Hitchcock, Henry Russell. 1940. "An Eastern Critic Looks at Western Architecture." *California Arts and Architecture*, Vol. 57, Dec., pp.20-22; 40-41.

Howard, John Galen. 1912. The Future of Architecture on the Pacific Coast." *The Western Architect*, Vol. 18, Nov., pp.113-121.

Hutchins, W. E. 1915. *By Ways Around San Francisco*. New York.

Huxtable, A. L. 1957. "Progressive Architecture in America: Reinforced Concrete Construction. The Work of Ernest L. Ransome, Engineer, 1884-1911." *Progressive Architecture*, Vol. 38, Sept., pp.139-142.

Jacobs, Stephen W. 1963. "California Contemporaries of Wright." in *Problems of the 19th and 20th Century*. Princeton, pp.44-49.

James, George Wharton. 1914. *California Romantic and Beautiful*. Boston.

Jenney, Wm. L. B. 1906. "The Old California Missions and Their Influence on Modern Design." *The Inland Architect and News Record*, Vol. 47, Feb., p.7; March, p.23, April, p.35, June, pp.71-72.

Bibliography B

Keeler, Charles. 1902. *San Francisco and Thereabouts.* San Francisco.

——1904. *The Simple Home.* San Francisco.

King, Elmer R. 1938. *Handbook of Historical Landmarks of California.* Los Angeles.

Kirker, Harold. 1960. *California's Architectural Frontier.* San Marino.

Lancaster, Clay. 1963. *The Japanese Influence in America.* New York.

Lander, Walter. 1949. "West Coast U.S.A. Post War Architects." *Architects Yearbook,* No. 3, pp.130-132, London.

Lassere, F. 1947. "Regional Trends in West Coast Architecture." *Canadian Art,* Vol. 5, No. 1, pp.7-12.

Lewis, Oscar. 1957. *Here Lived the Californians.* New York.

——1966. *San Francisco: Mission to Metropolis.* Berkeley.

Macomber, Ben. 1915. *The Jewell City: Panama-Pacific International Exposition, 1915.*

Marriott, F. (Publisher) 1887-8. *Artistic Homes of California.* Issued with the *San Francisco Newsletter,* San Francisco.

McClure, James D. 1948. *California Landmarks.* Stanford.

McCoy, Esther. 1960. *Five California Architects.* New York.

Milliken, Ralph LeRoy. 1961. *San Juan Bautista, California: The City in History.* Los Banos.

Monterey Savings and Loan Association (publisher). 1965. *Monterey's Adobe Heritage.* Monterey.

Moore, Charles W. 1966. "You Have to Pay for the Public Life." *Perspecta,* Nos. 9/10, pp.57-97.

——1967. "Plug it in, Rameses, and see if it Lights Up." *Perspecta,* No. 11, pp.33-43.

Morley, S. Griswald. 1928. *The Covered Bridges of California.* Berkeley.

Morrow, Irving. 1925. "The Riviera Revisited." *The Architect and Engineer,* Vol. 80.

——1941. "Why Modern Architecture?" *The Commonwealth,* Vol. 17, Sept. 2. (Articles by Irving Morrow, Richard Neutra, Louis C. Mullgardt and Arthur Brown).

Muybridge, Edward. 1877. *Panorama of San Francisco from California Street at Hill Street.*

Neasham, V. Audrey, & Henley, James (Janice A. Woodruff, Editor). 1969. *The City of the Plains; Sacramento in the 19th Century.* Sacramento.

Neuhaus, Eugene. 1915. *The Art of the Exposition.* San Francisco.

——1939. *The Art of Treasure Island.* Berkeley.

Newcomb, Rexford. 1916. *The Franciscan Mission Architecture of Alta California.* New York.

——1937. *Spanish Colonial Architecture in the United States.* New York.

Newhall, Ruth. 1967. *San Francisco's Enchanted Palace.* Berkeley.

Newsom, J. J., & Newsom, T. D. 1898? *Up-to-Date Residences.* San Francisco.

Newsom, Joseph C. 1890? *Picturesque and Artistic Homes and Buildings of California, No. 3,* San Francisco.
1895? *Modern Homes of California, No. 4.* San Francisco.

Newsom, Samuel, & Newsom, Joseph C. 1884? *Picturesque California Homes, No. 1.* San Francisco.

——1887? *Picturesque California Homes, No. 2.* San Francisco.

Nordhoff, Charles. 1878. *California for Pleasure and Residence*. New York.

Oakey, A. F. 1891. "Architecture in San Francisco: A Word to the Wise." *The Overland Monthly*, Vol. n.s. 18, p.132.

Olmsted, Roger, & Watkins, T. H. (Photos by Morley Baer and others) 1968. *Here Today: San Francisco's Architectural Heritage*. San Francisco.

Palmer, Phil. 1971. "A Bay Area Delight." *Journal of the American Institute of Architects*, Vol. 56, August, pp.44-45.

Park, Andrew G. 1906. *The City Beautiful: San Francisco Past, Present and Future*. Los Angeles.

Peatfield, J. J. 1893. "The California Exposition." *The Californian*, Vol. 5, Dec., pp.145-151.

Peitotto, E. C. 1892. "Architecture in San Francisco." *The Overland Monthly*, Vol. 21, p.441.

Pelton, John Cotter, Jr. 1882. *Cheap Dwellings*. San Francisco.

Perusse, Lyle F. 1955. "The Gothic Revival in California." *Journal, Society of Architectural Historians*, Vol. 16, Oct., pp.15-22.

Phillips, A. & Company (publishers). 1889. *Phillips' California Guide*. Boston.

Pratt, Helen T. 1912. *San Francisco As It Was, As It Is and How to See It*. San Francisco.

Prieto, Guillermo. 1938. *San Francisco in the Seventies*. San Francisco.

Rand McNally & Company (Publishers). 1923. *San Francisco, Oakland and Other Bay Cities — A Visitor's Guide*.

Ray, Milton S. (Text: Oscar Lewis). 1946. *San Francisco Since 1872*. San Francisco.

Reid, Kenneth. 1938. "The Architect and the House: William Wilson Wurster of California." *Pencil Points*, Vol. 19, Aug., pp.472-494.

Richey, Elinor. 1970. *The Ultimate Victorians*, Berkeley.

Rider, Fremont. 1925. *Rider's California: A Guide Book for Travelers*. New York.

The Sacramento Bee (Publisher). 1939. *Sacramento Guide Book*. Sacramento.

San Francisco Museum of Art (Publisher). 1949. *Domestic Architecture of the San Francisco Bay Region*. (Articles by Richard B. Freeman, Lewis Mumford, Elizabeth Kendell Thompson, William W. Wurster, Gardner Dailey Francis Joseph McCarthy). San Francisco.

———1959. *Two Buildings: San Francisco* (Crown Zellerbach Bldg. & John Hancock Bldg.). San Francisco.

Scanland, J. M. 1904. "Curious Houses of San Francisco (Old Landmarks of a Western Metropolis)." *The Overland Monthly*, Vol. 43, pp.470-475.

Scott, Mel. 1959. *The San Francisco Bay Area: A Metropolis in Perspective*. Berkeley.

Sears, Mabel Urmy. 1911. "Some Types of Shingle Houses." *The House Beautiful*, Vol. 29, Feb., pp.89-90.

Sexton, Randolph W. 1927. *Spanish Influence on American Architecture and Decoration*. New York.

Shuck, Oscar. 1869. *The California Scrap Book*. New York.

Stanford, Trent E. 1950. *The Architecture of the Southwest*. New York.

Stanger, Frank M. 1946. *Peninsula Community Book*. San Mateo, Calif.: Crawston.

Stanger, Frank M. 1963. *South from San Francisco*. San Mateo: San Mateo Co. Hist. Assoc.

Steilberg, Walter T. 1918. "Some Examples of the Work of Julia Morgan." *Architect and Engineer*, Vol. 55, Nov., pp.38-83; 84-107.

Sterling, George (Photos by Francis Brugiuerre). 1915. *The Evanescent City*. San Francisco.

Studer, Jack. 1968. "Julius Kellersberger: A Swiss Surveyor and City Planner in California, 1851-57." *Quarterly, The California Historical Society*, Vol. 47, No. 1, pp.3-39.

Taylor, Frank J. 1929. *Land of Homes*. Los Angeles.

Temko, Allen. 1960. "Sacramento's Second Gold Rush." *Architectural Forum*, Vol. 115, Oct., pp.124-129.

Tharp, Newton J. 1900. "Good and Bad in San Francisco Architecture." *The Overland Monthly*, Vol. 36, Dec. p.533.

Thompson, Elizabeth K. 1951. "Domestic Architecture of the Bay Region." *Journal, Society of Architectural Historians*, Vol. 10, Oct., pp.15-21.

Truman, Ben C. 1885. *Homes and Happiness in the Golden State of California*. San Francisco.

Turnbull, William, Jr. 1971. *MLTW/Charles Moore and William Turnbull, Jr.: The Sea Ranch, California. 1966–*. (Edited and photography by Yokio Futagawe). Tokyo.

Vail, Wesley D. 1964. *An Account of Domestic Architecture in Victorian San Francisco*. San Francisco.

Whitaker, Herman. 1906. "Berkeley the Beautiful." *Sunset Magazine*, Vol. 18, Dec., pp.138-144.

Williams, Samuel. 1921. *The City of the Golden Gate, a Description of San Francisco in 1875*. San Francisco.

Withey, Henry F., & Withey, E. R. 1956. *Biographical Directory of American Architects (Deceased)*. Los Angeles.

Woodbridge, John M. 1959. "Bay Region Style, La Tradizione Architettonica della Baia San Francisco." *Casabella*, No. 232, Oct., pp.39-45.

Woodbridge, John M., & Woodbridge, Sally B. 1960. *Buildings of the Bay Area: A Guide to the Architecture of the San Francisco Bay Region*. New York.

Woon, Basil Dillon. 1935. *San Francisco and the Golden Empire: A Guide Book*. New York.

W. P. A. (Editors). 1939. *San Francisco and the Bay Area*. New York.

———1939. *California: A Guide to the Golden State*. New York.

Wurster, William W. 1944. "San Francisco Bay Portfolio." *The Magazine of Art*, Vol. 37, Dec., pp.301-305.

Yelland, W. R. 1923. "The Work of W. R. Yelland, Architect," *Architect and Engineer*, Vol. 75, Dec., pp.52-62.

Young, John Philip. 1912. *San Francisco: A History of the Pacific Coast Metropolis*. Chicago.

Index

Index

Index

Index

Index

Index